# Searching for CIORAN

# Searching for CIORAN

Ilinca Zarifopol-Johnston

Edited by
Kenneth R. Johnston

Foreword by
Matei Calinescu

Indiana University Press
Bloomington and Indianapolis

This book is a publication of

Indiana University Press
601 North Morton Street
Bloomington, IN 47404-3797 USA

http://iupress.indiana.edu

Telephone orders 800-842-6796
Fax orders 812-855-7931
Orders by e-mail iuporder@indiana.edu



The paper used in this publication meets the minimum requirements of American National Standard for Information Sciences—Permanence of Paper for Printed Library Materials, ANSI Z39.48-1984.

Manufactured in the United States of America
Library of Congress Cataloging-in-Publication Data

Zarifopol-Johnston, Ilinca, 1952–2005.
Searching for Cioran / Ilinca Zarifopol-Johnston ; edited by Kenneth R. Johnston ; foreword by Matei Calinescu.
p. cm.
Includes bibliographical references (p. ) and index.
ISBN 978-0-253-35267-5 (cloth : alk. paper) 1. Cioran, E. M. (Emile M.), 1911–1995. 2. Philosophers—Romania—Biography. I. Title.
B4825.C564Z37 2009
194—dc22
[B]

2008023842

1 2 3 4 5 14 13 12 11 10 09

IN MEMORIAM

E. M. Cioran

1911–1995

Simone Boué

1919–1997

Ilinca Zarifopol-Johnston

1952–2005

# CONTENTS

## PART 2 · Memoirs of a Publishing Scoundrel

# Editor's Preface

Before she died at age fifty-two in January of 2005, my wife, the author of this book, had nearly completed a critical biography of her Romanian compatriot, the philosophical essayist and existentialist provocateur E. M. Cioran. Ilinca's goal was to write a biography of Cioran's Romanian life, from his birth in 1911 until he left Romania for France in 1937—a departure which became permanent after 1941. She had completed more than two-thirds of this project, which constitutes part 1 of the present volume, *The Romanian Life of Emil Cioran:* chapters 1–3 and 5–7 as printed here, plus her introduction, "Cioran's Revenge." I have constructed chapters 4 and 8 (Berlin and Paris) from her drafts, reading notes, computer files, and marginal commentaries in her copies of Cioran's works. Chapter 9, "The Lyrical Virtues of Totalitarianism," was one of several analytical studies of Cioran that Ilinca was conducting alongside her biographical work; I have attached it here to provide a kind of conclusion to what must necessarily remain an incomplete whole.

During the course of this project, Ilinca became engrossed in another one, an autobiographical account of her experiences in writing Cioran's biography. This she completed shortly before her death, as *Searching for Cioran, Myself: Memoirs of a Publishing Scoundrel,* printed herein as part 2: *Memoirs of a Publishing Scoundrel.* As the first part of her original title suggests, she discovered things about her own past in the process of discovering Cioran's Romanian past. (She also started an autobiography of her own, called *The Escape Artist.*) Cioran is no easy biographical subject, for not only were there things about his past he was extremely reticent about, especially his fascistic writings, but he also was a non-person, and persona non grata, in communist Romania, as a "decadent" Western writer. Ilinca never saw or read anything by or about him during her own lifetime in Romania (1952–77). His past seemed to have disappeared twice for her, once into France, and then into oblivion.

But after he died in 1995, another drama began, in which Ilinca was caught up, willy-nilly, the essence of which is conveyed by her memoir's subtitle. Simone Boué,

Cioran's companion from the early 1940s, was the de facto literary executor of his estate and after his death had to deal not only with publishing responsibilities but also with a huge range of publishing "opportunities" proposed by writers of all stripes who saw a subject of great interest, and profit, in his life and works after his death. Ilinca was ensnared in this drama, as she recounts.

Ilinca explains in her introduction how she came to be involved with Cioran personally, and not only as his biographer. Briefly: from a chance suggestion by a friend and colleague, Matei Calinescu, Ilinca had agreed to translate some of Cioran's five Romanian books, virtually unknown in the West. Two of these appeared, published by the University of Chicago Press: *On the Heights of Despair* (1933; 1992) and *Tears and Saints* (1936; 1995).

Soon after she started working on these translations, Ilinca met Cioran in Paris and became friends with him and Simone Boué. I and our son Teddy also met them frequently at their apartment on the rue de l'Odéon near the Luxembourg Gardens, where our acquaintance grew into friendship, almost like three generations of a family. As Ilinca walked and talked with Cioran (she was one of the few persons he deigned to address in Romanian, a language he had foresworn in the radical act of transforming himself into a French writer, though they spoke mostly in French), she began to see in his willed self-exile from Romania (ca. 1940) a reflection and anticipation of her own. She decided she had to become his biographer, for no true biography of him exists—still—and all approaches to his life—or lives, the Romanian or the French—are heavily skewed and pre-determined by the writer's view, pro or con, of Cioran's temporary allegiance in the mid-1930s to Romania's home-grown fascist movement, the Legion of St. Michael (the Legionnaires) and its political party, the Iron Guard.

I have edited Ilinca's manuscripts to produce the most complete, coherent, and continuous narrative I can, well aware that her final version—had she lived to produce it—would have benefited from her revisions and corrections, not only in matters of style and conception but also in more mundane matters of references and sources, which I have been able to trace only so far. Her memoir (*Scoundrel*) is complete as is, though I have removed parts that substantially repeat sections of her biography of Cioran. All Romanian and French texts have been translated into English by her, unless otherwise indicated, although I think she frequently relied on Richard Howard's superb translations of Cioran's French books. Similarly, the "I" in both parts of the book refers to her; if there seems any possibility for confusion, I have distinguished her persona from my own by using our initials, IZJ or KRJ.

Ilinca wanted to write a biography for general readers, not just for academic or philosophical specialists. But she also wanted to be scrupulously fair and honest, following the best academic standards. These two somewhat different motivations are reflected not only in the two parts of the book but also *within* each part: part 1 is not completely "objective," and though part 2 is "subjective," it contains many details and facts that reflect back onto part 1 as a kind of retrospective commentary. Furthermore, her method is a combination of scholarship and *reportage.* She knew "the literature" on Cioran, but she also knew Cioran and Simone very well personally, albeit at the end of their lives. So her approach is a combination of scholarship and personal essay. At one point, I thought of sub-titling the book, "A Personal History," but I decided that might sound like it was Cioran's own view of his history—and, as Ilinca makes abundantly clear, managing and massaging his personal history constitutes a large part of Cioran's authorial presence.

Editing Ilinca's Cioran manuscripts has necessarily been a lonely work, but I have been accompanied and helped along the way by some good friends and colleagues. I am especially grateful to Janet Rabinowitch, director of Indiana University Press, for taking a chance on an incomplete project. I am indebted to the Press's anonymous reviewers, not only for their approval but also for their detailed comments, criticisms and suggestions. Matei Calinescu did much more than write the foreword to the book. Friend and colleague, he is an acclaimed poet and critic both in his native Romania and in his adopted country, author of *Five Faces of Modernity* and *Rereading* (among other works), and Professor of Comparative Literature Emeritus at Indiana University. He answered countless queries of mine about everything from Romanian spelling and pronunciation to recondite details about Romania's complicated inter-war cultural history. I also thank Breon Mitchell, director of the Lilly Library (Rare Books and Manuscripts) at Indiana University. Ilinca's mother, Maria Economu, and her sister, Christina Zarifopol-Illias, provided sympathetic information whenever asked. Finally, I thank Nick Bashall of London for departing from his usual practice of portraiture and agreeing to make from a photograph the charcoal sketch that appears on the book's jacket.

Only one last editorial note: I am not a specialist in Cioran, existentialism, or inter-war European politics. I read and speak Romanian with difficulty (I lived there in 1974–75, when I met Ilinca), and my French is not much better. I am an academic specialist in English Romantic literature, especially Wordsworth. There are references to English Romanticism occasionally in this book, which some readers might think come from my editorial hand. One or two do, but most of them come from Ilinca—and from Cioran. Cioran was an amazingly erudite man, read English easily—and sometimes wished he had "exiled" himself to London instead of Paris. He had a particular fondness for, and insight into, the poetry of Percy Bysshe Shelley and Emily Dickinson. As to Ilinca's references to Wordsworth and English Romanticism: I was surprised to see them when I began editing her manuscripts, but I was touched by these hidden textual evidences of the way in which my work had touched hers—as now hers touches mine.

Kenneth R. Johnston
*Bloomington, Indiana*
*December 2007*

# Note on Romanian Spelling and Pronunciation

The Romanian language, like the country itself, is often referred to as "a Latin island in a Slavic sea," because Romanian is a Latin-based Romance language, like Italian, French, Spanish, and Portuguese. Most Anglo-American readers will be able to recognize and sound out most of the Romanian words that occur herein (all are translated, of course). However, about 25 percent of the Romanian vocabulary derives from its surrounding Slavic neighbors (including Old Church Slavonic), as well as from its non-Slavic ones, Turkey, Greece, and Hungary. Turkish suzerainty, as the Ottoman Empire, controlled the Romanian territory for centuries—ultimately producing the most famous Romanian of all, in the Western popular imagination, Dracula, or son of the devil, as the nationalist freedom fighter, Vlad Ţepeş, was commonly known. One result of these linguistic and national mixtures is that Romanian has more diacritical marks than most Romance languages. Although they are reproduced herein for accuracy, they need not detain most readers, especially the circumflexes, breves, and other marks over vowels—which are, in my long but still limited experience, very hard for Westerners to hear, let alone reproduce. But the cedilla under *ş* and *ţ* are easier, the former sounding as "sh" and the latter as "tz." So Dracula's family name would be pronounced "Tzep-esh." Finally, *c* before *i* or *e* is sounded as "ch," as in Italian. Hence the family name of the subject of this book, E. M. Cioran, is correctly pronounced "Chore-on" in Romanian, but acceptably as "See-or-an" in French and most other Western languages.

# Foreword

In the 1970s and 1980s, during my visits from the United States to Paris, I always made a point to call Cioran and offer to accompany him on one of his long daily walks, usually solitary, through the streets of his beloved Latin Quarter and the Luxembourg gardens. We would meet in front of the old building at 21, rue de l'Odéon, where he lived in a tiny garret on the sixth floor. In the late 1980s, when he first invited me to have dinner at his place, which he shared with his life-long companion, Simone Boué, he was ambivalent about the recent installation of an elevator. It was an amenity for his rare guests, he admitted, but a temptation—hard to resist—for himself, who had for years taken advantage of climbing the stairs several times a day as healthy exercise, good for blood circulation and the heart. And indeed it wasn't an ailing heart or other physical impairment that would cause his death (on June 20, 1995, at age eighty-four), but a long battle with an illness, Alzheimer's, that shattered his extraordinary mind and made him spend the last two years of his life in the geriatric pavilion of a Parisian hospital.

By then, Cioran had become a famous figure on the stage of French intellectual life, the admired author of several books of iconoclastic aphorisms, bitter and supremely elegant, apocalyptic and ironic, vertiginously intelligent and memorable. They seemed to represent, in the second half of the twentieth century, an unlikely revival of a great French tradition, that of the *moralistes* of the seventeenth and eighteenth centuries: La Rochefoucauld, La Bruyère, Chamfort, Vauvenragues. With the difference that this new La Rochefoucauld had read with particular attention, among many others, the works of Schopenhauer and Nietzsche.

Surprisingly, Cioran wasn't even French: he came from an obscure corner of Eastern Europe, from a country few people in Paris had heard (or cared) about. And he wasn't even young, though he burst upon the French intellectual scene in 1949 as a certifiable *enfant terrible*. He was thirty-eight, and before deciding to write in French, he had published, before the war, several books in his obscure native language.

Intriguingly, he showed himself ready to share in his adopted country's amazement at the very existence of his nation, repeatedly asking himself, "How can one be a Romanian?"

Needless to say, this was a recurrent topic in our peripatetic discussions. Much younger than him, I too was nevertheless, as I would put it in jest, an "escapee from the future." That is, from the Communist regime that had been imposed by the Red Army after World War II not only on our country but on Eastern Europe as a whole, claiming to represent the inevitable future of humanity. Our conversations were exclusively in French—which he spoke flawlessly, rapidly, but with a heavy accent that marked him as a foreigner. In an amiable, friendly way he would correct my mistakes in his adopted language.

At the time when I was introduced to him, Cioran enjoyed a solid, if still somewhat "clandestine" (as he liked to joke), reputation. He appeared to relish that imagined "clandestinity," as well as his being an "exile" in France—a marginal, an *apatride* or stateless person. Not fortuitously did he write, in the mid-1970s, about Borges, in a wry eulogy later included in *Anathemas and Admirations:* "The misfortune of being recognized has befallen him. He deserved better."

Did he realize that the same misfortune was in store for himself? On the point of becoming—appallingly, from his own perspective—a cult figure in France toward the end of his life, his buried Romanian pre-war past caught up with him. His foolish admiration for Hitler in 1933–34, the delirious if deeply ambivalent nationalism expressed in his *Transfiguration of Romania* (1936), his allegiance to the fascistic and anti-Semitic Iron Guard of Corneliu Zelea Codreanu, which continued to haunt him secretly long after he had renounced his native Romanian and had begun writing (and speaking) exclusively in French, suddenly became public knowledge. And thus, ironically, the obituaries published in the French press at Cioran's death in 1995 became a replay in miniature of *l'affaire Heidegger* of the previous decade. Unlike Heidegger's engagement with the Nazis, however, Cioran's fleeting intoxication with the mystical-terrorist Iron Guard could be understood as an unfortunate episode in a life sincerely devoted to the task of "thinking against oneself" (his most characteristic maxim). Perhaps even as a failed attempt of intellectual suicide, clearly a manifestation of self-hatred—of that strange self-hatred that he managed, later on, to distill into his darkly scintillating French aphorisms.

At any rate, as Ilinca Zarifopol-Johnston reflects in her diary notes for 1993 (included in the "Memoirs of a Publishing Scoundrel," the second part of her book), even after more than a half century of living in France, "Cioran's avoidance of the limelight, his willingness to live in poverty, on the margins, his rejection of prestigious and lucrative prizes is not just a pose, but it isn't as disinterested as it seems. I think it is related to his fear of revelations about his past. He knows that fame and publicity bring about the inevitable search into the past. But in the end he didn't escape from it."

As has been said, certain pasts refuse to pass.

Starting in the 1960s, Cioran's French books, admired for their stylistic purity and their arresting paradoxes, began to be translated into many languages, including English. His *Temptation to Exist,* in the fine version of Richard Howard and with an extremely favorable but not uncritical introduction by Susan Sontag, was published in 1968, followed by *The Fall into Time* (1970), *The New Gods* (1974), *A Short History of Decay* (1975), *The Trouble with Being Born* (1976), and so forth. Sontag's broad characterization of Cioran's philosophical position four decades ago has retained its accuracy. "Our response to the collapse of philosophical systems in the nineteenth century was the rise of ideologies—aggressively anti-philosophical systems of thought, taking the form of various 'positive' or 'descriptive' sciences of man. Compte, Marx, Freud, and the pioneer figures of anthropology, sociology, and linguistics immediately come to mind. Another response to the debacle was a new kind of philosophizing: personal (even autobiographical), aphoristic, lyrical, anti-systematic. Its foremost examples: Kierkegaard, Nietzsche, and Wittgenstein. Cioran is the most distinguished figure in this tradition writing today."

What has become clearer in the meantime is the specific biographical-historical drama that underlies Cioran's work. Ilinca Zarifopol-Johnston's new book goes a long way in illuminating its contradictory elements and in explaining its continuing interest.

Cioran was particularly pleased with Howard's English versions: a few widely scattered inaccuracies didn't bother him, as long as the "tone" was right. In the late 1980s, when I learned that he had authorized the translation into French of some of his early Romanian books, I discussed with him the possibility of publishing these books in English as well, in the series of "Romanian Thought and Literature in Translation" I was then directing at the Ohio State University Press. Cioran was at first reluctant. He didn't trust the abilities of a prospective English translator from the Romanian. What's more, he had a certain control over the French versions and was able to demand cuts and changes (he was critical of his youthful Romanian style: too "lyrical," too "loose," too imprecise), but he was not sure that he could do the same in regard to the English versions.

At one point he suggested that the English translations I was urging him to permit be done from the French, but I managed to persuade him that this would not do. I spoke to him highly of my colleague and friend, Ilinca Zarifopol-Johnston, an "escapee from the future" like myself, who was willing to translate his Romanian books, after having read *On the Heights of Despair,* which fascinated her. Cioran asked for a sample of her work before he made up his mind. Finally, after Simone Boué (a teacher of English at a reputed French *lycée* in Paris) had read and approved the sample, Cioran agreed and Ilinca translated—euphorically, beautifully—*On the Heights of Despair,* which was brought out by the University of Chicago Press in 1992 (in the meantime the series at Ohio State University Press had been discontinued). She then also did *Tears and Saints* (1995) for Chicago and, becoming increasingly fascinated with the thinker's enigmatic personality, she decided to embark on the ambitious project of an intellectual biography of Cioran. Unfortunately, her research was interrupted by her untimely death; but, fortunately, the manuscript was advanced enough to become, with the editorial help of her husband, Kenneth R. Johnston, the present book.

*Searching for Cioran* is an important and distinctly original contribution to the growing field of Cioran studies. Aside from its subtle analytical edge and the richness of the biographical material concerning Cioran's youth, it has the advantage, over a book like *Cioran l'hérétique* by Patrice Bollon (1997), that its author is thoroughly familiar with the thinker's Romanian background, with what one might call "Cioran's hidden face," including the self-inflicted wounds left on it by his wrong-headed youthful commitments. The latter form the subject of a remarkable study by Marta Petreu, recently translated into English as *An Infamous Past: E. M. Cioran and the Rise of Fascism in Romania* (2005), originally published in Romanian in 1999. (Ilinca had read it in the original and refers to it.) But Petreu's book is limited to the discussion of a single work by Cioran—*The Transfiguration of Romania*—and to situating it in the complicated, shifting landscape of the political and cultural life of Romania in the 1930s. What the more comprehensive present study does is to integrate the *Transfiguration* within the corpus of Cioran's entire body of Romanian work and to look closely at the ways in which the author tried, in his French writings, to secretly "unwrite" (if one may say so) the earlier books.

I should also point out that *Searching for Cioran* compares favorably with the treatment—which is essentially an indictment—of Cioran in Alexandra Laignel-Lavastine's *Cioran, Eliade, Ionesco: L'oubli du fascisme* (2002). Without glossing over Cioran's youthful extreme right-wing ideas and rhetoric, Ilinca Zarifopol-Johnston argues convincingly that the mature French Cioran did not simply conceal his past but tried hard to understand it, even though, to himself, it remained incomprehensible, as an act of madness, an act which, even when one is eventually cured, remains essentially incomprehensible. In the chapters devoted to the controversial *Transfiguration of Romania,* Ilinca demonstrates a psychological acumen and an ability to assess the significance of the tiniest detail in the context of a life-long secret obsession, which are rare among literary commentators.

Her study is complemented by an impressive, lively, and engaging autobiographical attempt to analyze the motives as well as the consequences, intended and unintended, of her "search"—specifically the *Search for Cioran*—in her own life as an academic researcher, forced by circumstances to become—like the hero of Henry James's *Aspern Papers*—a "publishing scoundrel." Under this allusive and self-deprecating title, we find an unforgettable, poignant portrait of the old Cioran at the Hospital Broca, during the last two years of his life. After a visit to the hospital, Ilinca noted in her diary: "Cioran's room No. 244, his name on the door. His name also on the books lying on the table in the room. The only books here. He can't read, but once in a while Simone shows them to him, points to the name and tells him that's his name, that he wrote those books. He bends his white mane and peers at the name, trying to remember who he is." His companion, Simone Boué, with whom Ilinca had a complicated relationship, at once rewarding and frustrating, is brought fully to life, as if by a quick, deft, delicate painterly brush. Other fleeting character sketches—of translators of Cioran, researchers, or just admirers visiting him in hospital—are also uncannily vivid. The reading of this whole section of *Searching for Cioran* is almost hypnotic, revealing in the "scoundrel" a graceful and accomplished prose writer.

The search for Cioran, which involved trips to post-Communist Romania (described in the memoir), increasingly becomes for the author a search for herself. At this juncture, she offers the reader an extended and affecting self-portrait against the background of a ruined country, made up of diary entries (encounters, reminiscences, impressions) which uncover the "hidden face" of the scholar. She is a sharp, insightful observer of self and others, courageous and candid, writing in a fresh, quick-silver style totally free of clichés and jargon—in a word, a wonderful memoirist.

Matei Calinescu

# Chronology: E. M. Cioran

| | |
|---|---|
| 1911 | Born April 8 in Răşinari, a village in Transylvania near the old Saxon city of Sibiu, at this time still part of the Austro-Hungarian Empire. His father is a Romanian Orthodox priest. |
| 1921–28 | Attends middle school and high school in Sibiu. |
| 1928–32 | Studies philosophy at the University of Bucharest, writing his undergraduate thesis on Henri Bergson. |
| 1933–35 | In Germany on a Humboldt fellowship for graduate study; breaks with schematic, systematic philosophy in the tradition of Kant and Hegel and embraces existential philosophy, which he calls "abstract indiscretion." |
| 1934 | His first book appears, *On the Heights of Despair* (*Pe Culmile Disperării*), published by the King Carol II Foundation, which awards it the Art and Literature prize. |
| 1935–36 | High school teacher in Braşov, a large city in the Carpathian mountains of central Romania. |
| 1936 | Publishes *Romania's Transfiguration* (*Schimbarea la faţă a României*), a polemical work of fascistic tendency; also *Cartea Amăgirilor* (The Book of Deceptions). |
| 1937 | Publishes *Tears and Saints* (*Lacrimi şi Sfinti*). Leaves Romania on a fellowship from the French Institute in Bucharest. |
| 1937–40 | Studying in Paris. His last book to appear in Romania before the war, *Amurgul Gîndurilor* (*The Twilight of Thought*), is published in Sibiu. |
| 1940–41 | Fall and winter: returns briefly to Romania; delivers radio address in praise of Corneliu Zelea Codreanu, murdered former leader of the fascistic Iron Guard; gains appointment as cultural attaché to Romanian legation in Vichy, France. |

| | |
|---|---|
| 1940–44 | Composes *Îndreptar pātimaş* (*Primer of Passions*), translated in French as *Bréviaire des vaincus;* it did not appear until 1991, when it became possible again to publish books by Cioran in Romania. |
| 1941 | Fired from his diplomatic post after three months, in a farce of mutual misunderstandings. |
| 1941 | Returns to Paris, where he lived the rest of his life uneventfully, except for great literary success. |
| 1942 | Meets Simone Boué, a teacher of English, who becomes his lifelong companion. |
| 1949 | Publication of his first French book, *Précis de décomposition* (*Treatise on Decay*), which is received ecstatically by the critics (Maurice Nadeau calls Cioran "the prophet of our era") and is awarded the Prix de Combat. |
| 1947–60 | Lives in a series of student dormitories or cheap hotel rooms in the Latin Quarter, taking meals at student refectories as long as he could pass himself off as a student. Supports himself as a translator and manuscript reader. |
| 1952 | *Syllogismes de l'amertume* (*Syllogisms of Bitterness*). |
| 1956 | *La tentation d'exister* (*The Temptation to Exist*). |
| 1960 | *Histoire et utopie.* |
| 1960–95 | Moves into an attic apartment at 21, rue de l'Odéon, with Mme. Boué. |
| 1964 | *La Chute dans les temps* (*The Fall into Time*). |
| 1969 | *Le mauvais démiurge* (*The Evil Demiurge*). |
| 1970 | *Valéry face à ses idoles* (*Valéry Confronts His Idols*). |
| 1973 | *De L'inconvénient d'être né* (*On the Inconvenience of Being Born*). |
| 1977 | *Essai sur la pensée réactionnaire: A propos de Joseph de Maistre.* |
| 1979 | *Écartèlement* (*Dismembering*). |
| 1986 | *Exercises d'admiration: essais et portraits.* |
| 1987 | *Aveux et Anathèmes* (*Praises and Anathemas*). |
| 1990–95 | Translation and publication of most of his Romanian books, first into French and then into many other languages, including English. |
| 1995 | June 20, dies in Paris after illness of four or five years: Alzheimer's and other complications. |
| 1997 | *Cahiers* [Notebooks], *1957–1972,* edited by Simone Boué. |
| 1997 | October: Simone Boué is found drowned on the beach near her family's house in the Vendée. |

## Romania before and after World War I

The salient feature of the map of Romania, besides showing the cities and towns where Cioran lived, is to indicate how radically the country changed shape during his years there, from 1911 to 1941. Before World War I, the new country—established between 1861 and 1878 by the union and eventual international recognition of the provinces of Wallachia and Moldavia—was squeezed between the Austro-Hungarian and Russian empires like a long-stemmed gourd. In the generous post-war settlements, it achieved its largest size, as "Greater Romania," gaining Bessarabia from Russia and Transylvania from Hungary, as well as other smaller gains in the north and south not shown here, such as Bukovina, the northern extension of Moldavia. After World War II, the country changed shape again, principally by losing Bessarabia back to Russia (since 1917 the U.S.S.R.), and a southeastern triangle (Dobruja) to Bulgaria. These changes did not affect Cioran directly, then living in Paris, but of course he observed and reflected on them, as he did the further change of Bessarabia into the Republic of Moldova after 1989. (KRJ)

# PART 1

## The Romanian Life of Emil Cioran

Every time I feel I can't go on—I will fail writing this:
Relu and EC and my *obligation* to them.
In his attic room being cold *the way he was.*
The obsession with the past—especially for us East Europeans.

—found among IZJ's working notes and drafts

"Je suis un ennemi de la gloire."

—Cioran's dedication to me—his future biographer—in a 1991 volume of *Îndreptar.* (IZJ)

# Introduction: Cioran's Revenge

It was cold in Paris in the winter of 1943–44. The war, as it seemed, was going badly for all sides, and shortages were implacable, beyond relief. To keep warm, the Latin Quarter intellectuals flock to the Café de Flore on the Boulevard St. Germain-des-Prés, where an impressive stove dominates the main room. Drawn to its generous heat, Jean-Paul Sartre and his group are there every day, arguing for hours around a few marble-topped tables reflected in the Art Deco mirrors on the wall. The Café de Flore is to Sartre's generation what the Dome and La Coupole were to Hemingway's. Existentialism, it is commonly said, was born at the Flore. Its birth may have owed as much to the cozy comfort of the steaming stove as to Sartre's eloquence. Whether "the paths to liberty led through the Flore," as Sartre claimed, is debatable, but that the path to the Flore led to temporary comfort and refuge for frozen, impecunious students, artists, and writers at the dark end of Europe's darkest days is without doubt.

At a table next to Sartre, who confidently draws on his pipe, sits a quiet young man, chain-smoking cheap Gauloises. Modestly but correctly dressed with coat and tie, his fedora hat carefully placed on top of a heavy navy overcoat folded next to him on the red velvet bench, there is a vaguely foreign, un-French air about this man, something formal and old-fashioned which strikes an odd note in the bohemian atmosphere of the café. He has a remarkable face: a head of light-colored hair like a lion's mane, brushed backward, piercing green eyes under a permanently frowning brow and a pinched, willful mouth set in a square jaw which he pushes forward in a *moue* of great determination. He comes every day, from eight to twelve in the morning, two to eight in the afternoon, and nine to eleven at night. "Like a clerk."[1] He smokes and listens to the heated arguments at the next table. He always sits next to Sartre but never says a word to him. Simone de Beauvoir is also there. Whenever she takes out a cigarette, the young man stands up, bends towards her ceremoniously, and, still silent, lights it for her. She thanks him with a nod of her head; he nods back respectfully and sits down. Every day that winter the silent ceremony is repeated. No one ever asks who the foreign-looking young man is. Every day, he sits without a word next to the "idol" of the French cultural scene. Is he never "tempted" to speak to the idol?[2]

The young man's name is Emil Cioran. At the time we see him eavesdropping on Sartre and his group, he is a Romanian doctoral student, in Paris on a renewable fellowship since 1937. But he hasn't yet written a single line of his thesis. He never will, in fact. He is not really a student; he is a writer. Nor is he as young as he seems: though thirty-three is not old for a doctoral student, some of Cioran's apparent youth is a feature of his foreignness, which he will cultivate as a permanent aspect of his *persona*. He is not even a *French* writer, yet. His equivocal position on the margins of Sartre's group, gravitating around the axis of French intellectual authority, always silent but always present, sums up this ambitious and divided young man, in quest of a center that will focus his own creative energy. In Romania, he is well known, the published and controversial author of five books and numerous articles. In Paris, in 1943–44, he is nobody, just an exile from Eastern Europe, hoping to make a name for himself in the City of Light. He is finishing a book about Nazi-occupied Paris as symbol of the final decay of Western civilization. But the book, written in Romanian, will remain, forgotten or abandoned, in manuscript form until its publication in 1991. For the young Romanian suddenly decides, the very next summer, to abandon his native language and to write henceforth in French, at last to break into, as it were, the conversations of Jean-Paul Sartre and Simone de Beauvoir.

Five years later, in the fall of 1949, the French publishing house Gallimard brings out a volume of essays with the curious title *Précis de décomposition (A Treatise on Decay)*. The author is an unknown Romanian, E. M. Cioran, the former Emil Cioran of the Café de Flore. His book causes a sensation in literary circles, and its author is welcomed as the oracle of our disgraced modern times. Maurice Nadeau in *Le Combat* extols him in rapturous terms as a philosopher for the end of time:

> he has arrived, he whom we have been waiting for, the prophet of our era of concentration camps and collective suicide, the one whose arrival has been prepared by all the philosophers of the void and of the absurd, harbinger of bad news par excellence. Let us greet him and watch him closely: he will bear witness to our times.[3]

In 1950, Cioran's book is awarded the Rivarol prize for the best manuscript in French by a foreign author. Overnight, Cioran has become a French author, immediately and often compared with Sartre and Camus, if only to be distinguished from them.

When he read Nadeau's article in *Le Combat,* Cioran was jubilant. "I made it! I won!" he told his companion, Simone Boué. "You must understand how important it is for a Romanian intellectual to be acknowledged and reviewed in France. I made it! I won!"[4] To his parents, he wrote in a similarly exuberant vein: "I must confess that the success of the book has surpassed my most optimistic expectations. Not being designed for a wide audience, the book cannot bring me much from a financial point of view. *But at least I am no longer a poor unknown stranger, which means a lot in a country where prestige is everything.*"[5]

Cioran had won a wager he made with himself, namely, that he would write and rewrite until he received public recognition in France. Just a few months before the publication of the *Précis*—which he rewrote four times—Cioran had felt snubbed and humiliated by Albert Camus in the Gallimard offices, when Camus, who had read the manuscript of the *Précis,* told him he still had to "enter the circulation of great ideas." Incensed, Cioran had sworn on the spot to "avenge" himself, that is, to write until he would triumph.[6] He had embarked on a lonely and painful adventure, but he was never discouraged, not even by Camus's dismissive comments. Cioran pursued his mission with dogged determination, with a fanatical belief in its importance that was the equivalent of mystical faith. He experienced his revenge as a triumph simultaneously over both French pretentiousness and Romanian provinciality.

In retrospect, young Cioran's silent position next to Sartre at the Flore was not at all accidental. Cioran chose it deliberately. He watched and waited like a spy, quietly measuring his forces against Sartre's to find out his own worth. "My path was the reverse of Sartre's," he said later, even though his essay on Sartre in the *Précis,* "On an Entrepreneur of Ideas," shows how much Sartre's model was on his mind.[7] He could speak as well as Sartre, he had read much more, he would write as well as they—Sartre's circle—were writing. His silence was not shyness or intimidation, but inordinate pride. With his body strategically placed on the margins of fame, Cioran made a statement. He was nearly inside the magic circle of Sartre and French cultural life, which had enormous prestige in the eyes of European intellectuals, especially marginal Europeans like Romanians. Just outside the circle, or rather on its borderline, the ambitious interloper worked silently and tenaciously in isolation for another five long years—scribbling away like Dostoevsky's underground man, in the cheapest hotel rooms in the Latin Quarter—to gain the place at the table he had marked out for himself, next to Sartre, publicly recognized in France. But unlike Dostoevsky's underground man, whose "revenges" were never more than pathetic failures to impress imaginary opponents, Cioran's "revenge" was a blazing success. Hailed by Nadeau as a "twilight thinker," by André Maurois as the new "moralist or immoralist,"[8] by Claude Mauriac for "masterly language . . . closer to Pascal than Vigny,"[9] the Romanian-born Cioran had not merely arrived on the French literary scene; he blazed across it like the meteor, symbol of obscurely powerful poetic genius, in Mallarmé's poem, "calme bloc ici-bas chu d'un desastre obscur"[10] [calm [granite] block fallen down here from some dark disaster].

This is the story my book has to tell: how an unknown young man from the margins of Europe, with a fanatic will to transform himself, achieved fame "in a country where prestige is everything." This biography covers the crucial first stages of his career, from 1911, the year of his birth, to 1949, the year of his consecration as a French writer, which marks his final break with his Romanian roots.

After 1949, nearly a dozen more of Cioran's books—all variations on the same theme, the decadence of the Western liberal world—came out with striking precision at roughly four-year intervals (see Chronology). More prizes followed: the Rivarol, the Saint-Beuve, the Combat, the Nimier. And more praise. In his lifetime, Cioran was acclaimed as "the greatest French writer to honor our language since the death of Paul Valéry" (St. John Perse), "a master of French prose," and "a modern Socrates" (Marc Fumaroli, professor at the Collège de France), and "the most distinguished figure in the tradition of Kierkegaard, Nietzsche and Wittgenstein" (Susan Sontag). When he died in Paris in 1995, the event released an avalanche of articles in *Le Figaro, Le Monde, Paris Match, Le Nouvel Observateur,* and *Magazine Littéraire,* as well as radio talk-shows and theatre productions reflecting a renewed interest in his life and work.[11] More than once, Cioran's name has been honored with standing ovations in the Assemblée Nationale. In the minutes of the March 17, 1999, session, for example, a member of the Assemblée pays homage to all of the "Francophone Romanians who contributed to the splendor of [our] culture," and among them to Cioran, "one of the greatest French philosophers of the 20th century." Cioran has become more conspicuous dead than alive.

However, though lionized in France and translated into many languages around the world, from Polish to Japanese, Cioran's name still draws a blank in many circles. He is particularly little known in the Anglo-American world of letters, where, though his work has been translated from French by the distinguished American poet Richard Howard, translator of Proust and Barthes, and praised by Susan Sontag, America's home-grown "European" intellectual, his writing has not caught on in the way the work of Sartre or Derrida did. Granted, he is a specialized taste, too sharp and bitter for many palates and yet, paradoxically, too lyrical or too "unserious" for others. Yet Cioran is a better, "purer" writer than Sartre or any of the postwar French existentialists. If his stylistic incisiveness has led some critics to put him in the same class with Paul Valéry, an ultimate accolade of linguistic purity, the shocking, bracing verve—and black humor—of his existential despair admits his philosophical prose to the company of Nietzsche and Kierkegaard.

It's peculiar to be simultaneously famous and obscure, but it's a situation that fits Cioran like a glove. If the scene at the Café de Flore tells us anything, it is that Cioran chose for himself a place on the borderline between fame and anonymity, a narrow precipitous place, which he then proceeded to inhabit for the rest of his life. Friend of Eugène Ionesco, Samuel Beckett, and Henri Michaux, Cioran was as famous as they, yet he was, as he often put it in interviews, "un ennemi de la gloire." He insisted that there could not be a greater calamity for a writer than to become somebody—"quelqu'un"—that is, someone important. He vehemently refused to consider himself an established author; he was at the most, he said, "un homme de fragment."[12]

Cioran flirted with fame but did not cultivate it. When it came to him, he evaded it: he refused to accept all of the prizes he was awarded with the exception of the first one, Rivarol, which "he found impossible to refuse."[13] He refused to give interviews in France (though he was more accessible to foreign journalists); he made no TV appearances, he had no public political stance. He thus acquired an *inverse* fame, the reputation of a recluse, who, from his attic in the Latin Quarter, like Bunuel's Saint Simeon on his column in the desert, regularly launched his books like so many anathemas against our times. If you wanted to put a face to this prophetic voice, he could be easily spotted on his daily rounds in the Luxembourg gardens or in the neighborhood of the cathedral of Saint Sulpice in the Sixth *arrondissement.* Dressed with the elegance of a British country gentleman in woolen cap, scarf, and coat, but with a most un-British stare in his intense "flashing" eyes and "floating hair," he cultivated an incongruous look, half-civilized, half-savage. One did not pass this elegant British-looking prophet in the street without asking oneself, "Who *is* that man?" His aura of mystery and provocation was carefully cultivated.

The same goes for Cioran's literary reputation. To the question I am so often asked, "Who is E. M. Cioran?" my best short answer is, "a famous marginal." I haven't found a better way to describe him. His very name illustrates the Cioranian paradox. It is a hybrid, a partly made-up name. The initials E. M. do not stand for Emil(e) Michel, as the Library of Congress mistakenly lists him, but simply for E. M., as in E. M. Forster. On the eve of his French debut, Cioran made the first two letters of his given name, Emil, into two initials alluding to an English author, who is himself somewhat on the margins of twentieth-century literary fame.[14] By thus modifying his given name into a pen name that copied the name of another writer—admittedly not the most famous one, but one who *seemed* famous to him and with whom he sought to identify—Cioran revealed both his writerly ambitions and his biographical ambiguities. Using the ordinary letters of his own Romanian *name,* he raised them to the status of famous *initials.* Thus Cioran, an unknown author, a "barbarian" from the margins of Europe, found the elements for the creation of a new authorial persona. Emil, the Romanian, the Transylvanian, turned himself into the cryptic E. M., and by this act of baptismal abbreviation he reinvented himself as a "civilized" West European author.

The name, grafting the old and the new, East and West, the marginal and the famous, is a mirror image of the man's biography. Cioran has in fact two lives, two identities, two voices: the Romanian Emil Cioran, a "mystical revolutionary,"[15] imbued with the ideals of political romanticism, author of five books and numerous articles, and the French E. M. Cioran, referred to simply as "Cioran" in the last stages of his fame, who in 1937 sent himself as exile to Paris, and twelve years later made his spectacular entrance on the French literary scene. In these two lives, he contains within himself much of the history of twentieth-century Europe, uneasily divided between East and West.

Cioran does not belong to the "once-born," to use William James's formulation. He belongs to the "sick souls" or "divided selves," that is, those who strive for a "second birth" and undergo a "growth-crisis" that will "convert" them to "their habitual center of personal energy."[16] Like Joyce's Stephen Dedalus in *A Portrait of the Artist as a Young Man,* young Cioran was engulfed in a cycle of identity crises (existential, religious, political) leading to exile and eventual triumph. Like Stephen, Cioran finds his true artistic self, once his "country has died" for him and he rejects all the embroiling and befuddling "nets" of family, religion, and politics. At the center of his life gapes the wide rift of exile, Cioran's unique way to self-realization and the driving force of his writing. In a very specific historical, political, and cultural context, Cioran crossed the chasm of exile and found his "habitual center," reaching what William Carlos Williams calls the creative "self's objectives."

Cioran's early life, with its abrupt change of identity, presents a fascinating story of Romantic self-transformation. The European intellectual world knows him as the ironic moralist and elegant stylist, a burnished, fixed image to go with his burnished, flawless style. The world also knows him as the disabused Old Man. Ever since his 1949 literary triumph, Cioran, like Yeats in "Sailing to Byzantium," adopted the mask of the wise and cynical old man, though he was then only thirty-eight years old. This old man's voice, which speaks in all of his French writings, creates the false impression that Cioran, even when he alludes to a younger version of himself and refers to unspecified youthful tribulations, has no other history than that of The Recluse of Saint Sulpice. But his images of the recluse, of the "abuser of the universe," its "universal calumniator," are carefully constructed versions of himself.

Though extraordinary, Cioran's personal saga is not unique, either in psychological or sociological terms. Psychologically, the stages of Cioran's evolution follow what Erik Erikson calls "a classical pattern of repudiation and devotion." First, repudiation of a career as a Romanian intellectual; next, temporary devotion to an extreme ideology, apocalyptic nationalism, that was for him always problematic; then, the sense of a spiritual mission which gradually narrowed its focus from the nation to the self, finally mobilizing the creative capacities of the self into the born-again writer.[17]

Neither is Cioran's life very different from the life of other right-wing intellectuals of the inter-war period, from a sociological point of view. It resembles, for example, a pattern which Jerry Muller, in *The Other God That Failed,* sees as paradigmatic of the life of many German scholars of the period, including perhaps the most famous of them all, Martin Heidegger. Muller's book, a "representative biography" of the German sociologist Hans Freyer (1887–1969), is especially interested in the "formative contexts, events and patterns of behavior that Hans Freyer shared with other intellectuals," not merely the particularities of one man's life. Muller thus identifies three stages in Freyer's life that are typical rather than particular: 1) "alienation from the liberal welfare state" and "articulate advocacy of an all-encompassing state that would mobilize society and culture for the militant defense of collective particularity"; 2) "ingenuous support for the National Socialist movement in the hope that the movement will provide the vehicle through which the ideal state might be realized"; and 3) disillusionment, disengagement and distancing of oneself in published works from the fascist tenets one previously held.[18] *Mutatis mutandi,* this pattern can be easily traced in Cioran's life as it moved from early political involvement to detachment and exile, except that for Cioran, the failure of the political dream brought about his literary triumph.

To a great extent Cioran's life pattern reproduces the cycle of political radicalization and subsequent de-radicalization of many twentieth-century intellectuals, a cycle which itself repeats a pattern already established by the European Romantic generations after the French Revolution. The cycle begins with intellectuals' critique of modern society, coupled with utopian, totalitarian solutions. It ends with their revulsion at the excesses of revolution, war, and totalitarianism, and a retreat into the de-politicized realm of art and ideas.[19]

As an enthusiast of the anti-rationalist philosophies widely popular in Europe during the first decades of the twentieth century, Cioran belonged to the tradition of the intellectual right descended from the Counter-Enlightenment. Its dominant ideology was "radical conservatism," characterized by strong antipathy toward liberal institutions and capitalist society and appealing for the restoration of civic virtues by radical, revolutionary action.[20] This neo-romantic critique of flaccid liberal society looked attractive on paper, but it turned ugly in reality. Hence Cioran, along with other brilliant Romanians of the period, cuts a sorry figure when, from being an "angry young man" in his bookish speculations, he becomes an advocate of the fascistic Iron Guard movement.

Surprisingly little biographical work has been done on Cioran. Academic monographs have tended to ignore Cioran's Romanian life and works and concentrate on the major (French) philosophical themes in his work. More recent works in Romania and the Romanian emigré press discuss Cioran in the context of over-all reevaluations of the intellectual generation of the 1930s. Some are flatly critical of his early right-wing political attachments, while others try to explain them away. In France, where Cioran has been exclusively known as a French writer, the question of his Romanian past has only recently come to the fore. Gabriel Liiceanu's *Itinéraires d'une vie* (1995) prefaces an interview with the ailing eighty-three-year-old Cioran with a biographical sketch that briefly outlines Cioran's Romanian period. Patrice Bollon's *Cioran l'hérétique* is a more ambitious project, connecting Cioran's Romanian work to his French *œuvre.* But Bollon concentrates exclusively on the anti-semitic aspect of Cioran's early work, which he considers a "youthful error," entirely attributable to the political climate and blind prejudices of the time. Thus for Bollon, Cioran's "second birth" as a French writer was a way of erasing the guilty trace from his past. Submitting himself to the rigor and discipline of the French language, Cioran, according to Bollon, gradually came to his senses, abandoned, regretted, and partially retracted his earlier anti-semitic stance.[21]

This book is neither a case for Cioran's prosecution nor an *apologia pro vita sua.* Our century is dominated by a trial mentality, as Milan Kundera rightly observed, and the temptation to "prosecute" an intellectual and prove that he or she remains a fascist (or a Communist) at heart is an inherent danger for any biography.[22] Mine is rather an attempt at understanding or comprehension, in Hannah Arendt's sense:

> Comprehension does not mean denying the outrageous, deducing the unprecedented from precedents, or explaining phenomena by such analogies and generalities that the

> impact of reality and the shock of experience are no longer felt. It means, rather, *examining and bearing consciously the burden that events have placed upon us*—neither denying their existence nor submitting meekly to their weight as though everything that in fact happened could not have happened otherwise.[23]

Avoiding both the witch-hunts of political attack and the high-minded celebrations of the "Olympian" Cioran of his later French years, I concentrate instead on Cioran's important formative years, his youth in a Romanian village in Transylvania, his student years in Bucharest during Romania's politically troubled inter-war period when, along with Eugène Ionesco and Mircea Eliade, he belonged to Romania's generation of "angry young men," and his first years in France, roughly coinciding with the outbreak of the World War II, the occupation of Paris, and the defeat of Nazi Germany, a period which was for Cioran the crucial turning point in his life as a writer. Throughout, I seek to answer the question of how this provincial young man made himself into the ironic moralist and elegant stylist so admired today.

But, if Cioran's life is a paradigm of self-creation, the questions still remain: How well did he succeed? How does he stand out? What makes him Cioran and what explains his triumph? While acknowledging the "formative events" and historical contexts in Cioran's life, this biography shows another aspect of the process, whereby a young man from a place as marginal to Western culture as Transylvania—a place that many Americans imagine exists only as the home of Dracula—was "radicalized" by intense experiences of spiritual and political awakening during the early years of Romania's "spiritual revolution." It shows how he reconstructed himself, by a process far more complex than a simple political retrenchment or self-imposed silence, into a writer, moralist, and essayist, who is now by most accounts one of the greatest stylists in the French language.

But there are dangers in contextualizing Cioran too much, reading him exclusively either as a right-wing Romanian or an apolitical Western intellectual. Thus, to read (and explain) him entirely in his Romanian context is not a complete solution. On the contrary, it can be an obstacle because of the danger of "Roumanizing" him, reducing him again to a general rule: how he is like other Romanian intellectuals of his generation. It would also force him back into the narrow confines of a small nation he always wanted to escape. One should read Cioran *against* the historical background of his early life and times to see *also* how he stood out and apart from his national context. Milan Kundera's comment on Leoš Janáček's cultural fate is relevant for Cioran as well: "If in the case of Broch, of Musil, of Gombrowicz, and in a sense Bartok, delay in recognition is due to historic catastrophes (Nazism, war) . . . , in Janáček's case it was his small nation that completely took over the role of catastrophes."[24] Being Romanian was for Cioran a calamity he did everything in his power to transcend, and his struggle to overcome this calamity is faithfully recorded in his books.

On the other hand, to compare him with German right-wing intellectuals such as Hans Freyer or Martin Heidegger is also limiting—for in their cases one cannot speak of triumphs. As Muller shows, in the aftermath of the war and through the entire de-nazification period, these intellectuals were barely surviving, only precariously maintaining a livelihood and their professional reputation. It is precisely at this point of crisis, however, that Cioran's path deviates from the general pattern: where they fall, he rises.

Disenchantment with his former politicized self, instead of being debilitating, becomes the motor of Cioran's literary career in the West. At the distance of more than half a century, we tend to forget how much, in the first two decades after the war, when Cioran was making his reputation in France, the memory of the catastrophe of the war and of totalitarianism(s) dominated the political and cultural life of Western Europe. Cioran's work must be understood in the pervasive climate of disappointment with political utopias. In his critique of the liberal, decadent West and the totalitarian aberrations it had led to, Cioran capitalized on the experience of the century and voiced the "spirit of the age," gaining recognition as "prophet" of the era. He snatched his personal victory from the jaws of Europe's defeat. In this "triumph of failure" lies Cioran's "revenge," and the secret of his self-reconstruction.

Cioran actually lived the experience of the century first-hand. It was, first and foremost, his own life experience. His existential prose draws upon it. The English Romantic poets, Wordsworth and Byron, wrote and rewrote many poems about the most formative years of their lives: the time of the French Revolution and the Napoleonic Wars, a time when it was "bliss to be alive, but to be young was very heaven."[25] During the years of his revolutionary youth—the decade of the 1930s, characterized by the rise of fascism in Western Europe and Stalin's reign of terror in Russia—Cioran, like Wordsworth and Byron, was deeply political and "subscribed to fanaticism, rage and madness," with a desperate abandon that was unusually intense and vehement. This was the time of Cioran's involvement with Romania's Iron Guard movement. It was then that he wrote his one political tract, *Romania's Transfiguration* (1937), a wildly fanciful utopia in which he dreamt of a Romania with "the destiny of France and the population of China"—and which he disbelieved almost as soon as he imagined it.

This period full of "juvenile errors," as Wordsworth called them, became the substance of Cioran's subsequent writings. As he himself observes, the spirit of the times precipitated young people into politics, exploiting the idealism and fervor natural to youth:

> He, who between the age of twenty and thirty, has not subscribed to fanaticism, rage and madness is an imbecile. . . . Misfortune is reality for young people. They are the ones who proclaim totalitarian doctrines, and who carry them out, they are the ones who clamor for blood, who revel in noise, screams, barbarity. At the time when I was young, the entire Europe believed in youth, all of Europe pushed the young into politics, urged them to take part in government.[26]

The turbulent years were followed by his self-imposed exile to France and adoption of a new persona—ironic, disenchanted, and skeptical—a move again uncannily similar to Wordsworth's retreat into the English Lake District, though in reverse, since Wordsworth retreated into nature's bosom, whereas Cioran chose the most sophisticated city in Western Europe. Both writers recreated themselves in exile, Cioran as the last of the French *moralistes,* Wordsworth as the first great English nature poet. The new self-image these authors presented to the public was in both cases apparently removed from the nightmare of history and politics, but only apparently.

It is only at the level of sublimation of the personal that Cioran could appeal to the Western public. No one would have listened in 1949 to the confessions of a marginal, a passport-less alien, a *sans papiers.* To have remained specific, to have played up his Romanian origins, would really have been the death of him. He would not have become "Cioran" but merely a footnote in history. Thus we need to interpret Cioran's texts in a closer relation to his life than has yet been done: not as direct reflections of the life but as his own interpretations of it. And this is, in fact, the approach Cioran himself advocates. As he put it in an interview, "all my books are more or less veiled confessions."

In spite of appearances, the aphoristic Cioran is a profoundly autobiographical writer. His works are autobiographical precisely because they don't seem to be. For, as he put it in *De l'incovénient d'être né,* "l'unique confession sincère est celle que nous faisons indirectement—en parlant des autres" [the only sincere confession is the one we make indirectly—while speaking of others].[27] The sublimated autobiography was for Cioran a means of (re)-imagining himself. One must read his indirect confessions on two registers at once: the autobiographical, personal and the aphoristic, universal. The two levels interact dialogically: the autobiographical detail or fact shapes the general thought while, at the same time, the thought requires the projection of an author's figure.

A passage from *La tentation d'exister* illustrates Cioran's manner of indirect confession. Embedded in an attack on biographical writing, we find his definition of life as a wound, of writing as a cure, and of the author as a martyr undergoing meaningless suffering. Simultaneously autobiographical and therapeutic writing both *conceals* and *reveals* the writer's life:

> In the age of biographies, no one covers his wounds without running the risk of having the bandage torn off and the wounds exposed for all to see; and, if they fail to expose them, we go away totally disappointed. And even he who ended on the cross, it is not because he suffered *for us* that he still matters to us, but because he suffered without end and gave out some cries that were as profound as they were free of charge.[28]

The metaphor of the wound of life, dressed in layers of writing, nowhere makes sense so well as in Cioran's own work. In this respect, Cioran resembles Luther, or rather Kierkegaard's perception of Luther: a "lifestyle of patienthood as a sense of imposed suffering, of an intense need for cure, and a passion for expressing and describing one's suffering."[29] By giving outward expression to his tormented inner life, Cioran managed to reduce its intensity and avoid a self-destructive internal combustion, for, as he memorably put it: "un livre est un suicide différé" [a book is a postponed suicide].[30] His passion for describing his own suffering is especially evident in his first book, *On the Heights of Despair,* written because Cioran, at age twenty-one, could find no better way to resist the temptation to commit suicide. It was Cioran's first successful attempt at a "writing cure."

Though all of Cioran's works are autobiographies in disguise, his earlier Romanian writings have an almost visceral quality: in them the wound of life is still raw, unhealed, close to the surface. They are intensely lyrical, almost savage in their passionate self-expression. They have a barbaric quality; they are made of "blood and tears." In them, Cioran groans and cries out in despair, reveling in descriptions of his inner torments. There is a lot of dramatic posturing in these early books that some readers find off-putting, but they are the signs of a genuine affliction, the difficulty Cioran has in finding a central direction to his life. Since he is not an "imbecile," he experiences his identity crisis as an illness. He gropes for an identity as for a cure throughout this early Romanian period, and his flights of passion alternate with flights of despair in his books, like red lines on a fever chart. In his early writings, Cioran lets us in on the evolution of an idea, the thinker's hesitations and tribulations *before* he reaches his thought. He thus gives the reader the impression that he is witness to a most intimate process, and creates between the reader and himself intellectual tension and excitement.

Cioran's later writings are more intellectual and less obviously autobiographical. In them, any trace of the process of thought elaboration is eliminated, but the *bons mots,* the aphorisms, the paradoxes, spectacular as they are as linguistic and intellectual tours de force, retain their confessional and intimate, "lived" quality; they are as much *cris du cœur* as they are philosophical fireworks, or as Cioran himself put it, they remain "tears turned into thoughts." They are still about the same "juvenile errors," but Cioran is now a contemplative commentator on his own past. The wound is now hidden from view under writing which has sublimated the martyred author's ordeal. The bandage—writing—is the wound's only trace, and the sufferer, now a master of style, is in control of his agony. His personal agony has become aestheticized to the point that one can speak of a tortured *dandyism*. By now Cioran has turned "passion" into a style, a lifestyle.

If Cioran's early writings are too self-revelatory and therefore guilty of "clearing up too many of those misunderstandings essential to a writer's secret fame" as Cioran said of Paul Valéry, his later writings, though obsessively returning to the same life experiences, treat them in a universal rather than personal way, with a drier, distanced, aphoristic style.[31] The later French texts project Cioran's private identity crisis into the tragedy of the human condition, moving, as Sorin Antohi says, from "the psychological abyss of stigmatized ethnic identity to the metaphysical plane of generic humanity. . . . When the question of identity is thus reoriented towards the entire humanity, the last traces of anxiety disappear, and Cioran, eternally obsessed with his roots, can finally escape from the metaphysical trap of stigmatization."[32]

This transformation from the viscerally personal to the impersonal is clearly marked by a change of language, tone, and style in Cioran's texts: from Romanian to French, from disheveled prose to the reticence of aphoristic fragments, from the vulgar forcefulness of prophecy and anathema to the elegant refinements of irony and paradox afforded by the eighteenth-century French style he deliberately chose as his model of writing. He chose to write in a language that was, by his own definition, universal, impersonal, and dead, and therefore best suited to his new condition as a writer without a language and without a country or a past. "Un idiome n'approche de l'universalité que lorsqu'il s'émancipe de ses origines, s'en éloigne et les renie" [A language only approaches universality when it is emancipated from its origins, distances itself from them and repudiates them].[33] Thus eighteenth-century French became both the model and the means—a sort of steep shortcut—to satisfy his ambitious aspirations to universality. Alerted to this transformation, any reader of Cioran, and his intellectual biographer in particular, must question Cioran's French reputation as a skeptical *apatride* (man without a country) and read all of his work in light of his life and times, as writings and rewritings of those years when the young Cioran was marching in step with his generation to the trumpets of History.

**FIGURE 1.** Family Portrait (*left to right*): brother Aurelian (Relu), father Emilian, sister Virginia, Emil, mother Elvira. Ca. 1925. Courtesy of Aurelian Cioran.

**FIGURE 2.** Young Cioran skiing in the Carpathian mountains. Courtesy of Aurelian Cioran.

**FIGURE 3.**
Cioran on army duty.
Fall 1935–Spring 1936.
Courtesy of Aurelian Cioran.

**FIGURE 4.** (*below*)
Cioran and Petre Țuțea,
the "conversational philosopher,"
in Bucharest in the 1930s.
Courtesy of Aurelian Cioran.

UNIVERSITÉ DE PARIS
FACULTÉ DES LETTRES
IMMATRICULATION
CARTE D'ÉTUDIANT N° 912
valable pour l'année scolaire 1938-1939
M. Cioran Emile
rue du Sommerard
Signature de l'Étudiant,
L. 39. — Paris, I. A. C. (9-38)

**FIGURE 5.** Cioran's student ID card at the Sorbonne, for the academic year 1938–39. He used the card more for admission to the cheap student dining halls than for lectures or libraries. Courtesy of Aurelian Cioran.

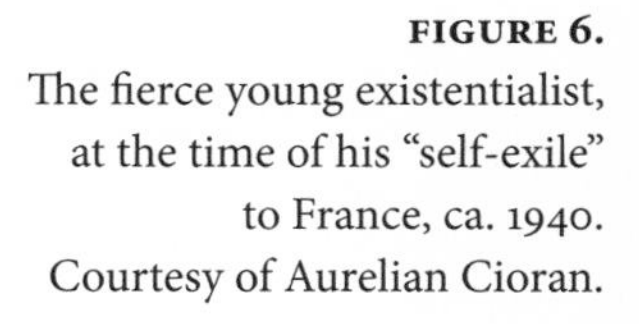

**FIGURE 6.**
The fierce young existentialist, at the time of his "self-exile" to France, ca. 1940. Courtesy of Aurelian Cioran.

# 1

## Rășinari, Transylvania, 1911–1921

I haven't written with my blood, I have written with all the tears I have never shed. Even if I had been a logician, I would still have been an elegiacal man. Every day I relive the expulsion from Paradise with the same passion and the same regret as the one who was first banished.

—Cioran, *Cahiers*, 683

I am not from here; condition of inner exile; I'm nowhere at home—absolute rootlessness. Paradise lost,—my constant obsession.

—Cioran, *Cahiers*, 19

I have lived all my life with the feeling that I was chased away from my true place. If the phrase "metaphysical exile" had been deprived of meaning, my existence alone would have sufficed to give it one.

—Cioran, "De l'inconvénient d'être né," *Œuvres*, 1320

### The Past's Omnipresence: 21, rue de l'Odéon, Paris, July 1960

He lay fully clothed on his narrow cot in the unfamiliar attic room, staring at the gray light filtered through a small skylight in the ceiling. He preferred overcast skies; blue skies were troubling, stirring up one's *wanderlust*. And now he had stopped wandering: for ten years, while living in furnished hotel rooms, Cioran had been dreaming of an apartment of his own. The dream had finally come true, but now it gave him little satisfaction. Having a home: if only God would forgive him such decadence! He was nowhere at home, he was *the* exile par excellence. He thought himself a *passant,* "en instance de depart, realité provisoire" [on the point of departure, provisional reality].[1]

He had been almost homeless all his life, moving from one city to another, farther and farther away from his birthplace: Răşinari, Sibiu, Bucharest, Berlin, Paris. Răşinari and Paris: the beginning and the end of his life's journey. Farthest apart in time and space, they shared one advantage for him: they were both places "out of time." The former was his childhood paradise, the latter was the "home" of his exile, which fed his vocation for marginality. Between them, they spanned history, and he abhorred history.[2]

He had *felt* homeless ever since the day he left his village in the Carpathian mountains to go to secondary school in the nearby old German town of Sibiu (Hermannstadt) in Transylvania.[3] Now forty years had passed, and he could not forget the feeling of estrangement he experienced then. He saw himself, a sturdy, fair-haired child of ten, dressed in the stiff new school uniform, sitting on a load of hay in the back of a horse-drawn cart. His parents sat on the box in front. Though a priest, his father had enough of the peasant left in him to drive the horses himself. His robust back, draped in priestly black robes, rose straight and massive in front of his son's eyes like an insurmountable obstacle or a terrible menace. The cart advanced slowly in the blue haze of an early September morning. The villagers on their way to their fields stopped and respectfully lifted their hats to greet them. They stared after the cart. The village priest's son was going away to school. Like a wedding or a funeral, it was an event worthy of their attention.

As the towers of Sibiu's churches gradually came into view, his heart sank with despair. He burst into tears, sobbing with uncontrollable and unmitigated grief. His father was "tearing him away from the village he adored to the point of idolatry." He had been used to running barefoot in the fields and hills of his native village from May to November, totally free. Suddenly he felt trapped. The outskirts of the approaching city were the new limits of his freedom, and his father's bulky black shape, their guardian. His new clothes itched, his new shoes pinched. He felt as if his feet had sunk into an anthill and were being slowly eaten by the tireless insects. He shook with helpless rage. He wished the new school would disappear, wiped away by some disaster. One of his childhood friends had thought up an ingenious method to do away with school: he had rubbed their old country school with lard, hoping the dogs would eat it. It was an action of protest worthy of Rabelais's Panurge. How well he understood the feeling that had prompted it!

Still crying, he was duly delivered into the competent hands of two German sisters who ran a boarding house in Sibiu. On that fateful day, after his parents had left, he spent a long time at the window of his new home, looking sorrowfully after their cart, looking back toward the "one place in the world [he] loved most," the village which for him was "the end of the world, or rather, the center." It was a place to which he afterward returned only briefly for summer vacations, and where he would never go back to live again. But he entertained fantasies of return all his life, for "the farther the place is, the more attached to it one becomes."

As he grew older, childhood memories gained more and more terrain, pushing out all other memories. They were stored up in images that trampled on his thoughts. They threw themselves at him in disjointed fashion. They did not exactly prevent him from thinking, but they prevented his thoughts from expanding. Nostalgia boiled like poison in his blood. His childhood exploded like a bomb in front of his eyes. He saw it in small fragments, a shred of memory here, a splinter there.

Life didn't suit him. He was made for a savage existence, for total solitude, outside of time, enclosed in a crepuscular paradise. Rășinari, his mountain village, what a splendid paradise! There, in that time before time, a young boy of six, dressed in white peasant clothes, ran barefoot through a narrow cobbled-stone lane, from after breakfast until noon, and then again from lunch till late at night—a pair of ragged pants, a coarse linen shirt flowing loose behind him. He ran toward the forbidden site, the gypsy settlement at the end of his village. Rounding up his friends with a promise of the raw sugar candy called bear shit (*caca de urs*) stolen from his grandmother's store, the children played hide-and-seek (*de-a hoții și jandarii*) on a nearby hill—his beloved Coasta Boacii (Hill of the Boacis)—till night closed in on them. No one checked or interrupted his games. Why did he ever leave Coasta Boacii?

His calling had been to live in nature, not to read and write. He was not just at home in nature. He was a child of nature, a "wild beast," fostered and reared by the river that ran behind his house and by the nearby wooded hills, which stretched toward the village like three knotty, rough fingers of a giant hand, reaching down from the lofty heights of the Carpathian mountains on the horizon.

The river was Rîul Caselor, river of the houses. He practically lived in it, like a water creature. Through its clear, shallow water, he could see the bottom lined with round pebbles and small boulders, all smooth, shiny, slippery, covered with a thick short fur of yellow algae. He made the smooth pebbles skip along the surface of the water. He waded and splashed around all summer long. He bathed in the shade of the old walnut trees by the edge of the water, where he had dammed up the river with boulders, forming a small, dark pool, big enough for one child. Sometimes he would climb and hide inside the tree's thick foliage, picking and eating the green walnuts that left a crisp, cool taste in his mouth.

In winter, the frozen surface of the river rang with the noise of bundled-up children, pushing and shoving each other in primitive improvisations of ice hockey, an alternative to sledding on Coasta Boacii. The snow was piled high in the streets of Rășinari, with only a narrow path to make one's way through it. His favorite snow route was the lane, *ulitza,* that led toward Trainei, a small shepherd settlement on the northern edge of the village. The lane was really a river bed, the *Steaza,* which came in tumultuously from the faraway mountains at one end of the village, slowed down as it traversed the village, and then continued on its way, flowing lazily into the plain stretching toward Sibiu. At the end of the *ulitza* in Trainei rose the ruins of an old Roman fortress, *Cetățuia,* so beaten by weather and the passing of time that it looked more like part of the hill than a man-made structure. From its battlements, he participated in mythic snowball fights, little Romans defending themselves from barbarian onslaughts.

He missed the snow more than anything. The swiftly melting snow in wet, desolate Paris was nothing like the enduring snows of Rășinari. Yet stepping in it, like Proust over the stones of Venice, brought back to him the memory of long, harsh winters in his remote mountain village, when the forest was still and mysterious under its heavy cape of snow. Wonderful, mythical Rășinari, in which the consciousness of time had not yet inserted itself, was borne back to him by the ephemeral snows of Paris. Why had he ever left it? Why did he ever leave Coasta Boacii?

### The Exacerbation of Memory: 21, rue de l'Odéon, Paris, January 1970

But beside these ideal images lay others more disturbing. Winter nights in Rășinari were long and cold. They—he, his older sister, and his younger brother—lay huddled together in their night shifts to keep warm, on a bed erected above the wood-burning stove, while Aunt Stanca told terrifying bedtime stories of children stolen by the gypsies, murdered by demons, and of witches and fairies bathing naked at midnight in the river outside. They were alone in the old house except for mad Stanca and their grandmother: three little kids struck dumb with fear, staring at each other with huge worried eyes, too scared to venture out at night even for the most pressing needs, too scared even to sleep.

It was past midnight. He lay still on his bed in Paris. His loneliness was so immense, it felt like cosmic destitution. He became accustomed to watch time flow during long waking hours, where one became one with the night, a palpable, "liquid night." He would count the seconds the way a prisoner, submitted to the water torture, counted the drops falling on his face. In this way he had learned to "perceive time's detachment from what was not time, its autonomous existence, its particular status, its empire, its tyranny."[4]

Memories of his distant childhood assailed him and turned the idea of origins into an obsession. He was born in a land where birth was considered a curse. He empathized with his clear-sighted ancestors. "Thracians and Bogomiles [primitive peoples of the region]—I can't forget that I have roamed the same space as them, nor that the former cried over their newborn babies while the latter, to exculpate God, blamed Satan for the crime of Creation."[5] Birth was an inconvenience, monstrous, abnormal. It was much easier to think of it as an anomaly than as a natural fact. His own birth had been an unfortunate accident. It had made him a prisoner of life, of history.

He first became aware of time at precisely three o'clock on a lazy summer afternoon when he was five years old. Like Wordsworth in Cumberland, this was a "spot of time" which Cioran chose as his self-defining moment. The world suddenly emptied before his very eyes.[6] While his village slumbered in the heavy heat, with only the buzz of drones to disturb the stillness in the air, he felt dizzy with "a sort of unbearable anxiety."[7] Everything around him lost its meaning as if it had vanished; time became still yet palpable. It felt as if it had stopped flowing and was "detaching" itself from things. The world suddenly felt solitary, engulfed in an "essential void." The experience lasted perhaps ten minutes, like an epileptic fit or a mystical ecstasy, yanking him from animal sleep into human insomnia, his adult malaise, a heightened, torturing consciousness of time. His real birth was not his biological one. If his trip to school in Sibiu at age ten severed him from his home place, his "fall into time" occurred on that lazy summer afternoon five years earlier, when he first experienced time as an "extraordinary *frisson* of spleen," a "profoundly disturbing feeling," a "complaisance à l'ennui," to which he became so addicted that one could say of him what Saint-Simon said of Louis XV: "He was born bored."[8]

To live where one was born should be the law for everyone. But it was not his. He was an exile. He worked hard at erasing the memory of his birthplace. And yet he lived in a space defined by nostalgia. He would suddenly remember things such as the color of the earth in the Răşinari cemetery, where he spent a good portion of his time during his early childhood. He knew it so well he could tell where every tomb had its place. His family had a garden next to the cemetery where he played. The old gravedigger became his friend and on many visits handed him freshly dug skulls to kick around. He played football with death. Afterward, cemeteries became favorite haunts. In Riul-Sadului, a small neighboring hamlet, there was a cemetery buried in wild, overgrown grass. On a rotting wooden cross, he had read a banality which exerted a great fascination on him: "Life is hope, death is forgetfulness."[9] But his obsession was more medieval, with death as reality and life as the illusion.[10]

Exhausted from lack of sleep, he greeted every morning with a helpless and self-destructive rage, impossible to control. He felt he would need centuries of British education to achieve self-mastery, but he came from a country where one still howled ritually at funerals. Why do I have to undergo this slow torture? he asked himself. The answer was always the same: "Because I was born."[11]

His own birth was a "minor obsession," a personal disease, symptom of a greater, all-engulfing "malaise of cosmic proportions." In his youthful writings, he had tried to cure himself of this personal illness, but to no avail. His profound unhappiness with his own birth gave way to his more general malaise of being, "malaise dans l'être." He wrote about this calamity, this absurdity, the act of birth, to cure himself of his obsession, just as he had cured himself of his obsession with suicide or with death. But until he wrote and published his book on the tragedy of birth, he would have no rest, no peace.

## The Interpretations of Memory

In later life, Cioran talked about his childhood with interviewers and wrote about it in his letters and his private journal. His early life, or rather his opinions and interpretations of it, shaped his philosophy. He was troubled by the fact that he was born in a marginal place whose role in history was so minor and abject that it was almost nonexistent. He felt that he was born with the "wrong" identity. The trauma of being born under humiliating historical circumstances marked his entire *œuvre,* gradually rising from a personal level into an existential and metaphysical drama.

As we have seen, Cioran depicts himself as an energetic child, high-strung and hypersensitive but blissfully happy in the primitive world of his native village, driven out of that paradise by his father. These are his sunny memories of a splendid, timeless mountain village through which a robust little peasant boy, full of *joie de vivre,* moved aloof and alone, master of the universe. And then there are his troubled memories of a cursed mountain village in which history had wreaked havoc. There, a child of precocious sensibility, easily depressed, subject to fits of melancholy and absent-mindedness, and black humors that sent him sprawling on the floor in nervous spasms, he developed a double consciousness: of time and of its humiliations, its limits.

Though the dominant memory is that of "une enfance couronnée," a "crowned childhood," "only calamities followed," he said, after his departure from Răşinari. The "calamities" he speaks of were all versions of his going away to school: first to Sibiu, then to Bucharest, later to Berlin, and, finally, to Paris. Going away to school may not strike modern people, especially if they are English or American, as a "calamity." But for Cioran, that relatively ordinary occurrence took on huge proportions and became a unique event, so extraordinary that he placed it on the same level as Man's original fall from grace. Its memory haunted him all his life, as he noted in his private diary: "Every day I relive the expulsion from Paradise with the same passion and the same regret as the one who was first banished."

Imaginatively, in light of that defining event, Cioran construed his entire life as exile into the world. If we are to believe his personal testimony, the sophisticated Parisian writer of existential *malaise* is none other than the little boy who "wept to dream again" and looked mournfully after his parents' horse-drawn cart disappearing in the direction of his mountain village. After Rășinari, as Cioran put it, his "vocation for sadness and regret had become a vice," curable only through writing. For the disconsolate tears of the little boy, the older man substituted pages of writing whose very titles speak of his enduring, mourning grief: *The Trouble with Being Born, The Fall into Time, Syllogisms of Bitterness.* The despair of being torn from a harmonious environment and being thrown into the world in utter solitude, as a hard-born baby is ripped from his mother's womb, was translated into the writer's predominant themes of decadence and exile—personal, political, artistic, and existential.

The foundation stone on which the myth of a blissful childhood is erected is, paradoxically, the myth of its loss. Cioran's strong sense of abandonment indicates a Romantic sensibility, of which he is keenly conscious: "If I think about it, my sensibility is of a romantic sort, that is, as I am incapable to believe in absolute values, I take my humors to be worlds, I consider them substitutes for the ultimate reality."[12] In other words, it suited his Romantic temperament to represent himself as an exile, and he deliberately adopted that stance as the central element of his life's narrative. He looked for models in literary history and found a kindred spirit in Emily Brontë. That female Byron was a connoisseur of powerful emotions sprung from childhood attachments to wild, remote original places, which she turned into the mythical world of *Wuthering Heights.* In his journal, he noted that Emily Brontë, disconsolate for having left Haworth, was, in fact, "the only one" whose despair at being taken away from home matched his own.

But if Cioran found his match in Emily Brontë's intensity of despair, he could not find anyone to match the intensity of his happiness as a child: "I don't know of anyone with a happier childhood than mine," he told one interviewer. "I lived near the Carpathian mountains, playing freely in the fields and in the mountains, without any duties or obligations."[13] Cioran's memories of mythical Rășinari emphasize the natural elements: the river, the snow, the hills and forests, but dwell little on the parental home. They situate the happy, carefree child outside his home, alone as if orphaned. Paradise does not have a history nor historical figures; it is only a landscape with wild life. "I was out in the mountains, from morning to night, like a *wild beast,*" he told another interviewer.[14]

In keeping with the romantic spirit that animates him, Cioran fondly and typically exaggerates the uniqueness of his happiness as a child, an exaggeration which in turn intensifies to the extreme his sense of loss. In his journal, he writes:

> When I think of my early years in the Carpathians, I must make an effort not to cry. It's quite simple: I can't imagine that anyone has had a childhood like mine. The earth and the sky belonged to me, literally. Even my apprehensions were happy. I woke up and went to bed as Master of the Universe.[15]

The child of nature, running free, naked, a miniature god, unfettered by social obligations and untainted by civilization, is of course a Romantic cliché, and comparable cases abound in Romantic literature from Rousseau and Wordsworth onwards. Echoing his Romantic models, Cioran recast for himself the myth of a perfect childhood, in which he, like Kierkegaard's Adam, was troubled only by the dream of *future* loss: "I knew my happiness and felt I was going to lose it. A secret fear gnawed at me. I was not as happy as I now pretend to have been."[16]

## The Turn into History

The myth of the "crowned childhood" of the child of nature, by short-circuiting history out of the picture, provides a wholesome, uncomplicated, unfissured matrix of identity. It is, however, only a cover for Cioran's ambivalence toward his birthplace, and his perennial quest for a suitable identity. He both loved and hated Răşinari, which he called "ce maudit, ce splendide paradis," this cursed and splendid paradise. It is no accident that he placed "cursed" before "splendid." For when he was not moved by ripping regret and idealizing nostalgia, Cioran saw his birthplace as the site of ignominious historical beginnings, a paradise flawed by history. It is in this enchanted earthly paradise that "the Barbarians, rejects of the Great Invasions, of those hordes who, unable to continue their march towards the West, collapsed along the Carpathians and the Danube, where they hid and slumbered, a mass of deserters on the edge of the Empire, scum with a touch of Latinity."[17] The slothful blood of these original hordes contaminated subsequent generations, paralyzing their will to act and assert themselves in history.

From this less sentimental perspective, the glow of the idyllic, peaceful little world fades and gives way to a historical nightmare, in which the streams, the woods, the valleys, and the "lofty heights" become the dwelling places of spell-bound peasants, trampled on by stronger people (Huns, Tartars, Slavs, Turks) who happen to pass through and sometimes settle in their midst. Accepting with resignation their role as victims of the whims and slights of history, "ageless, fond of their torpor, and practically bursting with dazed mindlessness," the natives live like "petrified larvae," lost in a "geological dream."[18]

The question naturally arises: What are the historical facts that determine Cioran's double vision—on the one hand idealized and sanitized to the point of cliché, on the other negative and problematic—of his own past?

Emil Cioran first saw the light of day on April 8, 1911, the second of three children born to Emilian Cioran, one of the Orthodox village priests and his twenty-two-year-old wife, Elvira Comanici. They already had a three-year-old daughter, Virginia (Gica), and two years later Cioran's younger brother, Aurel (Relu), would be born. As the oldest son, Cioran was given his father's name.

Emil(ian) is not a traditional peasant name. It is a Roman, Latin name—as are Virginia and Aurel(ian)—chosen by the parents expressly for its Roman connection. The choice of a Roman name for a Romanian child in multi-national Transylvania of the Austro-Hungarian empire was a political statement. Like many other children of educated Romanians, the Cioran children were given names that were meant, first, to affirm the Latin origins of the Romanian people, as opposed to the non-Latin origin of the other nationalities of the region, the Hungarians and Germans, and, second, to suggest that as the descendants of the Romans, the original colonizers of the province, the Romanians had more right to exist on its territory than the other populations, who arrived later during the Middle Ages.

Cioran's first name thus already marks the newborn child twice, investing him with a split identity. As a Roman name, it claims that he is a son or citizen of Rome, legitimizes his birth, placing him in a noble, heroic lineage. However, as a Romanian name—that is, the kind of name used by a certain class of Romanians—it sets him apart as marginal and lower caste in another empire, the Austro-Hungarian, where the Romanians' right to be is questioned and their existence merely tolerated. In its former capacity, the name participates in a national fiction of self-definition and survival; in the latter, it denotes a historical reality.

On the other hand, his family name marks him literally as a black sheep even among his own people. According to the genealogist Mihai Rădulescu, "cioran" derives from a Slavic word for black and was applied to black sheep (and their shepherds) who ranged far away beyond the Carpathians in winter, sometimes as far as the Crimea.[19] If any Cioran might be said to have fulfilled the destiny of his etymology, it was E. M. Cioran, whom we might call a "black sheep" in spades.

Furthermore, generations of Romanians in Transylvania had been haunted by a need for self-definition which they hoped would lead to political self-determination. Like all other Romanian nationals born in pre–World War I Transylvania, Cioran inherited at his birth an "identity problem" which was existential in a literal sense, since the very *existence* of Romanians in the Austro-Hungarian province was questioned on political and historical rather than metaphysical grounds.

Thus Cioran's various names each reflect something of the entire controversial history of Transylvania.

A real geographical region, not a fictional Dracula-land, Transylvania is situated on a high plateau of thick dark forests, broad shallow rivers, and golden wheat and cornfields, enclosed within the wide ring formed by the tail end of the Southern Carpathian mountains and comprising an area twice the size of Belgium. Formerly a Roman province known as Dacia Felix, and then an autonomous feudal principality ruled by various warring Hungarian princes during the Middle Ages, Transylvania was annexed by Austria in 1691. Romanians, though the predominant population—in 1785, for example, they accounted for 63.5% of the total population of Transylvania versus 24% Hungarians and 12.5% Saxons—were mostly peasants or serfs and had the status of only a "tolerated nation." That is, they had no political rights and did not function as an active group in the political life of the country.[20] With the exception of one brief interlude (1861–65) when, legally if not in practice, the equality of the Romanians of Transylvania with the other nations of the empire was recognized by the Austrian court, the history of the Romanian nation right up to 1918 is the history of a "tolerated" people, struggling for recognition of their right to exist.[21] To overcome their status as tolerated nation, the Romanians of Transylvania searched mainly for institutional solutions.

In the absence of an indigenous noble class to provide leadership, the Romanian clergy were instrumental in this struggle for national rights. Throughout the eighteenth and the nineteenth centuries, the Romanians of Transylvania sent memorandum after memorandum to Vienna pleading for the removal of the status of "tolerated nation" and for equality and official recognition as an independent nation in Austria's constitution. Their plea for political reform rested on arguments about their "historical right" to existence, owing to their direct descent from the original Roman colonizers of the province and their uninterrupted presence in Transylvania after the Roman retreat.[22]

During the eighteenth century, as an emerging class of lay intellectuals, teachers, historians, and editors took on the task of national emancipation, political nationalism was coupled with an "active cultural nationalism."[23] Aware of their nation's cultural backwardness, Romanian intellectuals believed that political emancipation would follow in the wake of cultural and spiritual renaissance. Education and culture were therefore seen as the principal means for shaping the people's national consciousness or, in the words of a popular patriotic song, for "waking the Romanians from their death-like sleep."

In Transylvanian history, Răşinari, Cioran's birthplace, is distinguished as a hub of organized national resistance, "a bastion of the Romanian national consciousness."[24]

Established in 1204, Răşinari struggled to survive as an independent community. The early date is important in a region where the Romanians' right to exist was constantly challenged: it shows the continuity of a thriving, industrious Romanian community of small land owners, with long-standing connections on both sides of the border, who during the Middle Ages acted as *servientes castri,* border patrols. The history of the village's fight to preserve its independent status is the history of a centuries-long unequal fight between the ever richer and more powerful Saxons of Sibiu encroaching upon the rights of the unprotected Romanians. It involved the gradual erosion of the Romanians' landowning privileges and, despite fierce resistance, their steady slide into serfdom.[25] In the region, the peasants from Răşinari have a reputation for "toughness" and "meanness," an invidious reflection of their positive character traits: seriousness, intelligence, pride. Unlike Romanian peasants elsewhere, "shyly humble, used to all kinds of masters," the peasant from Răşinari is supposed to be proud, independent, and loath to ask for favors or do humiliating work.[26]

Cioran, however, has no words of praise for the patriotism and resilience of the Răşinari peasants, nor does he praise their intelligence. On the contrary, when he does praise them as a group, he praises them for their superstitiousness. When electricity was brought to the village, he recalled with delighted amusement, the peasants crossed themselves and called it "the work of the devil"; when it was installed in his father's church, the general consternation was such that people believed the end of the world had come. "It's the Anti-Christ," the bewildered peasants whispered. When an imprudent photographer came to take pictures of the gypsies living in a nearby hamlet, he barely escaped lynching at the hands of an angry mob who thought he had come to steal their souls. Cioran's praise for such backwardness is a kind of parody: the peasants' only saving grace is a primitivism which gives them a sort of "insight" into matters beyond their understanding—again a Romantic view, of the "insightful idiot." But as such it is at the root of Cioran's problem with the people of his place and their history.

Răşinari lies on the mountainous border between Transylvania and the southern region of Romania called Muntenia, historically also known as Wallachia. Cioran compared it to the Vosges region of France.[27] In Cioran's time, the twelve kilometers between the village and Sibiu was covered on foot or in oxen- and horse-drawn carts. Today, a ramshackle tramway winds through a patch of thin woods called Dumbrava

(The Glade) and connects the town to the village in a manner not discernibly faster than that of the carts of old. Each evening, the tram disgorges most of the adult population of the village, returning from work in town, and they straggle along the riverbed which forms its main street, with flocks of geese, goats, and cows.

The name *Răşinari* has a double etymology which speaks of its natural setting: it derives either from *rasina* (resin) which the original inhabitants collected from pine trees and sold for a living, or from *rîuşor* (little river), which is both the actual name of a river separating Răşinari from a neighboring village and an accurate description of a village crisscrossed by two rivers and their little tributaries.

Its houses stagger up the hilly terrain between its two rivers and then stretch and thin out along the rocky riverbeds far up into the mountains. Its streets, paved with irregular river stones, follow the riverbeds and adjacent brooks, with all their intricate meanderings, often narrowing down to nearly impassable paths. After heavy rains, the streets become rivers themselves.[28]

Today, many of the houses are new, made of stone, with facades painted blue, yellow, or green in the style of German houses from the region. But, though new, the houses look decayed, their paint peeling off, eaten by blotches of humidity. Enclosed by high stone walls with tall wooden portals, they present a closed, sullen look to the stray passerby in the alternately dusty or muddy streets, whether an occasional tourist, a peasant woman with her head wrapped in a black scarf running barefoot after a flock of geese, or a logger in his sheepskin coat walking with his dog alongside a cartload of wood. Yet behind the forbidding walls, many of the houses have orchards, which in summertime are transformed into miniature paradises where the grass is high and silky, the bees murmur drunkenly in the dazing heat, and the trees are heavy with sweet, golden plums.

At the time Cioran was born, the houses in his village were still poorer and more humble. Timbered, with a local mixture of adobe between logs, they were white, with high-pitched roofs. They had front porches with intricately carved railings—a feature still preserved today—raised high above the muddy courtyards. Standing close together in irregular rows, each house had its own yard and adjacent buildings, all important in the peasant economy: a summer kitchen and a smoke house, pantry, granary, and stables.

The Cioran family house stood out among these humble peasant homes. Though it preserved the architectural features of a peasant house—the wooden porch, the high small square windows, the thatched roof—it was bigger, made of stone, and painted yellow like the houses of the well-to-do German burghers. Of his family home, Cioran remembered well the *Casoaie,* an outdoor summer kitchen used for baking and smoking meats, with a smoky, dark interior, and the fires smoldering in two earth ovens, sparks flying to the ceiling, where hams and sausages hung to cure. The memory connected him to the primitive village life, its ahistorical dimension, and it contributed to the making of the myth of the "splendid paradise" of Rășinari.

The house stood in the fork in the road where *Strada Crucii* (Street of the Cross) branches off to the old Orthodox church, where Cioran's father officiated as priest. The size of the house, and the fact that it was made of stone, bespeaks the importance of the Cioran family in Rășinari, where one of the streets now bears their name. Its front yard faced the village's Greek-Catholic church across the road, and its back gave on the river, where little Emil (or Emilutz, or Lutz) played as often as he could, and where, at age six, he got his first rheumatic pains, from spending too much time barefoot in cold water.

The reminiscing, nostalgic Cioran preferred to remember Rășinari as a *paradis perdu*. But history, like a snake in the lush grass of this natural world, lurks in the shadows of the idyllic picture, darkening them with a different meaning. Instead of an exuberant sense of freedom, it brings in the consciousness of fear, humiliation, and insecurity. The "natural" is historical and must be read as such. Thus, if the little six-year-old is "free" to wade about in the cold river water, it is not simply because he lived in a bucolic village, where no adult rules apply. It is because the year was 1917, the last year of World War I, and the child was in the slack care of an old grandmother, who was overwhelmed with household duties and running a small candy and tobacco business out of the cellar to make ends meet. The child's parents were "away" because they were political prisoners in Hungarian concentration camps, arrested for their undisguised Romanian nationalist sympathies.[29] The paradox could not be drawn any tighter: the child was free because his parents were in prison. Though the little Romanian savage ran wild, he was not—he could not be—as dauntless as he later presented himself. The sight of the uniformed Hungarian policeman, who did not speak a word of Romanian, patrolling his village was "strange" enough to set him on the run.[30] The child's fear of alien authority did not leave the grown man; in fact, it was deep enough to last a lifetime: "My cowardice in front of authorities. I feel completely lost before someone in official capacity. In this respect I'm clearly the descendent of a people of slaves, humiliated and beaten for centuries. As soon as I see a uniform, I feel guilty."[31]

Those were the last days of the Austro-Hungarian Empire, and Transylvania was still part of Hungary. The Hungarian government, whose policy of *Magyarization* reached a hysterical pitch as the end of the war loomed, was justifiably afraid of the restless Romanian majority within its borders. As a measure of prevention, it had ordered the arrest of Romanian clergy and intellectuals suspected of supporting the union with the Kingdom of Romania.

But a year later, on December 1, 1918, after the defeat of Germany and its Austro-Hungarian allies, Cioran's father was one of the seven delegates from Răşinari to vote in Alba-Iulia for the union of Transylvania with the kingdom of Romania, thus creating the modern state in its present dimensions.

## The Family (in) History

Father Emilian Cioran was an ardent nationalist, energetically dedicated to the cause of national emancipation. He was active in the political and spiritual life of the village, where he was not only principal priest but also the president of the *Reuniunea Meseriasilor* (The Artisans' Union), a society tending to the "intellectual, moral and material welfare of the village's artisans," and a board member of the Romanian Bank, "Andreiana," founded in Răşinari in 1911 as a sort of credit union for small property owners.[32] In 1924, three years after the union of Transylvania with Romania, he became archpriest and counselor to the Metropolitan of Sibiu. Family photographs show him as a strong figure, dressed all in black, with a darkly handsome face, framed by a mustache and a short beard enhancing a Christ-like effect. He looks stern, almost ascetic, sure of himself and his faith. Cioran says little of his father's character, except to suggest that like all mountain men, Emilian Cioran was energetic and full of vigorous vitality which he passed on to his son.

In a small community where the distinction between the *neamul bun* (good or rich people) and *neamul slab* (the weak or poor people) was rigidly respected, Father Cioran clearly belonged to the former. The Cioran family, "one of the most prestigious families of Răşinari," descended from a certain Bucur Cioranu (born 1825), who at his death left his four sons "four houses, nine vineyards, a hay field, and 140 sheep."[33] One of Bucur's sons, Coman Cioranu, Emil's great grandfather, made a fortune in sheep-dealing in the middle of the nineteenth century, leaving his family 161,503 florins, a millionaire by modern standards.[34] He was so rich that he acted as a one-man bank for the Romanians of Răşinari, who were usually denied credit by the German banks of Sibiu. He once crucially lent 2,000 florins to Andrei Saguna, the great Romanian Orthodox bishop, hero of the struggle for Romanian political and cultural identity in Transylvania. Saguna was at the time general vicar of Transylvania and needed money to travel to Karlowitz (in Yugoslavia) to be ordained bishop, but his application for a loan from the German bank of Sibiu had been rejected.[35] Coman's timely contribution to the Romanian national cause put him at the head of the Răşinari fighters for the Romanians' right to self-assertion in Transylvania. His grandson, Father Emilian, continued the tradition.[36]

Besides the prestige of wealth, the Cioran family also had the cultural prestige that comes with education, so important in Transylvania, where the Romanians constituted a largely illiterate majority. Most of the family's members were priests or teachers, with some engineers, bankers, doctors, and diplomats.[37] By marriage, the Ciorans were related to a number of other illustrious families of Transylvania: the poet and politician Octavian Goga, the pedagogue Onişifor Ghibu, the historian Petru Maior.[38]

Cioran's paternal grandfather was treasurer of the village. The treasury was robbed during his term in office, and he had to sell most of his property to make good the loss, leaving Cioran's grandmother to make ends meet by selling candy and tobacco from the basement of the family home.

A sister of Emil's grandfather, Aunt Stanca, married into another Răşinari family that produced dedicated priests, men of letters and politicians, the Barcianus. The rise and fall of the Barcianu family—their imposing manor house now houses the village's museum of folk art—was recounted by Cioran's father in a book written two years before his death in 1957. This family was also a great point of interest for the son, who in his private journal and in letters to his brother returned time and again to them and their destiny; he spoke of their house in Răşinari as the one place on earth he would like to own. Both father and son identified with the Barcianus. In this model of dedication to the cause of the nation, they recognized, each in his own way, a mirror of their own lives, which the father was to emulate and the son reject. (See Appendix 1.)

Cioran's mother, Elvira Comanici, descended from a long line of priests and small Transylvanian nobility from the nearby region of Făgăraş, sixty kilometers east of Sibiu in the Carpathian mountains. Nobility letters dating from 1628, and renewed in 1831, conferred upon the Comanici family the title of barons of the empire and confirmed their privileges and their land ownership in the village of Veneţia de Jos (Lower Venetia). Elvira was the daughter of Gheorghe Comanici, locally known as the "baron," notary of the district, founder of the "Venetiana" bank, and president of the Central Orthodox high school of the village of Venetia, and of Elisabeta Mosoiu, herself a priest's daughter.

An old photograph dating from 1912 or 1913 shows the women and children of Răşinari: three gentlewomen with their offspring in sailor suits and about thirty peasant women spiffed up in their traditional black and white garb, holding in their arms toddlers that look like miniature adults. The three gentlewomen in their town clothes look displaced among the illiterate peasants with weather-beaten faces and rough hands. And yet, class and education notwithstanding, a sense of respectful intimacy holds the group together. Seated at the center of the crowd of women with their hard-featured heads tied up in black bandannas, Elvira Cioran, wearing a big, fancy hat with white plumes, holds on her knees a chubby, fair-headed Emilutz, age one or two, and smiles confidently at the camera. She looks like a queen in the midst of her subjects. As the priest's wife, head of various women organizations, active in the nationalist cause,

Elvira Cioran was a respected and beloved authority figure in the village, who well deserved her position at the heart of the picture. The little fair-headed boy with a broad white lace collar she holds on her knees is the heir to his parents' position of leadership in the village. But he looks quizzically at the camera, as if already questioning the future.

So, far from being the "crowned childhood" he fantasized about, Cioran's childhood was fraught with tension and conflict. His experience could be roughly compared to that of a Palestinian child nowadays: politically homeless, born in a trouble spot, the son of a nation whose very right to existence on its native land was historically contested, a nation whose "tolerated" status among other nations was humiliating.

Though remote and beautiful, the village of Răşinari was deeply scarred by history. Cioran developed early a consciousness of humiliation for being Romanian since it was in the air, at home, and in the village. At home, in the form of a reaction: his ancestors, his own father, and many other family relations, all members of the Romanian clergy and the intelligentia, had fought fiercely for national self-assertion. As a child Cioran was never the free child of nature, as he would describe himself in his mellow old age, but the prisoner of a vexed historical situation into which he was born and which inevitably affected his sense of identity. As his father's son, he was the inheritor of a tradition of struggle for national selfhood, and he meant to uphold it. But he resented the situation into which he was born, rejected the role assigned to him by tradition, and thought of nothing else but escape.

Cioran's parents were respectable middle-class people, civic-minded patriots. He told me, "I was very happy because I had normal parents." But he casts them into a totally different light in his writings. Instead of an honorable, even heroic, family of stubbornly dedicated nationalists, he saw a "suspect family," descendants of "a degenerate race."[39] He wondered if there were any madmen in their family.

"Degeneration," if there was any at all, was more pronounced on his mother's side.[40] Cioran remembers his mother especially for her "unbearable melancholy."[41] Family portraits show a more intimate aspect of Elvira than the queenly presence of the official group photo: she appears as a woman of quiet demeanor, modest and proper as befits a priest's wife, with a round, chubby face and a small, fleshy mouth. She looks self-effacing next to her impressive husband, but her extraordinarily sad eyes tell of hidden ills and griefs. Her melancholy may have been due to a certain physical debility: she was prone to colds, throat infections, and headaches, and she complained all her life of unspecified pains (possibly rheumatic) in her body. But her complaints have a psychosomatic, or symbolic aspect, for she seems to have been a nervous woman, with an inclination toward hypochondria inherited by her son.[42]

Her children loved her. When she died, Cioran, strangely silent on the occasion of his father's death, had only praise for his mother: she was "admirable," "exceptional," a "special" person, "truly a somebody!" who filled their childhood with her "liveliness." She was obviously much more present in her children's life in a direct, immediate manner, for when she died she left "a huge emptiness," "she took away with her a part of our lives."[43]

If Cioran remembers the less striking mother instead of the dominant father, it is because of her "degenerate" streak. As a very young boy, Cioran could not have been much aware of what he later called his mother's "vanity, capriciousness," and, especially, the "delicious poison" of her melancholy. But later he saw these traits in his mother's personality as her specific legacy to her children, and especially to him. In his view, what was repressed and subdued in the mother becomes overt and exaggerated in the son.

If Cioran embraces and praises unequivocally his mother's "degeneracy," it is because for him it serves both as a hysterical (womanly, un-manly, un-fatherly) reaction to the anxiety of being Romanian and as an overall metaphor for his "trouble with being born" Romanian. The condition of being Romanian predisposes to melancholy. To the melancholy he inherited from his mother must be added a more general melancholy. In Romania, a melancholy "without contours" pervades: "in the cities, reigns a vulgar melancholy, and in the villages, a somber, underground melancholy spiced with nostalgic despair."[44]

The real, the true, the only misfortune for Cioran is "the misfortune of being Romanian. The drama of insignificance."[45] As late as 1969, at the age of fifty-eight, he still muses on his absurd desire to escape himself and be someone else because he has never overcome the humiliation of belonging to a nation so inconsequential as to be merely "tolerated" for centuries. Humiliations, says, Cioran, are the hardest thing to forget, and he himself—despite his attraction to Buddhism and other religions preaching asceticism and renunciation—could never rise above them.

> One word says everything about the people from whom I come and to whom I remain faithful because I find in myself all their defects: *minor.* It is not an "inferior" people, it is a people for whom everything turns out small scale, in miniature (not to say caricature), even misfortune.[46]

Cioran's affection for and attachment to his mother make his identification with her as complete and explicit as his rejection of his father is implicit and indirect, detectable mainly in his guarded distance from him:

> Everything both good and bad in me, everything I am, comes from my mother. I inherited her ills, her melancholy, her contradictions. Physically, I look exactly like her. Everything she was grew worse and more intense in me. I am both her success and her defeat.[47]

The identification with his mother presents Cioran with an alternative to being like, or identifying with, his father. When he comes to speaking about his father, the usually articulate Cioran is struck dumb. When news of his father's death reached him, the son's reaction is "degenerate," limited to an expression of numbness and self-abstraction:

> On the 18th of this month [December 1957], death of my father. I don't know but I feel that I will weep for him some other time. I feel so absent to myself that I don't even have the force of a regret, and so low, that I can't raise myself to the level of a memory or a regret.[48]

The memory of his dead father has an oddly enervating effect upon Cioran. The father figure represents the insertion of history into Cioran's earthly paradise. His active role in the making of Romanian history in Transylvania marked a path that Cioran might have taken, had he been an obedient son. Vis-à-vis the strong father, an upright man of religion and freedom-fighting patriot, with no apparent weaknesses to endear him to his son, Cioran felt himself in a state of mental and moral weakness. But the reverse is also true: the son, who lacked both the desire and the will to follow in his father's steps, did everything in his power to weaken the force and vigor of his father's injunctions and thereby escape his father's mold.

The few things that Cioran had to say about his father tend to challenge the latter's image as a saintly patriot and man of faith. Cioran looked for fissures in his father's double faith, his orthodoxy and his nationalism, that would confirm his rejection of the father's model. Thus, for example, he jotted down a hearsay report of his father's confession of doubt to a friend on the steps of the Sibiu cathedral. He liked to imagine his father as a Job-figure, but a disillusioned, broken Job, and found satisfaction in his father's loss of faith: "Ce fut là peut-être pour lui le véritable réveil après tant d'années de sommeil [Maybe the hour of awakening had finally come for him after all those years of sleep]."[49]

A vivid memory commemorates young Cioran's first feeling of emancipation from his father. The family still lived in Răşinari at the time, and the children shared a bedroom with their parents. The little eight-year-old pretended to be asleep and listened to his father's voice as he read aloud to his mother every night. The liberating moment happened one night when the father was on the verge of blasphemy. He read a story, which told of a monk who copulated with nuns in a convent (possibly a Russian imitation, starring Rasputin, of an eighteenth-century French pornographic novel). The story struck the precocious little boy as unusual, and one detail stuck in his mind above all others: Rasputin's father, on his deathbed, told his son to go to Moscow, conquer the city, have no scruples, hesitate before nothing, for "God is an old pig." "That phrase read by my father who was a priest shocked me, and it also *liberated me*."[50]

## Conclusion Inconclusive

Cioran thought that as a child he inherited the "fundamental incompatibility of [his] parents' characters"—the mother's melancholy, the father's energy and love of life—an incompatibility he was rather proud of and certainly not inclined to resolve. Instead of neutralizing their contradictions in his own nature, he "cultivated and intensified them,"[51] using the energy inherited from his father to reject and escape the condition into which he was born.

This descendant from a long line of priests on both sides of his family became a writer known for his avowed skepticism; the son of the fighting patriot became (in) famous for withering lines castigating his own people in *La tentation d'exister*: "I could not stop myself from cursing the accident that caused me to be born among them. . . . My country, whose existence had no obvious meaning, appeared to me as the sum of nothingness or the materialization of the inconceivable, a sort of Spain without its Golden Age, without its conquests and its follies, and without a Don Quixote of our bitterness."[52] Such lines stem from Cioran's avowedly hopeless and mad desire to be "other." Indeed, the author of *Syllogismes de l'amertume* [Syllogisms of Bitterness] could well claim to be the Don Quixote of Romanian bitterness. "All my life I wanted to be something else: Spanish, Russian, German, cannibal—anything but what I was. In permanent revolt against fate, against my birth. This madness of wanting to be different, of theoretically adopting all conditions save one's own."[53]

Yet Cioran was not without misgivings about his violent rejection of his people and his origins, and though he disobeyed, he did so at the cost of great moral anguish. The lines from *La tentation d'exister*, for example, prompted a direct confrontation between father and son. In a letter which was probably his last, Cioran's father had begged him "to make *mea culpa* to stop the campaign" started against him in the Romanian press because of his comments on Romania in *La tentation d'exister*. Though Cioran never publicly retracted his remarks and pretended to remain unmoved by the letter—did he ever answer it?—he did not take it lightly. It was one of those letters which, though hidden away in a drawer for years, could still revive both pain and passion, a letter which "had meant a lot to me in my life . . . and . . . had caused me many torments."[54]

There is a contradiction in Cioran's psychological make-up between rejection and regret, or rather a paradox by virtue of which regret becomes rejection, the elegy a protest, exile a boon. The man whose entire life as a writer was a " permanent revolt" against his own birth noted that a denial of one's origins not only does not make sense but is in fact a grave betrayal, tantamount to a sin, and thus he delivered this implicit condemnation of himself as a performer of rhetorical tricks and facile paradoxes: "One must never deny one's origins, no matter how much they make one blush. It's a shameful apostasy, a contradiction in terms: it is a rejection of identity, as if one were to proclaim 'I am not myself,' something one can certainly say, but which does not correspond to anything—unless it were a rhetorical turn of phrase or a circumstantial paradox."[55]

And the ironies proliferate. Cioran wants to be a citizen of the world, any world that is bigger than the world of the Romanians of Transylvania, or even of the whole of Romania Mare (Greater Romania). Paradoxically, the first "bigger" world that presented itself to the ambitious young Romanian—one could say, almost naturally—is the world of the Austro-Hungarian empire into which he was born, but as a merely "tolerated" citizen. Hungarian gypsy music overheard on the radio in Paris many years later stirs Cioran up and prompts him to record his feelings of frustration and resentment at the course of history:

> Under normal circumstances, had "Romania" not existed, I would have studied in Budapest and Vienna; I am a central European man; the fatalism of this unfortunate people runs in my blood but at the same time, I am Austro-Hungarian, I belong to the old monarchy. These songs I used to listen to in my childhood, they remind me that almost all of those with whom I listen to them are dead . . . this gypsy music . . . I don't know of anything more heart-breaking; through it, I join *my* dead.[56]

Cioran's connection with the past, to *his* dead ancestors, is made through a doubly alien element: Hungarian gypsy music—gypsies being looked down upon as much in Hungary as in Romania. It is a characteristically paradoxical Cioranian move: the family, the past—all the elements that contribute to a person's identity—are arrived at negatively. For Cioran self-identity is not single and one but double and contradictory. He sees himself at the uneasy junction of two contradictory identities: he feels that he "belongs to the Austro-Hungarian monarchy," that he is Central European. Yet his blood is impure, contaminated by the "fatalism of that unfortunate nation," to which by birth he also belongs, the Romanians. He said, "I have all the stigmata of a former Austro-Hungarian subject."[57] For him, Greater Romania would not have existed "under normal circumstances." He saw the historical union that produced Greater Romania in the wake of the Great War as an aberration that prevented him from following the traditional, normal path for an intellectual in the Austro-Hungarian Empire.

So strong was Cioran's desire to forge for himself a Central European identity that he saw no impediment to slightly adjusting historical facts to suit his purpose. He referred to his parents' speaking Hungarian at home, for example, as proof that he grew up in a family that was culturally tolerant, open-minded, and integrated, passing over in silence the fact that Hungary's one-language policy *forced* citizens of other nationalities to learn Hungarian, and that his parents used Hungarian at home, like many bilingual parents, whenever they did not want to be understood by their children. He even went so far as to attribute to his father, who had been imprisoned by the Hungarians during World War I, and who had voted for the union with Romania in 1918, political preferences that were most likely his own.[58] Thus in an interview with the Hungarian journalist Francois Fejtö—necessarily skewed by the fact that he was speaking to a Hungarian and a personal friend—Cioran said that his father would have preferred a federal system for Transylvania, and that "he was not really anti-Hungarian. I would even say that he was deeply ingrained in the Hungarian civilization. The Hungarian government never persecuted Romanians. But the Hungarian people treated the Romanians as if they were peasants, subalterns."[59]

History, however, followed its aberrant course, and the creation of Greater Romania sent Cioran to Bucharest instead of Budapest or Vienna, away from the heart of civilized Europe and into the murkiness of a quasi-Oriental nation. Though it "made" his nation, the union was fatal to him: it forced him to "belong" falsely elsewhere. Though he may have been tied to the Romanian nation by blood, he does not feel loyal or bound to it in any other way. On the contrary, he felt trapped, victim of a historical accident, forced to live a destiny he deemed was not his. And from that remote "heart of darkness," he had to make his way back to civilization, but the "civilization" he first reached was badly, even more badly, flawed: first, Hitler's Germany—what an irony!—and then Nazi-occupied Paris. The following chapters are dedicated to this journey from Răşinari onward. Who Cioran is depends to a great extent on his refusal to be what he was and his aspiration to be what he was not.

# Sibiu, 1921–1928

I could say of Sibiu or Paris what Akhmatova said of Leningrad: "my shadow lingers on your walls."

—Cioran, *Cahiers*, 921

I have sometimes known the "glorious frenzy" of which Teresa of Avila speaks when she describes one of the stages of divine union . . . it's been so long ago, though!

—Cioran, *Cahiers*, 51

My youth was desperate and *enthusiastic;* even today I suffer the consequences.

—Cioran, *Cahiers*, 195

The town of Sibiu lies in a wide plain at the foot of the Făgăraş mountains, the natural border that separates Transylvania from Romania's southern region, Muntenia or Wallachia. For most of its history, Sibiu has been a border town, its fortified walls raised to defend the margins of empires. It was known at first as Cedonia or Cibinium, one of twelve towns in the thriving Roman province of Dacia Felix, roughly coinciding with today's Transylvania. Dacia was the Romans' last major conquest—commemorated on Trajan's column in Rome—and became the furthermost stronghold of an empire threatened by barbarian hordes from the North and the East.[1] In the Graeco-Roman world, this region was considered the end of the civilized world, if not slightly beyond it. The poet Ovid, banished from Rome to Tomis (modern Constanța) on the shores of the Black Sea (Pontus Euxinus), lamented a fate that, to citizens of the ancient world, seemed worse than death. "I lie at the world's end, in a lonely wasteland . . . Some places make exile / milder, but there's no more dismal land than this / beneath either pole."[2] It was a shock from which he never recovered. In Sibiu, Cioran began consciously cultivating the feeling of inner exile from which he also never recovered, but which nevertheless fed the fires of his artistic inspiration.

In the eleventh century, German colonists (known as Saxons) were brought in by the Hungarian king, Stephen I, and settled along the Transylvanian Alps. To create a buffer zone between East and West, they fortified a string of seven towns, which gave Transylvania its German name, *Siebenburgen,* the "land of seven cities." Sibiu was one of them. The Saxons called it first Hermannsdorf (Herman's village) and then Hermannstadt (Herman's town), while the local population referred to it as Sibiu, a corruption of its original Roman name, Cibinium. Until the middle of the fifteenth century, the town continued to play a key defensive role in the wars between the Christian West and the Ottoman Empire.

In 1241, Sibiu was plundered and destroyed by the Tartars. To prevent the repetition of such a disaster, the town's rich German merchants ordered the building of even stronger fortifications around the city, which successfully withstood the attacks of the Turkish army in 1432, 1438, and 1442. With its thick walls, five bastions, and forty towers, Sibiu gained a reputation as the most powerful of Transylvania's seven citadels. Five hundred years later, during World War I, as one of the farthest outposts of the Austro-Hungarian Empire, it had not lost its strategic importance. In the fall of 1916, when Cioran was five years old, the Romanian offensive against Austro-Hungary stalled in front of Sibiu, where the Romanian troops dug in for a long siege which ended only with the general Allied victory two years later. The town and the whole border area teemed with soldiers. It was so "full of soldiers" that an impressionable young boy remembered them in his old age.[3]

Though geographically marginal, Sibiu was both economically and culturally advanced. Medieval Sibiu became a flourishing trade center, counting nineteen merchant guilds and twenty-five craft guilds in the fourteenth century.[4] The town has a long and distinguished cultural history: a hospital was built as early as 1292, and a library was founded in 1330, to which a printing press was added in 1528. There the first Lutheran catechism in the Romanian language was published in 1544. Sibiu's first German-language school opened in the fourteenth century, a Jesuit academy opened in the seventeenth century, and a law academy was founded in the nineteenth century. The humanist Nicholaus Olahus was born in Sibiu. Humboldt and Darwin were among the members of its Society of Natural Sciences founded in 1849. Franz Liszt, Johannes Brahms, and Johann Strauss gave concerts in Sibiu, which, according to an early nineteenth-century Viennese traveler, had the reputation of being a "musical town, with someone playing at least one instrument in every house."[5] Its reputation as a musically sophisticated town earned Sibiu the honor of lending its name to one of Haydn's symphonies, *The Sibiu Symphony*. In 1817, the Brukenthal museum opened in a monumental mansion in the Austrian Baroque style on Sibiu's main square. It housed a collection of rare books and antiquities donated by Samuel Brukenthal, governor of Transylvania in the late eighteenth century. At the beginning of the twentieth century, Sibiu boasted the second electric tramway in Europe. The first was in Vienna.

Originally a closed German town, by the time of Cioran's birth in 1911 Sibiu was ethnically diverse. Three different national groups lived within its walls: Germans (Saxons), Hungarians, and Romanians.[6] The Germans were the dominant group, with the Hungarians a strong second. Cioran's comment that until 1918 "the Hungarians and the Romanians were a species of slaves who tried to free themselves" more aptly describes the Romanians' situation, for after 1867 when the Dual Monarchy was established, in which Austria and Hungary were almost equal partners, the Hungarians ruled with an iron hand in Transylvania.[7] The German connection, however, tied Sibiu directly to Vienna, and through it to the rest of Central Europe. Sibiu was not unlike other towns in the Austro-Hungarian empire: upon reading a biography of young Kafka, Cioran was pleased to recognize in Kafka's Prague, situated at one end of the empire, his own Sibiu situated at the other: "les images de Prague et les mœurs qu'on y évoque me rappellent Hermannstadt. J'ai vécu à l'autre bout de l'Empire austro-hongrois" [the images of Prague and its manners remind me of Hermannstadt. I lived at the other edge of the Austro-Hungarian Empire].[8]

After 1918, when Sibiu, along with the rest of Transylvania, became part of the Romanian kingdom, it nevertheless retained the patina of old Central European civilization.[9] Even today, more than eighty years later, forty-five of them under Communist rule, Sibiu, with its charming Gothic and Baroque architecture, though badly in need of repair, remains an imperial town and strikes visitors from Bucharest, Romania's capital, as a sophisticated foreign city. Though officially still in Romania, in Sibiu one feels "abroad."

How wonderful and strange, as well as daunting, this ancient, "foreign," multilingual town must have seemed to the little ten-year-old boy who arrived there by horse cart in September 1921, with its towers and fortified walls, its tiled roofs, covered stairway passages and narrow cobbled streets, lined with solidly built burgher houses painted pale blue, ochre, yellow, and pink and decorated with graceful ornaments in white stucco. He had known no landscape other than his beloved Coasta Boacii and the river that ran behind his home. His native language was a Romanian *patois* spoken around his village, and his main social intercourse had been with village urchins, shepherds, and the village gravedigger. The new experience marked him for life. After Sibiu, he "could not live in a town where only one language was spoken"; he felt "happy and at ease only in multi-lingual cities." Before Dresden and Paris, Sibiu was the first to enter Cioran's pantheon of most-beloved cities.[10]

It was at Sibiu's *Apollo* that young Emil saw his first movie, a silent feature titled *Doamna Mării* [*The Lady of the Sea*]. What impressed the little boy, however, was not the brothers Lumières' new invention, but the sight of the sea rolling and tossing on the screen. Growing up in remote Răşinari, surrounded by mountains, he had never seen the sea before. The sublime image of an infinity in perpetual turmoil awed him, and its memory lodged so deeply that it was preserved intact for nearly fifty years.[11] If Răşinari was for Cioran a vision of life as suspended potentiality, that "primitive world where everything is possible and nothing is actualized,"[12] in Sibiu he encountered for the first time a culturally sophisticated and ethnically and linguistically diverse world in which his own life options unfolded and began to take definite shape. Compared to the enclosed world of Răşinari, Sibiu was like an opening toward the sea of life.

During his first three years (1921–24) in Sibiu, young Emil lived in the house of two German sisters, where he was supposed to learn German through total language immersion. But all the boarders were Romanian boys, some from the same village as himself, and they rarely spoke German among themselves. Like him, these boys had only recently arrived from their mountain villages, but unlike him, most of them were the sons of illiterate Romanian peasants taking advantage of new socio-political arrangements. The first in their families to get an education, they were like little savages, with bad manners and no social graces. The two spinsters were kind but found the task of educating them too demanding. They felt they had sunk very low, catering to "barbarians" and, exasperated, often admonished the unruly boys: "You should have stayed in your mountains, you are not civilized people, you don't know even how to behave properly!"[13] Indeed the boys did not know how to behave, and on one memorable occasion their boorishness was particularly shocking. One of the women came into their room one day and announced that her sister, of whom they had all been particularly fond, had just died. The boys were quiet at first, but as soon as the woman left the room, they burst into laughter.[14]

Among these little savages, young Emil, a sensitive, precocious boy, stood apart. His roommates' coarse, even brutal, behavior jarred him and gave him occasion to think that an untamed beast hid in every man. His thoughts seemed miraculously confirmed by the title of one of Zola's novels, *La bête humaine,* which he glimpsed in the window of a bookstore. Unlike his rougher comrades, he was inordinately fond of books. For three years, on his way from the boarding house to school, he passed by the same bookstore, where he stopped each day to admire the books in its front window. Though the book display changed with a certain regularity, Zola's book, with its pessimistic title, seemed to have been forgotten in a corner. Its daily presence, like a daily reminder, reinforced the boy's early apprehensions about human nature.

Prompted by what he later called "ridiculous patriotism," but probably also influenced by peer pressure, young Emil enrolled at Sibiu's Romanian high school, Liceul Gheorghe Lăzar, which had just opened in 1918.[15] The school still occupies an imposing building on the corner of the street with the same name, a block away from the town's center. The history of the building gives a telescopic version of the town's multi-ethnic history. It originally housed the Jesuit school founded in 1692. In 1850, the school switched from Latin instruction to the German vernacular, and in 1867, year of the Dual Monarchy, it switched languages again, becoming a Hungarian high school. During the late nineteenth century and the early twentieth century, 50 percent of its students were Romanian, since the Romanians had no high school of their own. After the union of Transylvania with the Romanian kingdom in 1918—when Transylvania underwent a total institutional and cultural overhaul, and was rapidly and massively Romanized, opening Romanian language schools became a high priority in the government's reform program—the old school switched languages once more. It became the Romanian high school, named after Gheorghe Lăzar, a late-eighteenth-century Romanian teacher and scholar of the Enlightenment, a pioneer in the field of higher education, and a native of the Sibiu region.

Education was a high priority on the new government's agenda, but education had always been a priority with the Romanians of Transylvania. For them, education was the means to emancipation. Gheorghe Lăzar is a Romanian national hero, a man whose individual effort affected the development of an entire nation's culture, but his own personal history is also typical. Of lowly origins—he was born in Avrig, a village near Sibiu—he rose to middle-class status by educating himself. He studied law, theology, and philosophy in Cluj and then mathematics, history, geography, and philosophy in Vienna. A man of great erudition and enlightened ideas, he returned to his native region in 1809 and taught at the Romanian Theological Institute of Sibiu. His progressive, revolutionary ideas, however, led to his losing his teaching position and to exile across the border in the old Romanian kingdom. There he continued his activities as educator and in 1818 founded in Bucharest the *Sfîntul Sava* (St. Sava) high school, the first school in the country in which Romanian was the language of instruction. In 1821, he participated in the Romanians' revolt led by Tudor Vladimirescu against the Turks;

its defeat left him tired and close to death. In 1823, he returned to his village near Sibiu to die at the age of forty-four.

A statue in Sibiu's town's square is dedicated to this teacher and patriot. Cut in rough white stone, hoisted on a pedestal atop a small stone platform, a Romanian national flag floating nearby, the statue stands alone in front of the town's eighteenth-century German Catholic church, in the vast space of the square where once upon a time the merchants and artisans of Sibiu's rich guilds displayed their wares. Flanked by colorful rows of patrician houses in the Austrian Baroque style, the statue seems oddly out of place. It can hardly compete with the elegant Brukenthal palace at the southern end of the square, the golden hues of its imposing walls setting off the neo-classical architecture and pale blue walls of the house next door, one of the oldest in Sibiu. Nor can it compete with the tall yellow and ochre clock tower of the Catholic church standing right behind it. But the statue's incongruous presence in Sibiu's main square is emblematic of the town's cultural politics at the time of young Cioran's arrival on its premises. It is a symbol of the graft of Romanian culture on this most German of towns. It makes Gheorghe Lăzar, who embodied the goals and aspirations of the new Romanian authorities, if not exactly the spiritual patron of the city, a challenger to the town's ostensible cultural patron, the Austrian governor Samuel Brukenthal.

By choosing to enroll at the Gheorghe Lăzar high school instead of the Brukenthal Lyceum, a choice in which his father must have acquiesced, Emil did not go to school with the town's German elite, but with Romanian peasant boys, the "savages" with whom he roomed with at the boarding house, the first beneficiaries of the Romanian government's new cultural policy. The figure of Gheorghe Lăzar, who had risen like them from nowhere, had particular relevancy for them and was certainly meant to set an example in those years when the heroes of national history were still fresh in everyone's mind, and when national ideals had only recently begun to take political shape. But fifteen years later, peasant boys such as Emil's schoolmates gave rise to a generation of misguided patriots, talented, eager, yet mostly unemployed and aimless, unformed intellectuals. For it was from the restless ranks of this generation that the fascist Iron Guard would recruit its members.

Young Emil was a good student though not an exceptional one. His grades throughout high school are average. On the Romanian grading scale of 1 to 10, he obtained 10 in only one subject in his last two years in high school: Romanian literature and language. His grades in Latin, French, and German range between 6 and 9. In his final baccalaureate examination, the future "greatest French prose writer after Paul Valéry" received a 6 in French.

Though ambitious and competitive by nature, in those early years Emil's ambitions focused more on winning at *popice* (bowling) against his school chums than on winning school prizes. He was determined to win, not for the sake of the prize, usually beer or money, but in order to prove to himself that he could overcome the fate that had made him physically weaker than his comrades. As he had all the time in the world to practice in Răşinari during summer vacations, while the other boys helped their families in the fields, he usually won at the Sunday games.[16] It was a moral triumph more than anything else. Though a robust and healthy child, his small body with its big head made him feel very insecure.[17] He disliked feeling inferior in all things and resented his school mates, peasant boys whose big strong bodies awed him.[18] Emil's adolescent insecurity about his body turned into a genuine obsession about inherited degeneracy which haunted him all his life. His determination to win, however, is remarkable and telling in a young child of twelve or thirteen. It is a prefiguration of the steely will and single-mindedness that later helped him overcome hardships and circumstance to achieve his own objectives and become a writer.[19]

The peasant boys who attended Emil's school had more than just a muscular physique. Some seemed to be endowed with miraculous powers because they knew everything, "*without ever studying.*"[20] Such effortless intellectual nonchalance in sons of peasants was awe-inspiring to young Emil and became a model he wanted to emulate. Three schoolboys, in particular, were brilliant students in all subjects, surpassing even their teachers. One of them was also a good writer, a fact which Emil, who had writerly ambitions of his own, did not fail to notice. But ambition did not deprive him of critical spirit. As he confessed in a letter to his brother at the time, "compared to him, I was a nobody, just a young talentless scrivener."[21] But Cioran remembered his old schoolmate probably less his for talents than for the irony of his later fate, which could easily have been Cioran's own, had he not escaped in time the nets of responsibility toward family and country which hung over him. The promising young man became an obscure country priest while the "talentless scrivener" became a famous writer.

There is something superstitious in Cioran's fascination with a specific human type, *le raté* (the failure), the gifted man who does not realize his potential, who promises to be everything and does not meet his promise, a fascination which begins with the stories of failure of many of his school friends. One boy in particular represented in Cioran's mind this pattern of promise and failure. Witty, argumentative, eccentric, Petru Ţincu, one of Emil's childhood friends, stood out in the crowd of young peasants, attracting Emil's unstinted admiration. For him, Petru Ţincu was truly "somebody," "a meteoric genius." Even in his old age, Cioran preserved the same childish admiration and spoke of him as "one of the most original men I have ever met."[22] Petru also bore the distinguishing mark of intellectual showmanship, the aura of incendiary talk and daring insouciance. "Tall and pale, he used to carry around books and newspapers, but he never carried a text book. He was the only one in the whole school who did not own a single text book."[23] At sixteen, he was already the author of a booklet titled "The Death of the Capitalist Civilization." But between sixteen and twenty-one, this "genius" burned himself out. In 1932, from Bucharest where they were students together, Emil wrote to Petru's brother, Bucur, to declare his friend a failure in no uncertain terms:

> Petru hasn't yet abandoned the mirage of a revolution; only superficially can I convince him of the illusion inherent in this impatience of his, so full of apocalyptic visions. A sure thing, Petru is a shipwreck of life.[24]

The flamboyant Petru Ţincu, articulate, provocative, insouciant, provided an early role model for young Emil. The identification was facilitated by the fact that the two boys were intimate childhood friends: childhood terrors as well as adolescent dreams compounded the cement that bonded them together. The Ţincu children, sons of a very poor but very proud family, lived right across the road from the Ciorans in Răşinari.[25] During their adolescent years, sitting in the shade of a tree on Coasta Boacii, young Emil and the Ţincu brothers made plans for the future: they spoke of fellowships abroad, of studies at foreign universities, Vienna, Berlin, Paris. The future was not generous with the brothers, least of all with Petru, who never lived up to the promise of his youth.[26]

Luckless, talented figures such as the Ţincu brothers, or the young writer who became an anonymous country priest, exerted a great fascination over Cioran. They were like negative parallel destinies, representatives of his brilliant generation, lost amid the very historical conditions that created them. Of them all, only Cioran escaped the leveling forces of fascism and communism and, self-exiled from his country's history, made a name for himself.

In 1924, when Emil was thirteen, Father Emilian Cioran, newly appointed archpriest and adviser to the Metropolitan bishop of Sibiu, moved his entire family into town. Emil left the German boarding house and went to live with his family at their new home on Strada Tribunei 28. It was a roomy, comfortable one-story house with an inner courtyard filled with lilac and rose bushes, its privacy protected by a massively arched stone entrance and a tall, three-paneled wooden gate. There the family led the quiet, easy life of prosperous and respectable middle-class Romanians.

In a town like Sibiu, middle-class Romanians borrowed the habits of their German neighbors, "those Swiss lost in the Carpathian mountains," as Paul Morand called the Germans of Transylvania.[27] Though rather caricatured, Morand's description nevertheless captures the town's Central European flavor: "bourgeois life, flowers on the window-sill, German stoves, painted plates and armoires full of linen, whose wood trim makes them look like heavily decorated miniature chalets."[28] A photograph (fig. 1) from the period captures the Ciorans' genteel, late-Habsburg, way of life. The two parents are seated, the father in a patriarchal chair, the mother in a straight wooden chair near a table draped in embroidered velvet, with a vase of roses on it, one arm on the table, the other delicately languishing in her lap. Only some needlepoint work is missing to complete this image of quiet domesticity. The parents' faces are difficult to read: the mother has a dreamy gaze, the father's lips are pressed together in a severe thin line almost hidden by his moustache and beard. They remain distant, "official-looking." The children, however, give the picture a certain dynamism. Neatly dressed, they stand respectfully behind their parents, reflecting their filial allegiances: Emil, who felt closest to his mother, leans affectionately against her high-backed chair while his sister and younger brother flank their father in his priestly robes. The two boys, especially, were too young to be frozen, expressionless, in the picture. The younger brother, Aurel, in a dapper suit with golfing pants, looks cockishly at the camera, already his future gallant self. Emil, correctly dressed in a military-looking school uniform, looks like a model schoolboy. In his fair, open face, with closely cropped hair, there is only a flicker of naughty amusement in his blue-green eyes to indicate otherwise.

Looking at this picture, nobody would guess that under the normal, tame appearance hid a difficult, independent-minded child, who caused his parents many worries and much pain. By the time he moved back in with his family in 1924, Emil had lived "parentless" for most of his young life. In Răşinari, his parents had been away—in prison—during the war, and he had grown used to his freedom as a "child of nature." While living at the boarding house in Sibiu did not afford him the same kind of freedom, it did remove him from daily parental supervision. Distracted by household chores and teaching responsibilities, the two German sisters running the boarding house—one intelligent and kind, the other "a bit simple"—had a hard time controlling a houseful of rowdy boys. As with his old grandmother, it was relatively easy for Emil to escape their supervision, and he was almost as free to wander around the town as he had been rambling through the woods of Răşinari.

The reunion with the family after all these years of relative independence was strained. The Ciorans were a typical, recently gentrified, upwardly mobile family. Though the father was a priest, they were not excessively religious; moral decency and a sense of duty rather than fanatic devotion reigned in the household. Yet "home," where parental authority ruled, soon became a problematic space for young Emil. The first sign of rebellion came quickly: he refused to say grace with the family before dinner and left the table while they prayed. It was shocking behavior, but it was only the beginning.

Soon after he moved in with his family, Emil started having periodic convulsive fits that resembled epilepsy in everything but the loss of consciousness. These "self-induced epileptic fits" occurred with increasing frequency, especially when he was at home alone on Sunday afternoons.[29] Sunday afternoons in sleepy provincial towns are notoriously boring and depressing, but the reaction they triggered in young Emil was extreme. The young boy threw himself on the floor, he kicked and jerked about, "moaning and sighing" under "the weight of a crushing emptiness."[30]

It is significant that these fits occurred at home. Provincial Sundays may be deadly, but they hardly explain such behavior. The lethal *acedia* that poisoned Emil's Sundays at home was a manifestation of his still inchoate feelings of alienation from his family and their way of life. We call "home" the place where we belong, where we feel most at ease and at one with ourselves. In his home, Emil no longer felt "at home." Like Kafka's Gregor Samsa, he felt divided and alienated from his bourgeois, commonsensical parents: a father who, though not a fanatic, was a man of the church and a dedicated citizen, and a mother whom he said he "despised until he discovered she liked Bach," however much such a memory is at odds with his other, fonder recollections of her.[31]

The fits, which continued throughout his youth, were the prelude to a long and severe identity crisis, whose resolution was so late in coming that it became the distinguishing mark of Cioran's adult life. The young boy who collapsed in torment on the floor of his house was looking for a meaning, "an answer" which was still eluding the mature Cioran in 1968: "I'm always searching for a way, I'm still waiting for an answer, but I no longer have the strength to forge ahead, not even the strength to sigh, to weep."[32]

Rebelling against his family, Gregor Samsa metamorphosized into a repulsive insect, a change experienced by his family as an act of aggression. Equally violent, Emil's teenage fits are the inarticulate expression of resentment on the one hand and self-doubt on the other. Home was where he first looked for an answer to his self-doubts, but he found none, or at least none to his liking. The boy who at sixteen was deeply moved by a sentence in Henri Amiel, "la responsabilité est mon cauchemar invisible" [responsibility is my invisible nightmare],[33] and who could not muster much interest for anything outside himself, did not feel he rightfully belonged to a family of earnest patriots and law-abiding citizens, which was "normal" to a fault. Still too young for his future to be more than a fuzzy blur, he rebelled instinctively against the life pattern which he obscurely felt that his respectable parents planned or expected of him. Boring Sunday afternoons in a provincial town became in his mind the epitome of that pattern.

Like Gregor Samsa, he must have seemed a monster to his mild, decent, and uncomprehending parents. On the occasion of one such fit—which Cioran was fond of recalling later in life—at about two o'clock one afternoon, Emil, prey to utter despair, threw himself on a sofa and exclaimed: "I can't take it any longer!" His mother, alone with him in the house at the time, gave him an answer that had the reviving effect of a slap in the face of a hysteric: "Had I known it, I would have aborted you."[34] Shocking thing for any mother to say, especially the wife of an Orthodox priest; it stayed with him.

Cioran pointed out the place and significance of Sibiu in his life history: "It was there that I experienced the greatest drama of my life, a drama that lasted several years and which marked me for ever."[35] The "drama" he refers to is his susceptibility to chronic insomnia, from which he began to suffer when he was about seventeen years old.[36] "From the time I was seventeen I have been plagued by a secret, mysterious illness which ruined my thoughts and my illusions: an irritation of the nerves, day and night, which has not allowed me, except for the hours of sleep, any moment of forgetfulness."[37]

Emil's insomnia is not unrelated to his mock-epileptic fits, which were the first signs of a pathological affliction, of which chronic insomnia was the more severe and advanced state. Not sleeping at night, he was all the more susceptible to his "daily epileptic fit."[38] Significantly, the bouts of insomnia also occurred at home. Emil could not sleep; that is to say he could not relax and be "at home" with himself and his family. Instead of collapsing on the floor and crying as he used to in earlier days, the slightly older boy escaped from home in the middle of the night and wandered for hours around town like a lost soul, a stranger in his own familiar surroundings: "I would go out around midnight and I just walked in the streets, there was no one except me and a few prostitutes in the empty town, the total silence, the deep province. I wandered for hours like a sort of a ghost and everything I wrote later was worked out during those nights."[39]

The intense, unrelieved feeling of boredom which led to his fits and, later, to his insomnia was a manifestation of acute alienation from his family and their expectations. He felt imprisoned, a captive of his time and place, weighed down by heavy chains he felt he would never be able to remove. No matter how hard he tried to persuade himself that he was free, he *felt* that he was not, and that it would require a superhuman effort to set himself free. Freedom was only an illusion. Who was he? What was he doing there? Could he escape his own self and its destiny? He repeated these questions to himself like a mantra on Sunday afternoons as he walked along the empty, steep, and narrow streets of the Lower Town, Sibiu's old Gothic district. He did not have a precise answer to these questions, but he obscurely felt that he had a mission and was alternately filled with pride and anxiety: "I was bored to death but I believed in myself . . . I knew that, whatever the outcome, the angel of perplexity would hover over my future years."[40]

Even much later in life, he drew strong connections between his fits of anger and the kind of writer he became:

> All fury against myself or against others ends for me in a fury against my birth; or rather, everything that happens to me participates in this fury, so that this unfortunate birth, which should leave me indifferent . . . installs itself in the center of my preoccupations and substitutes it for my life, my very being.[41]

Cioran's "secret and mysterious illness" occurred precisely at a time of crisis, when his career as planned by his parents in relation to the family's past traditions was problematic to him, to say the least, and when his future was still fuzzy, shrouded in morning mists. It became the dominant feature of Cioran's youth and young adulthood, to the point where he could speak of his problem as his "vocation": "It was my 'vocation', there's no doubt about that. To suffer because of boredom . . . , and then again to suffer from all the ills inherent to a fragile constitution and because of nerves predestined to be unhinged."[42]

This horror of origins seems more intense, more deep and irrational, than Cioran's reaction against his father's religion, which is no more than we would expect, given the atheistical tenor of his mature writing. "From the time I began to define myself, I was in reaction against the truths of my father, against Christianity." The apposite conflation (father/Christianity) is obvious, and pertinent. He goes on: "To this external reason was added another, more intimate"—"my inability to comprehend Christ, I would say, even to imagine him." This could be read as a classic psychological bind, rather than a theological one: reacting against his father's God for self-definition, Cioran the priest's son has an even more "intimate" version of the problem: imagining the Son of God.[43]

Although we might almost say that Cioran was born with an identity problem, as suggested in the previous chapter, he did not become conscious of it until he reached ethnically and linguistically diverse Sibiu. That is why Rășinari is a privileged place—out of time—in Cioran's mythology, whereas Sibiu is the first dot on the route map of his descent into time, history, and self-awareness. Everything in Sibiu conspired to bring about the dawn of an identity crisis in the sensitive and precocious boy on the threshold of adolescence: first the separation from and then the reunion with his family; the new high school; and, above all, the politically complex and culturally ambivalent situation in a town that had only recently changed hands, switching almost overnight from the crumbling infra-structures of the Austro-Hungarian Empire to the rudimentary infra-structures of the new, large, but on the whole backward kingdom of Romania.

The seventeen-year-old nocturnal vagabond was about to graduate from high school and go to the university in Bucharest. Behind him lay his "crowned childhood" in Răşinari, his adolescent years in a politically and culturally sensitive place, the inheritance of a sense of spiritual mission as part of his family tradition, and the high expectations of his civic-minded parents that their son should become a useful servant to the newborn state. Before him lay long years of wrenching inner conflict, during which he attempted to decide what the content of his spiritual mission was and, more importantly, to whom or to what it should be dedicated.

Emil had temporary cures for his illness. Two of them, reading and walking, became long-standing habits which also helped keep the adult Cioran sane.[44] A compulsive walker, he rambled day and night through picturesque Sibiu, in thrall to its provincial, melancholy charm. On the ruins of the city's old fortifications, under the trees of its parks—which reminded him of the woods on his beloved Coasta Boacii—or at Sibiu's three main libraries, Brukenthal, Astra, and the Metropolitan Library, he read voraciously Shakespeare, Novalis, and Schlegel.[45] Prey to fits of literary gluttony, he devoured rather than read books, the same way he sometimes threw himself upon food, eating more than his entire family. His instinctive need "to devour in order to feel that he existed" governed both his eating and his reading.[46] He memorized whole passages by heart, and he practically "lived" the books: the tormented adolescent was naturally attracted to the German Romantics' dissertations on the self, but he also read attentively Novalis on sickness, death, and suicide and Schlegel's theory of the fragment. He had also just discovered Russian literature and became infatuated with it, especially Dostoevsky.

From young Emil's personal library has survived a little volume of essays on Russian literature by Dmitri Merezhkovsky, translated into Romanian in 1925. From its worn-out pages, with heavy underlinings and copious marginal notes, it is clear that the young man read actively and intensely the essays on Pushkin, Tolstoy, Turgenev, Dostoevsky, and Rozanov. Also heavily underlined are Merezhkovsky's fragmentary "thoughts" printed in the last section of the volume. Some prefigure future Cioranian aphorisms while at the same time providing a gauge of young Emil's own "thoughts" and preoccupations at the time: "the farther you advance in life, the closer death is to you"; "music is often more persuasive than logic"; "censorship is the word's death sentence"; "the man obsessed by the idea that he will be read becomes stupid immediately"; "the Russian people achieves nothing alone, but everything is achieved through them."[47]

Emil started to read seriously at fourteen, replacing his former passion for playing the violin with a new one for reading. He had a veritable drive toward culture, what he called his *Bildungstrieb:* "la soif d'apprendre, d'emmagasiner, de savoir, d'accumuler des vétilles sur toutes choses" [the thirst for knowledge, for accumulating and storing up bits of information].[48] He was persuaded that acquiring culture was a means to escape the limitations of his milieu. Reading was not simply a divertissment from the boredom that plagued him. Through reading, he realized, he could transform himself and become as *unlike* his family as he wished, thus fulfilling any adolescent's dream. At once both an escape and a rebellion, reading was for him unquestionably related to a departure from his humble origins:

> Don't I have to *pay* for all of my ancestors for whom only one book existed, what they called *the* book, that is the Bible? It's both pleasant and humiliating to think that a few generations ago *my people* were savages, *indigenous tribes.* Juridically, they were slaves, forced to live in darkness; I feel the obligation to know everything.[49]

Cioran's personal emancipation through culture thus duplicates at the individual level the program of emancipation of the masses championed by enlightened Transylvanian intellectuals before the union with Romania and implemented by the Romanian government immediately afterward. Cioran thus put a paradoxical spin on the belief in the power of culture to erase borders and to lift barriers. For him, it admitted the self-confessed "savage" into the "civilized" company of the very people he is distancing himself from and the milieu he is attempting to escape.

Nothing interfered with his passion for reading. The figure of a young woman hovered fleetingly for a while in the young boy's imagination but was soon dismissed. Like a character in a Shakespearean comedy, Emil fell secretly in love with young Cella, one of the town's beauties, the daughter of a respectable bourgeois family. For two years, he timidly tried to steal a glance or an approving smile from her, without daring to speak of his love. But one day, as Emil sat reading Shakespeare in the park with his brother, Cella appeared walking arm in arm with the school jock, spitefully nicknamed "Pizdulici" (Little Cunts).[50] Profoundly humiliated, with the characteristic passionate intensity he put into all things, Emil swore off women and romantic love forever.

Spurned adolescent love being the rule rather than the exception, the Cella episode is not significant in itself, but significant for the place it acquired in Cioran's mythology. It is an artfully constructed little story. The moment of revelatory disappointment happened not by chance but by design, precisely as Emil sat reading

Shakespeare in the park. Cella appears as a consummate seducer who has the audacity to distract her timid lover from reading the greatest literary master. She exerts an evil and dangerous fascination. Consequently, the subsequent disappointment appears as a boon, Emil having only narrowly escaped the snares of a witch—an ordinary little bourgeoisie, in fact, whom he had mistakenly idealized.

Both Cioran and his brother were fond of recalling the Cella incident, placing it at the origin of Cioran's life-long misogynism. Cella's (very likely unwitting) insensitivity liberated Emil from the illusions of false romantic love and, more importantly, from yet another responsibility he was expected to assume in his adult life, marriage. His disappointment in love also allowed him to discover the virtues of prostitution: immediate gratification of intense adolescent sexual needs without sentimental entanglement and further commitments. As an old border town, Sibiu boasted three established and respectable whore houses where Emil—ostentatiously carrying a copy of Kant's *Critique of Pure Reason* in his coat pocket—became an assiduous customer and where he often met not only his schoolmates but also his teachers.[51] (A helpful local doctor suggested to his mother that his shocking behavior at home came from his having contracted *la vérole*, syphilis, from the whores.)[52] Here he became acquainted first-hand with women in the oldest profession in the world, who, in Cioran's imaginary gallery of misfits and marginals haunted by metaphysical obsessions, not only provided sexual release but also played an important role as nocturnal conversation partners. All his life, Cioran liked talking to prostitutes. "Only the brothel or an angel's tear can free us temporarily from the terror of death," he would say in *Tears and Saints*, in 1937.[53]

If provincial boredom drove Emil to reading, it also drove him to drinking. His education was completed in the pubs of Sibiu's Lower Town and the taverns of the surrounding villages as much as in its libraries. Young Emil was an *om de cafenea* [café man], a regular "barfly," ready to drink in anybody's company at the drop of a hat. Other barflies, drunkards, losers, and bums, all of them from the fascinating family of "failures," many of them schoolmates with whom he would stay in touch until he left Romania for good in 1937, became influential spiritual mentors.[54] Their education and newly acquired urban consciousness had not yet cut them off from their originary village "paradise," and they managed to preserve a natural wisdom and an expressive picturesqueness much admired by the intellectually more refined young Cioran. Though intellectually failed, they knew how to live every moment, consumed by inner fires of appetite which ultimately wrecked their lives but awed their luckier friend. One of them, Ion Tatu, was mainly known by his nickname, "Ionul Mumii" (Mother's Johnny). He acquired this nickname because, when drunk, he imitated his old mother, a simple peasant woman, who complained of his behavior by wringing her hands and repeating: "Ionul mumii, Ionul mumii, you haven't done anything with your life."[55] After a few rounds in a tavern full of smoke with the vulgarly sentimental lamentation of gypsy music in the background, Ionul Mumii used to fall into a "metaphysical delirium" during which "he spoke with equal passion of his wife and of nothingness." His failed marriage led to a "humorous and at the same time desperate vision of life," which charmed Emil while reconfirming his fear of any marital commitment. Nor did Emil ever forget one Dostoevskian evening, when at the height of his inebriation, combining despair with mystical exaltation, Ionul Mumii fell down on his knees crying: "Forgive me God because I was born Romanian!" Emil adopted the phrase as his own personal motto.

Together with this group of "great friends," fondly remembered years later in Paris, young Emil roamed the "Chestnut Alley" along the fortress walls, and Sibiu's Parc Sub Arini (Under the Alders)—stopping for refreshments at Schinzel's, a well-known German coffee shop. They sampled the wines of Sibiu's restaurants, The Roman Emperor, The Owl, and Boulevard. Their daily itinerary ended in the small hours of the morning at yet another restaurant, Schuller's, near the train station.[56]

The group had established rituals that would be kept faithfully all through their student years, even after Emil had left Sibiu and returned home only on vacations. One of them took place on Good Friday every year when they joined the town's German population at Sibiu's cathedral, the Dom, to listen to Bach's *St. Matthew Passion.* After the concert, the young revelers strung themselves around the plaza in front of the cathedral and sang, half satirically but with a mordancy of their own, the end of the first part of Bach's transcendent work: "You must lament, Man, your heavy sins . . ."

Also traditional were their summer escapades in the countryside around Sibiu, when they carried around with them the "historical object," as Cioran called it, a twenty-pound wine cask stolen from the wine cellar of a village priest. Memorable also were their hikes in the Carpathian mountains, when, joined by a Hungarian and a German friend, the rowdy travelers got "drunk" on sublime landscapes for a change, though Emil, always a man of extremes, needed the combined "high" of both landscape and drink. Caught by his comrades drinking from a little flask hidden in his pocket at the top of the mountains, near the highest peak of the Romanian Carpathians, the Negoiul, he replied: "I can't be expected to stay sober when I contemplate this grandiose spectacle!"

In September 1928, at age seventeen, Emil passed his baccalaureate examination in the "Moderns" section with a grade of 7.80 (on a scale of 10), good enough to place second in a class of ninety-six, and he officially graduated from high school. The diploma entitled the "Student Cioran, Emil, to enjoy all the rights given him by present laws and regulations." Armed with his diploma, young Emil left Sibiu to go to Bucharest, where he enrolled in the Faculty of Letters, Philosophy Section.

Sibiu, like Cioran's other two favorite cities, Dresden and Paris, paradoxically distinguished itself as a place where he suffered from the most acute boredom. Shortly before he left Romania, he told his group of friends that he loved the town very much, but "with one condition: the passers-by should change once in a while for they are the same every day."[57] One can safely say that it was probably boredom that taught Emil to love his town. Driven and restless, the lonely boy wandered its deserted, dusty streets, climbed on its ruined towers, idled in its parks and pubs, and uncovered its secret haunts. By the time he left Sibiu to go to Bucharest, Emil had become as familiar and ubiquitous as the town's ghost, and he always felt that his shadow, like Akhmatova's in Leningrad, still lingered on its walls.

# 3

## Bucharest, 1928–1933

What do you expect? We are here at the gates of the Orient, where everything is taken lightly. . . .

—Raymond Poincaré, epigraph to Mateiu Ion Caragiale's novel *Craii de Curtea-Veche* [Libertines of the Old Court] (1929)

I leave Transylvania, I go to Bucharest, and I become a philosophy student. I devote myself to it with the zeal of a Hottentot whose spirit was suddenly awoken.

—Cioran, "Ferveur d'un barbare," unpublished manuscript

Anything that doesn't kill me makes me stronger.

—Nietzsche, *Twilight of the Gods*

A six-hour train ride separates Sibiu from Bucharest, but in 1928 it was more than a trip from western to eastern Romania, it was like a trip from Western civilization to the gates of Oriental exoticism. *Acceleratul,* the fast train, runs—not so very fast—across the southern edge of the Transylvanian plateau, skirting the hazy blue slopes of its mountainous border. At Braşov, another large Saxon border town, the train turns sharply to the right and begins its journey south. It enters the Carpathian mountains through the Timiş pass, then follows the narrow course of a mountain river, pressed down on both sides by dark masses of mountains and forests, so close to the tracks that the traveler can nearly reach his hand out the window and touch them. The names of Romania's mountain resorts—Predeal, Buşteni, Sinaia (the king's summer residence)—chart the train's southbound progress. At Breaza, the mountains dwindle into hills, and soon after the train is engulfed by the vast Bărăgan plain where Bucharest lies sprawling like the "soft, gelatinous body of an amoeba."[1] He had come from the fresh, bracing mountain and forest airs of Transylvania to a "city of the plain" as decadent as anything in Proust or the Bible.

In September 1928, young Cioran alighted from the Sibiu train at the Gara de Nord, Bucharest's main train station, situated in an ugly, plebeian neighborhood, "with crowded tramcars, garish advertisements, and notices offering rooms to let."[2] Clutching a light cardboard suitcase that contained a few possessions and his baccalaureate diploma, the slight young man, dressed in a cheap dark suit that betrayed the provincial, moved along the station platform briskly and purposefully. With his thick mane of light auburn hair, and a scowl of determination on his face, he looked as if he meant to storm the city. Forging his way through the milling crowd of travelers, Emil stepped outside into Bucharest's late summer light and its dusty gray streets filled with the cries of ambulant vendors, peasants from all regions of the country balancing on their shoulders buckets of gasoline and vinegar, and baskets of radishes, fowl, fruit, nuts, wood, yogurt, and brooms. His advance was not easy. Taxis honked at ox carts and then passed around them on the sidewalks; electric tramcars frantically rang their bells to clear the tracks; shoeshine boys grabbed at his feet and gypsy girls grabbed him by the arm, thrusting their flowers in his face, begging him to buy them; *chivutze,* gypsy women offering to whitewash houses, blocked the way with their long-handled paint brushes. A whippersnapper, yelling at the top of his lungs as he peddled the evening newspapers, ran headlong into the weary traveler.

Startled by the unfamiliar, chaotic sights and sounds of the capital, Emil fell in behind one of the vendors, a shepherd in a short sheepskin coat over a long white linen shirt, who carried on his shoulders two bulging bags filled with *brînză de burduf,* cheese cured in tree bark. He could tell from the man's garb that he was from Transylvania. The cheap bars and pubs around the station overflowed with peasants who had come to the capital to work as servants or to sell their wares, and who gathered there to drink and dance as they did on Sundays in their native villages. Emil felt a certain kinship with his temporary guide. They were both barbarians descended from the mountains to seek their fortune in the capital.

But the young man from Răşinari had passed through Sibiu's civilizing press. If he felt a barbarian at heart, he couldn't help looking at Bucharest with Western eyes, as someone who had grown up in the Austro-Hungarian empire was bound to. Only six hours separate Sibiu and Bucharest in physical time and space, but culturally the two cities are worlds apart. Sibiu was—and still is—an integral part of the Western world or at least of that sub-division of the West usually referred to as Central Europe. Its past association with empire makes Sibiu, though provincial and marginal, an imperial town, a town of established tradition and coherent architecture, whose citizens, irrespective of nationality, are solid, disciplined, cultured burghers and self-conscious citizens, mindful of law and order. With its buttressed fortress walls and towers, Sibiu is a city of permanence. Compared to Sibiu's Baroque architecture and German orderliness, Bucharest, with its unending street cries, its perennial dust that turned to mud in the spring and the fall, its "warped pavements," its "roads swell[ing] and break[ing] open like tombstones on the Day of the Last Judgment," its "buildings and ruins lined up in succession in inert or exalted neighborhoods," was a barbarian city.[3] Although it is the capital city, it was a step backward, in the cultural terms of 1928, from where the young Cioran had just departed.

"Never build yourself a house in the [Danubian] Principalities!" a Greek Polonius is reported to have advised his son. Bucharest's greatest merit is that of having survived all the natural and historical catastrophes that have struck it in abundance: fires, floods, earthquakes, plagues, the corrupt rule of foreign princes, the exploitation of the Ottoman and Russian empires, and, more recently, the disfiguring and destructive drive of a megalomaniac Communist president, the ghastly Nicolae Ceaușescu. With its hodgepodge of architectural styles and its thoroughly mixed population (unlike Sibiu's distinctly defined ethnic groupings)—Romanians, Hungarians, Jews, Greeks, French, Russians, Bulgarians, and Turks—who came riding in on the crest of successive historical waves only to be left stranded there, Bucharest is truly what the then queen of Greece called it, a "patched up" city: "a marvelous crossroads of races, faces, customs and adventures." Its hybrid, patchwork character testifies to the country's long history of troubles, which Paul Morand aptly summed up as "the history of a chase: the neighbors lay in waiting for their Romanian prey: though they managed to wound it, they did not kill it."[4]

Originally founded in the late fourteenth century by the Wallachian prince, Mircea the Old, Bucharest was first known as *Cetațea Dîmbovitzei* (The Dîmbovitza Citadel), a military fortress and commercial center at the crossing of trade routes to Constantinople. Its position in the Danubian plain, despite the thick forests full of thieves that once surrounded it, left the city open to the attacks of invading armies, especially the Turks from south of the Danube.[5] Because of its proximity to the Ottoman Empire on the other side of the Danube, Bucharest did not become the official capital of Wallachia until the seventeenth century. As long as the Wallachian princes could withstand the pressures of the Ottoman Empire, their official capital remained in Tîrgovişte, a town in the Carpathian foothills. When national resistance was finally broken, Bucharest was chosen as the capital by the Turks, eager to keep their restive subjects under close surveillance. Thus, unlike most capitals, Bucharest became a capital at a moment of weakness in national history.

For two centuries after that, Bucharest continued as the vulnerable pawn in the power plays between the Ottoman Empire to the south, which hoped to turn Wallachia (and the other Danubian principality, Moldavia) from tribute-paying lands into *pashaliks,* the increasingly imperialistic Russians to the north, and the Austro-Hungarian Empire in the west, which regarded the Danubian principalities as a buffer zone between itself and the Turks. In addition to numerous beheadings and poisonings of ruling princes ordered by the Ottoman Gate or Porte—as the ultimate seat of power in Constantinople was known—"there raged a permanent hurricane of wars, military occupations, treaties, *hatti-cherifs* and all kinds of rules and regulations," in the midst of which the two principalities, surprisingly, managed to survive.[6] By the time Bucharest became the capital of the new kingdom of Romania in 1859, three-quarters of old Bucharest had already been destroyed by the fire of 1847, by cholera, floods, famine, bandits, and the never-ending peregrinations of the Russian army, pretending to defend Romania from the Turks.

On the still-smoldering ruins of old Bucharest, King Carol I (1866–1914) laid the foundation of modern, Westernized Bucharest with its landmarks: the Royal Palace, the Cotroceni summer palace, the Royal Foundation, the university, the Atheneum, the railroad station. When Greater Romania was formed in 1918, Bucharest became the capital of the second biggest country in Eastern Europe, which now, in addition to Wallachia and Moldavia, also comprised Transylvania, Bukovina, and Bessarabia. It was Bucharest's moment of triumph. And yet, though pleased to call itself the "Paris of the East," Bucharest has never really managed to look like a capital the way other Eastern European cities, such as Budapest or Prague, have. It has kept an oddly provincial and picturesque, half-Eastern, half-Western air, an ad hoc, makeshift character which nevertheless does not deprive it of a certain desolate charm. None of its boulevards have had the unifying touch of an imperial architect such as Haussmann; its royal palace does not have the grandeur or the elegance of the Louvre or Buckingham Palace; its big-city buildings overlook small-town houses with private gardens on quiet, shady, winding streets; its river, the Dîmbovitza, is neither the amply flowing Thames nor the mighty Danube nor the joyous Seine, but only a half-dried up, muddy little stream, a regular butt of jokes even to the natives. As a French visitor remarked in 1934, Bucharest "is not, like London, Vienna or Paris, a big city surrounded by its suburbs like a necklace of little towns; it is rather a physical phenomenon of gradual diminution. . . . The European city disappears and Asia begins. The road becomes a path, dust gilds its houses; without warning, the horizon opens towards the infinite, towards Iran, the Gobi desert, Tibet."[7]

To this city of the plains, grown in the Byzantine shadow of the Ottoman and Russian empires, inhabited by sons of Rome who, unlike the Romanians of Transylvania, did not inherit the Romans' "rigor of spirit," to this decadent city "at the gates of the Orient," corrupt, chaotic, charming, and cosmopolitan, "where nothing is taken seriously" and "where nothing is straight and everything is crooked: politics and streets, customs and cars alike," to this, came the young Cioran.[8] He was escaping the narrow confines of his native province and his family and, like a Romanian—or rather Transylvanian—Julien Sorel or Lucien de Rubempré, dreaming of a glorious future in the country's capital, in search of social and intellectual adventure.

He arrived at a critical moment; the city was in ferment. The era of political stability and economic prosperity ushered in after the creation of Greater Romania by the politically adroit liberal party, Romania's main ruling party, was rapidly coming to an end. Between 1922 and 1928, the liberal party had successfully guided the newly formed country through complicated legal and administrative reforms and economic reconstruction, laying the foundation for a democratic Romania. But the death of wise King Ferdinand in 1927, and then the successive deaths of three prominent leaders of the liberal party between 1927 and 1933, capped by the assassination of Ion Gheorghe Duca by the fascistic Iron Guard in 1933,[9] led to the creation of a power vacuum, in which the renegade King Carol II, who had abdicated his rights to the throne in 1926 only to reclaim them in 1930, competed with the Iron Guard for supremacy. Against the background of a European-wide economic crisis, the tense relations between King Carol II and the Iron Guard shaped the political landscape of Romania in the 1930s.[10] Thus by the early 1930s, Bucharest was a city in turmoil, plagued by strikes and violent student protests, often subject to martial law. Under the circumstances, young Cioran's descent into the city's political *maelstrom* was, if not inevitable, hardly surprising.

He arrived in Bucharest possessed by a "barbarian's fervor." He wanted neither more nor less than "to know everything," "devour everything that had ever been thought," "own all ideas, read all the books."[11] Reading was his life—and, as he put it in a letter to a friend, "ambition is the principal motive for reading."[12] But the ambition that propelled young Emil was neither crass nor simple. His passion for culture, the passion both of "an upstart and a primitive person," was not unlike the desire for emancipation through education which had animated generations of Central Europeans. Cioran lived it with all the intensity of his youth and unusually passionate temperament. This passion for culture is not restricted to Central Europe; it inflames the bosoms of many who live at the periphery of empires. V. S. Naipaul, another culturally exiled writer who, like Cioran, experienced in his youth the anxiety of marginal origins (in Trinidad), captures the essence of the marginal's reading syndrome when he says that in his young days reading was for him "less a true ambition than a form of self-esteem, a dream of release, an idea of nobility."[13]

The boy who liked to read Kant on Sibiu's ruined walls thought that what he called "serious" philosophy—Kant, Hegel, and the German philosophical tradition—was the fount of all liberating knowledge. Wayward son of a country Orthodox priest, he was not merely "interested" in philosophy, he *believed* in it as if it were a religion. He was, in his own words, like "the barbarian who first tackles abstractions because they dazzle him the most; he does not cultivate his spirit, he force feeds it; though suspicious of ideas, he lets himself be impregnated by them, mixes them with his blood which rejects them at first, and then absorbs them like poison."[14] Naturally, he enrolled in the department of philosophy at the University of Bucharest.

The first year was not easy for the young provincial. He did not know a soul in the capital; he had no friends. His loneliness was so absolute that he practically lived "without dialogue"; in his "vocabulary the word 'the other' did not exist."[15] He lived alone in a student rooming house near the Lutheran church of Bucharest, off Strada Pictor Grigorescu.[16] Established by a hotel owner who skimped on food and heat, the dormitory had its advantages: it was cheap and centrally located. Cioran partly paid for his room and board by doing menial tasks in the common kitchen. In his rooms "reigned an air of poverty and sadness."[17] The insomnia he suffered from in Sibiu had not disappeared. On the contrary, in his drab, cold little room, the wakeful hours of the night seemed even longer and more painful, the self-questioning more cruel. He avoided the glacial cold and bareness of his rooms by reading fifteen hours a day at the *Fundația Carol* (King Carol Foundation) situated on Bucharest's main thoroughfare, *Calea Victoriei,* right across from the Royal Palace, and only a ten-minute walk from his boarding house.[18]

Built "by a French architect fond of the Louis XVI style, the Institute [was] a sort of big student house," with four reading rooms, an amphitheatre, a lecture room, and a well-endowed library, "whose bound books, catalogued by subjects, contained what Anatole France used to call 'the universe in alphabetical order.'"[19] For a young man who dreamt of becoming Master of the Universe, it was the ideal place. From the Institute's tall bay windows, Emil sometimes watched the stream of well-clad passersby, children dangling skates on their backs as they came up from Bucharest's central park, the Cişmigiu; beautiful young women hanging on the arms of preening dandies; the comings and goings of official cars at the palace. He even had an occasional glimpse of the royal family. The happy, bright world of the boulevard was like a parade of vanities that moved him with a mixture of envy, hatred, and contempt. It was at this time that he conceived a particularly intense and long-lasting dislike of the newly reinstated King Carol II, which was to influence his thoughts and actions later on.

Never before had his loneliness and his poverty weighed so heavy on young Emil as when he looked from his library window at the happy, careless world of the boulevards below, so close yet so inaccessible to him. To make matters worse, like all adolescents endowed with a robust nature, he was beset by a powerful sexual drive which had no outlet. The unappeased flesh tortured and humiliated him. Friendless and penniless in the alien city, what was he to do? Who would want him in his threadbare suit, with his threatening expression, his small body? Certainly not the elegant city girls parading on the boulevard; even the prostitutes thereabouts were much too expensive for him. Only a servant girl might be willing to be taken to the theatre or an exhibition. He had not forgotten the Cella incident and once again solemnly renounced all frivolities, flirting, and amorous adventures, throwing himself into his reading with redoubled, pent-up energy.

In his later Paris days, remembering young Emil's mood of despair during that first year—his frightful isolation in the midst of a gay, cosmopolitan city, his inner turmoil caused by immense ambition battling insecurity, hope alternating with hopelessness—Cioran saw its reflection in Shelley's "Stanzas Written in Dejection, Near Naples," which became one of his favorite poems, often referred to in his private papers. Shelley's poet figure stands alone in front of an exuberant seascape, feeling wretched and full of discontent, out of joint with his splendid surroundings, which his "lost heart, too soon grown old, / Insults with this untimely moan":

> The sun is warm, the sky is clear,
> The waves are dancing fast and bright,
> Blue isles and snowy mountains wear
> The purple noon's transparent might
> . . . . . . . . . . . . . . . . . . . . . . . . . . . . . .
> How sweet! did any heart now share in my emotion.
>
> Alas! I have nor hope nor health
> Nor peace within nor calm around,
> Nor that content surpassing wealth
> The sage in meditation found,
> And walked with inward glory crowned;
> Nor fame, nor power, nor love, nor leisure—
> Others I see whom these surround,
> Smiling they live and call life pleasure:
> To me that cup has been dealt in another measure.
>
> (ll. 1–4, 17–26)[20]

Like Shelley in Naples, young Emil in Bucharest began to feel, much more than he had in Sibiu, that his cup of life had been "dealt in another measure." He was disgusted and discouraged with a life whose glorious beauty passed him by. Deprived of friendship and the simple joys of youth, his mood soured. He began to think that life was empty and absurd, and that he alone was conscious of it. Deprived of sleep, the blessed "daily cure of the unconscious," he was frequently exhausted, in a state of hyper-consciousness which often intensified his existential anxiety to the point of physical nausea.[21] Active as his reading was, there were nonetheless long spells in which he was too tired to do anything. He became obsessed with madness and death. His young heart "too soon grown old," he too felt that he was set apart like "one whom men love not." Though he proudly prized his solitude, when he was alone he was afraid. He longed to be returned to the streaming flow of anonymous life that unfolded under his eyes. In moods of self-pity, he was tempted to "lie down like a tired child, / And weep away the life of care, / Which I have borne and yet must bear." Instead, brooding and bitter, he returned to his books with renewed determination to "own them all" and become "Master of the Universe."

In his first year at the university, young Cioran, driven by his "barbarian's" passion, his poverty, and his loneliness, read everything he could lay his hands on, filling his mind and "absorbing the poison" of new ideas. And yet, though he read extensively, he never read indifferently. He adopted or rejected a book according to a clear principle: did he see himself in it or not? He read alertly, keeping an eye out for models, finding confirmations of himself in the example of various literary or philosophical figures. He was, like all young people in the process of making themselves, crafting a role to play, one that would suit both his temperament and his talents. He liked to describe himself as a cross between Thomas Mann's melancholy Tonio Kröger and Dostoevsky's demonic Kirilov; he also saw affinities between himself and the characters of André Malraux, who suffered from "violent resignation."[22] The character he would later become, when he finally adopted the new name of "E. M. Cioran," started to develop in this harsh first year at the university and continued growing and gaining substance throughout his student years.

Ironically, some of his strongest feelings of resentment were directed against those students and other urban dwellers who knew French; his lack of it made him feel still more uneducated and barbarian, despite his fluency in both German and Hungarian. In Sibiu, these had been the languages of the grand empire; in Bucharest, with its modish striving toward the West, French was *the* language, par excellence, of the great world; German and Hungarian were provincial by comparison. For all his erudition, he still could not "speak the language." Beyond a doubt, his linguistic insecurity at this time became the seed bed from which sprang, over the next two decades, his fierce determination to become a *maître* of French—it was the password, the *lingua franca,* for anyone presuming to become a "Master of the Universe." By 1947, it would be, for all practical purposes, his only language.

Crucial to this shaping of young Cioran's persona was another one of those revelatory moments with which he liked to punctuate his life in order to give it coherence. He recalled it repeatedly in interviews and in his journal. One day during that miserable first year in Bucharest, he sat as usual at his table at the library, lonely, worn sick by insomnia, full of self-doubt yet consumed by ambition. And suddenly everything changed with a lightning bolt of understanding and self-revelation. In a book by Leon Şestov, he came across an anecdote about Pascal that made him shout out in surprise.[23] Pascal, responding to his sister, who had begged him to take care of himself, had written that she, who did not suffer daily as he did, "did not know the inconveniences of health and the advantages of illness." Emil was so shaken by what he took as Pascal's description of his own condition that he had to put his hand over his mouth to stifle a scream. He trembled with a nervous excitement he could barely control. Pascal's words seemed to have come out of his own mouth. They confirmed what he had already obscurely intuited, namely, that there was knowledge to be gained from the nervous imbalance, especially the insomnia, that plagued him. Pascal's "experience of the heart," which led to his conversion to Christianity, was a different mode of apprehending the world. Emil suddenly felt with elation and pride that in Pascal, the "purely subjective," "the sceptical," "the torn" Pascal, the "Pascal who could have been a disbeliever, the Pascal without divine grace, without refuge in religion," he had found a kindred spirit.[24] He was not alone anymore; he had Blaise Pascal.

His plight insulated Emil from the outside world and opened, as it were, his inward eye, endowing him with a sort of hyper-lucidity, which allowed him to explore and meditate on the nature of the self, dwelling on the anxieties of his inner self in an act of obsessive self-love that he came to see as the prerequisite of spiritual life and unique individuality. Emulating his newly discovered idol, Pascal, Emil now saw suffering as a condition necessary for achieving a superior understanding of life:

> The fact that life does not offer me any of the comforts of a bourgeois existence . . . which might have interfered with my direct grappling with life, this fact represents, in spite of obvious disadvantages, an opportunity for creative living . . . a live feeling for reality.[25]

Besides Pascal, the philosopher who shaped the young Cioran, though less openly—even reluctantly—proclaimed as such, was Friedrich Nietzsche, who might strike us as a more obvious influence. Some of Nietzsche's texts on the advantages of illness and suffering, such as *The Gay Science, Ecce Homo,* and *Human All Too Human,* helped the bitter young man not only to accept but also to see the virtues of his loneliness, his poverty, his frayed nerves, and the nightly torture of insomnia. These ills, instead of bringing him down, now fortified his spirit. He cultivated them, he relished them, perversely one might say; he constantly burned at "high temperatures." To a physiology in crisis, he owed a more refined understanding of the world. To his friend, Bucur Ţincu, whom he took into his confidence, he spelled out his newly found vitalist credo, which spiraled into nihilism. The passage sounds like a distillation of his readings of Nietzsche but also of Georg Simmel, Gide, Şestov, Dostoevsky, and Baudelaire.[26]

> If we understand many more things than other people, we owe it to our nervous system which is far more disturbed. One says "I'm sad" but no one realizes what is the cause of his/her sadness; it may come from the stomach; or from a tune we have just listened to and which failed to impress us on the spot; or it may come from frustrated sexual desire. . . . It is not easy to see beyond symbolic forms of expression. People don't realize that you can negate the progress of humanity because your feet hurt. It is important to see beyond that which is given; and yet, once you see it, nothing matters.[27]

Young Cioran's "live feeling for reality" is similar to Nietzsche's tragic sense of life, the individual's acute awareness that the world is chaos, contradiction, fatality, and that Man, who stands alone in it, must create his sliver of meaning in a meaningless universe. Endowed with this special form of awareness, the young man felt superior to his peers, since "not every one can understand and feel reality, in all its specificity and irrationality, which are beyond common intelligibility."[28]

But, though he sounds like Nietzsche's super-man who knows he is alone in the world and must bear all responsibility for his actions, accepting his finite and historical nature, in his loneliness Emil is also like Dostoevsky's Man from Underground in his "mouse hole." He vents his frustrations and, to reassure himself, flaunts the superiority of the timid and overly ambitious nobody who engages in imaginary and futile battles with the world.

Proud, touchy, lonely, young Emil practically hid in the library. He disliked going to classes at the university. The subjects taught there were traditional and old fashioned, "out of touch with the problems of contemporary reality." The teachers were boring and arrogant, treating their students with careless contempt. Not one of them had been able to detect the "superior understanding" and hard-won erudition of the boy from Transylvania, who gained a vast culture from hours fruitfully spent in the library rather than wasted in the lecture halls. Emil described the situation at the university to his friend, Bucur Ţincu, in the melodramatic, emphatic fashion that seems to best suit his temperament:

> Since we've been talking about the university, I must tell you that I have broken all ties with this institution. If I go at all, it's for purely official reasons. . . . In fact, I never go to philosophy classes. I only go once in a while to Iorga's classes. He is the only teacher in the School of Letters and Philosophy who deserves respect . . . the things they discuss in class are so boring that despair grabs you only to think of them. Whenever I go there I experience the same feelings I had when I went to high school. And I must confess that my attitude towards the university is also dictated by the fact that a diploma offers the prospect of an existence no better than that of a beggar in the street. I have no illusions.[29]

But neither did Emil make an effort to assert himself. Whether stiff and awkward like any unsophisticated youth, or shy, overly proud, and self-conscious, like Dostoevsky's underground man, he preferred a disdainful obscurity to begging favors and courting his teachers, an attitude that lasted throughout his student years. In another letter to Ţincu, then a student at the University of Cluj in Transylvania, he explained:

> Here in Bucharest, one can only succeed through flattery and complete self-debasement. We, Transylvanians, though we may not possess an extraordinarily superior kind of intelligence, have a certain tenacity of character, which is contrary to success. . . . I've been for three years here in Bucharest and no one knows me, because I haven't tried, certainly. I don't like to feel inferior to anyone and therefore I avoid the arrogance and self-sufficiency with which the teachers treat their students. The only thing that sustains me is an ambition the likes of which I have rarely seen in other people. It is obviously a congenital thing, and all my illusions originate in it, though my inner style tends towards disillusion. Were I a more elastic and adaptable person, I would go far.[30]

There were, however, two exceptions: first, the respected historian Nicolaie Iorga and then the charismatic philosophy professor Nae Ionescu. Nae Ionescu would later direct Emil's never-completed doctoral dissertation on Kant, on a topic in the history of philosophy, which he "proposed" rather than "imposed" on the proud Transylvanian, in a simple gesture of trust and mutual respect which immediately won over his touchy student. In the same letter to Ţincu, Emil capped his critique of the Bucharest university scene with a rhetorical question and a quick sketch of this newly beloved teacher: "Don't you think it particularly telling that the Bucharest 'philosophers' want to chase Nae Ionescu away from the university? I set aside the fact that he is not well prepared, in order to acknowledge his philosophical disposition, which is unquestionable and which alone justifies the study of philosophy." Though critical of his teacher's lack of erudite background, Emil could not resist the charm of a man who was not only approachable and interested in his stellar students but who also taught them to "discover the heroism of one's loyalty to the inner self, the rejection of any imposed contingency, and the redemption through authenticity" as well as "the subterranean roads, the great organic experiences, and the adventure," feeding the disillusioned young man and others like him exactly the lines they wanted to hear.[31] Who could resist such grandiloquent talk? In the troubled political times that were soon to come, Nae Ionescu played a fateful role in the lives of his students, including Emil, whom he held under his spell.

One day Ionescu strode into class and asked, probably only half seriously, "What should I lecture on today?" "Boredom," quipped the young Transylvanian making one of his rare appearances in class.[32] But Ionescu capped the joke by proceeding to spend the hour in an impromptu meditation on the philosophical origins and uses of boredom. Teachers who call our youthful bluffs soon gain our allegiance. Cioran became a more frequent visitor to Ionescu's office rather than to his class, listening carefully to his professor's confessional musings about his political ambitions.

The young man with a slightly pudgy face, piercing green eyes, and permanent scowl furrowing his forehead, always sat at the same library table, surrounded by mountains of books. His Transylvanian accent, shabby dark suit, and constant presence in the reading room finally attracted the attention of another assiduous reader, a young man of Armenian descent, Arşavir Acterian. Intrigued by the unusual boy, whose face "was set in a permanent grimace of contempt, and who seemed determined not to abandon his loneliness," Acterian waited one day until Emil, having "flung" his book request form on the librarian's desk, went out for a break.[33] Acterian then crossed over and peered at the illegible writing, "the writing of a nihilist," to see what the stranger was reading. The list was impressive: several books by Kant and one by Maurice Barrès, significantly titled *Of Blood, Voluptuousness and Death.*[34] The indiscreet Acterian would have been even more intrigued had he come across Cioran's reading note cards on Barrès. In a bracket, young Emil had scribbled, in French: "Je suis un Barrès poussé jusqu'à Nietzsche" [I am a Barrès pushed up to a Nietzsche].[35]

Full of admiration, Acterian waited for Emil to return and introduced himself. They soon became best friends—Cioran had no others—spending hours together at the library or "cruising" on the Calea, the portion of Bucharest's main thoroughfare, Calea Victoriei, that stretched from the Royal Palace to Bucharest's most famous restaurant, Capşa. They paid each other visits and often dined at a cheap self-service restaurant, Herdan's, where for seven *lei* (less than a dollar) one could get wiener schnitzel on a bun. Over their modest fare, they talked and argued, Cioran especially. Once his slight stutter, probably caused by excessive timidity, was overcome, he talked incessantly, intensely, vehemently, drowning his startled interlocutor in an "overwhelming stream of words." He "negated everything with eager enthusiasm." He was full of contempt for life; he had endured too much, suffered for too long. Nothing mattered to him anymore; he didn't believe in a hierarchy of spiritual values: "activity or inactivity, generosity or hatred, enthusiasm or despair," were all the same to him, "all expressions of an insurmountable irrationality."[36] Though his frenetic and violent nihilism, reminiscent of Dostoevsky's characters, was potentially melodramatic or even ridiculous, Acterian, like many after him, never doubted its sincerity. Young Cioran was sincerely, shockingly desperate and tortured, given to confessions, willing to bare his heart and expose his despair. But he was a man of contrasts, and his pessimism was often "gay, exuberant, noisy," characterized by a "delicious absence of prejudices, and an engaging vivacity."

Arşavir Acterian introduced Emil to his other friends, which he called "the ship of failures": the poet and actor Emil Botta, the future playwright Eugène Ionesco, the philosopher Constantin Noica. The group did not take to the newcomer very well. Young Emil's gloomy talkativeness, given to extreme, violent formulations, and his pessimistic views often irritated or upset Acterian's friends; his explosive outbursts put people off. (He admitted to Bucur that he couldn't stand to be "second" in any conversation.)[37] His erudition, however, and even his anarchic posturing soon enough gained him the friendship of other young men, leaders of what was then known as "the young generation": the future philosopher of religions Mircea Eliade, the art historian Petru Comarnescu, and the philosopher Mircea Vulcănescu. Emil had thus finally, and suddenly, arrived at the center of Bucharest's effervescent intellectual life, where the "young generation" acted out "the ferment of ideological battles" of the time.[38] To them, one could well apply the monitory admonition of André Malraux, who certainly qualifies as an expert on the subject: "Between eighteen and twenty, life is like a market where one buys value not with cash but with acts. Most men buy nothing."[39]

In 1927, the year before young Cioran's arrival in the capital, a bespectacled and energetic young man, student of the history of religions, fresh from a fellowship year in India, had invaded the Bucharest publishing world with a deluge of articles and a best-selling novel about his love affair with an Indian girl, *Maytrei.* Then Mircea Eliade wrote a series of twelve articles titled "*Itinerariul spiritual*" (Spiritual Itinerary), which were published in Nae Ionescu's right-wing newspaper *Cuvîntul* (The Word), and became the "young generation's" program, making their author the generation's spiritual leader. The term "young generation" was not merely generic but came from a distinction Eliade established in his articles between the "old generation," the politicians who created Greater Romania, and the "young generation," the rising generation of intellectuals whose task was—or should be—to give Romania a great culture, one that would bring it in line with other European cultures.

This new generation of intellectuals was a group of non-conformist, enthusiastic, talented and eager young intellectuals, most of them from the ranks of Romania's emerging bourgeoisie, all of them, at one time or another, students of the charismatic philosophy professor Nae Ionescu. Their average age was twenty-five. In this mix, Cioran was in some ways the odd man out, coming from Transylvania, yet his personal tribulations and extremist personality made him, at the same time, a special example of this generation's anxieties.

The growth of the "young generation" was facilitated by a network of associations—most of them from Bucharest's high schools (especially Spiru Haret), some from provincial student centers—where young people "discussed and fought hours on end for different ideas, thinking they were the center of the universe . . . clamored for the privileging of intelligence, hard work, honesty, ability and order; hoped that the Fatherland would gain in cultural importance, which it lacked because of its uneducated and limited politicians."[40] The culminating point was the founding of the intense, if short-lived, *Criterion* group in 1932.[41] This young generation was "also a good thermometer for the general mood of the young, no small matter given the fact that the political passions of the time primarily affected the young, placing them in the foreground." These same cultural conditions, of a younger generation suddenly, and as it were before its time, replacing the "Lost Generation" from World War I, held true in England, in America, and, most of all, in Germany.

As his college years drew to a close, Cioran became more and more active in the *Criterion* group, usually as a member of the audience, but not always. He took the podium at one of its lecture series, addressing the company on the intuitionism of Henri Bergson, the topic of his undergraduate thesis for the Bachelor of Arts degree he was awarded magna cum laude in June of 1932. In fact, preparing this thesis on Bergson was probably some of the last extended, consistent, serious philosophical research and reading he did, before he began to switch his allegiance to the Nietzschean model of philosophy conceived as attack and provocation. While he always retained some of the characteristics of a "loner," he was too outspoken not to be noticed, though he rarely seemed to calm down to "normality," making his acquaintance a challenge, or an acquired taste. His pessimistic explosiveness was a positive detriment to progress in meetings of the group he attended, where many of the young men wanted to get down to the brass tacks of an aggressive politics impatient of democratic niceties. Always a "big talker," as he proudly recalled in old age, he was more interested in provocation than in genuine conversation—very much like the writing style he was evolving. Though his works are clearly "philosophical," it is very hard to discern anything like the structure of an argument in them; he and Simone Boué routinely and tirelessly corrected me whenever I called him a "philosopher." He was not interested in "objective" truth, and was bored with the need to argue and demonstrate.[42] As he would put it in *Tears and Saints* ten years later (1937), "As long as one believes in philosophy, one is healthy; sickness begins when one starts to think."[43] He is less consistent than Nietzsche; he often reads like a Nietzsche filtered through Oscar Wilde or, in the more common French comparison, Chamfort.

For many members of these new generations of self-conscious youth, writing and publishing was the human action of greatest importance, not as a *report* of their existence, and still less as *belles lettres,* but as the essential task of self-definition or self-creation, which was felt to have (and often did have) immediate national and international reverberations. It was true of F. Scott Fitzgerald and Ernest Hemingway, and it was no less so, for all his difference, for Emil Cioran. From this time forward, writing becomes his most important life activity, his central biographical *fact.* Where he lived, what he ate, where he traveled, even the people he knew, all fade far away in importance compared to what he was writing. He literally forced himself into authorship, to become a *known* writer. After several unsuccessful attempts, he first appeared in print in February 1931, in the Legionnaire journal *Mişcarea* [The Movement], and over the next two years he appeared in many others, some esoteric or academic, but some of the best, including *Calendarul, Vremea* [The Times], both conservative but not fascist, and the middle-of-the-road *România literară.*[44] And this proportion among his values became part of his life signature, even after he became famous in France in 1947: living and eating for years in student dormitories and refectories, interested only in his writing.

Mihail Sebastian (1907–45), the Romanian Jewish playwright and novelist, in his novel *After Two Thousand Years* (1934), which provides a sort of running commentary on members of his generation all across the ideological spectrum, sketches a character named Ştefan D. Pârlea (the surname suggests "conflagration" in Romanian), who has written an essay called "Invocation for an Invasion of the Barbarians as Soon as Possible." Pârlea is frequently assumed to be a portrait of Cioran as he appeared at the time, and he certainly seems to reflect the young man we have seen developing to this point (except for his being tall), providing a kind of contemporary snapshot or film clip, by turns sharply focused and grainy, of our anti-hero. At a pretentious intellectual gathering of friends one evening, discussing such topics as anxiety, modern neuroses, Gide, the war generation, and Berdiaev, a silly character who declaims that he knows nothing, understands nothing, "as in a Russian novel," is called "trivial" by someone else.

Ştefan D. Pârlea . . . replied:

"Yes, it's trivial. Yes, it's in bad taste. So what? Do we need to be delicate, spiritual, skeptical? The civilization of good manners makes me heartsick. To avoid being hurt because it's not something that's done? To not scream because of what they'll say? To not live because it's not cute? Forget all these stupidities. We had ten generations of skeptics who spent their time looking in the mirror under the pretext of being critics. To hell with all this elegance and live: that's what I want! Let us live tormentedly [*fougueusement*], without good taste, without choice, without 'chichis,' let us live with personal crises and with authentic drama."

Pârlea glared at me [Sebastian's eponymous narrator] with a violence that he contained with difficulty. He wiped his glasses nervously to see me better and his eyes flashed lightning until I was almost overwhelmed. He had a handsome mien: proud, tall, provocative, illuminated by the light in his eyes, to which his myopia gave an additional intensity. Here was an enmity to which I cling like a friendship. I don't explain it, I don't understand it, but I felt it in him from the first day, an irreducible opposition. Or, at a time when all sympathies are so easy, it's not a small thing to find a serious antipathy, on which we can count all the time, a severe antipathy from a sane man.

He is, actually, the only one for whom these vague words—crisis, anxiety, authenticity—have a real sense. His essay published in *Gândirea,* "Invocation for an Invasion of the Barbarians as Soon as Possible," showed for the first time the possibility of a spiritual position which allowed one to say, in a somewhat justifiable manner: "We others, the young postwar generation."[45] For me, Pârlea's thought is too lyrical and, as regards him, he must find me too skeptical. I would only like to make him understand that we can't be despairing and hold conferences on despair, be anguished and have conversations about anguish. I'd like to tell him that, if these feelings are true, then they constitute a drama and the dramas are lived, they aren't discussed. There is in Pârlea's nature some kind of rhetorical demon that pushes him to declaim that of which I am totally incapable. I, who have accounts only to settle with myself. To talk about "anxiety" until two in the morning at the Costarides' and then go to bed: there is truly the essence of comedy. Too bad that Pârlea has no humor.[46]

Sebastian goes on to reflect on Pârlea's reactions to the street demonstrations and riotous provocations of the times as they affected the young men just then finishing their university training.

Pârlea's case is more serious, and thinking about him, I asked myself if to be a hooligan is always more comfortable than being a victim. I'm sure that Pârlea seriously suffered after the revolts [*lors des émeutes*]. I don't care about his political nihilism, his innocent revolts, his formidable imprecations except for the effect of one puerile thought: it's not their value that interests me, but the sincerity with which he lives them, the drama he is undergoing. Naturally, when someone overwhelms you, it doesn't matter if it's a bandit or a hero, and I won't push delicacy to the point of preferring to have myself revolutionized by an ideologue rather than an illiterate.

But without judging my personal situation as any better than his, I can allow myself to meditate on my aggressor. And when his name is Ştefan Pârlea, I don't envy him at all. If the anti-Semitic troubles at the university were a tragedy for me, they were also one for him. I incited him one night to talk about his role in the movement. He responded with a voluble brutality:

"I don't regret what happened. I regret the way it ended: in indifference, in forgetfulness. . . . Breaking windows? That's great. All violent action is good action. 'Down with the *youpins*!' [yids] was a stupidity, granted. So what? What counts, is to succeed in shaking, weakening something in the country. Let's begin with Jews, if we can't do otherwise, but let's finish at the top, with a general conflagration, with an earthquake that spares nothing. At the time, I had this ambition, I had above all this hope. And know that I haven't lost it. I will suffocate if nothing else develops."

Ştefan Pârlea can think lyrically, he can maneuver symbols and myths, this tumult is nonetheless for him a political reflection. Who can assure me that the ideas or the numbers of S.T. Haim [a Jewish Marxist character in the novel] are closer to the truth than the illuminations of Ştefan Pârlea? His total incapacity to schematize comforts me. His thought is a sort of hurricane which demolishes, upends, takes away, without method, without criteria, in accord with the rhythm of his frenzy. I notice in his vocabulary the persistence of certain terms that he does not define sufficiently, neither written nor oral, but which possess some sort of magical virtue for him. It would probably be difficult for him to explain exactly what he means by this "barbarian invasion," which he calls one of his wishes, or by "fire storm," which he affirms that we each carry within ourselves in a latent state, without according him, as he deserves, the dimensions of an incendiary. All this is so vague, so inconsistent, so ridiculous sometimes. . . . And yet, he follows his thought all the way through to the act, to the act, to the most trenchant act. Therefore, his departure from the university—which all the world judged as the latest whim, because, for a little more patience he would have become in a few years, a full lecturer—this departure couldn't but have had a profound significance for him.

*The only thing I could do for the university, is to set it on fire.* He would've written to the dean in his letter of resignation. True or not, I didn't see anything too serious there. A young man's impertinence.[47]

[**KRJ** *note:* There is nothing more in Ilinca's manuscript at this point, to indicate what comment she might have had in mind to make, if any, about the accuracy or significance of Sebastian's "portrait" of Cioran—if that is what it is, though Sebastian's phrase "[he] can think lyrically" is a virtual voice-print or ideological signature for Cioran. By way of providing some sense of closure to Sebastian's perspective on Cioran (for the two are among the most interesting personages of their generation), I supply the two following vignettes from Sebastian's *Journal 1935–1944: The Fascist Years,* published in French in 1998 and in English in 2000. (It should be kept in mind that they come from seven or eight years after the period IZJ is dealing with in this chapter. Chronologically, they refer to events IZJ sketches in chapter 8.)

Sebastian makes only two direct references to Cioran over the ten-year course of his journal—a remarkable document, that manages to be harrowing and charming at the same time. Many entries begin with summaries of the music broadcasts to which he has listened, on his beloved short-wave radio, from Zurich, London, Rome, and Berlin—until, in about 1939, he could not bring himself to listen to anything coming out of Germany.

On Thursday, January 2, 1941:

> This morning I met Cioran in the street. He was glowing.
>
> "They've appointed me."
>
> He has been appointed cultural attaché in Paris.
>
> "You see, if they hadn't appointed me and I'd remained where I was, I would have had to do military service. I actually received my call-up papers today. But I wouldn't have gone at any price. So like this, everything has been solved. Do you see what I mean?"
>
> Of course I do, dear Cioran. I don't want to be nasty with him. (Especially not here—what good would it do?) He is an interesting case. He's more than a case: he's an interesting person, remarkably intelligent, unprejudiced, and with a twin dose of cynicism and idleness, combined in an amusing manner.
>
> I should have liked—and it would have been worthwhile—to record in greater detail the two conversations I had with him in December.[48]

It certainly would be worthwhile, to have heard what Sebastian and Cioran said in December (of 1940), the time of Cioran's radio address praising the assassinated Iron Guard leader, Corneliu Codreanu, in which he said that, given a choice between saving Codreanu or all of Romania, he would unhesitatingly choose the former. Sebastian quotes Eliade to the same effect: "'Romania doesn't deserve a Legionary movement,' when nothing would have satisfied him but the country's complete disappearance."[49] To which Cioran is quoted as chiming in, "the Legion wipes its arse with this country." At the time of this entry, in early 1941, Iron Guardists were being purged, in hundreds of summary executions, from the government in which they had participated with the fascist general Ion Antonescu since the preceding September. Sebastian's following entries make it abundantly clear that his old friends were badly caught out by this turn of events, because they were implicated in the Guardist element: "it must have stunned the life out of them in the ranks of the Guard," mentioning both Cioran and Eliade, ruefully acknowledging that the latter is "lucky as ever, if he's still in London"—where indeed he was, having won the same post there that Cioran got for Paris.[50] This view of events must qualify IZJ's regarding Cioran's eventual departure from Romania as a "self-exile," not as to its significance for him, but to the extent that it was an "exile" paid for by Romania's fascist government of the moment.[51]

On February 12, 1941, Sebastian comments again on his friend Cioran's good fortune.

> Cioran, despite his participation in the revolt [i.e., the Iron Guardists' attempts in January to resist their purge by Antonescu], has kept his post as cultural attaché in Paris, a post that Sima gave him a few days before he fell. The new regime has even given him a pay increase! He leaves in a few days. Well, that's what revolution does for you![52]

That is all he has to say about Cioran in his journal. Clearly he knows and likes Cioran, though more than a bit bemused by him. Sebastian was much closer to Eliade, and correspondingly much harder on Eliade's fascist enthusiasms and outspoken anti-Semitism. Though Sebastian kept on meeting with Eliade during these years, one is finally at a loss to say which is stranger, Sebastian's social encounters with his anti-Semitic friends, or his friends' expressing their anti-Semitic sentiments in front of their Jewish friend—for Sebastian was not one of those Jews who kept their Jewish identity hidden. On this question, finally, Sebastian records a very interesting conversation with Eugène Ionesco, who started to "spill the beans," confessing that his mother was Jewish, and "outing" a number of other Romanian intellectuals not known to be Jewish.[53] He observes that all three of his friends, Cioran, Eliade, and Ionesco—by many counts, the three greatest Romanian cultural figures of the twentieth century—were desperate at this time to get out of the country, one way or another. Of himself, he says, "Strange that I've never thought of running away (since the fall of Paris)—except as a mere nostalgic dream, which does not bind me to do or even plan anything."[54] But at other times he sounds quite like Cioran: "There is no more room in my life for anything but suicide, or perhaps a departure for good into a solitary existence somewhere."[55]

Mihail Sebastian is only one witness among many, however. Though more attractive to me than Cioran or Eliade, or even Ionesco—as I feel sure he was to IZJ as well—his perceptions are his own, though terrifyingly ratified by subsequent events. He was not as "serious" a thinker as any of his three famous friends, being more of a journalist, popular playwright, and novelist. His complicated sex life, his keen music appreciation, and his pride in mastering the arts of skiing and of speaking English make his journal about as *human* a document as one can imagine, for such inhuman times, a sort of Anne-Frank-for-adults. He was not a martyr to his cause, race, or religion, however: he was killed by a truck crossing a street in Bucharest on May 29, 1945, three weeks after V-E Day. Yet even this absurd accident serves to underscore the fact that his "existential" credentials were in every bit as good order as those of his more philosophical friends, as evidenced by his journal entry for March 26, 1941:

> Later, much later, a study might be written about a strange phenomenon of these times: namely, the fact that words are losing their meaning, becoming weightless and devoid of content. Their speakers do not believe them, while their hearers do not understand them. If you analyzed word by word, grammatically, syntactically, and semantically, the declarations to be found almost daily in the newspapers, and if you opposed these with the facts to which they refer, you would see that there is an absolute split between word and reality.[56]

Sebastian acknowledges that "it is not the first time that such thoughts (written here badly) have occurred" (they occurred to many observers of the French Revolution, for example) but for his time and in his place, they antedate by five years their definitive post–World War II formulation, George Orwell's "Politics and the English Language" (1946). **KRJ**]

❦

The first formative phase of Cioran's life in Bucharest ends with the composition and publication, in 1933, of *On the Heights of Despair* (*Pe Culmile Disperării*). This period, from spring 1932 to spring 1933, was the period of his most regular participation in the *Criterion* group's activities; besides his own lectures on Bergson, he also participated in Professor Dimitrie Gusti's sociology seminars.[57]

In *On the Heights of Despair* we see, for the first time, within its provocatively nihilistic constructions, the process of the creation of a new authorial role we can recognize as "Cioran." Although there is hardly a historical reference of any sort in it, past or present, its "genre" and authorial character are entirely contemporary to the Romania of the early 1930s.[58] Notices of suicides in Romanian newspapers of the period invariably opened with the same formula: "On the heights of despair, young so-and-so took his life. . . ." The rather pompous sounding phrase "on the heights of despair" was thus recognized as a sort of generic rationale for all suicides. Cioran clearly expects his readers to recognize this and to appreciate his ironic (yet serious) adoption of the role of the putative suicide; the narrator is a suicide, a self-killer. But for Cioran, this fictional self is a rhetorical, theatrical gesture, by which he hopes to save his real self. By casting himself in this character, Cioran commits suicide metaphorically while managing to survive the call of death by releasing through his invented character the surplus of lyrical energy he felt surging through him:

> The terrifying experience and obsession of death, when preserved in consciousness, becomes ruinous. If you talk about death, you save part of yourself. But at the same time, something of your real self dies, because objectified meanings lose the actuality they have in consciousness.

The impulse to write in order to free himself of his obsessions always motivated Cioran's work. As he said in an interview to Fernando Savater, "Writing for me is a form of therapy, nothing more."[59] Like the young Goethe of the *Sturm und Drang* era, who invented the suicidal young Werther to survive a personal crisis, Cioran also creates a character out of his anguished self. But unlike Goethe, for whom Werther was a private demon he managed to exorcise "so well that he did not suffer at all," a mere accident in a career so "limpid" and devoid of "sublime or sordid secrets" that it is "discouraging," Cioran—who confessed (in his notebooks) that he had "no organ of feeling for Goethe"—sees his destiny as inextricably linked to the sufferer who first comes to life in *On the Heights of Despair.*

> I hate wise men because they are lazy, cowardly and prudent. . . . So much more complex is the man who suffers from limitless anxiety. . . . An existence full of irreconcilable contradictions is so much richer and creative.[60]

*On the Heights of Despair* is a Romantic crisis-poem in prose, whose main topic is the self at grips with itself, God, and the universe. Cioran's personal obsessions, predilections, and manias are clear from a glance at the book's chapter titles, though they much more various than one might have predicted from what we have seen of his life so far. The gloom and existential anxiety are obvious: "Weariness and Agony," "Despair and the Grotesque," "On Death," "The Passion for the Absurd," "Apocalypse," and others. But they are not more numerous than those exploring the excited, elevated frames of mind and expression which Cioran called "ecstasy" or, more frequently, *lyricism:* "Ecstasy," "On Being Lyrical" (the opening meditation), "Absolute Lyricism," "Unimaginable Joy," "Enthusiasm as a Form of Love." Equally well represented, surprisingly, given the programmatic atheism of the young student we have seen, are religious meditations, however unorthodox: "The Meaning of Grace," "The Flight from the Cross," "On the Transubstantiation of Love." His most intimate, personal, bodily concerns are also fully present: "Man, the Insomniac Animal" and "The Blessings of Insomnia." As are his wit, irony, and plain good humor, so rare in most existential writing after Kierkegaard: "The World in Which Nothing Is Solved," "Irony and Self-Irony," "Love in Brief," "Beauty's Magic Tricks." And, through it all, we recognize his complete self-understanding of what he is doing, signaled most clearly in the book's penultimate meditation: "The Double and His Art."

Though not poetry, *On the Heights of Despair* is a very lyrical sort of prose, a "song of myself" in which the confessional mood becomes a philosophical meditation, wherein the great philosophical themes like death, God, infinity, time, history, good, and evil are no longer abstract, but acquire an organic, living meaning:

> There are experiences and obsessions with which one cannot live. Isn't it salvation then to confess them? . . . To be lyrical means you cannot stay closed up inside yourself. . . . The deepest subjective experiences are also the most universal, because through them one reaches the original source of life.

This theme sounds repeatedly through the book, no matter what the ostensible topic of meditation: "I like thought which preserves a whiff of flesh and blood, and I prefer a thousand times an idea rising from sexual tension or nervous depression to an empty abstraction." "I despise the absence of risks, madness and passion in abstract thinking. How fertile live, passionate thinking is! Lyricism feeds it like blood pumped into the heart!"

> On the heights of despair, the passion for the absurd is the only thing that can still throw a demonic light on chaos. ("The Passion for the Absurd")

> Those who write under the spell of inspiration, for whom thought is an expression of their organic nervous disposition, do not concern themselves with unity and systems. ("The Contradictory and the Inconsequential")

> There are questions which, once approached, either isolate you or kill you outright. ("On Death")

> One does not learn the art of psychology, one lives and experiences it, for no science will give you the key to the mysteries of the soul. One cannot become a good psychologist without turning oneself into an object of study, evincing daily interest in the complexity of one's own case. ("The Double and His Art")

In his biological imbalance lies the germ of the book; he wrote it as a cure instead of committing suicide. Emil now acceded to his "superior" form of understanding, especially during "those sleepless nights, when one counts the hours, and when, past despair and the limits of resistance, one sees everything on the same plane, as void and meaningless."[61] But if such understanding—possible only through the experience of suffering, anxiety, and tormented self-interrogation—is highly desirable, it is also ruinous to the nerves. Self-annihilation is the natural outcome of an experience in which "purification of all symbols is achieved, in which Man is placed in front of existence in its naked form, and in which the dualism between consciousness and reality grows to an explosive intensity that brings about nothing but destruction."[62]

The younger Cioran, fearful of what such extraordinary experiences might lead him to, had believed that a rigorous training in "pure" philosophy which deals with "abstract and impersonal problems of space, time, causality, numbers" was the right antidote to any excesses of his intense inner life. Consequently, he was torn between a "sentimental" philosophy that says that life is dynamism and tension and its opposite, classical or "pure" philosophy. He gave himself and a close friend this advice: "when you're sick with life, appeal to Leibniz not to Baudelaire," and, "sad people should tackle math not poetry."[63] At the time, his "anarchic temperament" weighed heavily in favor of "sentimental" philosophy, and his excesses were not over but only just beginning. But the program of self-mastery he outlined to his friend is interesting insofar as it foreshadows his later linguistic adventure in French, where he would submit himself to a punishing discipline. In that case, a highly codified language replaced the pure philosophical abstractions meant to curb his lyrical excesses.

But in the published book, we see a drama enacted between the suffering problematic man, that is, the organic and lyrical thinker who is Cioran's sufferer, and his archenemy, the philosopher or the sage, the abstract man, a distinction reminiscent of Nietzsche's Dionysian and Socratic man. The style of the book, by turns lyrical and ironical, poetical and paradoxical, rejects the technique of dry philosophic argument in favor of suggestive and vivid imagery, and reveals the intellectual and spiritual agony of the philosopher's mind in playful yet gripping ways, anticipating the later Cioran's unique combination of elegant style and profoundly felt thought.

Nietzsche, in *The Birth of Tragedy*, criticizes the optimism or "Greek cheerfulness" that goes with the Platonic ideal of the "dying Socrates, as the human being whom knowledge and reason have liberated from the fear of death." Those who pursue this ideal ultimately discover that "logic coils up at the boundaries [of science] and finally bites its own tail," whereupon "a new form of insight breaks through, *tragic insight.*" Similarly, Cioran attacks "those who try to eliminate the fear of death through artificial reasoning . . . because it is absolutely impossible to cancel an organic fear by way of abstract constructs."

Fernando Savater calls Cioran's philosophical discourse "anti-pedagogical." It tackles major philosophical themes but deliberately resists taking shape as an informative and constructive discourse. It does not aspire to anything "new" on its subjects, thus renouncing all false pretensions to originality. "It never recommends anything except the horrible and the impossible and even that only ironically."[64] Cioran never tires of saying that he believes in nothing. His "destructive" discourse, going against the grain of traditional philosophical practice, unremittingly seeks to expose the contradictions inherent in any philosophical system and cultivates with relish all contraries, conferring upon them equal value and equally little significance.

> Everything is possible, yet nothing is. All is permitted, and yet again, nothing. No matter which way we go, it is no better than any other . . . There is an explanation for everything, and yet there is none. . . . All gain is a loss, and all loss is a gain. Why always expect a definite stance, clear ideas, meaningful words? I feel as if I should spout fire in response to all the questions which were ever put, or not put, to me.

In *Syllogismes de l'amertume,* Cioran recalls how, as a young and ambitious philosophy student, he wanted to write a thesis on an extremely original topic and chose, to his professor's dismay (though it recalls Nae Ionescu's impromptu lecture on boredom), "a general theory of tears." It may be that *On the Heights of Despair* was written in lieu of this proposed theory of tears. He started writing it in April of 1933, just one year out of college. He knew it would create an outcry, and went to so far as to inquire about the cost of publishing it himself, if no publisher would accept it (something that happened more than once in his career); even his still-proud parents were willing to help defray the costs, though they little knew what they were getting.[65] He left that fall for nearly two years in Germany, on a prestigious Humboldt graduate fellowship. *Despair* was published by the King Carol II Foundation—the institution where he had educated himself, named for the king he loathed—in spring of 1934, during his absence from Romania, and won "best first book" prize in the Literature and Arts category, offered by the Ministry of Public Education. Thus when he returned to Bucharest in 1935, he came back as a new literary celebrity, having left as a complete unknown except to his little circle of friends.

# Berlin, 1933–1935

In Berlin, in Munich, I was frequently in ecstasy—I lived as never before on the *summits* of my life. Since then, I have only experienced imitations.

—Cioran, *Cahiers*, 579 [1968]

In the 1930s, as today, a Humboldt fellowship was one of the most prestigious awards given by the German government to promising students from abroad, on a par with Rhodes scholarships to Oxford.[1] That Cioran was chosen for the honor is a measure of the intellectual promise he was felt to have, even by his sorely tried professors. He was going to study philosophy in German universities, still then widely regarded as the fountainhead of all serious, systematic philosophy, even though logical positivist and linguistic philosophers such as Bertrand Russell and Ludwig Wittgenstein had begun the mighty shifting of philosophical inquiry that signaled the birth of a *modernism* in philosophy, parallel to the modernist revolutions that were already occurring in art, music, and literature. What Cioran did with his fellowship time in Germany shows his attraction to these new directions—even as it illustrates the difficulty of aligning him persuasively with any one of them. Once again, he was his own man, and being his own man was, once again, the essence of his philosophy.

But he was not the only philosophical egotist in Berlin in 1933. To arrive in Berlin in that year to begin post-graduate work in philosophy was an even more dramatically (in)auspicious beginning than the young Wordsworth's arriving in France in 1792 to improve his French. Adolf Hitler's National Socialist party had won the parliamentary elections that March, and by the fall, when Cioran arrived, Hitler was in the first full swings of his ruthless consolidation of parliamentary powers into full-fledged dictatorship. We may say Cioran became an "existentialist" in Germany in 1933–35, but it was an existentialism spawned in the cradle of Nazism. Wordsworth could say, famously, of himself in the French Revolution, "Bliss was it in the dawn to be alive, / But to be young was very heaven!" What paraphrase could we make for Cioran: Shame was it in that dawn to be about, and to be young was very dangerous? Nor did Cioran resist the temptations. Yet he had known the risks: the year before he left Romania he had written to his brother about his desire to study, in Germany, philosophy of culture, history, and philosophical anthropology—especially "the German problem"—but he knew it would not be easy: "we had the misfortune to finish [university] when the economic and social situation is tragic."[2]

Although he started out earnestly enough in the systematic vein, he soon—as he had already started to, in Bucharest—broke with the great systematic traditions of Kant and Hegel, which strove to produce coherent accounts of all existence, from the nature of the universe to the individual psyche, and he embraced, instead, what he called, at first, "abstract indiscretion." The phrase is perfectly Cioranian: cheeky yet funny, accurate yet vague. Its signature appears on almost every page of his mature and immature works: he is indiscreet about serious philosophical and religious matters. For example, when he wrote, soon after his return to Romania, "Jesus was the Don Juan of agony," he is being irreverent, funny, and deadly—or at least consistently—serious.[3]

He began, of course, where a generation of rebels had already begun, by reading Nietzsche. And yet Cioran is a less "Nietzschean" philosopher than he at first appears; he does not fit well into that pigeonhole. Equally, he was enamored of Georg Simmel (1858–1918), a less well-known figure than Nietzsche, but one with greater personal attractions for the young Cioran. Simmel is one of the founders of modern sociology; along with Max Weber and others, he organized the German Society for Sociology. His 1908 book, *Sociology: Investigations on the Forms of Sociation,* is regarded as one of the modern discipline's cornerstones. Yet Simmel was much more philosophical than we imagine (most) sociologists today to be, and at the same time much more "sociological" than we imagine (most) philosophers to be. This mixture of disciplines—always a danger in academia, even in today's "interdisciplinary" university—probably accounts for some of Simmel's lack of academic success, even though he was one of the most popular teachers at the University of Berlin, where he spent his entire career as a non-tenured faculty member, dependent on students paying to hear him lecture, despite numerous attempts (both by himself and by friends like Weber) to get him professorial posts at other universities. No one says it was because he was a Jew—his father had converted to Christianity—and he was brought up by a rich industrialist guardian, so he was always financially independent and thus freed from the necessity to kowtow for appointments for financial reasons. Above all, he was a "cosmopolitan," a term widely applied to urban Jews by both Nazis and Communists, though it was the intellectual style of virtually all the avant-garde of the era, for whom ethnic considerations were laughably (and then tragically) old-fashioned. Simmel's profile has obvious anticipations of Walter Benjamin, especially his fondness for the role of metropolitan wanderer, or *flâneur.* (One of his few books available in English today is called *The Stranger.*) He was what we today would call a philosopher of culture; his 1900 book, *The Philosophy of Money,* was contemporaneous with such similar seminal works as Thorstein Veblen's *The Theory of the Leisure Class* (1899).

In all this, we can see many reasons why he would appeal to young Cioran—who, we must remember, was fluent in German, still the most prestigious philosophic language of the day, and not yet fluent—at all—in French. But possibly what made Simmel irresistible to Cioran was, characteristically, not his successes—uneven though they were—but what is regarded as his worst career misstep: his jingoistic, enthusiastic propaganda writings defending Germany's role in the First World War: "a desperate effort by a man who had always regarded himself as a 'stranger' in the land to become immersed in the patriotic community."[4] Except for the idea of immersing oneself in community, this description could stand well as an account of the first book Cioran would publish on his return to Romania in 1935, *The Transfiguration of Romania.* And an enthusiasm for the very different Germany—from Simmel's World War I victim—that greeted Cioran in 1933 does much to account for that book's paternity.

Besides Simmel, there was a real-life philosophic influence on Cioran in Germany as well, Ludwig Klages (1872–1956), a man whom Cioran described in one of his first articles on Germany as a philosopher with the "temperament of a *condottiere*" and "the most accomplished man I ever met." Cioran was a graduate assistant in Klages's seminars (a tribute to the credentials of a graduate student from Romania), in the year after the philosopher's sixtieth birthday, which had seen the publication of the third and final volume of his magnum opus, *Der Geist als Widersacher der Seele* [Spirit as the Adversary of Soul]—a work whose title points up its anti-Kantian, anti-Hegelian message, for Klages was a renowned *vitalist* in the tradition of Bergson—hence naturally attractive to Cioran (and vice versa), who had written his bachelor's thesis on Bergson. Klages is an even stranger figure than Simmel today, though to call these men "strange" is in part only to admit one's difficulty in comprehending the range of their interests, to say nothing of their astonishing productivity. He was praised by Walter Benjamin, and caricatured in Robert Musil's modernist masterpiece, *The Man without Qualities* (1930–33), as a visionary prophet called "Meingast." Klages is today regarded as one of the philosophical founders of the ecological movement, from his book *Mensch und Erde* (Man and the Earth). He is also, inter alia, one of the perfectors of the science of graphology, or characterology, as it was then known. His prescient watchwords, or slogans, were "biocentric metaphysics" and "biocentric psychology." For him, men were but living machines—an idea that our contemporary fascination with cyborgs and artificial intelligence regards as anything but strange.

Klages as the enemy of "spirit" was anti-Christian like Nietzsche, but also anti-Nietzsche, and anti-Jewish as well. He may have helped wean Cioran away from Nietzsche's strong but ultimately misleading influence on him. (On a website devoted to Klages, there is only one name in a list of persons he is said to have influenced: Emil Cioran.) His emphasis on psychology—he claimed that both Freud and Jung had been credited with insights that he had had first—complemented the sociological influence of Simmel on Cioran. And his emphasis on a philosophy of "life," inherited from the early nineteenth-century Romantic philosophers of Nature, provided another avenue for unfortunate inroads of the kind of "vitalism" that Hitler, and European fascism generally, made into Cioran's thinking during these years.

Klages was, however, no apologist for Hitlerism: he and his circle of followers were tolerated at first, but their organization and journal were shut down in 1936, and in 1938 he was publicly attacked by Reichsleiter Dr. Alfred Rosenberg. Yet he was left remarkably free to write and travel during these years, and in 1940 he published a book which may explain why, though it would be hard to imagine a more *outré* idea for the times: he claimed that Nazism and "World Jewry" were similar in their world-dominating aims, but that the Jews had succeeded where Nazism failed. Of course, this came after the time of his close association with Cioran, but it would be hard to believe Cioran did not ponder, somewhere, these new developments in his old graduate school mentor's thought. In a notebook entry in 1963 he had, or remembered, a similar thought of his own: "The two peoples that I admire most: the Germans and the Jews. This double admiration which, since Hitler, is incompatible has led me into situations that are, to put it mildly, very delicate, and has stirred up in my life conflicts that I could have done without."[5] But he had by then also reflected on the tragedy of both their similarities and their differences:

> When one thinks of the German literary salons, of the Romantics, of Henriette Herz, of Rachel Levin, the friendship which the latter, Jewish, had with Prince Louis-Ferdinand, and when one reflects that a century later one would see, in the same country, the emergence of Nazism! Certainly, the belief in progress is the silliest and most stupid of all beliefs.[6]

Klages is credited by his youthful friend, the problematical Jewish philosopher Theodore Lessing (1872–1933), for contributing to Lessing's theory of self-hatred, particularly Jewish self-hatred.[7] This was a topic that Cioran also reflected on, in his passing enthusiasm for the rabid Jewish anti-Semite of the turn of the century, Otto Weininger—an enthusiasm he wondered why, many years later, had been so strong. "I shared evidently his hatred [*haine*] of women [or The Female]. But what seduced me, more, was that he, a Jew, detested his *race,* just as I, a Romanian, had a horror of belonging to that nation." Here we see that Cioran's anti-Semitism was not something in itself, freestanding—not an anti-social attitude directed at others, a hatred of a people—but rather a *model* for his attitude toward his own people: "This refusal of origins [in Weininger], this incapacity to resign oneself to be what one is, this dream to be another, I knew all about that; but it seemed to me that Weininger had gone as far as possible in this willfulness, in this search after self-destruction, that he represented a limiting case, *the case* [of self-hatred]."[8]

These are the intellectual influences we can see impinging on Cioran in Berlin. But to see what else he did there is harder, as his life there began to assume the aspect it would finally always have, even after his French fame began in 1949: he simply *thought.* For the rest, we know only—for the most part—that he was alone, and miserable. "When I think of my Berlin solitude, in the winter of 1934–35, I have a *frisson* along my spine. In the tomb, one is less alone, and less abandoned than I was in the miserable Schumannstrasse and Wullenweherstrasse. I seethed with horror, insomnia, pain, foolishness, profligacy. . . ." And then, characteristically, he adds: "I thought that I was called upon to knock over the world."[9]

As he looked back, it was not so much the content of his ideas at the time that amazed him, but the intensity with which he felt them. "I lived a life of hallucination, of folly, in almost total solitude. If only I had the courage or the talent to evoke that nightmare! But I am too weak [now] to be able to plunge myself again into those horrors. . . . It was the negative *summum* [*le summum négatif*] of my life."[10] "My Berlin solitude could not be imagined by a normal man. [Yet] how could I be at the same time so *nervous*? I had never been so close to *dégringolade* [tumbling down, crashing] and to saintliness. . . . I believe that I attained, in certain moments, to those limits often achieved by saints . . . of becoming *positive* monsters, happy monsters and inimitable misfortunes."[11] "I lived with such intensity that I had literally the fear that I would end up as the founder of a religion. . . . In Berlin, in Munich [and in Dresden, which he also visited], I was familiar with frequent ecstasies—which lived as never before on the *summits* of my life. Since then, I have only experienced their simulacra."[12]

But he did not, of course, really do nothing. He did what he would always do: he wrote and published. In his less than two years in Germany, he wrote and sent back for publication in Romania many essays, some quite lengthy, on his impressions of Germany—or more accurately, of his meditations upon what he witnessed there: not journalistic reportage, but "abstract indiscretions." These essays have only recently been collected and republished (in Romania), but this collection, valuable though it is, does not give the full flavor of Cioran's life and thought in Germany, for it omits about ten essays in which he is much more frankly admiring of Hitlerism than in the others. (A description of some of these essays, a translation of one essay, and a translated excerpt of a second essay appear in Appendix 2.)

Cioran was far from the only enthusiast of the newly elected National Socialism he saw unfolding before him in that fateful year of 1933. The horrors of the Second World War and the Holocaust have cast a veil of amnesia over almost all minds that look back at the early 1930s: what everyone can see clearly now, very few could see then—even fewer than those who now *say* they could "see it all coming." But on the ground at the time, Cioran was simply a cipher in a wide movement, or *persuasion* more accurately, of Europe's "advanced" intelligentsia, for whom parliamentary democracy, as represented in Germany by the fallen Weimar Republic, seemed to stand fatally revealed as definitively compromised. "Democracy" was the system of old boys and sweet deals, whereas "Hitlerism" (a name originally more *courant* than Nazism) seemed to give promise of a new kind of political life, irrational to an extent, but with a *vitalism* that could catch up, and hopefully resolve, many intractable social conflicts. But "who knows," Cioran remarked prophetically in his first winter in Berlin, "if the vitality of this people will not cost us dearly?"

From the beginning, he was both enchanted and horrified by the amazing, terrifying new era he saw unfolding literally at his feet. "One falls into hitlerism," he said, "as one falls into any mass movement with a dictatorial tendency." He marveled at the metamorphosis of an entire people into a "fantastic forest." Much later, he claimed he started to study Buddhism "so as not to let myself be intoxicated or contaminated by hitlerism."[13] The spectacle of huge parades and public assemblies inspired in him meditations on the fragility of the instinct of liberty in mankind. "Since the world is the world, men aspire to liberty and exult each time they lose it. . . . Mortals are never more idolatrous than when they lose their chains."[14] This is Rousseau stood on his head. The sight of the Führer acclaimed by thousands of "fools" seemed to him to participate in "a strange frenzy of submission." "It seemed to me that they all raised their hands toward him, imploring a judge capable of satisfying them, as if they aspired impatiently toward enslavement. All dictators have a soul of a messianic blockhead. . . . The fools demand to be commanded. . . . Adam was an adjutant [in God's military march]."

But this was later. At the time, he was swept up himself in the frenzy, or at least in his admiration of its . . . possibilities. He had just come, after all, from a self-consciously very *nouveau* movement of young right-wing Romanian intellectuals who regarded their parliamentary democracy as nothing better than powerless cronyism, as far as the greater good of society was concerned. Now, he saw someone capable of *making* History, able—like Robespierre before him—to make Terror "fecund," and willing to unleash "the mystique of collective mobilization." (He also, with what might be called "abstract indiscretion" in politics, regarded Lenin with the same awe.) Beyond Hitler's imaginings, and influenced by his mentor Klages, he saw the integration of the proletariat into the nation as the creation of a new type of humanity, an "acosmic being," in Jungian terms. When he got back to Romania, he thought he saw the same thing in the Iron Guard: "*The Possessed* of the Right, adepts of orthodox ideologies like those denounced by Dostoevsky, but psychologically very analogous."[15]

Images and ideas of *health* and *action* were prominent in the propaganda of the Nazis and their apologists; Cioran, hypochondriac and preeminent man of *thought* that he was, tried to bend himself to the prevailing wind. The new governing elites would *purify* the nations of their decadence, and Romania between the wars had something of a corner on that market, and not only in Cioran's eyes: "a country of roués, skeptics and cynics."[16]

In a similar paradox, he, though an explorer *par excellence* of interior spaces, warned his brother—and himself, by implication—against the dangers of interiority. "The youth of our epoch is not capable of being saved in libraries." Engagement in a national effort was a way to save oneself from a self-consciousness on the point of imploding from its own excesses, a therapy for "a menacing interior life." He warned Relu, in March of 1935, just before his return to Romania: "If you can, leave your interior life to one side, for if you enter into it with caution, that has no value, but if you carry it to its climax, it will destroy you. . . . Action which is complete in itself constitutes the only way to reintegrate life. . . . The only way to escape from the abyss of interiority is to engage another way, essentially different."[17]

And yet, true to his origins and its devils, he also saw in all this, at the time, and with genuine regret, that it was far beyond anything that Romania was capable of! Transcendentally shocking, bracing, or boggling, that in all we now know about the dripping, horrible history of German Nazism, that there could have been times and persons who could have wished, regretfully, that their country was capable of *that.* But so it was, for Cioran. Seeing a mighty nation on the march in a strikingly new direction (and remembering that many thousands of otherwise intelligent Westerners saw it the same way: think of Charles Lindbergh), Cioran felt, of all things, ashamed of his origins. Compared with *this,* Romania, land of ignorant peasants, could not compare: "With the peasants, one can never enter into history by the *little* door."[18]

This was the frame of mind he was in when he returned to Romania, primed to write a similar political rhapsody for his poor little country. This was the frame of mind in which he could dream, with as much seriousness as exaggerated humor, "of a Romania with the destiny of France and the population of China." For what he aimed at was nothing less than, in the words of the title of his next book, the Transfiguration of Romania.

## Retrospective

Cioran was never a mindless enthusiast for Hitler. He always retained his habits of scholarly objectivity, studying carefully other parts of German history. Later, after the war, during the height of the Cold War, he called on his German experience in another way. He proposed writing "An Apology for Prussia," or "Toward a Rehabilitation of Prussia," proverbially the most warlike of German provinces, home to Bismarck, the Iron Chancellor, and still clearly associated in the 1930s with the causes and provocations of World War I, though now associated with the very different terrors of communism, Prussia constituting much of what was East Germany.

> I am perhaps, outside of Germany, the only man to cry over the ruin of Prussia. It was the only solid reality in Europe. Prussia destroyed, the West *must* fall to the power of the Russians. [This was written in 1958.] There is a ridiculous prejudice against Prussians (the responsibility of the French); a prejudice favorable towards the Austrians [and] Bavarians, [who are] infinitely more cruel; Nazism is a product of southern Germany. (It is evident, but inconvenient to everyone.)
>
> The moment has finally come to speak the truth.
>
> In pursuing the political destruction of Prussia [by establishing the German Democratic Republic], the Russians knew what they were doing; the Anglo-Saxons are only following the prejudices they have inherited from the French (that's their excuse), who since the Revolution make the opinion in the world, that is to say the prejudices . . . on the other side, England, *for the first time in a thousand years,* works against its own interest and renounces—truly suicide—the idea of European equilibrium.[19]

But, despite his strictures on Austria, he dates from his time in Munich (1935) a special fondness for the Empress Elizabeth of Austria (1837–98), when he read a book about her by Maurice Barrès, the extreme French nationalist, *An Empress of Solitude.*[20]

Finally, many years later, he could finally see clearly what everyone saw by then. He had been reading a book by Jorge Guillen on Garcia Lorca, about Spain in 1933.

> Three years after this was the catastrophe. All epochs of intellectual fecundity anticipate historical disasters. All the conflicts of ideas, the passionate struggles which engage a generation, born in the domain of the spirit, these boilings never presage anything good. Revolutions and wars, these are the spirits on the march—that is to say, the triumph and final degradation of the spirit.[21]

# 5

# *Romania's Transfiguration*, 1935–1937

## Negative Passion, Negative Identity

*Schimbarea la față a României* (Romania's Transfiguration) was published in the spring of 1936, almost at the same time as Mircea Eliade's *Yoga*. In a letter to Cioran, who was then unhappily teaching high school in Brașov—having served, even more unhappily, his time in the army from fall 1935 to spring 1936—Eliade mentions the imminent publication of their respective books, asks Cioran to send the exact title and money for the printing paper, and recounts a bizarre last-minute snafu: the two typesettings had gotten mixed up. Luckily, Eliade was on hand at the publishing house to straighten things out. Eliade also comments on the political aspect of Cioran's book, praising his chapter on "workers and Jews" and disagreeing with Cioran's views on Romanian village life.[1] On June 10, 1936, Cioran wrote to Eliade from Sibiu, praising *Yoga*, which had just been published.[2] He did not say anything about his own book, but if it had stayed on schedule, it must have been out by then as well.

The publication of *Romania's Transfiguration,* which was reprinted in 1941, marks a peak in a highly charged political and cultural context. According to Zigu Ornea, who has studied the cultural scene in Romania of the 1920s and 1930s in two voluminous books, the "young generation" of intellectuals to which Cioran and Eliade belonged passed through two distinct phases: from 1928 to 1936 and from 1936 to 1940.[3] Thus for Ornea, 1936 is a pivotal year; indeed, the publication of *Romania's Transfiguration* may well have helped him to demarcate his critical chronology. But whereas the first phase was hailed as Romania's cultural renaissance, the second was characterized by a gradually increasing politicization, which started in 1933 with Nae Ionescu, the generation's guru, endorsing the fascist Iron Guard movement in the pages of his newspaper *Cuvîntul* (The Word).

The political turn in cultural attitudes among the "young generation" is evident in Eliade's 1936 letter to Cioran about the publication of *Romania's Transfiguration.* In it, Eliade speaks in the same breath of Romanian politics, of Cioran's book—which he perceives as a political tract—and of a projected weekly, "rightist, political and *somewhat* cultural as well" to which many of the members of the "young generation" would contribute, and he identifies them by name: "you, I, Țuțea, Sorin Pavel, Golopenția, Stahl, Noica, and a couple more." Politics have taken the upper hand; culture is present only "somewhat," in name. Alluding to intense political arguments in their group, Eliade comments: "You and Țuțea have driven me nuts, I shall become a politician in my hours of sleep and delirium. What a horrendous thing is politics in Romania!"

This process of intense politicization of Romania's cultural life, of which *Romania's Transfiguration* is both a symptom and a symbol, reflects the country's increasingly radical political climate in the 1930s. Starting with Prime Minister I. G. Duca's assassination by members of the Iron Guard in December 1933, Romania gradually slid away from its liberal politics and toward the extreme right. In 1935, the Iron Guard, outlawed in 1931 and then again in 1933, reappeared as a legal party after combining with another extreme right group under the name of *Everything for the Fatherland.* The new party's popularity grew, due to the economic crisis and the traditional parties' inability to remedy the deteriorating situation. Fear of Communist Russia, the growing strength and prestige of the political right in Western Europe, and a lack of confidence in Western liberalism—all contributed to the balance tilting in favor of Hitler and Germany. In February 1938, under the pretext of solving Romania's political crisis, King Carol II put an end to Romania's democratic government by instituting a royal dictatorship.

This is the broad social context in which *Romania's Transfiguration* appeared, but though it helps to account for some of the book's rhetoric, it does little to explain what the book itself is actually about. A critical analysis of Romania's minor-nation status, a long, minute, and merciless inventory of Romanian national flaws, and a reform proposal presented as an "attempt to place a stone on the foundation of a future Romania" (59), *Romania's Transfiguration* is part philosophical essay, part political pamphlet, and part utopian vision. But more than anything else, it is the journal of an identity crisis, and its violent rhetoric betrays an authorial mind in a state of acute anxiety, restless, searching, and desperate to find an answer to its obsessive questioning about his own and his country's destiny.

The main "plot" of *Romania's Transfiguration* is the young Cioran's quixotic quest for a suitable selfhood, or rather, *for a reformed nation that would suit his sense of himself.* In it, his incommensurate pride battles with his self-contempt, obsessive inferiority complex, and self-consciousness about his Romanian origins, and he fills frantic pages with wild megalomaniacal dreams about a "delirious" Romania "with China's population and France's destiny." At the heart of the book lies Cioran's cry of despair and wounded pride: "I want another nation!" The correlation between self-hatred and over-blown pride characteristic of this youthful text was later recaptured by Cioran in one of his briefest aphorisms, "n'est pas humble celui qui se hait" [He who hates himself is not humble].[4]

*Romania's Transfiguration* is, like Cioran's first book, *On the Heights of Despair,* the result of many nights of insomnia. Cioran speaks with the personal authority of one who "has spent many a wakeful night meditating on Romania's destiny" (52). This book has both the specious clarity and the nightmarish intensity of those dread thoughts that assail us in the early hours of the morning. The questions that kept the young Cioran awake were questions that would continue to haunt him for the rest of his life: Who am I? What does it mean to be Romanian? Or, "How can one be Romanian?" as he put it later in *La tentation d'exister,* alluding to Montesquieu's question, "Comment peut-on être persan?" The question's fine irony underscores the absurdity, the aberrational character, of anything marginal when viewed from the center. The question stuck like a thorn in Cioran's flesh.

At the time he is writing *Romania's Transfiguration,* in late 1935 and early 1936, in a state of personal suspension, the "hiatus" between his two years in Germany and his departure for France, Cioran has not yet achieved Montesquieu's ironic distance. "L'ironie dérive d'un appétit de naïveté, déçu, inassouvi, et qui, à force d'échecs, s'aigrit et s'envenime" [Irony derives from a naive appetite, disappointed, insatiable, and which, as a result of its failures, becomes bitter and aggravated],[5] he would write much later. But the young Cioran is still naive, still hopeful, still searching for an answer to his insoluble dilemma: How can one be Romanian and *still be* oneself? His ordeal has only just begun, and *Romania's Transfiguration* is an early record of it.

One feels naturally inclined to ask in return: Who does he think he is? What motivates this excessive pride? *Romania's Transfiguration* provides an answer. Cioran's exacerbated sense of self comes from his sense of himself-as-writer. Creativity is for him inextricably linked to the sovereign self, as and at the center of the universe, and hence to the incommensurate pride of the creator:

> *Man cannot create except to the extent that he believes himself to be the centre of history.* I'm not speaking here of the blindness of the bourgeois, who lives as if he were the only reality, but rather of the greatness of the spirit which enlarges every moment to the size of eternity. If you don't have the feeling that everything that preceded you was made expressly for you, and that you are a unique crossroads in history, if you don't feel that life wants *you* and that your moment in history is absolute, unique and irreplaceable, then you are nothing more than a firefly in the sunlight, an invisible flash, pale fire. You are a world in yourself only if the axis of the world pierces your heart.[6]

It sounds like pure megalomania, but it is also admirably brave, coming from a man so insecure about his origins, yet with no doubt whatsoever about his intelligence and creative powers. The passage reveals a strong *ironical* tension between his ambitions for himself and his actual condition of marginality.[7]

Cioran lives in two worlds at once: an interior, ahistorical world, in which he (or what he considers to be his pure, central self) is like God, if not actually God himself; and an exterior, historical world, in which he is like a beggar on the margins of existence, his self-pityingly cherished downtrodden self, a mere historical accident. In *Romania's Transfiguration* his moods oscillate wildly between a sense of security sprung from self-centered creativity, and an endemic insecurity caused by his self-conscious marginality. Cioran's personal drama is the drama of the ambitious creator laboring under the curse of marginality, writing in a language hardly anybody knows, handicapped by a culture of which no one has heard.

> [P]assion for Romania cannot accept its condemnation to eternal mediocrity. . . . Criminal lucidity sees it as a disappearing microcosm, while passion places it at the center of the heart, and therefore in the rhythm of the world. . . . The pride of a man born in a small culture will always be wounded. It's not easy being born in a second-rate country. Lucidity becomes tragedy. And if messianic fury doesn't suffocate you, your soul will drown in a sea of disconsolation. (28)

Though the language sounds grandly generalized, we can clearly recognize in the last lines all the personal and psychological accents which we have seen in Cioran's self-portraits thus far, especially the extreme swerves between fury and epiphany. There is the wound to pride (the insult of being born Romanian) and what Cioran came later to call "the wound of life" (the metaphysical insult of being born at all). Cioran identifies himself with his nation, but the identification is highly unstable or problematic, since Romania is marginal, whereas Cioran's sense of self is absolutely central, god-like. His solution is not to change himself, but to change—transfigure—his nation.

The apparently paradoxical question, How can one be Romanian and still be oneself? further modulates into: How can one be Romanian and still be creative? To be great, to be successful and creative in an insignificant culture and in a language that has no circulation is indeed an impossibility, a contradiction in terms, an aberration. To be Romanian, therefore, is for the young and ambitious Cioran a catastrophe of cosmic proportions.

But Cioran thrived on catastrophe and contradictions. The "inconvenience" of being Romanian—which he only later universalized into the "inconvenience of being born"—constitutes the origin of his writing. Cioran writes about Romania because he cannot disassociate Romania's fate from his own. In its future his very sense of self as a martyred author is at stake, but it is through writing about it that he will ultimately achieve the much-longed-for disassociation. So, he writes about Romania in order to negate it, and his sense of himself-as-writer grows, perversely, out of this negation, out of deliberately self-inflicted torture and humiliation: a double-bind which could easily be cast in Freudian terms, with Romania playing at once the smothering mother-figure and the castrating father-figure of authority.

For example, in chapter 1 of *Romania's Transfiguration,* "The Tragedy of Small Cultures," while discussing one of the book's main themes, the dichotomy between great and small cultures, Cioran explains why he has chosen this topic. He stresses the subjective, unscientific angle he takes on the question of small cultures and reveals the stakes for him in such a discussion. He acknowledges that he is directly and passionately implicated in the issues he raises, and far from a neutral observer. He deliberately chooses to see them *not* as a dispassionate observer of history might (since he does not believe such an observer exists), but as a man of resentment, a man who was "inconveniently" born into a small, insignificant culture with which he cannot come to terms. This is, in fact, the "inconvenience" that turns him into an author, and it already gives us a portrait of the author as a wounded, tortured young man, racked by negative passion for Romania:

> Yet, ultimately, for whom is the question of small cultures painful? Certainly not for a historian. . . . It is in the eyes of the representative of a small culture that this question

> appears in a subjective light, and takes on a life of its own totally surpassing the sphere of historical objectivity. Had we not had such a deep feeling for the phenomenon we call Romania, had we remained objective towards it, we couldn't have cared less whether it played a role in history or not. Then its place alongside other small cultures would have seemed natural to us, and its anonymity would not have affected us. (28)

Cioran identifies here the two extremes between which he is divided in unresolved conflict, and which constitute the two poles of his negative passion: on the one hand, a "passion for Romania" (read: passion for self) which "places it at the center" of the world irrationally, "with messianic fury" and "criminal lucidity," and on the other, a condition of marginality, the consciousness of not being at the center, from which he sees Romania (and self) "as a disappearing microcosm," and which "drowns his soul in a sea of disconsolation." The young author acknowledges that he is directly and passionately implicated in the apparently generalized issues he raises.

The obvious contradiction between these two impulses must have been clear to Cioran, but it is not one that could be cleared up by mere common sense: for example, to become more nationalistic/patriotic, or to be less egotistical. On the contrary, for Cioran these two poles of his inspiration in *Romania's Transfiguration* are clear examples of the concept of *negative identity* which Erik Erikson observed in the self-creation of the young Martin Luther and, by implication, in many such cases of creative individualism. Negative identity, in Erikson's formulation, is that identity or role which the individual has been warned to avoid, a self-image that is diametrically opposed to the dominant values of his upbringing, one which he can adopt only with a divided heart, but which he nevertheless feels himself compelled to adopt, all the while protesting his wholeheartedness.[8]

In the posthumous *Mon Pays,* whose composition dates probably from the early 1960s, the French Cioran draws from memory a portrait of the young Romanian Cioran.[9] Recognition and even admiration for the "wild madman" he once was is subdued in this portrait by a sense of estrangement. The distance in time separating the two selves is emphasized, the younger self can only be reconstructed imaginatively. But the young man's negative passion for Romania is a salient feature that time has not blurred. It is significant that the older, French Cioran still vividly remembers the wound of pride from which his writing sprang.

> I had written at the time a book on my country: it may very well be that no one has ever attacked his country so violently. It was the ravings of a wild madman. But in my negations there was such a fire that, from a distance, I can only imagine it as a sort of love in reverse, idolatry *à rebours* [against the grain] . . . I longed for the inexorable. And to

> a certain extent, I was grateful to my country for providing me with such a marvelous occasion for torment. I loved it because it did not answer my expectations. Those were the good times: I believed in the prestige of unhappy passions. I loved challenge, and the biggest seemed to be that of having been born in my country.[10]

Cioran sounds here, once again, like a character out of Dostoevsky. He cultivates suffering and unhappiness as the only road to selfhood—like Dostoevsky's man from underground, he is most alive when suffering most. And since, like the same memorable character, he "believed in the prestige of unhappy passions," Cioran finds in his historically insignificant fatherland, "a marvelous occasion for torment." He gains his sense of self as writer, therefore, from a perverse identity with the nation he loves to hate; the more he identifies with his Romanian origins, the more he hates himself. Or, he hates so much that his hatred becomes "love in reverse, idolatry *à rebours,*" plunging like a knife, mercilessly, into his wounded pride.

To write, then, Cioran needs this self-inflicted wound. As Sorin Antohi has noticed, in representing his Romanian identity as a wound, Cioran "offers the most articulate image of Romanianism as *stigma* . . . which equally covers the miraculous marks of divine election (through the symbolic memory of Christ's wounds), the external attributes of illness and deformity, a sure sign of justice on the body of great delinquents, as well as the sign of public disapproval toward persons who do not conform to the 'normality' specific to a given community."[11] Or again, in larger cultural terms, we can see the same pattern in Erikson's young man Luther, this time identified by no less an existential authority than Søren Kierkegaard: "a passion for expressing and describing one's suffering," creating a sense of *improved* suffering without need for a cure.[12]

## Self-Portrait: The Artist as a Wounded Martyr

The picture Cioran drew of himself in *Mon Pays* is accurate in its emphasis upon his Dostoevskian streak, his fondness for suffering. One could imagine the young Cioran's motto to have been: I suffer, therefore I am. In his twenties, he believed fanatically in the cult of suffering, in the positive transformations suffering works upon the human soul—starting with his own—and never tired of singing the praises of suffering, his religion at the time. From Berlin in April 1933, when he was not yet twenty-two years old, he wrote enthusiastically to his friend Petre Comarnescu about the satisfaction he derived from suffering and despair. This letter, written four years before the publication of *Romania's Transfiguration,* is proof that the identity crisis which constitutes the core of that book had long been rumbling underground. *Romania's Transfiguration,* almost the last of Cioran's Romanian books, is the final, apocalyptic expression, the long-incoming but inevitable public explosion of a powerful pent-up drive:

> I am the sort of man who has changed completely under the effect of suffering, even though this transformation may simply be the intensification of elements already there. Thus amplified, they give an entirely new perspective on life. I believe, frenetically and fanatically, in the virtues of suffering and of anxiety, and I believe in them especially since, though I've suffered greatly and despaired much, I nevertheless acquired through them a sense of my own destiny, a sort of weird enthusiasm for my mission. On the heights of the most terrifying despair, I experience the joy of having a destiny, of living a life of successive deaths and transfigurations, of turning every moment into a cross-road. And I am proud that my life begins with death, unlike the majority of people, who end with death. *I feel as if my death were in the past, and my future looks to me like a sort of personal illumination.*[13]

Young Cioran saw himself as a sort of Christ figure who embraced suffering, welcomed death, and whose true life began only with resurrection after death. One wonders what kind of suffering a twenty-two-year-old has undergone to justify such an ambitious analogy? He is probably alluding to his chronic insomnia, the "quotidian [or daily] crucifixion," as he later called it.[14] In language with strong mystical overtones, the letter praises death as momentous beginning, as revelation or illumination. St. John of the Cross's *The Dark Night of the Soul,* a text with which young Cioran was familiar, comes to mind. And yet there is also an unmistakable sense of pride that is less Christian in feeling, a satisfaction derived from having to start under a minus sign, with a handicap. Death is a metaphor for an unspecified deficiency. The letter says, "I am proud that my life begins with death," which can be read as, "I am proud that my life begins with absence, as lack or emptiness," and it is typical of Cioran to find an advantage in this absence and sing its praises. The letter also makes clear that Cioran saw himself as a man of destiny, one of the elect, a man with a mission. The embedded analogy with Christ suggests that his mission is that of a savior. And whom will he save if not "the majority of people" whose life, unlike his, ends with death? He does not specify, however, the nature of the mission (is it spiritual? cultural? political?) or the means to fulfill it; he only intimates that he acquired the true sense of his mission through suffering, or, maybe, *in* suffering. It is less the content of his mission than its form that he stresses: whatever it consists of, it will be *revelatory* in impact.

One could find in this line of reasoning a residual, or paradoxical, trace of Christianity in Cioran, who normally sounds thoroughly un-Christian. On this reading, his pride is not un-Christian but the reverse: the less you have, the more you have, as in the Beatitudes from the Sermon on the Mount: "Blessed are the poor in spirit, for theirs is the kingdom of heaven" (*Matthew* 5:3).

Cioran's theory of suffering is still vague and general in these lines from the beginning of his letter to Petre Comarnescu, but its focus soon shifts from his penchant for suffering to his locating and purging it in Romania. Towards the end of the letter, Cioran moves from a praise of suffering for its general "advantages" to a more contextualized notion of suffering—suffering from and for being Romanian:

> Some of our friends will think that I became a fan of Hitler's out of opportunism. The truth is that there are certain realities I like here, and I'm persuaded that our native good-for-nothingness could be stifled, if not eradicated, by a dictatorial regime. In Romania, only terror, brutality and an infinite anxiety could still lead to some change. All Romanians should be arrested and beaten to a pulp; only after such a beating could a superficial people make history. It's awful to be Romanian: you never win the trust of any woman, and serious people smile at you dismissively; when they see that you are smart, they think you are a cheat. But what did I do to become the one who has to wash away the shame of a people without history?[15]

These are shocking formulations, even from a "master of hyperbole," especially if one happens to be Romanian. But, despite the change of register—from the private to the political—the second passage from the letter exhibits a clear continuity with the first one. The praise of "infinite anxiety" and of suffering returns at the end of the letter, but is now given a specific name and form: dictatorship. He was writing from Berlin, and when he speaks of Hitler he clearly delights in the perversity of turning things on their head and preaching the horrible. He praises Hitler precisely because he embodies the epitome of Evil, the scourge, the torture, which Cioran invokes as the necessary shock treatment of his recommended "cure."

The idea of a mission is also present here but is given at once a more specific and a more negative content. By mission, Cioran means "making history," that is, elevating oneself and one's people to a position of centrality. But his fellow countrymen, "superficial good-for-nothings," cannot, short of a sound beating, carry out this mission successfully. Similar language and imagery was used by many other intellectuals in the 1920s and 1930s, in Germany, Italy, England, and America, to defend and extol the "discipline" that fascism would bring with it. So, Cioran sees himself as the chosen one: his body, his entire self will substitute itself for that of the nation, he becomes the sacrificial victim, and thus he will—in fact, he already has, metaphorically speaking—undergone the "beating," in the form of the suffering announced earlier in the letter.

What Cioran is describing in his letter to Comarnescu is, therefore, a vision of himself as a savior of Romania, a vision he will try to act out in *Romania's Transfiguration.* He has both a martyr's enthusiasm and his willpower. He will try to save the nation with his pen, which becomes an instrument of glory as well as of torture by vilification. For his mission is both a curse and a blessing. Listen again to the somber tone of his concluding rhetorical question, "But what did I do to become the one who has to wash away the shame of a people without history?" Even as he talks of being Romania's savior, he balks at the idea: 'Why should *I* be the one who must expiate her sins?' His sense of mission toward his country is always in tension with his sense of mission toward himself: to become the writer he felt he was and must be. Thus the euphoric suffering of the letter's opening goes hand in hand with the bitter consciousness of his Romanian identity—there is literally "nothing to write home about" when women don't trust you and serious men dismiss you as a cheat—an almost comical insight into the condition of marginality with which the letter concludes.

Read now, with the knowledge of the historical catastrophe that was Hitler's Germany, this letter seems to anticipate sinister re-formulations. But Cioran's overstatements were meant to be shocking and extreme even at the time they were written, and Cioran, a master of exaggeration, did not miss his mark. The letter's circumstances are important. One must not forget that it was written during the early stages of Hitler's government. Cioran was in Berlin on a German government fellowship and had been sending home articles full of praise for Hitler's Germany—which could also be interpreted as attempts to curry favor with the Germans in order to have his fellowship prolonged. Hence the letter's plea against the charge of opportunism. Cioran was writing to a friend who presumably would repeat the contents of the letter to their other common friends in Bucharest, among them those who had accused Cioran of opportunism. It is quite conceivable that, at the time, young Cioran was more concerned about a charge of opportunism than a charge of pro-Hitlerism.

Cioran writes, as always, for the shock value. Moreover, he *was,* most likely, guilty of opportunism: anybody who knew Cioran in the 1930s knew that he was desperately trying to get out of Romania, and since he was always short of money, he was always on the lookout for fellowship opportunities.[16] His real cure for the disease of "Romanianism" was getting away from it, not reforming it. But the letter is ultimately interesting for its ambiguity, for the unresolved dramatic tensions it displays, the way in which personal *motives* and intellectual *motifs* interact, overlap, and play against each other, both revealing and concealing the personality of the letter writer.

## History and Politics

*Romania's Transfiguration* furiously debates the question, "How can one be a Romanian?" That is, how can one live in this marginal condition and still be something, a creator, a writer? This lengthy debate, with its grandiose and often extreme formulations, sounds, as Matei Calinescu perceptively observed, like "an exercise in tenacity or self-persuasion."[17] Typically, Cioran transposes his unhappy actual situation, as a teacher in auxiliary service in Braşov, into a philosophical, existential quest. The book explores exhaustively one possible answer to his dilemma: stay in Romania and await or herald its "transfiguration," become the young prophet of a new era.

By "transfiguration," Cioran means a radical transformation of the country's destiny that will realign it in history, if not with big cultures like France, England, or Germany—that would be too unrealistic a hope—at least with intermediate ones like Spain and Italy. In language that has the same mystical overtones as the letter to Petre Comarnescu, Cioran dreams of a national revolution that will bring Romania out of its state of sub-culture into culture, from "biology into history," from anonymity to glory, for "without glory, history is nothing but biology" (27). In other words, he dreams of a revolution that will bring about Romania's salvation. And "in great cultures, the individual is saved. Nay, even more than that, he is always saved." Thus Cioran at one point fancies that he has found an answer to his personal identity crisis: to be oneself one must identify with one's nation at its moment of glory—provided the nation experiences such a moment.

But Cioran's psycho-drama of megalomaniacal obsession with himself does have its counterpart in the public, political drama of a nation trying to make itself and modernize itself in the process. Many other people besides Cioran were asking themselves a version of Cioran's question: "How can one be a (Greater) Romanian?" Paraphrasing an Italian revolutionary's comments on Italy's unification—"We have made Italy; now we must make the Italians"—Irina Livezeanu writes in *Cultural Politics in Greater Romania* that "once (Greater) Romania had been made, there remained the formidable task of making the Romanians."[18]

Cioran was formulating his question in the interwar period, when the centuries-old dream of "Greater Romania" had been realized, at least geographically and politically, but the entire country was still in the grip of tremendous efforts to turn a political abstraction into a viable economic, social, and cultural reality. The nation became "great," at least in name, almost overnight: "Greater Romania" was constituted on December 1, 1918. (See map.) But the goal was achieved through a process in which the Romanians were not even the principal actors. As Livezeanu argues, "Greater Romania" was not a "natural" entity, the natural consequence of a "natural" process of unification, but a social construct, the consequence of a historical and political process of nation building that was intensified rather than decreased after unification:

> The unification of the Romanian lands in 1918 constituted a national revolution—despite the unquestionable linguistic, historical, and cultural ties existing among the Romanians from the old and new territories—and this revolution initiated the turbulent nation building and civil strife that characterized the decades between the two wars. . . . the "embarrassment of riches" Romania faced with the postwar settlement was an ambiguous

> and difficult gift. Like the "Trojan horse," it brought apparent and momentary glory but concealed untold social, demographic, political and cultural challenges.[19]

Livezeanu's thesis is that the proportions of Romania's national identity crisis were doubled by the twin facts of sudden (and externally supported) unification, coupled with the new government's immediate and enthusiastic attempt to "Romanize" a welter of multi-ethnic elites (Austrian, German, Hungarian) who had until barely the day before yesterday been just as thoroughly "Magyarized." Thus Cioran's preoccupation in *Romania's Transfiguration* with the dichotomy between small and great cultures is not simply an expression of personal resentment, but rather the resentment of a whole nation of nobodies, a nation that had no history of greatness because it "had lived for as long as anyone can remember under foreign rule." In this context, his vituperative criticisms of the Romanian national character, his fulminations against the Balkan or "Oriental" flaws of Romanians—indolence, laziness, corruption, failure—his desire to whip the nation out of its "sub-historical" state of somnolence, are not unique. He shares the opinion of many Transylvanian leaders after the union with the mother country in 1918, such as Iuliu Maniu, the leader of the National Peasant Party, and Onişifor Ghibu, a leading cultural reformer, whose "criticism reflected the outraged 'national conscience,' [but] it also contained a regionalist component. The Transylvanian purists perceived the pettiness, indiscipline, and sloppiness of the bureaucracy as the baggage of Balkan Romania and were reluctant to carry it. They saw themselves as more skilled and morally superior, an outlook which made for a certain ideological compatibility between this group of Transylvanians and a younger generation of radical Romanian nationalists."[20]

Similarly, Cioran's undisguised envious longing to belong to a cultural aristocracy is symptomatic in a country where one of the most urgent and daunting tasks of nation building was "the replacement of foreign elites" and "the recruitment and expansion of national elites."[21] When in typical hyperbolic fashion he writes, "I'd give up half of my life if I could experience with equal intensity that which the most insignificant of Greeks, Romans or Frenchmen experienced even for a moment at the height of their history" (32), Cioran also gives voice to a widespread longing of a whole nation to emancipate itself. This longing, expressed early on in *Romania's Transfiguration*, inexorably leads to the later formulation of a wish to join a national renaissance movement that would catapult Romania into history:

> *He who remains outside his country's national revolution remains outside of himself as well.* I haven't met any individuals more depressed or depressing than those who in Germany, rejecting Hitlerism, eliminated themselves voluntarily from the rhythm of their nation. He who misses the apogee of his nation misses himself. (227)

Here we come again upon praise of Hitlerism, and yet these lines are different from those sent to Comarnescu in 1933. The German (that is, Hitlerian) model has here a positive content—it is represented as the "apogee" of Germany—and thus contrasts sharply with the negative, perversely twisted praise Cioran gave it in the earlier letter. There, dictatorship was seen as the means, not the end, of reform: dictatorship provided the suffering necessary to reform individuals and, consequently, the nation. The critique of Romanianism, a theme common to both the letter and *Romania's Transfiguration,* receives a different solution here: whereas in the letter, the "I" stands alone as Savior and martyr, at this advanced point in the book the young author has managed to talk himself into the idea that true selfhood is gained only through identification with the nation. This equation, nation = self, implies the total stripping of the self as individual and its subordination to the nation, with the nation at its "apogee" taking on the role of Savior of the individual. So, though the problem here is the same as in the letter to Comarnescu—the need for national reform—Cioran's role in it oscillates between the active and the passive poles, between being the Savior or one of the saved.

Given the historical moment, it is not surprising that Cioran should see a movement for national renaissance as the means to achieve his dream of Romania's grandeur. In this he was again reflecting not only the spirit of the age but also its political realities for, as Livezeanu writes, "in order to assimilate the new provinces . . . the Romanian government initiated cultural and educational policies that resulted in intense national mobilization. These policies in turn fueled the existing populist, nationalist discourse that gradually came to dominate political, social and cultural life after 1918."[22]

The passages about Germany cited above are as close as Cioran comes to showing his political allegiances in *Romania's Transfiguration.* Though he never mentions the Iron Guard directly, statements like these leave little doubt that he has it in mind as he is writing his book. The political moment of the Iron Guard coincides with the publication of *Romania's Transfiguration,* and the latter is, as Matei Calinescu observes, "the main trace left in Cioran's work of his having been 'carried away' by an extremist ideological wave. . . . Even so, one would look in vain in it for even one mention of the Iron Guard, or its leader, Codreanu, or, for that matter, any other specific name or event in the political life of contemporaneous Romania. Cioran speaks prophetically and in general terms."[23]

But he also speaks ambiguously and inconsistently. Sorin Antohi, for example, points out that "at a rapid glance, there's nothing to distinguish the revolutionary élan of the young Cioran from Legionnaire enthusiasm. It's all there, from Messianism to the violence of the political program"; but there are also many "significant—and even decisive—differences. They are rather lost in a prolific textual mass, often redundant or contradictory. . . . [Cioran] rejects the return to ethnicity, believes that democracy is a 'vital necessity,' and has heavy words for nationalism, which 'has become an incubator of misery.'"[24] Cioran's quarrel with nationalism, embedded in this overtly nationalistic political tract, reflects his misgivings about the nationalist movement and his role in it, misgivings he candidly sets forth in letters to Eliade, who openly sided with the Iron Guard. In 1935, he writes to Eliade,

> My formula for politics is: to fight *sincerely* for that in which I do not believe. The difference between me and the nationalists is so great that my participation could only confuse them. The only thing I have in common with them is the interest in Romania. . . . I can't tell you how many times I'm not a nationalist. Yet I love my country for I can't remain indifferent towards the world.[25]

And again in 1937, while asking Eliade to help him get out of Romania, he writes: "What would I do if I were to stay here? Since I cannot actively integrate myself within the nationalist movement, I have no practical reason to remain in Romania."[26]

So what, then, is Cioran doing in *Romania's Transfiguration*? On the one hand, his discourse is clearly part of a general public discourse dictated by the specific historical moment. On the other hand, it is so *unlike* anything else being written on its subject that it stands out in the political context as a sort of aberration. What makes it so is the fact that he uses to the utmost the resources of the genres within which he is operating—political manifesto and utopia—while at the same time undermining them with his skepticism and lack of faith. *Romania's Transfiguration* is a political tract, but a tract *à la Cioran,* and its uniquely Cioran-esque aspect must be stressed. The word "political" has the special meaning Cioran disclosed in his letter to Eliade: "my formula for politics is to fight *sincerely* for that in which I do *not* believe."

*Romania's Transfiguration* is more than just a political tract, more than just a reflection of a country's convulsions in the process of building itself as a nation, and its contradictions reflect the painfully divided consciousness of its author. It might just be possible to work out the differences between Cioran's politics, as represented in *Romania's Transfiguration,* and the positions of the dominant nationalist ideologies of the time, but the result would be useless, politically speaking. Cioran's negative passion for Romania, his "idolatry *à rebours,*" is too unusual and intense, too organic, to be a mere echo of the spirit of the age. He writes as if he were personally responsible for his country's salvation, as if he had been *chosen* to drag it into history. He writes, moreover, as an artist, not as a politician, for he takes political events as a personal affront. We are faced here with a creative inconsistency or contradiction which becomes the source of much of Cioran's writing. The political aspect of *Romania's Transfiguration* is informed by Cioran's own insecurities about himself as a creative artist. He hopes, on the one hand, to find an answer to his dilemma in an identification with a glorified ideal of the nation. On the other hand, his sense of duty toward the community conflicts with his sense of artistic mission. In a way, *Romania's Transfiguration* represents an alternative scenario to Cioran's life, a fiction which helps him examine the "practical reason," as he put it to Eliade, that would justify his staying in Romania rather than going abroad. One should not forget that Cioran wrote it at a time of life when a young man sees many paths opening in front of him but knows that he can only choose *one,* making the choice a pure agony. Through his writing, he is imaginatively and passionately living out and working through those options he will ultimately *not* take.

## The Anxiety of Origins

But, in addition to the general political context in which *Romania's Transfiguration* was produced, and its refraction through Cioran's personal crises of vocation and identity, there is another context, specifically related to Cioran's family history, which must be taken into consideration. The obsession with a mission of cultural and spiritual reform in *Romania's Transfiguration,* the vehemence of its prophetic tone, and the virulence of its negation come from a tradition Cioran knew well because of his own family connections with it. It is the tradition of the heroic struggle of the Romanians of Transylvania to assert their national identity and gain equal rights with other nations in the Austro-Hungarian Empire, a tradition in which intellectuals played a major role.

To appreciate the bearing, the pressure, that this background exerted on the Cioran of *Romania's Transfiguration,* we must return to the little world of Răşinari and Sibiu, and specifically the larger national horizons that Cioran's father and others like him tried to envision and project from their provincial homes. The idea that the intellectual has a mission in society, that he is inevitably involved in politics, and that, above all, he has a moral duty toward his country—to further the nation's interests, to work for the advancement of its people—came to Cioran directly from his father. As we have seen, Cioran belonged to a family of fighter-priests, leaders of the despised and oppressed Romanians of Transylvania, and their sense of mission, that he had to play a part in their further emancipation, was drilled into him since early childhood. Thus in *Romania's Transfiguration* his is not purely a personal "creative" dilemma in the abstract, but one fed from his most intimate family roots, but in ways that twisted into a classic vocational double bind, of the kind analyzed by Erik Erikson. On the one hand, Cioran is both *rejecting* this tradition as insufficient and stifling and yet *continuing* it in the more extreme, polarized, and violent context of European politics in the 1930s. On the other hand, his inherited notions about the mission of an intellectual are in conflict with his ideas about his own artistic mission, the egotistical force, and the obsessions that shape an artist's career, "driving his own designs towards his self's objectives," as William Carlos Williams put it in his *Autobiography.*

Cioran's inferiority complex had its historical roots in an experience quite common to all Romanians in Transylvania, namely that being Romanian did not get you very far in society: "those Romanians who did succeed had to assimilate, and did so, in fact, so well that they passed for Magyars and then were lost as Romanians."[27] Irina Livezeanu describes three possible reactions to the pressures of Magyarization on the Romanians of Transylvania: 1) assimilation which led to success, 2) self-conscious nationalism, and 3) return to traditional village life after a few years of schooling. In his search for a solution to the dilemma of his Romanian origins, Cioran considered them all: he rejected the last one as spiritual suicide, acted out the nationalistic scenario in *Romania's Transfiguration,* and ultimately opted for assimilation, but of a different kind. The lesson of assimilation was not lost on Cioran since it was the course he chose for himself in life, when he moved to France, adopted French for his language, cut his Romanian roots, and stopped speaking Romanian altogether: that is, assimilation by rejection. The path to this third solution is, however, paved for Cioran with the agony of deliberations, vacillations, and doubts about his failure to believe in the second option—the family option, as it were.

Emil Cioran's letters to his family from abroad, detailing his student life, the hotels he lives in, the clothes he buys, the colds he gets, and the money he often asks for, resemble the exchanges between Sava P. Barcianu and his son Daniel cited in Appendix 1. There is, however, an important difference. Though always respectful and mindful of those at home, Cioran is *never* eager to return; on the contrary, the thought of having to return makes him sick with anxiety. He faced choices similar to those of Daniel Barcianu, but whereas the latter returns and obediently joins the established ranks of nation builders by becoming a teacher and writer inside the Romanian community of Transylvania, Cioran longs to escape, abhorring a teaching career especially. Thus from Paris in 1938, referring to the teaching position in Braşov, which he had held at the time he was writing *Romania's Transfiguration,* he avers,

> I'm willing to accept anything but be a teacher. Whenever I think of Braşov, I feel sick, and I believe that I would have never written pages as bitter as those in my last book had I not been exasperated by such an impossible profession.

And again, a few months later:

> As far as Braşov is concerned, let me know if I must send you the documents now. My fellowship expires in November. If they appoint me, I'd very much like to ask for a one-year leave, by pretending that I still have a fellowship for another year. The thought that from Paris I'd fall back directly into a high school simply makes me ill.[28]

The family ambitions, with their national overtones, which would assign him the role of a small-town teacher, priest, or writer in a minor language, are too narrow and imprisoning.[29] Thus the high school teaching position in Braşov becomes for him the embodiment of the hated limit to his own unlimited ambitions and excessive sense of self, as he poignantly put it in his letter to his parents. (As to any companions there, he merely says, "I'm not speaking with anyone but Shakespeare.")[30] The Barcianu family options, of which his own father strongly approved, are also his, but they are not enough.

Thus, through his family connections, early and late, Cioran was born into an old tradition of nationalism which claims him as its own. The "burden of the past" weighs heavily on his shoulders, and *Romania's Transfiguration* is the expression of a struggle with that past, an open polemic with an older generation of nationalists, into which he was born and which first formed his national consciousness. The young Cioran writes:

> Romanian nationalism until now has not been positive, but only patriotism . . . that is, sentimentalism, without a dynamic orientation, without messianism, without the will to fulfill itself. Our forefathers did not love us enough, since they shed so very little blood for freedom. (41)

Or again,

> I do not feel proud of Romania's past, nor of my ancestors, so devoid of ambitions that they slept a long time waiting for liberty. Romania does not make sense unless *we begin it.* We must create Romania *internally* in order to *be born again* in it. (39)

In these statements, he is not simply suffering an attack of gerontophobia. Rather, he is gripped by a paroxysm of the anxiety of influence, stridently rejecting the ancestors with whom he has all too much in common. He particularly rejects the kind of nationalism they embraced, always tempered with pragmatism and prudence.[31] It is against this pragmatism, this prudence, that necessarily implied limited goals and limited horizons, that the young Cioran rebels in *Romania's Transfiguration. Romania's Transfiguration,* in which he acts out a nationalistic scenario on a much grander scale, is his means of purging his political ambitions, his writing cure, a "political" fantasy of an alternative life for himself. Though *Romania's Transfiguration* is a defiant gesture of rejection of a burdensome past, it also clearly continues an inherited tradition of self-help and uplift. Cioran struggles against it, claiming for himself and his generation the privilege of being the beginning, the origins of his country's history. One strategy he adopts is to accuse, unfairly, his ancestors of faintheartedness and lack of pride.[32]

But if Cioran rejects his ancestors' pragmatism, replacing it with his own version of violent Machiavellism, *Romania's Transfiguration*—with its prophecies, its anathemas, its criticisms of the flaws of the Romanian nation (just what the Transylvanian nationalists warned against), but also with its tone of urgency, anguish, despair, and disgust—belongs *generically* to the same kind of consciousness-raising, messianic literature as the sermons given by Romanian priests in Transylvania. Priests like those in the Barcianu family never missed an opportunity to improve, enlighten, and embolden their parishioners. Cioran, son of such priests, was quite familiar with this kind of sermon. In spite of his protests, the model of radical nationalism put forward by *Romania's Transfiguration* does not so much diverge from the beaten path as it exaggerates it, pushing it to extremes, but along already familiar tracks. Despite its violent rhetoric, it still inscribes itself within a historical and even familial tradition, simultaneously continuing while apparently negating a tradition of specifically Transylvanian nationalism.

For example, there is a striking similarity in tone, mood, and voice between *Romania's Transfiguration* and a sermon given by Sava Barcianu in 1792 in the church of Răşinari, which is quoted *in extenso* by Emilian Cioran in his history of the Barcianus. Like Cioran in *Romania's Transfiguration,* this preacher has spent many anguished hours reflecting upon the fate of the blighted Romanian nation and comparing it to other "greater," and more fortunate nations:

> how often during hours of loneliness did I pause to think about the state of being of other nations and compare them to that of our own, and I found such a great difference as between white and black.[33]

The difference between Romanians and other nations lies within the Romanians' "nepriceperea, neînţelepciunea, nestrăduirea şi lenevirea" [incompetence, lack of wisdom, lack of drive, and laziness]. Cioran, in *Romania's Transfiguration,* describes a similar agony of lonely hours of meditation on his unfortunate and dispossessed nation. It is the same context and the same quandary, and even, perversely, the same "patriotic" impulse, but in typical Cioran fashion, he delights in his agony and finds pleasure in Romania's historical humiliations:

> I don't understand how some people can sleep peacefully after having thought about the underground existence of a persecuted people, centuries of darkness, terror, serfdom. When I imagine Transylvania, I see an expanse of silent pain, a closed and stifled drama, a time without history. . . . In my hours of sadness, I like to intensify the pain by sinking into the lower depths of the Romanian people, and wallowing in its suffering. I love the curses uttered throughout the centuries by this people, and I shudder at their resignation, their stifled moans and cries from the shadows. (42)

Sava Barcianu's sermon concludes by saying that Romanians must work hard and always strive to win greatness, that as long as they remain in the dark, no good will come to them. He instills in his parishioners a sense of national destiny, a consciousness of what they should strive to become by teaching them the noble, honorable Roman origins of the Romanian people. Thus he sees himself laying the foundation of a legitimate history of the nation, aware of his position at the beginning of the hard road ahead, of the efforts and the striving "spre a cistiga vrednicie de ajuns întru cîstigarea cinstii şi norocirii noastre" [to win enough worth to ensure our honor and our happiness]. In so doing and speaking, Barcianu is a maker of beginnings and acts like what Cioran calls "a God of our history." But whereas Barcianu strives to educate and develop "strength in consciousness" by instilling and cultivating a positive sense of belonging to a noble race, Cioran's model of a "God of our history" is negative. The main difference between Cioran and his ancestors lies in a shift in emphasis: from moral responsibility and anxious concern to improve to a decadent delight in the fallen condition, combined with dismay, despair, and dandified lucidity.

> We, on the other hand, know and must know how to begin, we must have the lucidity of beginnings, the live consciousness of our dawn. . . . If we don't have strength in our consciousness to give shape to our fragile life, we will not make history. (40)

Cioran urges his generation to draw their strength from the "lucidity of beginnings," that is, the consciousness of *absence* of noble origins. His emphasis is on a profound sense of emptiness *before* the struggle rather than (as might seem more normal) on a sense of achieved fullness to follow. If they are to be creators, they must be "divinely" aware of being creators ex nihilo.

We encounter here a familiar Cioranian paradox, the advantage of *absence,* the praise of nothingness. Though in this passage Cioran speaks in the name of his generation, it would be wrong, I think, to mistake his lonely, eccentric voice as representative of a plurality. The shift from a constructively engaged attitude to a praise of absence, that otherwise "criminal lucidity of beginnings," bears Cioran's peculiar and provocative signature. *Romania's Transfiguration* is an extreme and often extremely unpleasant book. But Cioran's qualities that it shows in such a bad light—decadent, selfish, narcissistic, and individualistic—are singular. They are very different from the hysterical mass rhetoric of the Iron Guard, with its ideal of sacrificing all, even oneself, for the fatherland. The creator who makes the suffering induced by a super-consciousness of marginality and insignificance the foundation of his work can, of course, be none other than Cioran himself, "driving his own designs towards his self's objectives." It is the same Cioran who in his 1933 letter to Comarnescu wrote: "I'm proud my life begins with death." His life as an artist is an inner, spiritual journey, mapped as a series of illuminations, and its starting point in "death to the world" is twofold: he dies first by being Romanian and thus marginal to European culture, and he dies again by becoming an exile and thus formalizing the condition of marginality, becoming, once and for all, a stranger to all cultures.

To conclude, Cioran's book is not simply a falling away from a family political tradition, or a shift from it; it is a change in which the location of the *creative spirit* is transferred from the community to the individual artist. This is why for the young author the question "How can one be a Romanian?" is a knife twisted in the wound. Yet he derives a strange sense of pleasure and fulfillment—*jouissance*—a sense of self-as-author, from his negative passion for Romania, the contradictions it involves, and, last but not least, the excessive, orgasmic prose it prompts him to write. He does not simply turn a disadvantage into an advantage; he makes the disadvantage indispensable to the very essence of his being, an inextinguishable source of all his writing: "You are a world in yourself only if the axis of the world pierces your heart." The metaphor of the world's axis piercing the creator's heart is apt because it stresses the suffering, the martyrdom, and the loneliness implied by the act of creation: to be at the center, and thus a creator, one must throw oneself upon the center's sharp point and be impaled. "I fall upon the thorns of life! I bleed!" More than just an identification with his beloved Romantic model, Shelley, Cioran's fondness for these lines looks back, as Shelley did, to his identification with, and "transfiguration" of—Shelley's buried allusion to—Jesus Christ's crown of thorns. This, finally, is the significance of the carefully chosen religious word, Transfiguration, in Cioran's Romanian title, *Schimbarea la față a României.*

# *Romania's Transfiguration,* Continuing Controversy

I can't find myself in it. . . .

—Cioran, foreword to the second edition of *Romania's Transfiguration* (1990)

*Romania's Transfiguration* occupies a peculiar space in Cioran's *œuvre.* It is his only Romanian book that has never been translated; it is significantly absent, for example, from Gallimard's recent Quarto edition of the *Œuvres* (1995). Yet it is at the same time the most notorious of his works, since it is reputed to be the book in which he "reveals" his fascistic tendencies, or, at the very least, the extent of his flirtation with the peculiar brand of European fascism represented by the Romanian Iron Guard movement. As such, it becomes Exhibit A when Cioran is hailed into the court of retrospective world opinion and subjected, like Mircea Eliade, Martin Heidegger, Paul de Man, and many others, to rigorous questioning about the extent to which his "youthful errors" represent, in fact, a permanent, ineradicably contaminating sub-stratum to all his other works, despite their determinedly apolitical, "existential," and aphoristic appearance.

Cioran appears in this court as a somewhat sympathetic witness for himself, since he both acknowledged his early political writings and disavowed them as unforgivable "stupidities" and "the ravings of a wild madman." He did not, however, like to talk about them, nor did he spend much time in his mature later (French) life in apologizing for them—which, for polemicists dedicated to unearthing any hint of fascism and anti-Semitism in the writings of otherwise culturally honored modernist writers (for example, T. S. Eliot), amounts to a kind of tacit admission of continuing guilt, since only if the writer in question were to continue forever acknowledging his guilt would the moral polemicists be satisfied. In these prosecutions, to have been a fascist once, to whatever degree, constitutes a permanent stain and ineradicable guilt; memories may fade, but the cancerous cells are always there.[1] Paying attention to Cioran's youthful fascism is fair and just, if we are to gain a full picture of his stature and development. But some of his critics seem to follow a logic similar to that of the House Un-American Activities Committee used in its witch-hunts during the 1950s McCarthy era, especially against former Communists or Communist sympathizers in Hollywood during the years we are concerned with here: the 1930s. But whereas HUAC was concerned with former Communists on the Left, in Europe the hunt for proto-fascists on the Right has been much more intense, and only relatively recently have commentators dared to take a wider view and observe that European cultural critics have been more forgiving toward youthful Communist sympathies than toward youthful fascist leanings—for obvious reasons, in the historical perspective of World War II and its aftermath.

I will not enter into the extremely difficult moral determination of which is worse, fascism or communism, given their horrific records of state-justified murder—even if we agree that, on balance, fascism, at least in its German National Socialist form, is worse. But the fact is, to do meaningful research and writing on the key question, *what could have led* these sometimes brilliant young people into such errors?—and thus perhaps illuminate our thinking about them—we cannot soundly judge their errors, or the extent of their commitment to them, if we begin with the a priori, almost Manichean, assumption that all such people were "just evil."[2]

It is not my intention to excuse Cioran's extremist statements in *Romania's Transfiguration,* since he has made his own defense, however unsatisfying it may be to some contemporary analysts, such as Patrice Bollon and Alexandra Laignel-Lavanstine.[3] Nor, however, is it my intention to take the easy road of rebuttal and maintain that *Romania's Transfiguration* is an exception in Cioran's *œuvre*, which can therefore be set aside as an unhappy experimental chapter in the on-going story of his self-creation.

On the contrary, though the book is the only one of Cioran's works with a markedly socio-political content, it is my contention that it should be seen as *part of the same cloth* as Cioran's other works, both earlier and later. That is, though the book "looks" political, and can be made to sound like the ravings of a committed young fascist, I would maintain that despite its relatively few historical references and its wild political rhetoric, *Romania's Transfiguration* is still clearly, if unstably, focused on Cioran's early-chosen and long-pursued themes of the creative (and therefore suffering) self versus the uncomprehending Otherness of the world, whether we identify these poles as young Emil Cioran versus backward Romania or, as he later generalized them, the creative genius versus conventional morality and philosophy and religion in all its orthodox forms.

Cioran himself always evinced an ambiguous attitude toward *Romania's Transfiguration:* part rejection, but also part admiration. He did, tellingly, allow its republication in Romanian after the fall of Ceauşescu's communism in 1989, but only in an altered form. This dubious decision—neither one thing nor the other—caused a scandal in Romania, where his moral right to reprint the book, yet alter its form, was passionately debated in the press. It was argued that if he sincerely regretted it, he should never have allowed its republication in any form, and that to publish it in altered form was adding insult to injury and made a mockery of literary history. However, his belated re-recognition of the book did not go so far as to allow it to be translated.[4]

Thus, though partially present in his *œuvre, Romania's Transfiguration* is also a conspicuous "absence," to which all Cioran specialists refer, but which is not accessible to all of his readers. Literally a closed book to those who cannot read Romanian, it forms a kind of black hole in the study of his *œuvre:* nearly invisible, but with an inexorable gravitational pull. This ambivalent status of *absent presence* contributes a good deal to the aura of mystery surrounding it.

The republication of *Romania's Transfiguration* in 1990 brought the seventy-nine-year-old Cioran abruptly face to face, publicly, with his Romanian past. He was not without misgivings about his decision to republish: it was like opening up Pandora's box. His brief foreword to the second edition, dated February 22, 1990, betrays his ambivalence, as he hovers on a borderline between apology and praise:

> I wrote these rambling, raving pages in 1935–36, when I was 24 years old, and full of pride and passion. Of all my entire work, both Romanian and French, this is maybe the most passionate text and, at the same time, the one I feel most alien to. I can't find myself in it, though my hysteria at the time seems to me quite obvious. I thought it my *duty* to suppress a number of silly, pretentious pages. This is the *final* edition. No one has the right to change it.[5]

Cioran condemns his book, or at least he has many more words of criticism than of praise for it. He dismisses it as "elucubrations, ramblings, ravings," and stresses the fact that he was very young at the time of its composition and "full of pride and passion." He singles out pride, passion, and hysteria as the book's main features and emphasizes his feeling of alienation from such excesses. He implies that the distance he feels toward his own text is a result of old age, and a more mature and tolerant mind that can only view the book as "silly" and "pretentious," though its critics would use much harsher epithets. He also justifies its republication in a cut version as a moral duty he feels. It is not clear toward whom he owes this duty, but it is very likely toward the image of himself which he will leave behind. The "corrected" text, and through it his writerly self, is his legacy to posterity.

The emphatic interdiction with which the foreword closes suggests that Cioran very much feared what Milan Kundera defines as the "absolute spirit of the trial" pervading our century. It is Cioran's defense at his own imaginary trial by the "absolute tribunal" mentality of the twentieth century, which reduces "biography to criminography," and "whose memory is colossal"—and perverse—because it involves *"the forgetting of everything not a crime."*[6] His line of defense is only too obvious: impetuous youthful passion often goes too far, and one must intervene to curb and correct it when the opportunity arises.

As a result, he cut out one entire chapter from the original (Chapter 4, "National Collectivism," which dealt with the Jews in Romania) and a number of passages from the last chapter on the Hungarians and Hitler, thus removing the parts that would offend and outrage those large ethnic groups. But he was not content to simply mark out the cuts for the publisher, he literally tore the condemned pages out of the book. Mme. Boué told me that, searching among Cioran's papers after his death, she found an original copy of *Schimbarea la faţa* with many pages torn out and the remaining pages freshly renumbered in Cioran's own handwriting. To feel compelled to assault and maim the book physically speaks volumes about Cioran's anger and frustration with his text as an expression of his youthful self. Mme. Boué also said that he often expressed the wish that he had never written it, and he told me, "I've written a lot of stupidities (*bêtises*) in my youth."

With the publication in 1949 of his first French book, *Précis de décomposition,* Cioran had managed quite effectively to cut himself off from his Romanian origins. However, in his new edition of *Romania's Transfiguration,* his younger fanatical self returned to claim him for itself. *Schimbarea* came to symbolize an entire past he had done everything in his power to repudiate. But like Lady Macbeth, no matter how hard he tried to scrub off the trace of a past full of blood, tears, and rage, the trace stayed, taunting, accusatory. And since he himself allowed it to come back into the light of day, we can legitimately speak of a return of the repressed.

The 1990 foreword to *Romania's Transfiguration* is only the last and most public attempt by Cioran to distance himself from his youthful past, to break the link between his younger and his older self by effacing the living memory of the damning book. The critical note he sounds in the foreword forms a *leitmotif* in his letters to family and friends during many years of correspondence. Thus in 1973 he writes to his brother Relu commenting on attacks on himself in Parisian literary circles:

> How stupid people are! The times when I wrote "Schimbarea," seem to me very far away. Sometimes I ask myself if it really was me who wrote these ravings they quote. I would have certainly done better if I had just taken a walk "under the alders" [referring to the park of that name, Sub Arini, in Sibiu] instead. . . . Enthusiasm is a form of delirium. We once had this illness, from which nobody wants to believe we have recovered.[7]

Another letter from 1979 re-asserts his repudiation of *Romania's Transfiguration:*

> I know about the attacks from hear-say only. . . . Concerning our nation, I think now more than ever that we can have no illusions about it. I have for it a sort of desperate contempt. The point of view of *Schimbarea* seems to me unacceptable, except for its negative side.[8]

Intriguing, in this connection, is an undated sheet of paper from Cioran's study, not published in his *Notebooks* but presumably deposited by Mme. Boué in the Foundation Drouet, in which he wrote down, in French, the beginning of five sentences in *Schimbarea* (translating from the Romanian as he wrote). From page 83: "if Romania doesn't want to enter into history. . . ." From page 86: "the Romanian people are the only people in the world who . . . ," and, "Its belief that it is useless. . . ." [Sa croyance qu'il est inutile . . . ] From page 117: "I wish for a Romania with the population of China and the destiny of France." And from page 174: "What do the Romanian people know compared to the Jewish people?"[9]

Bracketed among these quotes, though not clearly assignable to any one excerpt, are Cioran's notes or comments:

> For me, it was an inferiority complex which aggravated [my] madness. To despair is to be Romanian. It is strictly speaking impossible not to feel in these pages a secret passion for the Jews, and a despair and shame at being Romanian.
>
> Important detail: after having written this book, I fell into a religious crisis. *Tears and Saints.*

Scribbled in a corner are two further comments: "If one didn't know the age of the author, one would say that this book was written by a general paralytic."[10] And a reference to "une revue de droite," from 1937 to 1949, with the names "Benjamin Fondane, Maurice Blanchot, George Bălan, and [Otto] Weininger."

Finally, on the reverse of the sheet two last comments are scrawled: "In 280 pages, the Iron Guard is not mentioned in a single place." And, only partly decipherable: "The words of my [illegible] after having read the book: 'One cannot tell if you are for or against the Jews [,] the impression that I have [illegible] is one of a great release [*déchaînement;* literally, unchaining, unleashing].'"[11]

What do these stray comments add to the general lines of self-defense we see Cioran taking with regard to *Romania's Transfiguration*? They are clearly a set of self-defensive notes about the actual contents of the book and the apparent motivation and (im)maturity of its author, jotted down perhaps in preparation for a more extended rebuttal of his critics. They suggest that his references to the Jews are to be taken metaphorically, or as instances of well-known lines of cultural comparisons and contrasts about Jews—and that, in any case, he makes much worse comments about Romanians than he does about Jews. But given the shadowy reputation of *Romania's Transfiguration,* and the fact that few people are likely to have read it, even though they may be ready to attribute to it the most vicious kind of anti-Semitism, it is necessary to describe what Cioran actually says about Jews in it. He does see the Jews as a threat to Romanian nationalism, but for very different reasons than we might assume, if we take Nazi propaganda as our measure of anti-Semitism. For Cioran, the Jews are far *superior* to the Romanians, cannot be blamed for the backwardness of the country, and are thus not good candidates for the rough assimilation politics he recommends to be used on his countrymen. In this characteristically paradoxical Cioranian formulation, anti-Semitism is "the greatest tribute paid to the Jews."[12]

His references to Fondane, Blanchot, Bălan, and Weininger are particularly intriguing in this context, as possible versions or models of what he saw in himself. I have not been able to identify the war-time rightist review Cioran refers to, or whether the four names mentioned were contributors to it, subjects of discussion in it, or only analogous figures. A Romanian poet, dramatist, film director, and essayist (Fondane), a French novelist and literary theorist (Blanchot), a Romanian musicologist (Bălan), and an Austrian polemicist (Weininger); the first three could be said, roughly, to adhere to a "conservative" aesthetic which stresses the self-contained integrity of the work of art (or of language generally), with a minimum of external historical reference—just the kind of position Cioran came to adopt in his French reincarnation. Fondane (1898–1944) was, like Cioran, a self-exile to Paris, where he altered his surname, from Fundoianu (somewhat as Emil Cioran became there, for the first time, "E. M." Cioran), having already abandoned his birth name, Wechsler. But unlike Cioran, Fondane was associated with the surrealists and liberal politics. He was also Jewish, denounced by his Parisian neighbors, and deported to Auschwitz, where he perished. Bălan (born 1929) is a musicologist and philosopher who has developed a theory of "musicosophia" or "conscious listening" that allows non-specialist listeners to unlock deeper philosophical meanings in music.[13] His relative youth, compared to the other three, allows us to date Cioran's sheet of notes as from the late 1960s, or more probably the early to mid-1970s; he could hardly have been a contributor to a review of 1937–49. An appreciative exchange between the two was published after Cioran's death.[14] Blanchot (1907–2003) was, like Cioran, an enthusiastic right-wing journalist in his youth who later joined the Resistance; his post-war novels and essays of "philosophical fanaticism" are even more arid and devoid of "real world" reference than the writings of Cioran at his most aphoristic extreme. *L'espace littéraire* (1955) propounds the theory that literary works are organic entities separate from the external world. Unlike Cioran, Blanchot was embraced by the French Left despite his reactionary past, but like Cioran he kept very much to himself, avoiding allegiances to any "movements."

Otto Weininger (1880–1903) is the odd man out in the group in every way. He was an anti-Semitic Austrian Jew who converted to Christianity and wrote a single book, *Sex and Character* (1903), which propounded the thesis that all living things are compounded of masculine (positive and moral) and feminine (negative and immoral) elements. It had a sensational impact in the feverish cultural politics of the pre–World War I era. Christianity fell into the former category; Jews, into the latter—along with women, of course. Weininger committed suicide after his book was published.[15] Cioran mentions him in *Tears and Saints,* written right after *Romania's Transfiguration:* "Weininger used to say that epilepsy was the criminal's last solitude. Having no more ties with the world, all he has left is the fall."[16]

In sum, a group of ambivalent figures, except perhaps Bălan, about whom the safest, most general thing to say may be that their politics and attitude toward Jewishness (their own or others') are not easy to categorize, and changed during their lifetimes. And yet all recognizable cultural figures of more or less repute. Is Cioran saying, 'these are men of some stature despite their controversial lives and works: am I not entitled to the same consideration'?

There is little doubt, therefore, that Cioran had long bitterly regretted, privately, ever having written, not all of *Romania's Transfiguration,* but certainly a good part of it. He saw its republication in 1990 as an opportunity to make his change of mind public. It was an occasion to retract in an "official" way, and as he said in the foreword, he felt it was his duty to do so. He was very keen to make the heavily cut 1990 version his final word, and as its author he felt he had the right to modify it in any way he saw fit.

In this respect, Cioran's action is not a unique case by any means. Many authors have kept on re-working and changing their works right up to their death. Wordsworth's example again comes to mind: there are nearly twenty more or less complete versions or new copies of his famous long (8,000 lines) autobiographical poem, *The Prelude* ("On the Growth of My Own Mind"). Like Cioran's, the most interesting of Wordsworth's changes to his poem over the decades between 1805 (when he first finished it) and 1850 (when it was published posthumously) are those concerning his representation and evaluation of his "juvenile errors" in the political sphere—in his case, his youthful enthusiasm for the French Revolution.

But Cioran's grappling with his problematic text over the years was not limited to his private correspondence and his 1990 foreword to its republication. Matei Calinescu has convincingly argued that Cioran first rewrote portions of this book as early as 1956, in the essay "Un peuple de solitaires," in *La tentation d'exister,* where he recast his disparaging remarks about Jews in Chapter 4 of *Schimbarea.*[17] Although Cioran never made an explicit connection between "Un peuple de solitaires" and the pages he cut from *Schimbarea,* the essay nevertheless can clearly be read as a discreet retraction and public apology for his earlier book. As Calinescu puts it,

> the author of "A People of Solitaries" wrote his text with a double intentionality—one exoteric or public, the other hidden; . . . he wanted not only to communicate directly with his Western reader, but also to revisit his Romanian older texts in order to distance himself from them—but under the seal of secrecy. Am I wrong if I discern in this double movement the elements of a personal drama? Or if I sense an impulse toward confession, a confession, however, that dares not utter itself openly and fully but is only murmured in soliloquy?[18]

The implicit impulse to "communicate with his . . . reader" and "to revisit his Romanian older texts in order to distance himself from them," detected by Calinescu in "Un peuple de solitaires," is made explicit in Cioran's 1990 foreword to the republished *Schimbarea.* A "discreet retraction," silently inscribed within a re-written text of 1956, becomes, some thirty-five years later, open and public. It is part of an on-going life process for Cioran, since for most of his adult life he struggled to come to terms with his earlier texts and the image of himself they projected. It was, moreover, a dramatic process; the agony of the divided self shaped and formed Cioran's entire intellectual life. He might have republished it anyway, but circumstances as widely varied as the 1989 Romanian revolution and his own failing health and presentiment of impending death helped prompt his decision to allow the publication of an abridged version of *Romania's Transfiguration.*

*Romania's Transfiguration* constitutes only one act in the personal drama that Cioran played out in his life. It was an eruption of immoderate pride, for whose excesses, as in a morality play, the protagonist does penance forever afterward. Once abroad, he was soon forced by circumstances to learn the ways of humility, on the evidence of his letters home. Sometime around 1945–46, in times of immense social uncertainty and disarray, Cioran writes from France to reassure his parents about his situation during the war. Here we see that one of those among the "peuple de solitaires" has taken on a real-life existence and importance for Cioran, far removed from the metaphors of alienation into which he had made them and with which to excoriate his own countrymen in his *Transfiguration.*

> For many reasons, I've been quite lucky to have a Romanian Jewish friend [*un prieten evreu român*] established in Paris since 1940. I used to know him back home a long time ago. Although much older than me (he's 58), he's been more friendly and more generous than all of the other "Christian" friends put together. Not a week passed without his inviting me over for a rich dinner; I can count on him for everything. In fact, all preconceived ideas are absurd and false; there are only people as people, irrespective of origins and beliefs. In this respect, I've changed quite a lot. I don't think I'll ever embrace another ideology again.

According to Simone Boué, this Romanian Jew was a certain Krakauer (possibly originally Cracanera, in Romanian), who managed to survive and do shady, profitable business in Paris all through the war, only to commit suicide a few years afterward by throwing himself off the pier at Ostende. Anyone at all familiar with Cioran's lifelong precarious ways of living—always on the edge of poverty, always on the lookout for a dinner invitation in exchange for his talents as a conversationalist (he told his parents he would have died of hunger if God had not made him so talkative)—can appreciate the extent of Cioran's sincere gratitude toward his Jewish friend. The generous Jew taught him a lesson in humility which helped to radically transform and really "transfigure" the historical Cioran. His letter describes the kind of small humanizing experience that sometimes carries the force of revelation for us. He tells his parents, as if asking them to join their thanks to his, that his gratitude was strong enough to cause him to begin to revise his own preconceived ideas, which he was later to tear so violently from the pages of *Schimbarea la față.*[19]

The double movement that Calinescu has identified in "Un peuple de solitaires" is characteristic of many of Cioran's texts: the impulse to confess and apologize, counterbalanced by the desire to hide. In the controversial instance of the republication of *Romania's Transfiguration* we have, on the one hand, a public avowal of guilt and an apology—but not entirely, for it seems clear to me that Cioran, though severely critical of his book, was also still fond of it. He was not at all ready to make the total rejection of it that some expected of him. His public apology is restrained, minimizing the "fault." Thus he speaks of hysteria that "is quite obvious to me," but without further condemnation, and dismisses quite lightly, as mere pretentious silliness, passages that he had himself at one time literally torn from the book. His apology, thus expressed and qualified, may strike many as insincere and insufficient. Yet I think what really matters is not so much the question of his sincerity, as the question of what made Cioran still cling loyally to his troublesome text, resisting the temptation to take the much "cleaner" course of dismissing it altogether. It would, doubtless, have been easier for the French Cioran to deny the text completely, without any further ado.

One reason he does not reject his earlier text outright seems to be a sense of kinship he has with his former self, as well as the honesty of acknowledging something that had been, after all, part of his life. This kinship Cioran only reluctantly acknowledges in his 1990 foreword: "I can't find myself in it, though my hysteria at the time seems to me quite obvious." In other words, it's not me, but yet it is me. It is not so much shame at the book's *contents* as a difficulty in recognizing its *author*—himself—that troubles Cioran. This hysterical "I" exerts a sort of fascination on the older man. It is also strange that he should balk at his former "hysteria," since what he elsewhere calls his "lyrical" self is a common feature of his writing, and of the dramatic personal style with which he struck all the friends of his youth and young manhood. Mixed in with his criticism of the book's "hysteria" there is also an unmistakable shade of admiration for the book's "pride and passion." While the process of his transformation into the French Cioran was taking place, and with it the necessary distancing from his problematic text, as the "new" Cioran broke his ties with the "old," the reverse was also true: the new French Cioran was still enthralled by his older (which is to say, younger, literally) self, absorbing into his new make-up a lot of what he already was.

This double movement can also be traced in his letters. Already as early as 1947, writing from Paris to his old friend Petre Comarnescu, he says,

> It's not your fate to grow old while I . . . I feel as if I have lived through several centuries and endured their overpowering length. My quasi "political" fervors of long ago seem to date back to times immemorial. Whether they were aberrations, truths, or delusions, I couldn't tell. They belong to a vanished past, which I can neither despise nor regret. They blame me on all sides—and aplenty—the enthusiasm I had for a certain collective delirium over there, they even hold me responsible for it and thus attribute to me a success to which I have never aspired.[20]

Here Cioran distances himself from his book in his characteristic way, by stressing the enormous distance in time that separates him from his former self: his past political fervor dates from "prehistoric times," in a few years he has grown "centuries" older, and supposedly wiser, because he stoically endures time's "overpowering length" (*la durée accablante*). We find in these lines the trope of old age—signifying restraint and wisdom, but also degeneration and loss of vitality—which is clearly nothing but a trope, since Cioran was by then only thirty-six years old, compared with twenty-six when *Romania's Transfiguration* was first published. However, in spite of this implied gulf of time, Cioran nevertheless confesses that he cannot reject his "vanished" past entirely, simply because, whether right or wrong, its youthful fervors and fevers were his own: "Whether they were aberrations, truths or delusions, I couldn't tell. They belong to a vanished past (*une époque évanouie*), which I can neither despise or regret."

Though only ten years have passed, old age and growing old are Cioran's metaphors for the radical transformation *he* has undergone throughout this period, and few would contest the claim that a decade like 1937–1947 made a qualitatively greater impact on almost everyone who lived through it. In identifying his "older" self with his new French *persona,* and his younger self with his Romanian one, and placing "centuries" between them, his younger self thus becomes "older" in a different way: a prehistoric, barbaric layer buried beneath the new skeptical and civilized man.

By the time he was writing the foreword to the 1990 edition, Cioran really *is* an old man, who in re-reading his text is newly intrigued by its passionate quality, and who regrets the loss of his youthful ardor, however foolish. By now, the trope of old age has become a reality. But the Nietzschean cult of youth and force has not lost its attraction for Cioran: though now an old man himself, he still shows signs of the "radical gerontophobic attitude" that characterized his writings of the 1930s.[21] The recklessness, silliness and pretentiousness of the *Schimbarea* notwithstanding, Cioran was loath to lose its spirit of youthful passion—especially its negative, anarchic quality. As he confessed to his brother Relu in 1979, the only thing that still interested him in it was its "negative aspect." The passion that animates the critical pages of *Romania's Transformation*—where Cioran is on the attack against Romania's flaws, not where he is, in effect, borrowing constructive "solutions" for them from others—is destructive, sweeping through its pages like an ocean gale. Negative force never failed to appeal to him.

So, to a certain extent, it must also have been his admiration for the sheer force of his former passion, combined with its bracing negativity, that prompted the aging Cioran to allow a reprint of his infamous book. Again we recognize a doubling of motives: on the one hand, to preserve something of his youthful self, no matter how hysterical and "silly"; on the other hand, he wished he could retract those statements that remained embarrassing to the reputation of the older man.

The old man felt he needed to correct the young one, not kill him off. Looking back, re-reading himself, the old man felt he was entitled to what he surely knew would be a suspect gesture of censorship, because he was re-writing his own self from a very different perspective—one that perhaps only he could maintain. Our selves are discontinuous, no matter how much we try to think the contrary; change is an obligatory feature of our humanity, as John Stuart Mill famously put it in his essay "On Liberty." It is our capacity for change that confirms our humanity.

Of course, if Cioran indeed believed that the new text of *Romania's Transformation* would replace the old one to become the *only* one, he was being either very naive or very devious. But one can never be sure, for to say, "this is the final edition. No one has the right to change it," is not the same as saying, "this is the only edition I recognize and accept." It is not easy to cheat history, for if to re-write is a legitimate, even expected, activity, to erase is impossible. As literary historians, if not as moralists, we must be happy rather than cross with Cioran, since our sense of his development is enriched by a late addition of a new version of an old text. We still make our own judgments on his sense and his sincerity, but from the inter-textual play of the new version with the old we stand only to gain.

# *Tears and Saints*, 1937

The year after he published *Romania's Transfiguration*, his least attractive work, Cioran—by then already out of Romania and in France—published *Tears and Saints (Lacrimi şi sfinţi)*, written largely while he was teaching in Braşov—which his friend Jenny Acterian called "the saddest" book he ever wrote.[1] It did not fare well with the critics at the time, but it may well be the most attractive—if we can use that word in speaking of his writings—of all his Romanian books, to contemporary readers.

It is hard to believe these two books were written by the same man, to say nothing of their being composed, to a considerable degree, simultaneously. Cioran said he had something like a nervous breakdown after completing *Romania's Transfiguration,* and *Tears and Saints* is at once evidence of it and its result, perhaps its cure. But "cure" is a very relative term, applied to Cioran, who shunned "normalcy." Whether insomniac, suicidal, or in varying stages of nervous exhaustion, he always wrote with the greatest *intensity,* always, from the first, "on the heights of despair." Now, turning from a book that was the most closely involved in all his *œuvre* with Romanian nationalism and contemporary European politics (albeit in his own unique manner), he produced a book that has hardly a single reference to Europe beyond the Middle Ages. Indeed, except for a very few passing references to Nietzsche, Rilke, and Schopenhauer, one could imagine it was written centuries before our times—except, of course, for its completely modernist, utterly disillusioned, brilliantly blasphemous, and thoroughly *existential* cast.

He had a hard time getting it published, and it may have been just as well for him that he was out of the country when it appeared. In the printing shop of the publisher who had at first agreed to publish it, one of the compositors fell to reading the text he was setting up in type. Shocked, he went to the front office and told his bosses about it. They too recoiled from a text that seemed to them not only blasphemous but also, paradoxically, more *religious* than anything they had yet seen by Cioran. They refused to have anything to do with it. But luckily, as Cioran told me with that charming twinkle in his eye when he knew he was being outrageous, they had not yet broken down the plates, and they let him make a set of galley proofs, which he carried around Bucharest in a bag in search of a publisher. In the end, he got it printed and distributed, but only by agreeing to pay the costs himself.

When it appeared, it caused a scandal, as it was intended to. Written in short, aphoristic fragments—nearly four hundred of them, ranging in length from one line to a couple of pages—with no chapter headings, breaks, or other divisions—it is strongly reminiscent of Nietzsche both in form and in content. Likewise Blake's "Proverbs of Hell" in *The Marriage of Heaven and Hell* (1794) and Emily Dickinson's entire *oeuvre*—both poets Cioran knew well, as his journals show. It is a discontinuous but subtly interwoven and iconoclastic philosophical discourse on mysticism. The aura of decadence that goes with the book's anti-Christian, blasphemous tone was almost unheard of in Romania. But, as J. K. Huysmans says of his decadent hero, Des Esseintes, in *À Rebours* (Against Nature, 1884), one must be a Catholic first in order to desecrate Catholicism. And there is a strong Christian current stirring under the anti-Christian surface of Cioran's prose. ("Boredom is the only argument against immortality. From it derive all our negations.") Not for nothing was he the son of a vigorously intellectual Romanian Orthodox priest and therefore very familiar with the doctrines of the Christian faith—doctrines that, furthermore, he had struggled both to understand and to confute.

> I am altogether too much of a Christian. I can tell from the way I am attracted by beggars and deserts, and from the insane fits of pity to which I am often a prey. All of these amount to various forms of renunciation. (118)

His younger brother Relu recalls long nights spent over bottles of wine, during which Cioran argued intricate theological questions with his father and theological students from the seminary in Sibiu. According to Relu, Cioran's obsessions at the time were theology and music, a fact confirmed by Cioran's text—as always an exorcism of his obsessions—in which fine, tender aphorisms on music (especially Bach) intertwine with his musings on tears and saints.[2]

> Many saints—but especially saintly women—confessed a desire to rest their head on the heart of Jesus. They all had their wish fulfilled. Now I understand why Our Redeemer's heart has not ceased to beat for two thousand years. My Lord! You fed your heart on the blood of the saints, and you bathed it in the sweat of their brows! (4)

A modern-day hagiographer, he has "dreamt" himself "the chronicler of these [saints'] falls between heaven and earth, the intimate knower of the ardors in their hearts, the historian of God's insomniacs." The question naturally arises: why would a healthy young man in the middle of the 1930s, who, if hardly "normal," nonetheless confesses openly his love of life, and who is politically alert and active, want to become a "heavenly interloper" spying on the saints' secrets? A partial answer may be found in a passage from Nietzsche's *Beyond Good and Evil:*

> The mightiest men have hitherto always bowed reverently before the saint, as the enigma of self-subjugation and utterly voluntary privation—why did they thus bow? They divined in him . . . the superior force which wished to test itself by such subjugation; the strength of will, in which they recognized their own strength and love of power, and knew how to honour it: they honoured something in themselves when they honoured the saint. In addition to this, the contemplation of the saint suggested to them a suspicion: such an enormity of self-negation and anti-naturalness will not have been coveted for nothing. . . . In a word, the mighty ones of the world learned to have a new fear before him, they divined a new power, a strange, still unconquered enemy:—it was the "Will to Power" which obliged them to halt before the saint. They had to question him.[3]

Nietzsche's insight is confirmed by Cioran, who on the first page of *Tears and Saints* spells out the reason for his interest in saints, in the form of a question his book promises to explore: "How does man renounce himself and take the road to sainthood?" In the saints' ability to renounce the world, Cioran detects their "will to power": saintliness, he writes, is "imperialistic"; it "interests me for the delirium of self-aggrandizement hidden beneath its meekness, its will to power masked by goodness."

Clearly fascinated by this will to power in a political world torn by extreme claims, from fascism to communism, Cioran nonetheless regards it with an awe tinged by ironic skepticism.

> Sainthood in itself is not interesting, only the lives of saints are. How does a man renounce himself and take the road to sainthood? But then how does one become a hagiographer? By following in their traces, by wetting the soles of one's feet in their tears! (4)

He looks upon saints as partial alter egos, devout existentialists who "live *in* flames" while "wise men live *next* to them." His relationship to them as it develops in the book is one of both love and hatred. "I loved saints for their passionate naiveté," he writes at one point. His love for the saints has a shade of decadent aestheticism in it: "we no longer believe in them. We only admire their illusions."

However, such dandified love is counterbalanced by a vigorous and virulent hatred. He confesses many times that he hates the saints for the habit of hopeless suffering that they bequeathed to us, since suffering "can't be anything but futile and satanic." "How could one not hate saints, angels, and God? . . . Heaven irritates me, its Christian disguise drives me to despair."

A brief look back at *Romania's Transfiguration* helps us to appreciate the distinct note struck by *Tears and Saints* in its historical context. Whereas the latter is a critique of mystical discourse, the former borrows the rhetoric of mystical discourse and applies it to the realm of politics, a utopian political fantasy, dreaming of a Romania "transfigured" from its "sub-historic" destiny. In *Tears and Saints,* Cioran defines saintliness as the "overcoming of our condition as fallen creatures." In mysticism, redemption and the saints' will to possess God are in fact one and the same thing. That is why the formula for redemption need not remain confined to the spiritual domain and can be easily translated into political terms: the mystic's spiritual union with God becomes like a (small) nation's fulfillment of a greater destiny: "Our entire political and spiritual mission must concentrate on the determination to *will* a transfiguration, on the desperate and dramatic experience of transforming our whole way of life."[4]

*Mutatis mutandis,* Cioran's solution for Romania's identity crisis is this: it will overcome its "fallen" status only when it is driven by a fanaticism equal to that of the saints. In this case, the mystical "will" is not object-less, as it is in *Tears and Saints* (which rules out God). Rather, it has a specific political content, and its stage is not the heart or the soul but history itself:

> *Romania is a prophetless country.* . . . This sobering thought should prompt us to be different, to burn with a blind fanaticism, to be illuminated by a new vision . . . and

> the thought of another Romania should be our only thought. To persist in the same historical sequence is the equivalent of slow suicide. . . . We shall have to renounce our lucidity which reveals to us so many impossibilities, and, in a state of blindness, conquer the light.[5]

Couched in the mystical language of ecstatic visions, the will to bring about spiritual reform is coupled here with the will to achieve cultural greatness. To bring about this end, all means are justified in the eyes of the young Cioran, who sounds like a new Machiavelli:

> All means are legitimate when a people opens a road for itself in the world. Terror, crime, bestiality and perfidy are base and immoral only in decadence, when they defend a vacuum of content; if, on the other hand, they help in the ascension of a people, they are virtues. All triumphs are moral.[6]

We are thus faced with a highly interesting intellectual situation: two books by the same author published within twelve months of each other, both suffused with mysticism, the one rabidly political, the other a critical analysis of the political roots of mystical discourse. One might be tempted to say that while *Tears and Saints* is a philosophical dissertation on the mystical phenomenon, *Romania's Transfiguration,* its unfortunate political counterpart, is a rather crude application of mystical principles, very much in step with other politico-religious right-wing or left-wing discourses of the period. But Cioran's ambiguous attitude toward mysticism in *Tears and Saints* shows that *Romania's Transfiguration* is in his mind, at the very moment he is writing the latter, a political utopia—a "delirium of self-aggrandizement." Its mystical overtones strongly contribute to its delirious utopian character, at odds with Cioran's existential philosophy of skepticism and despair. In *Tears and Saints,* Cioran's love-hate relationship with the mystic saints problematizes the simple and fanatical solutions he offers in *Romania's Transfigurations.* Thus *Tears and Saints* represents in some ways Cioran's philosophical struggle with himself, a text full of contradictions and ambiguities. Appearing at the same time as *Romania's Transfiguration,* and arising out of the same preoccupations, it reveals the shortcomings of his other, crudely naive political text, and thereby undermines it.

As a discourse on spirituality, asceticism, and suffering for the love of Christ, *Tears and Saints* is strongly inscribed in the historical, philosophical, and political discourses circulating in the Romania of the 1920s and 1930s. "Spirituality" was so much the talk of Romanian interwar culture that the journal of Cioran's group, *Criterion,* devoted a long article to it in its "Dictionary" column, which, like radical writing during the

American and French revolutions, tried to (re)define the "principal ideas" of the period and establish their "circulation value." In particular, the article identified "the problem of a 'new spirituality' with that of the 'new generation'" to which Cioran belonged.

According to the *Criterion* article, Cioran's young generation saw themselves as representatives of a "new revolutionary spirituality" which both overlaps with, and at the same time rejects, other types of spirituality present in contemporary Romanian culture: the traditional, orthodox spirituality of their charismatic philosophy professor and mentor, Nae Ionescu, and the more "cultural" or humanistic type espoused by other young intellectuals like Petru Comarnescu and Constantin Noica. Mircea Vulcănescu, author of the article, estimated that large numbers of this new generation, "led by Mircea Eliade," embraced a new "agonic spirituality" whose main characteristics are "lucidity, negation, and a tragic doubt that wants itself *in*validated by the revelation of a new type of man, yet to be born" (my italics).

As we have seen, this generation of intellectuals had political ties with the Legion of the Archangel Michael, later known as the Iron Guard, "a populist movement with strong mystical characteristics," bent on bringing about "moral and spiritual change, ethnic 'regeneration' by returning to Orthodox Christian values, and 'salvation' through asceticism and sacrifice."[7] Cioran's generation was sympathetic to the Legionnaire movement because they believed it to be the only political means capable of triggering a "Christian revolution" that would lead to the creation of a Christian state. Against a background of extreme political corruption and economic deterioration, moved by a strong sense of an ending, caught between nostalgia for Paradise Lost and impatience for a New Jerusalem, these young, modern-day "saints" were animated by a desire to reform which, unfortunately, found its political counterpart in the fascistic Iron Guard.

It is fairly easy to trace the similarities between the historical conditions that gave rise to Western European mysticism and the mystical mania that swept Romania in the 1930s. Both periods were characterized by an identity crisis and the responsibility to reform politically and spiritually. As Michel de Certeau puts it, there is in history a certain tendency toward *coincidence* between a "Machiavellian moment" and "the invasion of the mystics."[8] Thus "the task of producing a Republic or a State by political reason that would take the place of a defunct, illegible, divine order, in a way [was] paralleled by the task of founding places in which to hear the spoken Word that had become inaudible within corrupt institutions." One can argue, as Certeau does, that European mysticism did not die in the seventeenth century but simply receded: "this phantom of a passage, repressed during periods secure in their knowledge, reappears in the gaps within scientific certainty, as if ever returning to its birthplace."[9] "Secure" and "certainty" are the key words here. Europe in the first half of the twentieth century was wrenched by momentous upheavals. In the tormented European political and intellectual context, Romania, given its political and economic coordinates, dramatically lacked certainty about itself and thus became fertile ground for a rebirth of mysticism in political garb.

*Tears and Saints* is a meditation on saintliness, but not saintliness of the usual type. That is, not the martyrs and heroes of traditional hagiography, worshiped for their virtues, but rather the mystics famous for their high degree of spirituality, their intimate personal knowledge of God, who brought about a new "eruption of the absolute into history." The title refers to what is known in the tradition of the Roman Catholic Church as "the gift of tears." The *Dictionnaire de la spiritualité* describes this gift as "a complex phenomenon consisting of certain spiritual feelings and their concrete manifestation." It cites three categories of holy tears: penitential tears (purifying tears of fear and regret), tears of love (or grace), and tears of compassion wept for the Passion of Christ. Starting with Francis of Assisi in the early thirteenth century, the latter became the predominant "genre" of holy tears.

The tears of pity for the suffering Christ, to which Cioran alludes repeatedly in his text, are thus a characteristic feature of Western European mysticism. Mysticism is "a movement towards an object outside the limits of empirical experience," and also "a direct and passive experience of God's presence" (*Dictionnaire de la spiritualité*). This "movement" is an escape—through prayer, meditation, and contemplation—from the here and now. It aims at reunion with God, and it is centered on the mystery of the Incarnation and Redemption because the humanity of Christ is perceived as a mediation between man and God. Through sympathetic identification with the *suffering* Christ, one is redeemed from one's fallen state and reunited with God, thereby partaking of his divinity. Though much of this sounds like normal Christian doctrine, the emphasis in the mystic tradition is on the extremity of emotions involved. Tears were perceived as a sign of grace, an external manifestation of God's presence in the human heart. Many descriptions of this gift insist upon its ineffable sweetness. Cioran puts a twist on mystical discourse from the very beginning, since for him tears are not sweet but bitter:

> As I searched for the origin of tears, I thought of the saints. Could they be the source of tears' bitter light? Who can tell? To be sure, tears are their *trace*. Tears did not enter this world through the saints; but without them we would never have known that we cry because we long for a lost paradise. Show me a single tear swallowed up by the earth! No, by paths unknown to us, they all go upwards. Pain comes before tears. But the saints rehabilitated them. (3)

The saints in Cioran's book belong to a special class of saints, mostly lay and mostly female, called "mystics," "spirituels," "contemplatifs," or "alumbrados." Their approach to the Christian faith is anti-theological, based solely on intuition and sentiment.

> The Church was wrong to canonize so few women saints. Misogyny and stinginess make me want to be more generous. Any woman who sheds tears for love in loneliness is a saint. The Church has never understood that saintly women are made of God's tears. (49)

Many of the names in the book, Meister Eckhart, Catherine of Siena, Teresa of Avila, St. John of the Cross, have left classic works of Western European mystical literature, but there are many more minor, unusual figures as well. Cioran subsumes mystics under the name of saints. Since for him mystics in the ordinary sense are apolitical, passive contemplators of divinity, he prefers to call those he seeks out "saints." Saints, he writes, are politicians—though "failed" ones, because they deny appearances: pragmatic men and women of action, whose acts of charity express their love of humankind. Indeed, many of the European mystics were active reformers, serious players in the game of European politics. (Catherine of Siena, for example, played a role in bringing the pope back to Rome from Avignon.) And all of them—many belonging to mendicant orders—were dedicated to charity work in the world outside the monastery walls, assiduously tending the poor and the sick.

European mysticism is thus a religious movement with political overtones. It is marked by a strong spirit of reform, which developed in the margins of—and often at odds with—the official institutions of the Catholic Church, which these saintly persons perceived as degraded and corrupt, no longer capable of caring fully for the spiritual needs of the population.

> The world is divided between owners and beggars. Stuck in the middle, the poor form the colorless content of history. Owners and beggars alike are reactionaries. Neither wish for change or progress. The poor are left to struggle. Without them society would be a meaningless concept: their hopes are society's arteries, and their despair the blood of history. The owners and the beggars are parasites on the eternal poor. There are many recipes against wretchedness, but none against poverty. (92)

Historically, the period of mysticism covers several centuries and several Western European countries, from its inception with Bernard of Clairvaux in the twelfth century to its vigorous expansion at the end of the thirteenth century in Germany and Holland and then into Italy, through its apogee in sixteenth-century Spain, and its final afterglow in seventeenth-century France just before the dawn of the Age of Reason.

Although it spans many centuries, European mysticism is almost always a "borderline" phenomenon, occurring on the threshold of modernity, at a time when unified Christian Europe was beginning to disintegrate, strongly secular states were being formed, and the basis for new sciences and arts was being set down. Thus "the ambition of a Christian radicalism [is] traced on a background of decadence or 'corruption,' within a universe that is falling apart and must be repaired."[10] Faced with the breakdown of the Christian faith and "the humiliation of the Christian tradition," the mystics rise to fight for the restoration of the true faith. For example, Teresa of Avila and St. John of the Cross were reformers of their orders. They thus formed a "Christian radicalism," verging on heresy, "wavering between ecstasy and revolt."[11]

These are not Cioran's formulations, but the relevance of such an outline of mystical action to his sense of Romania's situation in the 1930s is obvious. He focuses explicitly on the political elements in saints' lives, but in his view their charitable deeds are the least interesting aspect of their lives. What fascinates him are their tears, their thirst for pain, and their capacity to endure it: in short, the pathology or, as he puts it, the "voluptuousness of suffering," for "suffering is man's only biography." Behind this suffering, and their uncanny ability to renounce everything through ascetic practices, Cioran detects in his saints a fanatical will to power.

Saints' writings are often titled "Dialogues" because they are presented in the form of a dialogue with God, "conversar con Dios," as Teresa of Avila called it. In his analysis of mystical discourse, Michel de Certeau observes that a main feature of the saints' writings is the initial assertion of will, the opening *volo*—"I want"—which is both ecstatic, signifying a decision to escape, and ascetic, signifying a decision to lose.[12] This act of willing—"vouloir"—is at the same time an act of power, "pouvoir." Certeau cites one of the classic mystics, Meister Eckhart, who said, "With the will I can do everything," and, "what I want to have, I have."[13]

But what do these saints want to possess and control? "Their space to conquer is the sky, their weapon suffering," according to Cioran. The saints' "will to power" has no object in particular. They want to own infinity ("the sky") and God: that is, they want an absence, for, as Baudelaire once remarked, "God is the only being who, in order to rule, does not even need to exist." Thus inner space is the region in which the will reigns supreme, enjoying an autonomy that does not depend on object or circumstance.[14] And the heart or the soul is the stage on which the mystical drama is enacted, as for example in Teresa of Avila's *Las moradas*.

It is this fanatical, but at the same time gratuitous will to power, to know and to love, or to know through love—directed at everything and at the same time at nothing, that is, God—that engrosses Cioran's attention in *Tears and Saints*. But whereas for the saints God is meaningful nothingness, for Cioran, as for Nietzsche, "God is dead," and nothingness is the void of meaning. ("Let God pray for the man in whom there is nothing left to die!") Thus the book is a critique of this will to power which reaps nothing but empty and cruel suffering. It both reveals and rejects the political roots of sainthood, and finally inscribes itself in the psychological or aesthetic sphere, since saints are, after all, "failed politicians" who stubbornly deny the world of appearances. Nonetheless, to speak of the saints' "will to power" does point toward a political aspect of their existential religious experience, which is why the historical context of the production and publication of *Tears and Saints* is important.

Many of the themes in *Tears and Saints* are ones which Cioran will return to again and again, in his later, mature *French* writings: music, spirituality, suffering, death, solitude, doubt, despair, decadence, God, and nothingness. As a discourse on mysticism, it is neither mystical discourse nor objective, impersonal philosophical discourse. Generically, it resembles Nietzsche's hybrid philosophical commentaries. The free and easy colloquial and lyrical style, studded with striking metaphors, and the personal, intimate tones, alternately tongue-in-cheek and baldly vehement ("Let's march to the Last Judgment with flowers in our buttonholes!"), mask the extent of the book's enormous erudition, its bookishness, as well as the depth and accuracy of its commentary on mystical phenomena. The ambiguous, often paradoxical nature of *Tears and Saints* originates in its fundamental oscillation between two opposite drives: the intense longing to believe with passion and abandon—an attitude also informing *Romania's Transfiguration*—and the passion of disbelief, that is, of despair.

The book's central figure is Cioran's "failed mystic," "the one who cannot cast off all temporal ties." Thus he writes that "the secret of successful mysticism is the defeat of time and individuation," but also that "I can't help hearing a death knell ringing in eternity: therein lies my quarrel with mysticism." The "failed mystic" is a grotesque character: "the passion of the absolute in the soul of a skeptic is the life an angel grafted on a leper." He belongs to the same family of existential outcasts, forever wandering in a No Man's Land stretching between history and eternity, as Unamuno's martyr, Manuel Bueno, Dostoevsky's Ivan Karamazov, or Jean Genet's "criminal saint." One thinks also of the youthful Cioran's fascination with *le raté* (the failure), the gifted man of promise who does not realize his potential.

There is no redemption for Cioran's failed mystic. While the successful mystics praise as the apogee of their ecstasy the moment in which they feel alone with God, what St. John of the Cross calls "soledad en Dios," Cioran complains that he cannot feel "at home in God," that he is a perpetual "exile in Him." For the successful mystic, God is *the* object of desire, the target of his will to power. But for Cioran, no matter how hard he strives to love and to believe in a mystical way, his fervor is always undermined by doubt and despair. He is haunted by Nietzsche's realization that "God is dead." Or, as Cioran more humorously puts it, God is "a Universal absentee." He unmasks the saints unforgivable naiveté: they "have never asked themselves the question 'what begins *after* God?' and for that I cannot forgive them." The despair of this failed mystic and his existential doubts are mixed in with touches of bravado, a romantic, Luciferian pose. On the one hand, "My God without you I'm mad, and with you I shall go mad!" On the other, "my doubts cannot take me further than the shadow of His heart." Our role, says Cioran, is to amuse a God who is lonely: we are "poor clowns of the absolute." But he refused to play his part in God's entertainment piece, in a daring act of "rejection of God sprung from agonic frenzy": "I, with my solitude, stand up to God."

Centered on this figure of the failed mystic, Cioran's discourse on mysticism is a self-consciously blasphemous parody of mystical discourse. The voice of the faithless mystic introduces a new perspective into the traditional genre of saints' lives, that of despair, and thus gives a new accent to the mystical experience, deliberately and perversely distorting its meanings. For example, "paradise from the viewpoint of despair" becomes "the graveyard of happiness." In the mystical experience, meditation and prayer are important steps toward God, but for Cioran they are exactly the opposite: "one must think of God day and night in order to wear him out, to turn him into a cliché." For the mystics, life in God is the only true life; for Cioran, it is "the death of being."

The most frequent target of his attack, however, is another key aspect of mysticism: the imitation of the Man-God's agonistic passion as the only means to reach the divine.

> One does not need to be a Christian in order to fear the Last Judgment, or even to understand it. Christianity did nothing but exploit human anguish to make top profits for an unscrupulous divinity whose best ally was dread. (90)

The mystic's suffering has as its goal redemption, that is, to achieve perfection in divinity. Cioran, however, approaches suffering from an aesthetic rather than ethical point of view, since it is the "voluptuousness of suffering," not its virtues, that fascinates him. He sees suffering as essential to the tragic human condition—"suffering is man's only biography"—and as aimless, since it does not hold out the promise of redemption inherent in Christian notions of suffering, which are carried to extremes in mysticism. Suffering, behind which Cioran detected a will to power, is ineffectual; it achieves nothing except more senseless and cruel suffering. There is no room for redemption in a world in which, "since the creation of consciousness, God has appeared in his true light as one more nothingness."

The despair of the failed mystic, bereft of his greatest hope and overcome by what Unamuno called "el sentimiento tragico de la vida," takes the form of Nietzschean attacks on Christianity. In these attacks, Cioran's voice is by turns virulent and ironic. "I don't know any bigger sin than that of Jesus." "The ultimate cruelty was that of Jesus: leaving an inheritance of bloodstains on the cross." Jesus, "the bloodthirsty and cruel

Christ," [was] "lucky to have died young. Had he lived to be sixty, he would have given us his memoirs instead of the cross."

In a passage that recalls past catastrophes caused by excesses in the history of Christianity, and also anticipates the excesses soon to occur in his own country, Cioran, fascinated with violence and suffering, writes—decades before Georges Bataille's *Larmes d'Éros* or René Girard's *Violence and the Sacred*—that "Christianity delights in the sight of bloodstains, its martyrs have transformed the world into a bloodbath. In this religion of blazing twilights, evil defeats the sublime."

If the mystical formula ultimately fails for Cioran in the spiritual domain, it follows that its political counterpart is also doomed to fail. Could this man of so many doubts and shadows have been doing anything else but raving in a fit of impotent rage or a "delirium of self-aggrandizement" when he wrote *Romania's Transfiguration*? Could he, like Unamuno's failed saint, Manuel Bueno, have been preaching something in which he himself cannot believe? If *Romania's Transfiguration* tried to offer a solution to Romania's existential political problems, its contemporary twin, *Tears and Saints,* reveals the other side of the coin, namely, that there are no solutions to be had where there is only honestly despairing doubt. Thus through *Tears and Saints* we gain a perspective on Cioran's complex and divided mind exactly at the time he was writing his more outrageous political tract:

> the soul of those haunted by God is like a depraved spring, littered with half-withered flowers and rotten buds, swept by foul odors. It is the soul of blackmailing saints . . . and of anti-Christian Christians such as Nietzsche. I regret I'm not Judas to betray God and know remorse.

In the Romania of the 1930s, Cioran's young soul was haunted by two absolutes, neither of which he could actually believe in. Given this situation, his next step seems inevitable: if not suicide, then self-exile. He undertook his own "exile" not as a definite decision at a specific moment, but gradually "grew" into it over the next few years. In 1937, a few months before the publication of *Tears and Saints,* he left Bucharest and never returned except for a few days at the end of 1939 and quick trip between November 1940 and February 1941. He leaves Romania, and he virtually disappears. War breaks out, and he becomes his own underground man. We hear very little of him for almost ten years, when, in 1947, he has the revelation that he must write in French, and he never writes in Romanian, or even speaks it, except very rarely, again. By 1949, when the French book he started composing in 1947 appears, as *Précis de décomposition,* he has cast off both his Romanian language and identity, and yielded to a long-cherished obsession: not to be a Frenchman, but to be a man from nowhere.

# 8

# Stranger in Paris

Is there on the Boulevard St. Michel a stranger more strange than me?

—Cioran, quoted in Liicieanu, *Itinéraires d'une vie Cioran*

Cioran wrote two more books in Romanian after leaving the country in 1937. The first of these is *Amurgul Gîndurilor* (The Twilight of Thought), published in Romania in 1940. The second, *Îndreptar pătimaş* (Primer of Passions), translated in French as *Bréviaire des vaincus,* written between 1940/41 and 1944/45, was not published until 1991, when it became possible again to publish books by Cioran in Romania. Between the 1937 publication of *Romania's Transfiguration* and the 1945 completion of *Primer of Passions* are seven years exceptional in world history, and no less exceptional in Cioran's life. He was moving between one country, Romania, which was in the throes of fascist coups and counter-coups, before joining Hitler's Axis in June 1941 (switching over to the Allies when the Russians invaded it on August 23, 1944), and another, France, which fell to Hitler's rapidly advancing armies in June, 1940, endured four years of its own collaborationist regime, centered at Vichy, to be triumphantly liberated by the Allies moving east from Normandy in that same fateful month of August 1944. Cioran spent most of these years in France, returning home to Romania only twice, very briefly. Not surprisingly, there are very few records of Cioran's whereabouts or his activities during this time. Instead, we must take the usual detour and look for him in his books—where, as he always insisted, in war or peace, we are more likely to find him anyway.

If *Romania's Transfiguration* is a utopian political tract, or personalized utopia, *Primer of Passions* is a disabused existential meditation. Yet both are expressions of a deep and wrenching identity crisis in Cioran's life. They are linked thematically by recurring questions of identity and origins, the questions that obsessed Cioran for the rest of his life. Nevertheless, the answers that the two books give to these questions are different, and the difference clearly indicates an evolution in Cioran's mind pointing in the direction of his final break with Romanian culture. By the end of *Romania's Transfiguration,* Cioran is already beginning to doubt the certitude he hoped to gain by affirming a mystical union with his nation; doubt and despair increasingly gain the upper hand in the books that follow. In *Primer of Passions,* he finds the essence of self in exile and disassociation. After it, he makes good on his word never to write in Romanian again and embarks upon his uniquely linguistic quest to find—create—a new self.

In contrast to the hysterical affirmations of *Romania's Transfiguration,* there is a tone of bitter disappointment in *Primer of Passions,* which clearly relates to the historical events of 1940: Romania's dismemberment, King Carol's abdication, and the failed Iron Guard coup d'état. The disappointments are, just as clearly, personal as well: Cioran's brief return to Romania, his public radio lecture praising the "martyred" Iron Guard leader Corneliu Zelea Codreanu, his appointment as Romania's cultural attaché to the new French government at Vichy, losing that appointment in a comedy of diplomatic manners, and making his way, alone and without prospects, to Nazi-occupied Paris. Like *Romania's Transfiguration, Primer of Passions* is not a direct reflection of its author's life, but rather his rhetorically coded interpretation of it.[1]

## Sightings

It's hard to find reliable records of private persons' lives in Europe—in France, in Paris—during World War Two if they didn't write about it themselves, and sometimes not even then. Cioran's "lost" years in France, roughly 1937–45, will doubtless be gradually uncovered, if never fully recovered, as scholars, historians, and controversialists continue to examine his life and writings, especially as the extreme nature of his writings provokes polemical claims and counter-claims. With so much heat, there should be some light as well. The following pages thus offer some "sightings" of this elusive character that future biographers may use to take his bearings more accurately.[2]

His time in Vichy, and his diplomatic post there as cultural attaché, like his year of high school teaching in Braşov, do not amount to much. If he did any actual work in Vichy, there is no record of it, unless we count his radio broadcast on Codreanu at the end of 1940. Marta Petreu opines that he may have been fired for non-performance of duties or for insubordination: likely possibilities, given his previous employment track record. Or, she suggests, he could have been a victim of political whiplash, a common "accident" in many European countries at the time. When he delivered his November 1940 radio address praising Codreanu, Romania had just been declared a Legionary state, with General Ion Antonescu as its leader; but at the end of January 1941, after Cioran had received his diplomatic appointment, Antonescu outlawed the Legionary movement and made himself military dictator; the letter terminating Cioran's diplomatic appointment was signed by Antonescu.[3] In any case, Cioran's real goal—amazing enough, considering the time and the circumstances—was to get to Paris as fast as possible, and this is where we can pick up his trail, faint though it be.

His sole means of support was his graduate fellowship from the French Institute in Bucharest, and his putative "mission" was to complete his doctoral dissertation, as stated in his application dossier to the Institute in 1937. But he regarded this job as cavalierly as he did his diplomatic responsibilities. As far as we know, he never wrote a word of his thesis, and he was very frank in admitting it. He enrolled in the Sorbonne, but with no intention of attending lectures or following a course of studies; instead, he was interested in getting the tickets which allowed him to eat in the student refectories or get restaurant meals at reduced prices—a lifestyle that he continued to follow for several years after the war was over.[4] His fellowship tenure was not affected by his lack of progress, except in one ironic way: when he sought to prolong his fellowship after the first two years, he was unable to get the two letters of recommendation required—because he had been absent from all his classes during that time. Yet he was indulged by his Romanian admirers: "The director of the French Institute in Bucharest, who had sent me to Paris, was an enlightened man: he lied for me and was not bothered about the completion of my thesis, he said. On the contrary, he said [I was] the only fellowship student to know France from top to bottom, which, after all, is much better than a doctorate."[5]

It was during this early period that Cioran wrote back to his friend Constantin Noica, asking, "Where are you with your doctorate?" This, a universally terrorizing bit of black humor among graduate students at all times and places, was especially shaming to members of the self-styled "Young Generation" of Romania to which Noica and Cioran belonged, given all their polemical activity and intellectual manifestos from the late 1920s until the debacles of fascism engulfed them.

He set himself up in the Hôtel Marignan, 13 rue Sommerand, in the Fifth *arrondissement,* the Latin Quarter, near the Sorbonne. On his fifty-first birthday, in April 1962, he found himself wandering, by accident or design, through his old haunts. "I have wandered in the 5th: rue Rataud, where Eveline lived [unidentified], rue L'homond where I lived one month in 1935, and even all the old streets where I passed my *jeunesse:* rue du Pot de Fer, rue Amyot, the top of rue Cardinal Lemoine, etc. [Saw] a funeral procession: I bore [wore] the mourning of my spirit."[6]

Although in some sense a freeloader—and he is hardly the only graduate student never to have worked on his thesis—he had anything but an easy life. It was literally a hand-to-mouth existence, as lonely as his years in Berlin, but in much worse times and with much less money. He lived as what he called a "young rentier" in a city which he compared to Rome for its decadence. In the *Bréviaire des vaincus,* which he started on March 12, 1940, a "voluptuous claustrophobia" suffuses the pages, when Cioran recognizes the depths of his powerlessness as an unwanted alien in a strange city: "Is there on the Boulevard St. Michel a stranger more strange than me?"[7]

It is important to remember that he arrived in Paris before its occupation by the Germans, and that he was still just learning to speak French, despite his fluency—indeed, his volubility—in Romanian, Hungarian, and German. Later on, there were persistent rumors that he earned some money by giving tours of Parisian cultural sights to German officers, but he could not understand the question when I asked him about it, and Mme. Boué said she had never heard him say anything about it. Some of his ways of teaching himself French are different from what we might expect, given his life and career to this stage. He made an acquaintance of another Romanian, who "stupefied" him with his religiosity. "I was then reading the Bible (in their language, of course), every day. I remember that I was in the church in the rue Jean de Beauvais (I lived near it) in search of 'religious' books. Thus I returned to the sources of language. Today, when I regard what I have written at that time, I am forced to recognize that my effort of that time has not produced the fruits I had hoped for."[8]

Another friend, named Lapparent, further enriched, or complicated, Cioran's attitudes toward the new country and language he was gradually adopting—though we must remember that this was not yet a conscious, long-term project for him. Lapparent often came to visit Cioran in his rooms during the German winter offensive of 1940. Once, two visiting Romanian students were also present. "I don't know whom," Cioran said. "I had gone out for a half an hour. On my return, the students had left, and I stayed alone with Lapparent, who said to me, 'Your compatriots are asses [*cons*], yes, asses. They love France!' Lapparent always had a fear of being mobilized, for which reason he hoped for a rapid defeat [of France]. I have never known anyone more *French,* in the good and the bad sense, than he."[9] We can work out for ourselves, as Cioran does without comment, the apparent gap (to mere common sense) between Lapparent's patriotism and his Frenchness.

But it was not always winter, nor was he always desperately unhappy. Though poor, he frequently cultivated a pose or lifestyle of decadent, lazy enjoyments—which, however, usually included voracious reading. During the summers of 1938 and 1939, he undertook bicycle tours of France, from the Atlantic seashore to the Pyrenees to the Côte d'Azur. One evening he came upon a youth hostel catering equally to Catholics and Communists, to which he found he could be admitted because he carried a membership card for an organization called "Interntational Rapprochment for Youth." He also recalled that it was a special pleasure for him to stop in cemeteries in the countryside for a smoke.

An especially fond memory was his first acquaintance with Simone Boué. They met each other in 1942, at the student cafeteria where they both ate. She was studying English, which became her teaching career. (She spoke impeccable British English, with no discernible French accent, but with softer modulations than many British natives.) He kept coming around to talk to her about the pressures on him. The Romanian military attaché wanted to send him back to Romania, to enlist him in the army and send him to the front lines. He told her he wished he had gone to England instead of France in 1937. He ran the risk of being arrested by the Germans at the request of the Romanian authorities—because Romania was now one of the Axis powers. Far from being afraid, Cioran was furious with this attaché who, he said, had promised to leave him alone but then went back on his word. But there were larger reasons for his anger: he didn't think his fighting was going to save Romania, but he thought his writing might make a difference. And, like Wordsworth in the midst of the French Revolution, he was right, for himself, despite the apparent discrepancy between public external events and private internal motives.

Mme. Boué recalled that he went about everywhere with a packed suitcase, ready to decamp or go into hiding on a moment's notice. But the suitcase was also useful, in a way perfectly emblematic of his ability to make art out of his troubles: he used it as a portable writing desk.

As we saw in chapter 6, he depended on the generosity of others—the Jew Krakauer, for example. But he also stirred himself to help others. In the spring of 1944, he and two friends managed to obtain Benjamin Fondane's release after his arrest by the German authorities. But Fondane's sister was not released, and rather than leave his sibling he joined her in the prison convoy to Auschwitz, where he was killed in October.[10]

By the end of the war, Cioran was—like many, many others, of course—at the end of his tether. In addition to all the deprivations he suffered along with everybody else, there was the exasperation and humiliation to his immense sense of self-pride. Again, common sense might find this ridiculously excessive, but common sense is not the measure for Cioran. He suffered his own humiliation; he didn't ask sympathy for it. The author of five notable volumes in his native language and a sixth book he was just completing (Primer of Passions), he was less than a nobody in Paris. It was at this point that he began his own underground reconnaissance or resistance movement against (or toward) the French literary establishment. He created something actually resembling a "job." He began taking himself off to the Café de Flore, scrupulously, "like a clerk," every day, sitting himself down next to the intellectual headquarters of post-war French existentialism, the table occupied by Jean-Paul Sartre and Simone de Beauvoir.

Now that the real external enemy, the Nazis, had gone, defeated, Cioran set his sights on the enemies, or rivals, within—he called Sartre "a schoolteacher tainted by masochism" ["un instituteur atteint de masochisme"]—the ones *he* wanted to defeat (in the sense of surpass) in the scene that became the primal scene, at age thirty-four, of the next, last, and most famous stage of his self-transforming life, his re-birth as a *French* writer, and, even more crucially for him, a famous one.[11]

# 9

## Conclusion: The Lyrical Virtues of Totalitarianism

> Given the spectacle of their teeming successes, the nations of the West had no trouble exalting history. . . . It belonged to them, they were its agents: hence it must take a rational course. . . . Consequently they placed it under the patronage, by turns, of Providence, of Reason, and of Progress. What they lacked was a sense of fatality, which they are at last beginning to acquire, overwhelmed by the absence which lies in wait for them, by the prospect of their eclipse. Once subjects, they have become objects, forever dispossessed of that luminescence, that admirable megalomania which had hitherto protected them from the irreparable. . . . France, England, Germany have their age of expansion and madness behind them. Then comes *the end of insanity,* the beginning of the defensive wars. No more collective crusades, no more citizens, but wan and disabused individuals, still ready to answer the call of utopia, though on the condition that it come from *somewhere else,* on the condition that they need not bother to conceive it themselves.[1]

This quotation from "On a Winded Civilization," in *La tentation d'exister* (1956), illustrates the essential *French* Cioran: beautiful style placed in the service of the most melancholy of themes, the decadence of Western civilizations. The death of the West from a combination of impotence and old age, whose symptoms are liberalism, democracy, and the parliamentary system, and a view of the republic as a "paradis de débilité" [paradise of stupidity] are principal *idées fixes* in Cioran's obsession-riddled French *œuvre*. But hidden at the heart of Cioran's somber ruminations on the rise and fall of Western empires, cloaked in the language of disappointment, lies his now barely spoken longing for a utopia, "un délire neuf" [a new delirium] capable of exciting the collective imagination of a nation and incite it to revolution—the trace or echo of his early *Romanian* voice. Cioran dreams, if only indirectly and in-between the lines, of a healthy, vigorous, *virile* society, whose vitality is measured against a naked assertion of its will to power: in other words, a totalitarian society. Such a society would agree "not to annihilate itself," as the tolerant, democratic West tends to do, "but to liquidate its failures by undertaking *impossible* tasks, opposed to that dreadful good sense," which is the cause of the West's decline.[2]

Cioran bitterly reproaches Western civilization for its many missed opportunities to achieve this social dream. Thus, in *Histoire et Utopie*, he writes that the West "has not initiated the revolution that was its imperative, the revolution that its entire past demanded, nor has it carried to their conclusion the upheavals of which it was the instigator. . . . Not content with having betrayed all those precursors, all those schismatics who have prepared it and formed it from Luther to Marx, it [the West] still supposes that someone will come, from outside, to initiate *its* revolution, to bring back its utopias and its dreams."[3] Impotent because, liberal and tolerant, the West allowed Russia and its satellites to botch its dreams of utopia. But even the type of "utopian" society built by Soviet Russia, its inequities notwithstanding, is closer to Cioran's ideal of social and political order because it possessed a vitality/virility that never fails to draw his praise: "Those tsars with their look of dried-up divinities . . . they were, as are these recent tyrants who have replaced them, closer to a geological vitality than to human anemia, despots perpetuating in our time the primordial sap, the primordial spoilage, and triumphing over us all by their inexhaustible resources of chaos."[4]

Cioran's love of tyrants and totalitarian regimes manifests itself only cautiously in his later, French work. In the essay "À l'école des tyrans," from *Histoire et Utopie*, for example, Cioran gives us the psychological portrait—drawn in the true French moralist tradition—of the tyrant as a type illustrating one kind of human folly, the madness of self-aggrandizement. Cioran analyzes the travails of tyranny inside the human psyche with a dispassionate, clinical eye, and his stance is so full of irony, his authorial pronouncements are delivered from such a superior vantage point, that it is not easy to grasp the undercurrent of his own persistent admiration for tyranny.

In the opening lines of his essay, Cioran writes: "Whoever has not known the temptation to be first in the city will understand nothing of how politics work, nothing of the passion to reduce others to the status of objects."[5] By the logic of his own sentence, Cioran, as the author of this essay on tyranny, implies that he was once closely acquainted with it. He thereby both claims authority on the subject of tyranny on the basis of direct experience and confesses to a past sin: that he himself had once succumbed to tyranny's seductive charms. Later in the essay, his confession becomes explicit. He speaks of the "the days when I unreservedly loved the tyrants," when I was "unable to render myself worthy of them by action, I hoped to do so by words."[6] Rhetorically, however, this confession of a troubled past only serves to reinforce his stance of authority: that of the wise man who speaks from experience, who has learned from the follies of his youth and implicitly disassociates himself from them. Thus, though making an explicit confession, Cioran covers up rather than reveals his own enduring admiration for tyranny.

What gives the confession away as a rhetorical cover-up, a rhetorical device, and betrays Cioran's secret love of tyranny, is the ambiguity of his text. On the one hand he sets up his extravagant, incriminating past in opposition to a present in which the voice of wisdom and moderation reigns supreme. It is from this critically superior vantage point of this present that he views his past and exploits it as raw material for his moral portrait of the tyrant. On the other hand, Cioran parodies the very position of the wise old man from which he writes:

> Now, deceived by these extravagances . . . , I have come to dream of a city, a marvel of moderation, ruled by a team of slightly senile octogenarians, involuntarily amenable yet still lucid enough to make good use of their decrepitudes, exempt from desires, from regrets, from doubts. . . . And such is at present my fallen state that democrats themselves seem to me too ambitious, too mad.[7]

Such tongue-in-cheek praise for a utopia of moderation is damning praise. The real praise is reserved for a utopia "de l'insensé" [insane] which for Cioran never quite totally lost its allure. But this praise is not directly spoken; it is only implied by the author's clownish self-mockery, his mascarading as an "octogénaire," "lucide" but "un tantinet gâteux" [a stale cake], so decrepit that not only tyranny but even democracy strikes him as "delirious." Spoken in this muted, deflected, and ironic way, Cioran's love of tyrants is barely noticeable. It is, however, the enduring trace left by Cioran's early Romanian work, where his predilection for totalitarianism was expressed openly and with great lyrical force.

Between 1934 and 1937, the year of his self-exile to France, Cioran published four books in Romania, of which one, *On the Heights of Despair,* was a paen to lyricism, another, *Romania's Transfiguration,* was a paen to totalitarianism, and a third one, *Tears and Saints,* was a meditation on mysticism, an extreme form of religious lyricism. These three books mark three important stages—existential, political, and religious—in young Cioran's personal identity crisis, which is best summed up by a Montesquieu-type question Cioran himself formulated later in his life: "Comment peut-on être Roumain?" [How can one be Romanian?].

Lyricism for Cioran, then, is not merely a literary style or pose; it is closely bound to his real life. An answer to the question "Comment peut-on être Roumain?" must first of all take into account the biographical accident of Cioran's birth in 1911 as a Romanian subject of the Austro-Hungarian Empire, as well as the fact that Cioran's growth into adulthood coincides with the birth of the young nation-state, Greater Romania, founded in 1918, and this new state's struggle to achieve a national identity during the troubled inter-war period. The young Cioran belonged to a generation of Romanian intellectuals under the sway of the totalitarian seduction. In the specific national context of a politically vulnerable new state, and in the more general context of the post–World War I era in which a widespread feeling of the "sense of an ending" fueled arguments for totalitarianism as the only means to shore up the unraveling of Western civilization, Cioran's generation embraced totalitarianism because, as one recent Romanian commentator remarked, "it strengthened the instincts of affirmation: efficiency, cruelty, enthusiastic drunkenness, the dissolution of individuality."[8]

The connection between totalitarianism and lyrical style is not tenuous in Cioran's Romanian books. It is not by chance that the opening essay in *On the Heights of Despair* is titled "On Being Lyrical." "One becomes lyrical," writes the twenty-three-year-old Cioran, "when one's life beats to an essential rhythm and the experience is so intense that it synthesizes the entire meaning of one's personality. What is unique and specific in us is then realized in a form so expressive that the individual rises onto [a] universal plane."[9] This definition of lyricism is the first formulation of Cioran's life-long obsession with self-realization. How to "rise onto [a] universal plane," "reach the original source of life," in other words, escape the cultural and spiritual periphery that was his historical inheritance and achieve a position of centrality and power—be like God as much as possible!—these are his first and foremost preoccupations.

Cioran's lyricism is an illustration and a confirmation of the accuracy of Milan Kundera's observation that the lyrical mode "is not only a literary genre, but a whole way of life, an attitude toward the world"; in other words, that the lyrical is not merely a question of aesthetics but also of moral philosophy and politics.[10] The lyrical attitude asserts the Self to the utter exclusion of the Other; it proclaims the unity of the world and the rule of the One over the many by dissolving the distinction between self and the world through an irrepressible overflow of powerful feeling. In either cultural or political terms, intense lyricism is inherently tyrannical, since it does not conceive of any opposing will or ideas, it sweeps up and carries everything away in its train. As

Cioran writes in "On Being Lyrical," lyricism "is beyond forms and systems. A sudden fluidity melts all the elements of our inner life in one fell swoop, and creates a full and intense rhythm, an ideal convergence" (5).

Young Cioran, according to Horia Patapievici, "divides the ontology of the world into two different and diametrically opposed classes of reality": the organic and the non-organic, or, given the age metaphor at work in Cioran's distinctions, we could call these two classes the young and the old. In the former, "life develops *naturally* following its own specific rules of cruelty, fanaticism, intolerance and anonymity." The latter class, by contrast, is derived negatively from the former and is characterized by "diminution, old age, sclerosis, atrophy and death."[11] Lyricism is the stylistic register of the organic class. "Compared to the refined cultures of sclerotic forms and frames, which mask everything," writes Cioran, "the lyrical mode is utterly barbarian in its expression. Its value resides precisely in its savage quality: it is only blood, sincerity and fire."[12] Totalitarianism, which "rehabilitates fanaticism" and is "all fever and tension," is the political regime that corresponds to the organic class, as Cioran wrote in his articles from Hitler's Germany.[13] The non-organic class prefers irony for its stylistic register, and liberalism for its political regime. According to this classification, democracy is "nothing but the rejection of the absolute," and liberalism, with its repression of vital instincts, such as violence and intolerance, becomes in young Cioran's eyes, "pure political masturbation,"[14] a "theoretical expression of debauchery."[15]

Since it conceives only of absolutes—absolute truth, which is poetry, and absolute will, which is tyranny—lyricism is more than an expression of the self, it is the assertion of the self's will to power. Consequently, the lyrical worldview is a totalitarian worldview. Bearing in mind Napoleon's fondness for Ossian, the wildly rhapsodic "Gaelic" poet manufactured out of some old linguistic scraps by James Macpherson in the mid-eighteenth century, we can safely say that the tyrant is a failed poet and, conversely, that the lyrical man is a frustrated tyrant. This is precisely the evaluation that the older Cioran makes of his younger Romanian self when he wrote that "not having the power [to] render myself worthy of them [the tyrants] by action, I hoped to do so by words." But whereas the older Cioran depicts his younger self with irony tempered by pity for the vagaries of the human soul, the young and ambitious Cioran has nothing but praise for the lyrical savage he harbors in his bosom and adorns him with positive attributes: mad, young, passionate, savage, barbarian.

The "hero" of Cioran's first book is his alter ego, the organic or lyrical thinker who contemptuously rejects the intellectual optimism of the abstract thinker, the philosopher or the sage, a distinction reminiscent of Nietzsche's Dyonisian and Socratic types:

> Despair is the state in which anxiety and restlessness are immanent to existence . . . I despise the absence of risks, madness and passion in abstract thinking. How fertile live, passionate thinking is! Lyricism feeds it like blood pumped into the heart.[16]

This kind of unbridled lyricism inevitably leads to and feeds on dreams of self-aggrandizement, including political utopias of the kind Cioran devised in his (in)famous political treatise, *Romania's Transfiguration.* In it, Cioran recommends, with utmost seriousness, extreme measures such as the extermination of three-quarters of Romania's population, the "fanaticization" of its remaining population, and dictatorship as the sure means to create a "Romania with China's population and France's destiny."

To conclude: there are two important phases in Cioran's career as a writer, clearly marked by differences in language (Romanian versus French) and style (effusive, unbridled, and poetic versus guarded, aphoristic, distanced, and ambiguous). But if lyricism is the stylistic equivalent of totalitarianism, irony, with its mistrust of absolutes of any kind, is the very opposite. Hence a contradiction arises in Cioran's later work, for although he has abandoned his native language and the lyrical mode and shifted the focus from self (and self-expression) to the "metaphysical plane of generic humanity" (more specifically, the decadent West), he has not abandoned his original scale of values in which all those "dynamic madnesses," totalitarianism included, are privileged.

If it were simply a matter of generation and historical-political context, Cioran's lyrical/totalitarian worldview could be regarded as a passing phase in his youth, which he abandons along with the lyrical style after the move to France. The older, French Cioran could then be seen as a sadder but wiser man, and my explanation of his two careers would simply be an apology—something of the kind that, "he is not really so bad after all." But the lyrical/totalitarian worldview is not just the symptom of a passing phase, the traces of it in his later work attesting to continuity rather than rupture. But neither is my explanation of the connection between the two Ciorans a mere denunciation, since it does not aim at simply unmasking "the real Cioran"—reactionary, fascist—hiding behind his new, French persona. What my explanation aims for is a critical representation of the troubling, complex, and ambiguous Cioran who stands behind his French *œuvre.*

Cioran's French work is disturbing, since in providing a critique of the ills of the democratic West—with which we can all more or less sympathize—he also provides a discreet, guarded apology of dictatorship as a form of political "madness" that could have beneficial effects, even though we know and he knew and contemplated its disastrous consequences in our past century. To this alternative only another form of "madness" is preferable, the beggarly state of exile which presupposes renunciation of the self's will to power. But here we come back full circle, because there is a kinship between exile and dictatorship in the element of megalomania common to both. As Cioran himself points out in "Avantages de l'exil," "The man who has lost everything preserves as a last resort the hope of glory, or of literary scandal. He consents to abandon everything except his *name*. But how will he impose his name when he writes in a language of which cultivated people are either ignorant or contemptuous?"[17] Even in exile, Cioran is not free from the obsession of self-assertion. On the contrary, it is in exile that this obsession becomes even more pressing, but he disguises it in its very opposite: the ascetic self-renunciation, through adoption of French as the language of his mature work and the detached, faintly moralistic irony for which he ultimately became so famous.

Exile and irony are characterized by distance. Ironic distance destroys the poetic illusion of unity between the project of the self and the actual historical self. In exile, from the infinite distance of old age and different geographical and cultural space, the wise but decrepit old Cioran ironizes the ambitious but foolish young Romanian who tries to reconcile his condition of being Romanian with his personal quest for the "self's objectives." But to criticize, even deride, the futility of the project does not preclude admiration for it. On the contrary, just as Cervantes both laughs at and loves the noble but foolish Quixote, so does Cioran simultaneously bemoan and admire the idealism of his former self. Finally, and paradoxically, it is only in self-exile—taken in its literal sense of exile *into* the self, with the self thrown upon itself without a historical, political, or linguistic reality to back it up—that the project of the self, now a purely egotistical drive toward realization of the self's objectives, can actually complete itself as the writerly project. Self-exile and irony thus become in Cioran's French career a new kind or stage of lyricism.

# PART 2

## Memoirs of a Publishing Scoundrel

He had nothing to fear from us because he had nothing to fear from the truth.

"Do you think that it's right to rake up the past?"
"I don't know that I know what you mean by raking it up; but how can we get at it unless we dig a little? The present has such a rough way of treading it down."
"Oh, I like the past, but I don't like the critics," the old woman declared, with her fine tranquility.
"Neither do I, but I like their discoveries."
"Aren't they mostly lies?"
"The lies are what they sometimes discover," I said, smiling at the quiet impertinence of this. "They often lay bare the truth."
"The truth is God's, it isn't man's; we had better leave it alone. Who can judge of it—who can say?"

What was more in my mind was that she had a fancy to play me the trick of making me engage myself when in fact she had annihilated the papers.

"So it was a regular plot—a kind of conspiracy?"
"Oh, a conspiracy—we were only two," I replied.

"Ah, you publishing scoundrel!"

—Henry James, *The Aspern Papers*

# Prelude

## IMAGINING CIORAN

In the era of biography, no one wraps up his wounds without running the risk of having the bandage torn off and the wound exposed for all to see; and if they fail to expose the wound, we go away disappointed.

—Cioran, *The Temptation to Exist*

The following pages are adapted from an informal diary I kept of my acquaintance with Cioran, and his companion, Simone Boué, during the last years of his life, during his slow decline and final passing away in a geriatric hospital in Paris in June 1995. They also record my tribulations as a biographer, a member of what the narrator in *The Aspern Papers* calls the "dreadful race of publishing scoundrels." My project required more than just burrowing for documents in libraries and archives. Like Henry James's scholar-turned-thief, I needed the tact of a diplomat and the nerve of a smuggler, besides the ordinary skills of a translator, critic, and cultural historian. What began as a scholarly endeavor soon grew into a full-blown drama around a dying man's bed.

The passage of years has only confirmed Cioran's insight that we live in an "era of biography." Fiction writers now jostle with biographers and memoirists in the practice of "life writing." But whereas novelists try to dress—somehow—what Cioran called the "wounds of life," biographers still try to tear away the bandage and expose festering horrors to the cruel eyes of an avid reading public. Countless importunities, indelicacies, and indiscretions are committed in the name of truth. The specter of Henry James's snoopy narrator in *The Aspern Papers* stalks the would-be biographer, partly as threat, partly as mockery.

I became a biographer by accident. In 1988, E. M. Cioran first refused, then agreed, to let me translate into English his first Romanian book, *On the Heights of Despair* (1934). I finished it in the summer of 1990, while on vacation in Mallorca. Every day, exhausted and exhilarated after hours of work on Cioran's text, I would take my solitary evening walk along the rugged Mallorcan coast at Colonia de San Pere, watching the sun set behind the Sierra Tramuntana across the Bay of Alcudia. I was not alone. Cioran had already started to obsess me. In the blaze engulfing the mountains, I saw apocalyptic images from his *Heights of Despair.* My ears burned with the exalted, raging words of an angry young man. I found the mixture of defiance, outrage, and vulnerability in his youthful, passionate prose extremely erotic; my daily struggle to master it had become like a sexual tryst.

Imagining the author is part of any reading experience. I began imagining Cioran when I started translating him. For me, at the time, Cioran was a totally unknown author, since I had not even known his full name until shortly before I was handed his book to translate. I could not have been a more innocent or more ignorant reader in my first literary encounter with Cioran. In Communist Romania where I grew up, the past Cioran belonged to, the interwar period, was a mystifying dumb-show, both shadowy and shady. People raised their eyebrows, rolled their eyes, grimaced suggestively, but nobody talked. Especially about Cioran. He was persona non grata in Romania from 1947 to 1989. His name was not pronounced, his works were banned.

Yet I suspect that my ignorance was to some extent self-imposed. My first impulse when I arrived in the United States in the late 1970s was to break all ties with my Romanian past. I earnestly, and perhaps naively, tried to erase the bruising memories of the tragic and absurd Communist world from which I had escaped. I suffered from what the Polish poet Czeslaw Milosz ironically calls "the privilege of coming from strange lands where it is difficult to escape history." I didn't know it then, but I was repeating, in my own, less flamboyant way, Cioran's gesture of exile thirty years earlier. He too had completely severed his Romanian connection, even ceasing to speak his native language. But by the time Cioran arrived in my life in the late 1980s, I had understood that it was difficult to escape history, that in fact I had a moral obligation not to. Looking into Cioran's past was a unique opportunity to recover its suppressed truths. He had brought me to the door of a forbidden chamber and given me the key, only pleading that I should not use it. Of course I had to become his biographer. But while treading my way through the echoing rooms of Cioran's past, piecing together his story, I kept stumbling over threads of my own. Re-imagining a past for him meant that I had to revisit what I myself had endeavored to forget.

As I tried to imagine my Cioran, I suddenly remembered the day when I first brushed by his invisible presence, unwittingly. I was eleven years old when I first visited Cioran's native village of Răşinari, in Transylvania. I remember strolling through its cobbled stone streets, after a ride in a rickety old streetcar that took us there from the nearby city of Sibiu through a leafy bit of woods and over a green, mildly sloping hill. My mother, my sister, and I visited the house of the nationalist poet Octavian Goga and admired the monumental tomb of the enlightened Transylvanian Orthodox bishop-scholar Saguna, with two lions at its gate. Nobody mentioned that in the two graves next to Saguna's mausoleum lay the parents of another famous son of Răşinari, E. M. Cioran. He was not spoken of in Romania; I was to hear his name for the first time only twenty-five years later, in Spain.

From Spain, in that summer of 1990, I went to Paris to consult with Cioran about my translation. The existence of a living author complicates the game of authorial fiction making. I longed to meet the real-life Cioran not only because, like Jacob wrestling the angel, I wanted his blessing, but also because I felt that he would not be complete until I met him in flesh and blood. Trying to imagine the author I was about to meet for the first time, I steeled myself for an encounter I anticipated yet also dreaded. The man in Paris was a stranger, half a century older than the angry young man I knew from the pages of his book. He was lionized in France; his fame was intimidating, forbidding. But when I met him that summer, I immediately recognized the young barbarian familiar to me, in the flashing green eyes, the exuberant laughter, and the sheer physical energy of an eighty-year-old man, who bounded up the six flights of stairs leading to his attic apartment near the Odéon theater like a young deer from his native Carpathians. In his modest Paris apartment, imaginatively improvised out of the attic of an old building on the Left Bank, he led me through a long, narrow passage with a low ceiling and an uneven floor to an unexpectedly sunny room with a cheerful garden improvised on its terrace. Cioran looked frail, but misleadingly so, as I discovered when I learned that he preferred to ignore the new elevators in his building. Seeing the old man intensified the mystery around the young one whose words I knew intimately, though not the experiences from which they arose. His past, out of which he had spoken to me with such passion every day in his book, was a gap I did not know how to fill. What had provoked that passionate intensity?

Bouncing back down the six flights of stairs, he stepped out briskly into the street and took me on his favorite walk through the Luxembourg gardens. When he talked, his clear green eyes flashed from under thick eyebrows, their penetrating glare transfixing me, while his jaw pushed forward with youthful determination, and the old man was miraculously transformed into the young man I knew, my Cioran. But the contradiction remained, for the young man spoke like an old man, and when I asked what he was writing, he answered that he no longer wrote, because "I don't want to slander the universe anymore; I've done it long enough, don't you agree?"

**FIGURE 7.** Ilinca Zarifopol-Johnston, E. M. Cioran, and Simone Boué, in Cioran's apartment on the rue de l'Odéon, 1992.

**FIGURE 8.** *(below)* Simone and Cioran.

**FIGURE 9.** Ilinca Zarifopol-Johnston and Cioran.

**FIGURE 10.** *(below)* Ilinca and Relu, 1997.

# Paris, 1992–1994

**1992**

May 13. Two evenings in a row with Cioran and Simone Boué. Yesterday I went just to say "hello" and stayed for supper, though I was dead tired after my trip from the States. Shared their *potage*. Simone is a great cook, the *potage* delicious. They are an irresistible couple, warm, easy-going, full of charm and tenderness for each other. We talked a lot; we laughed a lot. Today I was there again, from 6 to 11:30. Big dinner. I'm worried about him as an informant. His past is for him "de la préhistoire," literally so. She is now his memory as far as dates, events, and names are concerned. She's a good storyteller. He listens to her with a look of surprise as if the things she recounts did not happen to him but to someone else. He seems detached and estranged from his own past: the stranger he's always wanted to be, now more than ever. Only now, ironically, not because he wills it, but because he cannot help it. He's ill, no doubt about that, mind slipping out of control.

The illness must have started about two years ago. I remember an incident which seemed inexplicable at the time. We had arranged for him to meet me at my hotel one day to work on my translation of *The Heights of Despair.* The rendezvous was set for 2:00 PM. I was very nervous. Working with the grand old man for the first time, what an experience that would be! Two o'clock came and went, and then 2:30, 3:00. No sign of Cioran. I went out in the street to look for him. I went back inside and asked if there was a message. Finally, I worked up my courage and called the apartment. He answered sheepishly and apologetically. He had gotten lost and had returned home. He was very sorry. I couldn't believe my ears. The apology was so fantastic that it couldn't but be true, and yet how strange! Lost in familiar territory, a fifteen-minute walk from the Odéon to the Panthéon, through all his old haunts. I didn't make anything of it then.

I asked him about *Tears and Saints.* What made him write it? At first, he couldn't remember he had written it at all. "Which one of my books is that? When did I write it?" I reminded him that as a student he wanted to write a thesis on tears. He was glad to hear about that incident from his youth, just as he likes listening to Simone's stories. She told me the story about the publication of *Tears and Saints* in Romania, how the typesetter was shocked by its content and took it to the director of the press to make sure he wanted to publish such an incendiary book, and the worried publisher then refused to publish it.

It's much better if I don't ask specific questions about his past. He seems suspicious of anything that requires precise answers. He likes to talk on general themes. One has only to get him started. Today I mentioned exile. His interest revived, he talked at great length. Exile has been a lifelong obsession of his. His goal in life, to become a stranger. He talked at length about the "voluptuousness of exile," the exquisite pain of being from nowhere, a main theme in his work. I asked him to connect this obsession with something specific in his personal history. He couldn't or wouldn't say. But he repeated that exile was for him a mental attitude which he had intentionally cultivated all his life. Exile as a means to ensure intellectual independence. That's a clue; an oblique reference to his youthful involvement with the Romanian Legionnaire movement and his subsequent rejection of it?

Leaving Romania was his escape; he never wanted to go back there. He likes being an *apatride*—a man without a country—a social status that best suits his frame of mind. Only an accident of fate brought him to France. He was temperamentally more suited for Spain. However, he feels grateful toward France for harboring him, though he is not particularly fond of French culture. He explicitly distanced himself from French writers. He never felt any affinities for them, nor wanted to be like them. I should have asked him: what about the eighteenth-century French writers you chose as models of style? But I didn't. I'm still very shy and loath to challenge him. He expressed his great passion for Dostoevsky. Not only for his books, but especially for his personality and his life. Naturally. He must see a parallel between himself and Dostoevsky's early political attachments and excesses. A connection also between Dostoevsky's epilepsy and his own fits of rage, his insomnia, and other nervous disorders of which he so often complains? The cursed family inheritance? Romance or reality?

He also mentioned his stay in Germany in the early 1930s. He said, however, that he left Germany with no desire to return. Neither to Romania, which was in chaos, nor to Germany, where Hitler was bad. I'm suddenly on the alert. Surprised and suspicious. I think of the euphoric articles on Germany he wrote during his stay there. Germany didn't seem so bad to him then. I wonder whether he's feeding me lines. Who knows? Maybe he isn't. He was twenty years old then, now he's eighty. Anyone who has spent time with twenty-year-olds knows how wrong-headed they can be. About anything, but especially about causes. I saw a collection of writings by Nietszche on a table in the passageway. I must come back to the topic of Germany and German writers some other day. No point in pushing if I encounter resistance.

We talked about the media campaign against Mircea Eliade, the historian of religion. Cioran has heard about Norman Manea's essay on Eliade, "Felix Culpa," but hasn't read it.[1] I promised to send him a copy. He is mentioned in the essay, of course. As a foil to Eliade, as the man who has apologized and retracted. There will be more and more writings about his own political past. It's inevitable. I must make him face it. He pretends not to be worried about what he calls "attacks" on his "emballements de jeunesse" [youthful crazes], and says that the best way to deal with them is to ignore them. But he is very worried. Still, he deflects me. He switches to the anecdotal mode, his favorite form of conversation. Last fall, he had to suffer the wrath of Eliade's wife, Cristinel, for not writing to protest the articles against her husband. One evening she asked him over for dinner and scolded him like a schoolboy. His candid reply to her admonishing: "I did some of those things myself; it's not up to me to defend him." His humor and pique at Cristinel's behavior is mixed with regret and pain in telling about it. But he can't keep out of trouble. At an evening honoring Eliade given by the Romanian mission at UNESCO, someone from Radio Free Europe secretly taped a conversation with Cioran and broadcast it next day in Romania, to the Ciorans' great amazement. Simone was furious. She usually keeps watch over him like a hawk but was caught off her guard while they were milling about during the reception. She too is worried, though I doubt she knows the exact nature of the situation. She has never read his youthful enormities.

May 14. Today we talked about his adoption of another language, part of C.'s program of how to become a stranger: "il faut se lancer dans une langue." To "launch oneself" as one launches a new boat? To dive into language like an Olympic swimmer? To throw oneself as a suicidal man throws himself out the window? To hurl oneself against a hermetically shut iron door?

Returning to his obsession with exile: in life, one *must* have an obsession, without it one drifts hopelessly, derivatively: "on va à la dérive." Obsession as character. Also obsession as saving grace. It takes courage living with one's obsessions, nurturing them instead of weeding them out. Another favorite theme.

May 16. Last visit with the Ciorans. Lovely evening. Both are charming, chatty, warm, easy-going. Her devotion to him is sublime. He must have been very difficult to live with. And how they lived! He was hardly known, very poor, eating at student dorms, and at rich ladies' houses where he could get a free meal in exchange for his brilliant conversation. He was so poor that he did not have enough income to declare for tax purposes. Following a kind of paranoid logic that I can relate to very well, he decided to make up a false income and pay taxes on it so that he wouldn't be suspected of tax fraud and expelled as a non-French citizen. His greatest fear, expulsion from exile!

One of the first stories he proudly tells his visitors is the story of how he acquired his apartment. When it was no longer possible to live in furnished hotel rooms, he began to look for an apartment. He didn't want to move out of the neighborhood of the Left Bank where he had always lived. But it was devilishly hard to find anything. One day, a lady working at the post office told him that she was an admirer of his work. The next day he sent her a copy of his latest essay, *Histoire et utopie.* A few weeks later she told him she had a small apartment for rent and asked if he was interested. It was the attic on the rue de l'Odéon. He's been there ever since. Now he worries that the owners of the building will try to expel them in order to remodel the building and raise the rent. He sees plots of expulsion everywhere.

In the 1940s and 1950s, he used to wear hand-me-down clothes from luckier friends like Eliade and was introduced around Paris as "Ionesco's friend." His humiliation at being thus introduced; his humiliation when Gallimard told him that his books didn't sell well enough to merit a paperback edition. His humiliation when Camus rejected his manuscript, telling him he hadn't read enough. The effrontery! He was full of contempt for Camus, whom he considered a mediocre writer, a school-teacher type. A touchy, proud man, Cioran. He was sure of his achievements. He cultivated his marginality; he wore it like a badge of honor or a title of nobility. I must say I am puzzled by Camus's response, if indeed that was what he had said. He was very wrong. Cioran's erudition is vast. He has spent most of his life reading. He read, in fact, much more than he wrote.

His Romanian past came up again in conversation. He dismissed it once more as "de la préhistoire." Great reluctance to talk about it. He insisted on his break with his past, the lack of continuity between his Romanian and French selves. He greatly resents Dan C. Mihăilescu, a literary critic who came from Romania to interview him about his activities in the 1930s. "J'ai dit beaucoup de bêtises dans ma jeunesse" [I said many stupid things in my youth], he acknowledges with a finality that precludes any further questioning. Or as he often put it to Simone, one could say about him that he had had a "past," the way one said it about "certain women." By "certain women" he means kept women, or prostitutes. He prostituted himself politically. A confession, however reluctant.

Later, however, he opened up a little and talked about his philosophy teacher, Nae Ionescu, a mysterious, ambivalent figure in Romanian intellectual life of the 1930s, supporter of the Iron Guard movement. Ionescu's memory obviously still fascinates Cioran. According to him, Nae Ionescu is the key to what happened to Cioran's generation. He was a seducer, an extraordinary and subtle man, hard to pinpoint. Politically he belonged to the right, but Cioran's opinion is that it was all a pose or a game, that in fact he didn't believe in anything, was a nihilist and an adventurer. But also the most intriguing teacher he ever had in Romania or elsewhere. Cioran, like most of the other young intellectuals of his generation, including the Jewish writer Mihail Sebastian, became a disciple. I've heard all this before. Or rather, read it in C.'s interviews. It's one of his versions of what happened "then." The focus today is on the charismatic teacher. At other times, it's on the charismatic political leader, the head of the nationalist movement, Corneliu Zelea Codreanu. He never fails to mention confidentially, as if it were a big secret, that Codreanu was a foreigner, a Slav, not a Romanian. I'm not sure he's right, but he seems to like the idea. Or rather the paradox? And yet other times, Cioran talks about the sheer mesmerizing power of violence in a movement he despised intellectually.

I can relate to the corrupting-mentor scenario. I remember how I joined the Romanian Communist Party when I was in my third year at the university. It all came about because I wanted to please three young teachers whom I admired very much. They were just back from the University of California at Berkeley, full of talk about transformational grammar and speech-act theory. The linguistic concepts had an aura of things Western, beyond our reach, and therefore infinitely alluring; they intimated a vast world of free intellectual exchange and excitement, which appeared to us, as we sat in the dim and dusty classrooms of the Germanic languages department at the University of Bucharest, excitingly vibrant in its novelty. We hung on every word these teachers said, we lapped it up. The teachers didn't have Nae Ionescu's charisma, but they were like messengers from the Western world. When they started talking politics, we lapped that up as well. They said that we stood a better chance of changing the party from the inside than from the outside, if there were enough of us of the same mind inside the party. So, why not join the party instead of avoiding it? What they said came like a revelation; suddenly it made enormous sense. Yes, what *if*? All of us, the good ones? How come we hadn't thought of it ourselves? I was one of the more stubborn and reluctant disciples, but I was twenty and badly wanted to believe these teachers, because I wanted so much to please them. Thus I allowed myself to be drafted. Not without some quiet misgivings that were ferreted out by the party secretary of our departmental cell, who turned my induction into the party into a public humiliation. I still smart from it. Not because I was insulted and accused of lacking strong political convictions—it was true enough, I did lack them, the party secretary was right—but because I went through with it despite the insults. Later, I too found in voluntary exile my only way out.

There's an obvious link between political involvement and exile: one goes into exile either to escape persecution or to escape further involvement. There are superficial exiles and existential ones. Lenin, who bided his time in Zurich, was of the former kind; Cioran in Paris, of the latter. Naturally, Cioran fears a resurrection of his past. But, I suspect, not simply because, as has already happened with Eliade, he will be put to shame, criticized, and publicly castigated for it, or more specifically for having once been on the wrong side, that is, the extreme right—since "his past," as the phrase is commonly used, does not refer to the totality of his past life but only to his past political allegiances. He fears a public scandal as much as any of us would, no doubt. He is only human. But what he may fear even more is a simplification and distortion of this past which forms the obsessive and formative core of his life, his persona and his writing, toward which he has stood all his life in a paradoxical relation of inclusion and exclusion. For him, tormenting obsession is a saving grace. The greatest danger for the "uprooted poet," as he puts it himself in "Avantages de l'exil," is "to get used to his fate," to feel cozy in exile.

**1993**

April 17, 1993. Today I called Simone from Bloomington. Cioran is very ill in the hospital. He fell, broke his hip, and they had to operate. He seems to have lost the will to live. He hangs his head and looks at Simone with a dull expression. Refuses to eat, is in a great state of anxiety, twists himself in the chair, lashes out at the nurses and orderlies, was tied to his bed for being too violent. Premonition of madness, he quotes to her from Mihai Eminescu's "Second Letter": "organele's sfărîmate şi maestrul e nebun" [the instruments are broken and the maestro's mad].

May 12. Cioran is at the Hospital Broca, on rue Pascal, not far from the hotel I've taken on rue Cardinal Lemoine. An easy walk down the colorful rue Mouffetard: ethnic restaurants, bohemian boutiques, a street market. Fish, meat, vegetables, and fruit in self-indulgent superabundance, almost shamelessly on display. My eyes are filled with colors: pink of salmon, thick pulpy white of asparagus, violet-green of artichokes, orange-red of tiger lilies. Street vendors, a street organ, and two ageing singers, bawling out *chansonettes,* the cries of Paris. I bought a bouquet of lilies and continued up rue Pascal. I felt nervous, almost scared. This is so different from my previous visits, the pleasant nights spent with the Ciorans, the elegant little dinners Simone prepared, the long talks, what we laughingly called our "Armenian talks." Cioran knew the Romanian expression "an Armenian visit," signifying a long, interminable visit. Simone didn't, but she liked the idea and adopted the expression.

In a few minutes I arrive: Centre de Gérontologie, a modern, beige and maroon building, square windows in decorative round casings. I'm fifteen minutes early, so I stop in the street and look up at the windows, trying to take it all in, ruminating on the word "gérontologie." A man's full existence ending abruptly in that pompously scientific construction. And how Cioran had hated that word in particular!

As I glance up, I do a double take: a ghost with white hair stares out the window. From where I am, the face is blurred, but it could be Cioran: a floating white head, an apparition, a martyred saint. It's a strong impression, and it stays with me as I go in, for the place is full of ghosts like that, with haggard, absent faces, shuffling in corners: an old lady crumbled in a wheel chair, and next to her, a daughter perhaps, staring silently; a passing old couple, moving as if in a slow motion picture, she with a long, white pony tail, a camel's hair winter coat instead of a robe, felt slippers, he a slightly younger man, maybe a son, in a modest business suit. There are Romanians here too, a toothless lady with her mother in a wheel chair, chattering. Unidentified intermittent moaning. Milling about swiftly, at a pace greatly contrasting with that of the old people, the hospital staff, very young people, eating, drinking, smoking, and laughing at lunch hour in the cafeteria. A small garden, a row of columns, a cross-shaped brick path, a patch of grass, potted flowers. The elevators are very dirty (empty cans of soft drinks, cigarette packages), the smell of urine pungent as I come out on the second floor.

Cioran's room No. 244, his name on the door. His name also on the books lying on the table in the room. The only books there. He can't read, but once in a while Simone shows them to him, points to the name and tells him that's his name, that he wrote those books. He bends his white mane and peers at the name, trying to remember who he is. As I come in, he has been readied for the visit. He looks up with his green eyes, now pale, without their demonic light, and gives a smile almost of recognition. I kiss her, and then kneel down by his chair holding his hand. I'm saying some friendly words about my coming to see him again; she also repeats and explains who I am and why I'm there. In a great effort to be sociable and gentlemanly—as if the ghost of his past witty, courteous self returns for a flickering moment—he looks up, squeezing my hand, and says, "Then if she's come, we'll hear some interesting things!" And relapses into a half-bent position, head hanging down. But he hasn't released my hand.

We held hands the entire time I was there. It became a way of communicating, for he tries to speak, starts a sentence, in a barely audible voice, and then stops, lost, he cannot finish. The words don't come, or doesn't he know what it was that he wanted to say? I think he knows, but can't say it anymore, for as he is trying to formulate a sentence, the muscles in his arm tighten in a visible effort, his hand squeezes mine. Like Morse code signals. But nothing comes out. I don't know whether I should try and talk, maybe guess his meaning—if there's one at all—entertain him with small talk, or just be silent and hold his hand for comfort.

We get ready to go out for a walk. Simone and I help him into his wheel chair. He can get up if he is held, but he has a hard time appreciating the distances between chairs and needs a lot of prompting in turning around. We take him down in the elevator and out into the garden. He is cold, though it's a mild day, so Simone has to go back and grab a hat and a scarf. He doesn't remember how to ask her for his things, so he says, "bring down any instruments you find!" I wheel him back in while we are waiting. Old people are cold. I remember a friend telling me this spring that after his two cancer operations he felt cold and the feeling has never left him. I wheel Cioran around, I point out the Romanians to him and joke about the fact that they seem to pop up everywhere. He laughs at that. His face is still good looking, his leonine profile is there, his green eyes, his white mane—but it is all faded, like an old photograph. He has a skin rash, maybe from drugs, or dehydration; the skin on his face is peeling away in little white scales and is red and raw underneath. But with an English woolen cap (the Sherlock Holmes type) and a lavender scarf, he almost looks his old self again. Even a roguish smile appears when I compliment him on his looks. We go out again, and we stop in the sun. Simone and I help him out of the chair, and we start walking slowly around the brick path, supporting him on either side. At times, he walks better than at others, he almost steps with confidence, but if we start talking about it, he becomes tentative again, as if self-conscious. Today he wants to walk, to Simone's surprise. He launches himself along the path, then stops and looks with surprise in the opposite direction, where there is another path, as if he wanted to go there but couldn't make up his mind. We stop on a bench, we chat—that is, Simone and I do, while he rubs his hands and listens with bent head.

We talk about Beregovoy's suicide and Mitterand's new government.[2] Simone reminds him of the time he used to walk in the Luxembourg gardens at night, when he would see Mitterand walking with a woman, every time a different one, and as Cioran was walking right behind them, Mitterand would cover the woman's head with his coat so she wouldn't be identified, probably thinking that they were being followed by a private detective. Then she reminds him of his "vie mondaine." How once he was invited to a party at a chateau outside Paris, where Mitterand arrived in a helicopter. Cioran was afraid he would recognize him as the "shadow" from the Luxembourg, but instead Mitterand praised Cioran's work and said that he always took a book by Cioran with him on holidays. (A likely story?)

Back in his room, he looked wan and tired and stopped making the effort to converse. She spoon-fed him a piece of cake. We talked about the divorce of his American editor. Cioran seemed to understand, because he listened intently, and then said, "I was well known." It must be part of Simone's efforts to give or preserve a sense of identity in him, when she tells him that he is well known, an author of books, published in many countries. As proof, she shows him his name on book covers. E. M. Cioran as in E. M. Forster, as he has explained to me. He began his career by giving himself a new, famous-sounding name. But now that his life is reduced to bare essentials, the thought of his fame sticks out like a broken tree or a rock in the desert. The obsession that anchored his life—to make a name for himself in the world—lies shipwrecked on a hospital bed, lit by the pale afternoon sun.

We were getting ready to go. Neither of us had eaten, so we decided to have a cup of tea together. At four, the nurses would be coming with a snack, and Simone felt tired. She gave him a kiss, and said she was leaving. He looked up eagerly, and said, "I'm coming too." We both winced with sorrow. She told me later that she prefers not to tell him when she goes away to spare him the pain. She distracted him by giving him one of his books to look at, pointing to the name, and that's how we left him: staring absent-mindedly but obediently at his own name.

Talk with Simone in a brasserie not far from the hospital. She is upset, even confused at times, talks eagerly, but almost incoherently, jumping from one subject to the next, in a great rush to relieve her oppressed feelings. She tells me about Cioran's rapid decay during this past year: they found out in July that he had Alzheimer's disease. Arteriosclerosis of the brain and big drops in blood pressure led to repeated falls until the last, almost fatal one. Had it been fatal, it would have been better, she thinks, for now he may be physically stable for a while, but his mind goes on deteriorating. The whole saga of hospitals, tests, treatments, Cioran's violence, the doctors' lack of sympathy and visible annoyance with this stubborn and violent man, her own struggles with him to get him to do anything, like washing, or dressing. Stories of rebellion, Cioran tied up in the hospital, not accepting anybody's help except hers, dressing fantastically with sweaters on his legs. In the midst of all this, she tried to keep up a semblance of normality. Those lovely dinners she gave for me, and for others, were, it turns out, carefully orchestrated so that the idol would not fall for another little while.

Simone, the self-effacing, supporting woman. Devoted to the point of doting on the great man. Her devotion, her love for Cioran is a marvelous and moving thing to see. They've been living together for fifty-one years. She's only eight years younger; I thought the difference was much bigger. She's tall and very pretty, with round, warm, almond-colored eyes. Her brushed-up auburn hair has a thin mesh of white in it. When she smiles, her whole face lights up, her eyes twinkle full of spirit. She's a very good talker and storyteller, though the emotional strain she's under right now makes her stories less fluent. She didn't use to be much of a talker before, but now, since he's ill, she talks for him. It is as if his soul has taken flight and found refuge in her.

She reminisces about their life together. Together yet separate, since she never went out into society with him—she sounds oddly proud of her self-effacement. He never asked her about her family or her work teaching English at school. I listen and marvel as she recalls the many nights she used to stay up, waiting for him, sometimes till dawn or even later. How she cried and beat the pillows with her fists. How he would return, unshaven, disheveled, and surprised to find her in such a state. She led a double life, divided between Cioran and her family. She lied to her mother about sharing an apartment with someone she didn't know. She used to put a bookcase in front of the connecting door between their rooms when her mother came to visit. She used to spend half summers with Cioran, the other half with her mother and her brother's family, bringing up three nephews. One of her nephews visited her recently, and when he saw a book by Cioran on the table made the connection between the writer and the name on the door, and exclaimed: "Is this the same man? I love his books." Soon afterward, Cioran himself wandered into the room in his bathrobe, hearing voices and thinking that it was morning—he had lost his sense of time—and asked for his breakfast. He met the nephew, who was stupefied at discovering his aunt's double life.

Simone says that for many years now Cioran has stopped reading and writing, just sits in his room and rummages through his papers while she tried to keep up appearances in a lost battle. He had been aware of his condition and was infuriated by it. Once, after having begged him to take a bath, which he repeatedly refused, she went away crying. He came after her, embraced her and said, "I'm a sick man, forgive me."

They had planned to commit suicide together, like the Koestlers, but then Cioran fell ill, and now it's too late.

I must remind Simone that I am still planning to write an intellectual biography of him, and that he had agreed to it. She is now a crucial informant. Will she agree to it? Will she talk as freely as before? Will she let me look at his papers? There are papers. What will she do with them? I must ask her. I must bring myself to talk to her about these issues. But it's not easy. Now is a bad moment. She lives from day to day, focused on keeping him alive. But if I don't do it now and go away again, someone else is bound to come and ask permission to write a biography.

May 13. Chocolate coffee cake in Place Monge, and then back at the hospital around three. It's a gray and rainy day, I'm wearing my gold-colored velvet suit. I find Cioran on his bed, all dressed and ready to go for a walk with a nurse. He's happy to see me, though he has no idea who I am, but, ever the gentleman, behaves as if he does. He's like a crab shell on a beach, the contents are dry, but the outward form is still there. There are snatches of phrases, gestures, facial mimicry; he winks, he starts up a sentence in his old familiar way, "C'est . . . ," raising his hand to brush away his mane, and then stops abruptly, having lost track of the words that were supposed to follow. You can see that the thought is there but the words don't come, and so you try to guess, but if you miss he gets very angry. There are flashes of light in his darkness, and they must be terribly painful. Sixty years ago, in *On the Heights of Despair,* he described his condition with incredible prescience: it is not madness but the moments of lucidity in madness that are to be feared.

We walk around the corridors. He walks pretty well now, at times he hardly needs any support. He looked around full of curiosity. He recognized the room he had previously stayed in, then peered at another. When the nurse said, "That's not your room, Monsieur Cioran," he replied, "No, that is a whole other universe." We went back to his room, and I foolishly tried to get him to sign a Spanish translation of his *Fall Into Time.* He took the pen but couldn't hold it properly so he didn't sign. He started leafing through the book and paid no attention to me any more. I kept quiet since he seemed quite content to be holding the book, leafing through it endlessly, peering at pages as if he could read. It's obvious that reading is for him a pleasant and familiar occupation. Finally, he turned toward me and said, "This is a very interesting book; there are some deep things in it!" Then he looked at my arm, and stroked the velvet admiringly, "c'est beau ça!" The first of many compliments he paid me this day.

He likes looking at me, and I like him to. He makes me feel as if I were a nice bouquet of flowers or a beautiful landscape. I like pleasing him. One so rarely knows what others want or think or what it takes to give them pleasure, but in this case there is no doubt that he likes looking at me. It's worth paying him my visit. He held my hand and said, "I thank you for coming; you can't imagine what your presence is like here, in this . . ." But he couldn't find the right word and said, "asylum culture." "Atmosphere?" I suggest lamely. "Yes, yes, asylum atmosphere." I wonder though if "culture" wasn't better after all.

Though he is in a pretty expensive asylum, it is an asylum nevertheless. It's more like a madhouse than an old people's home. There's a woman wailing ceaselessly in a monotone, "Let me go, let me go, give me my clothes, open the door." Cioran hears quite well, and she bothers him. He can't help noticing all the shuffling, crippled, grimacing ghosts surrounding him when he walks outside his room. They are like phantasms out of a Goya painting.

Visit from Verena von der Heyden-Rynsch, one of his translators from German. Literary agent, former nun, she is in love with him. Simone says that "elle s'est toquée de Cioran" [she's smitten with C.]. Simone is quite weary of her, though they are very close. I can't blame her; it seems to me that all her life she had to endure other women adoring Cioran and crowding in around him. He is very attractive to women. Come to think of it, most of his translators are women. Like me, half in love with him. And he has many women friends. Probably his writing appeals more to women than to men. What attracts us is the erotic undercurrent in his writings—though he hardly ever writes about love or sex—the visceral quality of his prose, the voice of an angry young man any woman would love to take in her arms and soothe with soft caresses. The "intimacy" of his thoughts might seem indecent to many, but to women it's attractive: confessional, sentimental, feeling-driven, passionate.

Verena is in her fifties, tall and portly. Sharp bird-like features and a thin, bright red mouth. She bends over Cioran in a proprietary but affectionate way, and speaks to him lovingly and intimately in German, his second language. Though it's none of my business, I can't help wondering what his relations to her are.

S. came around five, and he didn't seem to know her at first, addressing her with "vous." Very politely, C. wouldn't sit down until we did, and wouldn't eat his cake until we did too. He ate a big dinner and seemed to be in a good mood, once in a while desperately trying to formulate one of his *bons mots.* What an irony: this sparkling conversationalist, who used to dine out on his verve, now deprived of words. His eyes start to twinkle, he opens his mouth to say something, starts up with a word or two and then stops, face darkening, closing up and collapsing into himself and his despair. When we were about to go, holding my hand and stroking my face, he said, "your, your . . ." His mouth hangs open as if trying to pronounce the letter "a." I tried to guess, "apparence" [presence]? "Yes, but more than that, more than *prietenie* [friendship]," he said. "We, in the universe, the rest is of no importance." I said, "M. Cioran, I too love you. One can't but love you when one translates your books." He seemed touched. His last words that night, "Come back." S., who tries to leave without him noticing, was waiting outside. Later she told me that she was pleased to see him caressing my face and looking so happy. Of course, I will come back. These two people have affected my life profoundly.

Dinner with S. at a little Italian restaurant nearby. We chatted a long time. As usual, she's very open and talkative. She's known C. since 1942. She met him at the student cafeteria where they both ate. She remembers he had a hard time in Paris: there were pressures from the Romanian military attaché who wanted to send C. back to Romania, to the front lines. He went about with a packed suitcase—ready to go into hiding. He didn't think his fighting was going to save Romania.

On C.'s fame. He was not really well known until well after the death of Sartre. After the publication of *Exercises d'admiration.* That was in the mid-1980s. Late indeed. *Précis de décomposition* (1949) was a success, but he was not reviewed very much afterwards. C. crushed and angry.

Sitting up in my hotel bed, writing. I wish the French had regular pillows on which I could prop myself against the wall instead of these little sausage-like head supports. I'm sneezing, and I'll probably catch a cold. The bare wall is damp and cool. I've been out every evening until tonight. I'm exhausted.

C. was very restless, almost violent yesterday. He kept getting up by himself, trying to walk alone. Impatient with his visitors. Besides me, there was another French woman, Christiane Fremond, who helped him revise the French version of *Heights.* Back from a tour of the corridors—same pungent smell, same shouting lady plus other howls and moans from unidentified sources, all very disquieting—he wouldn't sit down, shouted at me, then whispered, "Je regrette." He seemed very unhappy. As we were coming into the room, he said, "C'est la démission totale." The moments of lucidity in this broken mind are horrible. No wonder he was angry. Who, in their right mind, would want a witness to so great a degradation? I stayed a while after Christiane's departure, but he kept saying good-bye to me so I finally left. While still there, I helped him with his tea. He kept getting up from his chair, mumbling, "Ça n'a pas . . ." I filled in, "du sens." He looked at me and laughed and said that I was right and we'd be friends. Then he sent me away. His last words, "We should now part *en camarades*!"

At S.'s that same afternoon. Tea with petits fours and whiskey. She had some copies of C.'s books for me to take away. We looked at pictures: C.'s family in Răşinari, C. in his late forties in Paris, many more recent ones as well. A very photogenic and extremely good-looking man, not very tall, but wiry; fair-haired with green eyes under bushy eyebrows, a strong masculine, stubborn jaw, a leonine head of hair. The eyes, in all pictures, are striking, penetrating, the eyes of a visionary. I particularly liked one picture. C., in his mid-thirties, maybe, looking lean and fit, wearing a dark suit, bareheaded, leaning against an old ox-cart in a ruined courtyard somewhere in Spain. He is lightening a cigarette, with an air so manly and self-assured, he could have been a Hollywood star: Humphrey Bogart comes to my mind. Hard to accept that this is the same man crumpled in his chair at the hospital.

I asked S. what she knew of C.'s life during the Occupation. Did he still have a scholarship from the French state? In that case, who paid it? The Vichy government? She said he no longer had a scholarship. On what did he live, then? There were rumors that he had been a tour guide for the Germans since he could speak German well. She said all that was invented. I have a feeling she may not be entirely truthful. I must double-check. Who would know? I've been told by a pretty reliable source that after the liberation C. was arrested for a few days on charges of collaboration, then released. If he worked as tour guide, that could be construed as collaboration. There must be records in the police files; there must be official records of all fellowships as well.

The retrospective afternoon became an ordeal for both of us. S., who had intimately known the man in the pictures, was overwhelmed with grief. Two hours of looking at pictures, their entire life together spread out "like a patient on a table," she was close to tears and eager to see me go. I felt like a spy or a thief, totally disgusted with myself, ready to abandon my project. Prying into people's lives in the name of literary history did not seem like a good excuse. Really, confronted with her raw pain, I didn't feel like I had any rights at all.

May 14. Today I spent a wrenching afternoon at the hospital. The whole biographical thing, all this digging into other people's past—its sadness, its almost indecent quality—is getting to me. My nerves are on edge. I feel like crying all the time. My uncle, who is a homeopathic doctor, prescribed against anxiety some tiny white round pills that come in tiny tubes. I'm supposed to pop the contents of a whole tube under my tongue and suck them till they melt. Funny little pills, it's like playing doctor. I hope they work. I keep seeing C.'s younger face, the one from the photos, and cannot help imagining him as young, healthy, a charmer, a talker, a seducer. There must have been many women in love with him. Imagine this frail body with swollen red feet, scaly white skin with brown spots, the sunken face, pale eyes, as it once was, making love? What terrible punishments, old age and senility!

I stayed almost three hours at the hospital. He spent a long time folding and unfolding a napkin. He looked at a picture book, I read to him from the English preface to *The Trouble with Being Born,* recently republished in England. He listened attentively and seemed to understand; then he said, "Ce type écrit mieux que moi!" [That guy writes better than I do!]. When I told him it was his own writing, he opened his eyes wide with surprise and exclaimed humorously, "C'est vrai? Alors je suis au-dessus de moi-même!" [Really? Then I'm better than myself!]. He laughed and puffed as if he couldn't quite believe it. He hasn't lost his sense of humor, isn't it amazing?

Now I know that when he gets restless and has that pained look on his face it is because he wets his diapers. Uncomfortable, he moved from chair to bed and back. I tried to help him move, but he was angry. He must be conscious of what is wrong with him and embarrassed that I'm there to witness it. He, of all people! How he hated old age and the decay of the body. How he raved and ranted against it, and he was right: nothing in this world can prevent me or anyone else from reaching this last stage, nothing except suicide. I felt his humiliation; I felt guilty and scared and angry all at once. Why should strangers like me come and watch what's left of Cioran wet his diaper? Being a biographer is much harder than I thought.

Hard, indeed. I must talk to S. again and be more definite. Does she approve of this book, which is bound to be controversial since in it I must acknowledge C.'s political involvement? She is very welcoming and friendly with me, but is she really willing to talk to me truthfully and in detail about her knowledge of his early days? I must be forthright. Ask her if there would be a French publisher interested in my book. Make sure she understands the nature of my project: an intellectual biography. A chapter in European intellectual history. How did this man make himself into the essayist and moralist so admired today? Focus: the transformation from a young radical to a tempered moralist; the effect of exile; the two lives, first the controversial early period, then the reclusive writer. Make her understand that one must acknowledge C.'s political involvement. Make sure S. knows, approves, will help, talk. There'll be others, journalists, opportunists, who will certainly want to write biographies. But I feel I owe it to him. I respect him, and I have background knowledge of his origins. I'm aware of how awful all this is for her at this moment, but when would be a good time for me to come back? There are papers, when would I be able to look at them? And would I?

May 16. Lunch with Verena. Friendly enough, but I wonder if she is not sounding me out for some hidden agenda? She suggested I talk to Eugène Ionesco's wife, Rodica, about C.'s early years. Not a bad idea if I could only get through to her. Marie-France, their daughter, stands guard there like a ferocious bulldog. Verena offered to make contact with German and Spanish publishers, and Gallimard as well, when the book is ready. Boasting or offering real help?

Later, at the hospital. We sit around as if we were in the cave of the oracle at Delphi, watching, waiting, trying to make sense of the mumbo-jumbo that comes out of his mouth. From the darkness, gems occasionally fall out. A mind that twitches and struggles to find itself. C.: "La vie est une saloperie!" "Ici, c'est un monde à part!" "L'existence m'a fait ça!" "Avec vous, l'univers ne compte pas!" [Life is rubbish! Here, it's a world apart! Existence has done this to me! With you, the universe counts for nothing!]

May 17. Titian exhibition in the morning. Long hot ride on the Metro from the Grand Palais to the hospital. Found C. alone, finishing his dessert, half-spilled jars of sweet mush. At my urging, he tasted a few raspberries. S. had not come yet and he was unwashed, unshaven, his face smudgy all over like a baby's. After lunch, he always has his walk. I had to help him out of his chair and onto the wheelchair all by myself. Very awkward. My back hurts, I'm not very strong, so we both tottered and almost fell. The blind leading the blind. Vladimir and Estragon. He's very afraid of falling and was annoyed with me. Outside he was restless, and having only me to support him made him nervous. He constantly sought the support of a wall with his other free hand. Then we stopped to rest, and he made me walk around, looking at me very attentively all the while. When I came back, he said, "Vous avez un très beau visage." I'm glad he likes looking at me, for I'm not good at all at guessing the meaning of his half sentences beginning "C'est vrai que . . . ," "Vous savez que . . . ," and then trailing off. It pains me too much. Yet he means to say something and is clearly frustrated by his inability to do so. Several times he would start a sentence, I would try to guess its content, he'd say "no," and we'd start over again until he would get quite mad. Back upstairs, the nurse put him in his chair, and he, taking his head in his hands, sighed, "quelle histoire!" I was myself on the verge of tears, feeling faint and dizzy. I left, trying hard not to break into a run. I don't think I can stand to go again tomorrow. Maybe Wednesday or Friday to say good-bye, although, of course, as far as he is concerned, it doesn't really matter.

May 17. Talk with S. who is naturally worried about my project. She recommended that I should contact Dan Mihăilescu in Romania. She is willing to talk to me, but she is difficult to talk to because she is edgy, touchy, picks on my choice of words.

May 18. Thinking back on my talks with S. and Verena. It's clear that S., though friendly, is cautious. She feels she has to defend him since he has always abhorred the idea of a biography, people digging into his past. She defends him fiercely, like a lioness, challenging every word I say. I'm interested, I say, in the making of the philosopher. "No," she interrupts me, "he wasn't a philosopher and hated being called one. Read his books!" His own word for his condition, *apatride*. She insists he never used the word "exile," but I remember him talking to me about "la volupté de l'exil," and he uses it in his interviews, in the title of an essay in *La tentation d'exister*, "Avantages de l'exil," and so on. It will be difficult dealing with her, but neither is she definitely against my project. When I finally asked if I should go ahead with the project at all, she said yes, she wanted me to. Verena talked to me about S.'s fears. She told me about Tacou, the editor of the *Cahiers de l'Herne* series, a Romanian who supposedly tricked C. into giving him the rights to his Romanian books by playing on C.'s fears about revelations from his past. Tacou apparently tried to publish *Romania's Transfiguration* without C.'s approval. Blocked by Gallimard, who now has all the rights.

C.'s avoidance of the limelight, his willingness to live in poverty, on the margins, his rejection of prestigious and lucrative prizes is not just a pose, but it isn't as disinterested as it seems. I think it is related to his fear of revelations about his past. He knows that fame and publicity bring about the inevitable search into the past. But in the end he didn't escape from it.

Phone conversation with Ioana Andreescu, a chatty Romanian lady friend of C.'s recommended by S. She mentioned several people's names, all working on C. The throng of biographers gathers and waits in the wings to gape upon the "wounds" of C.'s life. I am one of them. Ioana suggested inviting from Germany a young man, Leopold Ferdinand, C.'s translator and a favorite, who apparently has important letters from C. He might be interested in a collaboration. She asked me not to tell S. about this. She fears S. might be jealous of C.'s affection for LF. Can that be right? What nest or net of plots, jealousies, suspicions, criticisms, and vying for affection and favors have I fallen into? Ioana also tells me that Ferdinand, one of C.'s few male translators, is critical of Verena. Ioana herself seems to take an inordinate interest in this young man whom she's foisting on me.

May 19. Reading some of C.'s youthful articles, I notice that one of the recurring oppositions (a theme retained in his later work) is between decadent culture—old, rational, intelligent, with style, represented by France—and passionate culture—fanatic, barbarian, young, like Spain, Germany, and Russia. Romania has no culture of its own at best, whereas at its worst, it is a bad imitation of the decadent culture of France. And yet when he opted for himself, he opted for France, for style and the strictures of reason. He ran away from Romania, but not in the predictable direction, not toward the barbarian cultures he professed to love passionately. A case of spiritual masochism? He says somewhere that he intended to go to Spain, but the war prevented him. Still, I wonder if his choice of France is as accidental as he wishes it to appear. The war was perhaps a convenient pretext not to go away from the center.

At the hospital. C. is better physically, making progress every day. His mind, however, is like Baudelaire's old desk, full to overflowing with bits and pieces, odds and ends, little drawers that open to show their disparate contents, hanging out in a messy tangle. He looked at the flowers I had brought with me and said that they reminded him of "the village." "Răşinari?" I asked, suggesting the name of his home village. "Yes, yes, it's like a local pain as if. . . ." He kept repeating "local pain," stumbling over those words and searching for more. I had a knife in my hands with which I was cutting the stems of the flowers I had brought him. I started to imitate the movement of his hands, and then it occurred to me that what he wanted to say was, "as if one plunged a knife in your heart." Outside, the garden seemed too small, and he was so unhappy he suggested "une fugue dans la rue."

I met Sanda Stolojan as I was leaving the hospital. She was coming to visit. She is the translator of *Des larmes et des saints,* my French counterpart, as it were. The lady who cried when he made her cut the text. I introduced myself. She was very pleasant, promised to see me in December. She reminds me of cheerful and sturdy German governesses in Romania, with backpacks and solid shoes, a pack of kids trailing behind them in the dusty streets and parks of Bucharest.

May 21. Last visit at the hospital. François Furet was there. We chatted about the University of Chicago where he teaches part of the year. As we talked, C. had a light stroke right in front of us: he suddenly slipped on one side and crumbled in his chair, his eyes staring fixedly, all pale, very, very pale. Later, after the nurses were done with him, I saw him one more time on his bed, resting, a lonely bundle of frail bones.

At S.'s in the evening, one of her lovely little dinners: mozzarella, prosciutto, tomato and basil salad, kulebiaka, strawberries, raspberries, and cheese. Guest of honor, Marie-France Ionesco, Eugène's daughter, close friend of the Ciorans. In her forties, loaded with jewelry, name-dropping. Grew up on Celibidache's knee, she said.[3] I didn't tell her my mother was Celibidache's cousin. I had seen him only once, during his one visit to Romania. Another famous exile who preferred to ignore his origins. MF seems wonderstruck by the extraordinary event of having been born Eugène Ionesco's daughter. She has never quite recovered from its magnitude. Very cool toward me. Sized me up and down. We did not hit it off, to say the least. *Méfiante* because S. sings my praises. Jealous? A disappointing evening.

As I translate *Tears and Saints,* I come across the following Nietzschean paragraph: "dying with the body strained like an athlete ready for a sprint, the face lifted and staring defiantly at infinity." I think of Cioran asleep in his hospital bed, a small, helpless body, slightly crouching as if returning to the fetal position, and I'm once more struck by the cruel irony of his fate. He seems to have been punished with the kind of slow, unheroic death he feared most and the additional humiliation of losing his mind.

**1994**

May 23, 1994. The Marais: lovely day, a burst of red roses on the quais of the Seine. To Hospital Broca to see C., who looks good but no longer speaks. Yet his eyes are alert, he understands, agrees and disagrees, with his eyes. An afternoon in the garden with S. and a visiting friend, whose name I missed, an Ethiopian lady with striking big black eyes and short, cropped white hair. Her husband, now dead, one of C.'s friends in Paris when he first arrived here. S. told us a story about C.'s coming to her English classes at the Sorbonne. He would appear in his thick navy blue Romanian winter coat, his hat, and a German newspaper, the *Pariser Zeitung*, under his arm, causing quite a stir. He used to go to the Romanian Orthodox church for food hand-outs. Once he participated in a political manifestation there, the burning of King Carol's effigy. It must have been before Simone's time. She's known him since 1942. He's been in Paris since 1937. Five long years for which I have to find witnesses.

Today S. was practically bubbling up with stories. How Gabriel Marcel used to take C. to the theater; how he helped him get paid for his article on Valéry, which had been first commissioned and then rejected by an American publisher. She is very disturbed by the Romanian "plot" to lay claim to C.: rumors are being spread that he wants to go back to Romania, that he speaks only Romanian now. Some enterprising Romanian journalists went to the Maison d'Assurances to find out the address of the hospital, and they came to see him when she wasn't there, bringing along with them the Romanian ambassador to France. They took pictures, and left President Iliescu's letter praising C. and asking if he could come to see him. Now she has hung on his door a sign saying "Visitors prohibited." I wonder if it will do him much good. Her fears are not totally unfounded. *Lumea Liberă Românească,* a Romanian newspaper in exile, printed a notice about C. last week, reporting that he was very ill in a French hospital and had forgotten how to speak Romanian.

May 24. Dinner at Simone's with Christiane Fremond and Nicolas Popesco, a Romanian born in Montreal, whose father had known C. in Paris, and who wrote a thesis on C. at Yale. I was coming down with a cold and drank too much. S. was full of verve, told anecdotes as usual, but I was too fuzzy-headed to remember much. At some point she mentioned that C. loved Germany; that it was the country he would have preferred to be famous in.

Before dinner, I had gone to the Hôtel Méridien at the Porte Maillot to join the crowd of Romanian expatriates waiting for the exiled King Michael to come. He is in Paris for a conference on Romanian culture in exile. A mixed group of people and on the whole not very distinguished. Do all exiles look as woebegone as we Romanians do? Bedraggled women and cocky dark-skinned men. I kept repeating to myself C.'s adaptation of Montesquieu: "Comment peut-on être roumain?" [How can one be Romanian?]. The organizer seemed to be a madman, shouting instructions, with great violence and urgency. He did not stand on ceremony. Very dubious looking men skirting the edges of the assembled Romanians, shirts unbuttoned. With impudent dark looks, shouting slogans that seemed calculated to disturb rather than boost the atmosphere.

The queen and her daughter, princess Margareta, arrived first and worked the crowd. The mother, mild and polite, the daughter an ambitious girl, too pleased with herself. They don't speak Romanian. The king arrived late. Tall and good-looking, he spoke simply and briefly about his pitiful condition as an exiled king. He's been a most humiliated king, and we are a forlorn people. Watching him, the futility and sadness of the Romanian situation struck me with full force. As an icon, he has a certain undeniable grace, and because of that, he strikes me as even more poignantly hopeless.

Romanians in exile, what a confusion! There are the "legionnaires," with their rabid right-wing sympathies, and then the many others. The legionnaires are full of that "passionate intensity" Yeats saw in "The Second Coming," while the others just as conspicuously lack it. The legionnaires have a program. They are against the king who once persecuted them. They have an obsession with freemason plots, that is, Jewish plots. In many ways, they are not that different from the Communists. The legionnaire spirit lives on here and in Romania. Corneliu Zelea Codreanu's movement, *Totul pentru Ţară* (All for the Fatherland), has now reappeared in Marian Munteanu's new organization of twenty-year-olds, *Mişcarea pentru Romania.* The need for spirituality and the dream—or is it the nightmare?—of a fulfilled Romania returns with a vengeance.

At the Romanian bookstore in Paris, *Librairie du Savoir,* Mr. Piscoci, the owner, is undoubtedly a legionnaire sympathizer but also, I suspect, a former Securitate agent. He lectured me about the plots and lies of big country governments, especially American and English. To strengthen his argument, he showed me a book, *Les secrets de l'empire nietzschéen,* by a Hungarian anti-Zionist Jew who sees plots and assassinations everywhere, and who believed that Hitler was an agent financed by Masonic Jews! Mr. P. was very eager to talk, dying to find out who I was. To protect my identity and confuse him—a game I enjoy—I spoke English. He asked me to stay and join him for a cup of tea, but I refused.

Last day: touching moment in the garden of the hospital. S. talking as usual to keep C. entertained. She tells stories recalling their past. He listens with wonder in his eyes, but is clearly pleased. At some point she stops, looks up at him and smilingly says, "Yes, I'm talking about you, do you remember?" He stretches his hand, takes her by the chin and looks at her face with a poignant mixture of love and gratitude. His eyes, in spite of his silence, tell all. Hers fill up with tears, and so do mine, watching these two people who've lived such an odd and close life together for fifty-two years.

# Romania, 1994

## To Bucharest

On my way to Romania, I changed planes at the Frankfurt airport, outpost of the Western empire. All flights to Eastern Europe go out from the airport's shabbiest, oldest wing. Through it pass the barbarians: Romanians, Hungarians, Chinese, Africans. I wouldn't have been surprised to see Han Solo come toward me in the company of a few weird characters, robots, gorillas, or men dressed in the uniform of the Ruritanian Guards. The grim hallways, an anticipation of the grimness that lies beyond them, resonated with harsh-sounding languages, like dogs furiously barking.

In Vienna, where the plane landed briefly, most passengers got off. All that was left on the plane was a handful of people, down-trodden, bad-smelling, big-bellied, gold-toothed. They were mostly men, and about ten of them had the unmistakable look of former Securitate members. Only one of them spoke English. He wore a cowboy hat and spoke for the whole group. The rest were proud of their linguistic ignorance. They delegated their cowboy to tell the American flight attendant that "just speaking one language, for example, Romanian, is much better," and they all watched her reaction with an air of shrewd superiority. To prove their point, they cracked crude jokes about her in Romanian. At Otopeni airport, they were met by a group of medalled officers, and a few recruits with shaved heads to lug the luggage. The man with the hat, impatient at the slow-moving luggage conveyor belt, waved his hands, and rhythmically shouted, "hai, hai!" A VIP van whisked them away. I walked out behind them with a knot in my stomach. It was my first time back since 1986.

First impressions. A dilapidated taxi took me into Bucharest. The engine stalled twice on the highway, and I worried that I would be stranded in the grayish dun landscape. Fall is the best season in Bucharest because it isn't icy, wet, muddy, slippery, dusty, or melting. The rust-colored chestnut trees make Bucharest look like an Eastern European Paris. But from out of my taxi window, all is unrecognizable. Gray, dusky, and bare as if two natural disasters had happened at once: a tornado and a dust storm. The majestic trees were torn down, and the dirt accumulated in heaps that couldn't be swept away by any wind. My throat started to scratch. The taxi driver told me I should not worry. I had a case of the "fumes." Thousands of cars have invaded the city, most of them in bad repair. He ought to know.

The traffic is crowded, the drivers irascible; they drive fast and brake hard. Someone scrapes another car. The traffic stops, two hulks get out of one car and rough up the driver of the other car. Then they get back into their own car and drive on.

The streets of Bucharest are crowded with Dickensian children and gypsies: barefooted, in rags, with dirty faces, smoking, leaning against house corners in a stupor, asleep on benches, prowling, and begging. Like Fagin's band in *Oliver Twist.* A three-year-old is smoking a cigarette; a passer-by upbraids a woman who may be the kid's grandmother. To show that she knows about discipline, she snatches the cigarette away from him. The kid cries, slaps her, and kicks her in the stomach.

We drive by rows of decayed, dilapidated buildings. But their original beauty is neither completely effaced nor completely defaced. Bucharest is a medley of architectural styles. Art Deco, Bauhaus, Hausmannian, Near-Eastern. All buildings are in a state of disrepair; it's a bit like driving through the depressed downtowns of big American cities. Or Havana. Or Beirut. Ruins and potholes. Someone said that when it rained you could go around in a boat. Bucharest is now a big slum.

Downtown Indianapolis when I first arrived in 1977 was not much different except that it seemed emptier.

The country looks like a vast apartment that has just been ransacked by the Securitate and left in shambles. Heaps of junk, piles of garbage, stones, earth, broken pipes, and other machinery. Broken-down cars and trucks are everywhere, and there are always people under them repairing them, or around them, talking about the needed repairs, consulting with glee for hours on end. This must be the Romanian counter-part of Mediterranean *tertulias*, gatherings of men at crossroads or in the marketplace.

In the midst of all the chaos, a lot of wheeling and dealing. Retail business begins in someone's window if the window is conveniently located on the ground floor, or in the doorway of an old house, where people have set up tables with odds and ends, like garage sales in America. They sell bread and cigarettes, and above one window there is a sign saying *Societate de export-import*. Only one sign to advertise a makeshift bakery: a loaf of bread hanging from a wire by a window. Inside a gate someone sells detergent, toothpaste, and gum; on the hood of a car, a few nails, half-full cans of Russian paint, slippers, discolored dresses, thin sheets of metal, spare car parts. Bucharest has become a city of peddlers. All over the country, there are improvised markets and small businesses like mushrooms in a forest after the storm: the "non-stop" shops, the fly-by-night export/import societies, signs advertising sales *en gros* and *en détail*. A bazaar economy. One truly feels in the "gate" of the Orient, as they used to say of Constantinople. In the Moldavian markets especially, gypsies, citified peasants, and Russians from Moldova and Georgia are milling about the eclectic merchandise and heaps of the autumn crop, especially beets, potatoes, cabbage, red peppers, and celery roots spread out on newspapers or directly on the ground. Many Russians among the sellers, pushing suspicious-looking goods. There is whispered talk of a Russian mafia trafficking in Romania. I saw a bright red Ferrari with Georgian license plates parked not far from one of these markets. Begging and thieving also do good business.

Cioran's question, "How can one be a Romanian?" nags at me.

I live in a slum. The whole country looks like an extended slum. But the taxi driver who picked me up the other day said that I lived in a "select" neighborhood. Apparently many of the apartments in these hideous, gray buildings belong to former Securitate officers. That's "select." I'm in good company.

In Bucharest, I walk along with my double, who sometimes is a five-year-old, at other times a teen-ager. Like Proust's Marcel, who, stumbling over a stone in Paris, remembered Venice, I, stumbling over the potholes of this harsh, grim, and grimy city, remember former Bucharest, only a shade less gray and grim, and return to my former sense of alienation and imprisonment. If I am on a bus or the metro, I hold myself aloof. I hardly dare breathe; I wait to get off in a sort of suspense that is supposed to preserve and deliver me unsullied at the end of my public transportation trip. I kept myself aloof the entire first twenty-four years of my life. I find, to my great distress, that it isn't hard to fall back into the familiar pattern. On the contrary.

Visit to my old family home. The wooden front staircase leading to the first floor, my mother's pride, which she used to wax and polish weekly and which we were not allowed to use except on grand occasions, is now gray with ingrained dirt. Windows and doors broken and boarded up. Massive metal locks on those that aren't. "This is no longer my home; it is only of a past time."[1]

Afterward, I strolled through Parcul Ioanid, a small and dusty public garden situated between my old house and the university. I used to walk through it daily when I was a college student. But my links with the dusty old park go even further back. I used to be taken there to play by an old lady who ran an informal French kindergarten. Zecu, I called her, unable to pronounce her whole name, Mrs. Lăzărescu. I have a photograph of myself from that period, and that park, which I remember as a greener, happier place, with a graceful wooden kiosk and a small pond bordered with chestnut trees and flowering bushes around which we played tag and hide-and-seek. In the photograph, I am dressed in a checkered frock with a white round collar, and I have a big pout. I like the defiance of the pout in that picture. It expresses an attitude of rejection, a negation. It says that I refuse to be happy on cue. I still have a mental pout. The park looks smaller than I remembered it, the pond is dry, there are no bushes, only a few trees, and the gray dust in which toddlers and dogs still play.

I am free now. But am I free? I feel sad today.

The launch of my father's book, *Naufragiul* [The Shipwreck], at the Mihai Eminescu library on Bulevardul Magheru. My father soared to heights of eloquence. He has not been a lawyer for nothing; he can speak so well, so movingly. He is articulate; he can be funny. You would think he is another person, not the old man in a ragged bathrobe crumpled in a shabby armchair in his apartment, eternally complaining about how unfair life has been to him. Yesterday he looked smart in his business suit, a fresh new shirt on, a bit of cologne on a white handkerchief tucked in his breast pocket. Afterward we had a little reception at his place. A mixed bag of people, some literary reviewers, some relatives, his publishers. The latter are a very suspect bunch. They have promised my father some money for the book but have not yet delivered on their promise. They talk big, but my father is so easy to bamboozle. I remember that once, in the 1950s, he came home proudly carrying several bottles of sunflower oil he had bought on the black market. Only they turned out to be colored water. My mother was furious and used to retell the incident to prove his worthlessness for years afterward.

His novel has come out in a cheap edition, with innumerable typos, even occasional text changes. His editor is either illiterate—and that wouldn't surprise me a bit—or he took liberties. My father, however, is immensely pleased and doesn't seem to mind. He never thought he would see his novel in print. He has been writing this book for thirty years. It was his hobby. He wrote it the way other people play tennis or golf or watch movies. Any time he would feel depressed, he would shut himself in his room and write a few pages. It is a romanticized version of his family saga covering two world wars and the post-war Communist takeover. My father exorcized his demons by writing. To my mother, his writing was a sign of weakness. He wasn't good for anything else; he wasn't made for real life the way she was. But look at him now, basking in his success, with his nearly two thousand pages of manuscript behind him.

Whenever my father had his "writing fits," he would cancel his business appointments. But he wouldn't bother to inform anyone. So people would arrive and wait in the dark hall at the center of our apartment, around which our rooms were arranged. He would send me to tell them he was not at home, that all appointments were cancelled because he had been detained at the courthouse. Some would not leave; they had pressing business and preferred to wait. So they would sit there and wait in the semi-darkness of our hall, on hard, uncomfortable, medieval-looking carved wooden chairs, like ghosts in the ante-chamber to Hell. They were a shabby bunch, and I felt sorry for them, and angry with him. He sat only three meters away, locked behind his door, pounding away on his typewriter. I still wonder how he got away with it. They must have heard the sound of the typewriter, and they must have guessed he was there. At the time not many people, except licensed professionals, were allowed to have typewriters.

My father is a good storyteller, but because he never thought he would be published, he never revised his book. But he's lost his drive, he feels old and beaten down, and since he's lost his eyesight in one eye, he feels even more helpless than before and justified in his helplessness. I should be like Milton's daughters, copy his manuscript out for him, rewrite it, do all the needed editing work. But I don't. I can't write in Romanian anymore. Not literary Romanian. I am also busy with my own research project on Cioran. Still, I can't help feeling guilty for not helping him more.

My father comes over to tell me that he's been hailed as the Tolstoy or Proust of Romanian literature. I tease him: either Tolstoy or Proust! But he takes all this praise seriously. And why not? If only it would make him happier.

**In Sibiu**

October 1. Driving out of Bucharest to Sibiu, the Transylvanian town where Cioran grew up. This trip can't be very different from what I imagine driving through Haiti would be like. The countryside is a God-forsaken place, a stretch of flat, gray, weedy fields, dotted here and there with the rusty iron skeletons of rambling, industrial shacks and the ruins of the old collective farms. The highway—the "best" highway in the country, the only four-lane highway built in this area because it connected the capital to Ceauşescu's birth place—can hardly be called a highway: it has no shoulders, no marked exits. All exits and entrances look like country dirt tracks. They are making repairs all along this highway, but there are no warnings, and cars coming from the opposite direction appear suddenly on your side of the median, coming straight at you. The road is littered with industrial debris, rubble, odd pieces of machinery, tubes, holes once dug for an unknown purpose and left unfilled. It is as if some big, ambitious project had been abandoned in disgust, or despair. Or, alternatively, as if there had been a war, and the country had been bombed for a long time. The four-lane highway stops in Piteşti, a large industrial city. It ends in a muddy plain; a flock of birds flies above it, black dots in a gray sky against which are silhouetted factory towers. Geese and cows come straggling across the plain and onto the road.

I almost had an accident near Sibiu. It was already dark, and the road was full of potholes, so I drove slowly. The lights of incoming cars blinded me. I stopped abruptly in front of a hole that opened its large jaws just inches ahead of me, and when I looked up I was stunned to see a truck on the other side of the chasm. The driver had also stopped because of the hole, thank God! Because of repairs, the two-lane road had turned into one lane at that point, but there was no one to control the traffic and no warning signs. I was very lucky.

October 2. First contact with Relu Cioran, the younger brother who stayed in Romania and served seven years in prison. A soft-spoken man, he looks like his brother Emil—same thick head of white hair—but he does not have the latter's piercing, tormented eyes. Yet he suffered while his brother meditated on suffering.

We had lunch that turned into dinner in an old Saxon peasant house, bought by Relu's wife from a German who emigrated back to Germany. The house is in Cişnadioara, a German village now almost taken over by Romanians, just a few kilometers away from Răşinari, the Ciorans' native village. We had grapes and nuts from the orchard, and then a copious lunch, *tzuica* (plum brandy), and sausages in abundance. Food is both an obsession and a point of honor with Romanians.

Only later in the afternoon, when it was already getting dark and rainy, did we get to Răşinari, situated about fourteen kilometers from Sibiu, a rich old Romanian city in this German enclave, with big houses in Teutonic style lining its cobbled streets. A small creek runs through the village. The Ciorans' old house is at the end of a street abutting on the creek in which the Cioran children, like today's village children, used to play. Geese and goats, and cows and people drifting through on their way home in the late afternoon traffic. The old Romanian church where C.'s father was a priest is farther up at the end of the same street. The father, Emilian, originally from Răşinari, a village with a tradition of resistance in the Austro-Hungarian Empire, died in 1957.

"You are mean people, you, the people of Răşinari," says Ica, Relu's third wife. There's resentment in her voice, but Relu seems pleased: he takes it as a compliment, yes, the people of Răşinari are "mean"—hard, not easy to break. He was not broken by years of prison, by years of menial work in a milk factory. He is still here, while his brother is lying in a hospital bed in Paris. The mother, Elvira, from a family south of the Carpathians, died in 1966. Relu showed me a book written by their father about a family of priests from Răşinari who played the role of defenders of Romanian cultural and social ways in Transylvania. From just browsing it, I can see clearly that the father closely identifies with his subject. As members of the village intelligentsia, active in movements for the national and cultural emancipation of their Romanian flock, the Cioran parents received recognition in death. Their tombs lie in a place of honor, across from the village cemetery, near the tomb of Bishop Andrei Saguna, an important Romanian cultural figure in Transylvania.

Relu reminisces in a soft, almost dreamy voice. His name, and those of his brother and sister, like most Romanian names in Transylvania, are names of Roman emperors or place names (for example, the Via Aemilian). Emilian, Emil, Emilutz, Lutz. Aurel, Aurelian, Relu. "Lutz," as they called Cioran in the family (Romanian "Luţ"), left the village at age nine to live with a German family in Sibiu. Relu, three years his junior, followed a few years later, when the whole family moved to Sibiu.

Relu last saw his brother in 1941 when the latter returned briefly to Romania from France. This is new information to me. C. never mentions this return in his interviews, never said a word to me about it. But according to Relu, during his stay in Romania in the fall of 1941, C. obtained the post of cultural attaché at Vichy. He was either fired or resigned a month later. Relu thinks his brother wasn't cut out to be a salaried employee.

Tomorrow: ask Relu about letters and manuscripts. Who has them? What are they? Ask about family history and early childhood in Răşinari. Anecdotes?

October 3. I spend the morning with Relu. Naturally very talkative, he gets shy and quite formal as soon as he is in front of the tape recorder, although I explained to him that I'm taping only to save myself the trouble of note-taking. It will be hard to tape him, unless I do it when he is unaware. He's promised to show me the letters and manuscripts he has. Meanwhile we went to the offices of the *Euphorion* magazine. He's given them letters and photos to publish, and they are friendly to him. They let me photocopy (for free!) part of a book, a monograph on Rășinari.[2] Friendly bunch of young people, sharing two small, bare-looking rooms, three typewriters and a copy machine. A lot of comings and goings, coffee drinking, smoking and chatting. Relu just hangs around, humored by them, happy not to be alone. Over lunch, in a nondescript cellar with half gypsy, half German motifs, he tells me of his marital woes, his wife's jealousy. He's planning to run away to Paris to see his brother without her.

From bits and pieces he tells me, I can put together cameo stories about "Lutz."

Lutz in Brașov, unhappily teaching philosophy to high school students. One day, a student asks: "What is ethics, sir?" Lutz's angry answer: "There's no such thing as ethics!"

Lutz used to come back to Sibiu for summer, winter, and Easter vacations. He used to read a lot at the Astra Library, the Bruckenthal Museum, the Theological School Library, and some private libraries no longer in existence. He spent long nights arguing about theology with his father and theologians from the seminary. He was obsessed with theology and music. Relu confirms what C. said about himself: he was not an atheist. He was a believer who couldn't believe. As he put it somewhere, "My effort to believe ended in failure." Relu is very religious. As we go by a *troitza* [a roadside crucifix], he makes the sign of the cross.

Another story about Nae Ionescu, the (in)famous philosophy professor whose demonic magnetism and verbal facility fascinated his students. Though he lectured, he gave the impression that he was holding a dialogue with his students. In a letter dated March 16, 1940, from Constantin Noica to Emil Cioran on the occasion of Nae Ionescu's death, and now in Relu's archive, I come across "He [Nae] was the only man who had already, while still living, the dimension of a legend." Also: "I now reflect upon everything that the Romanian *logos* has lost." And, "For the first time, I feel in exile, an orphan, I have a new understanding of the Romanian non-being."

Lutz's proverbial scowl, expression of his existential discontent, is almost like a signature for this early period. Among the youthful jottings and notes in Romanian, French, and German kept by his brother, I find the following: "The ideal woman's reply to my propositioning her: I must turn you down, for to sleep with you would be like sleeping with all human angst rolled up in one!"

Lutz was most unhappy during his military service in the artillery, when his scowl never left his face. He was very anti-social; army discipline was an insufferable yoke. Anything that had to do with groups and organized activities repelled him—one of the reasons why he never became a registered member of the Legion, while his brother signed up as soon as he got to Bucharest, where most students were right-wing. According to Relu, Emil knew Corneliu Zelea Codreanu,[3] but he never was interested in him, since he thought he was less refined intellectually than Moța.[4] Codreanu's genius was for organization, and Lutz hated that. Nor was Codreanu a good orator, but he was good-looking, had charisma. In a letter from Relu to his brother in Paris, dated March 5, 1991, I find the following lines: "You, just like Eliade, try to suppress an option we had in our youth. I understand you but I don't concur. . . . Don't take the above as a reproach but as a secret sadness."

Talking about the Legion and their involvement with it—his own quite open, his brother's limited and indirect, according to him—Relu brings up the subject of his brother's controversial 1936 book, *Romania's Transfiguration,* recently republished in Romania. He is eager to defend his brother and gets quite irate, shouting at me that the word *"legionar"* doesn't once appear in the text, and that an author has the right to change his book until the day he dies. He is referring to the debate in the Romanian press about the cuts made by C. in his book before allowing its republication. From the original version, a raving praise of fanaticism as Romania's only way to historical greatness, C. has cut some significant parts, including chapters on Jews and Hungarians. Many have protested the republication of this book, whose fanaticism, with or without the incriminating chapters, is perceived as dangerous and irresponsible. Also C.'s foreword, so ambivalent that it seems hypocritical, since on the one hand he rejects his earlier book as youthful ravings with which he no longer identifies, while on the other he still likes it well enough to allow its republication.

I remember C.'s qualms about this book, and I remember him talking about the cuts he was making when I visited him a few years ago. He was talking about those cuts as if he had hit upon a bright solution to his dilemma. They were republishing all of his early work in Romania, right after Ceaușescu's fall, in the euphoria stirred by a newly free press. The best publisher in the new world of the free Romanian press, Gabriel Liiceanu, a friend and disciple of C.'s friend, the philosopher Constantin Noica, had undertaken the enterprise of reprinting this fascinating author who for so long had been a cultural taboo. He was, in fact, launching his own publishing house by reprinting Eliade, Ionesco, and especially Cioran, the least known at home of all three. Cioran was caught in the euphoria of the moment, and he lowered his usual skeptical guard, giving in naively to the adulation and enthusiasm arriving from home. Moreover, Liiceanu, as Noica's disciple, had good credentials, and C. wanted to support his budding publishing house.

But one thing is sure. By 1991, Cioran was already ill, though it may not have been evident. I first met him in August 1990, so I remember vividly my first impressions, my fear and shyness in front of the grand old man, as well as my amazement when

I realized that the great man was not quite there all the time, that his thoughts wandered, he repeated himself, forgot what he was saying—all clear and, to me, dismaying symptoms of senility. He had already lost the lucidity and incisiveness that had been his trademark. Had he been in his right mind he would not have allowed the republication of *Romania's Transfiguration* for merely sentimental reasons; he would have treated his book with the same severity with which he treated all his other work. When *Tears and Saints* first appeared in France, for example, he made such drastic cuts and revisions that the short French version was practically another book. Trouble is, deep down C. was fond of *Romania's Transfiguration,* relic of his former intellectually vital, if crazy, self. He was ambiguous about it, however. He never allowed it to be translated abroad. He allowed its republication because it was to be in Romanian, and he hoped the book would be contained by language and country. He was wrong.

In any case, the controversy sparked in the Romanian press by the republication of *Romania's Transfiguration* is an interesting example of what Bakhtin calls the dialogue between a book and its context. What is in the book varies greatly, depending on so many factors: author's age, political atmosphere at the moment of publication, by whom and why the book is published. The Romanians' desire to print the book after their so-called revolution, and the various political motives that went into the publication decision, as well as the mixture of political and sentimental pressure put on a weakening C. in order to obtain his permission for republication, are not to be ignored, and are possibly to blame.

Relu's manuscripts. From Emil's university years, seminar papers: "On Henry Bergson," "Cosmologies" (1st year), "On Max Stirner" (2nd year), "Theism as solution to the problem." Unpublished manuscripts: "Considerations on the Problem of Knowing in Kant," "Philosophical Anthropology," "On Protestantism," "On the Tragic," "Contemporary Intuitionism," "Pamphlet and the pamphleteer," "Provincial Letter." This is what survived the parents' eviction from their home and Relu's years in prison. While Relu was away, Emil's books and manuscripts rotted in boxes. After his return, another calamity struck: Relu's first wife, in a fit of jealousy, made a bonfire with them in their backyard.

**Back in Bucharest**

October 19. Depressed. Cold. Lonely. Awful. I have been leafing through issues of *Dilema* and *România Literară* at the Library of the Department of Romanian Language and Literature in the old university building. Unheated nineteenth-century reading room with high ceilings, the librarians wearing ski clothes to keep warm.

I'm reading Zigu Ornea, literary historian and journalist, who seems to have cornered the market on the inter-war period. Very well researched information, but he harps on only one theme, which makes his work both monotonous and frustrating: Cioran, whatever the circumstances, was a fascist sympathizer and therefore wrong. Also a certain amount of bad faith. In reviewing a book of Eliade's correspondence, he came across a number of letters from C. in which the latter expresses strong reservations about the Iron Guard. Ornea dismisses the letters with, "No matter, he was a sympathizer nevertheless." Not very professional, to say the least. Leafing through his own thick book on the Romanian intellectuals of the 1920s, written in the 1980s, I notice that its first hundred pages or so are dedicated to a history of the Romanian Communist Party which has very little, if any, bearing on his subject, but which is obviously the "tribute" the author had to pay in order to see himself published at all. How can he then so severely blame C. for his youthful mistakes, when he himself is morally and intellectually tainted? C.'s involvement with the Iron Guard was problematic but earnest, originating in youthful idealism, however misguided, whereas Ornea's own involvement with the Communists was most likely due to baser motives, an adult decision to compromise, the hypocritical lip service that one had to pay if one wanted to see himself in print. Tricky, slippery terrain, and a simple black-and-white view of things will not help sort them out.

Met Alexandru George, literary critic and novelist. Editor of the work of the inter-war literary critic Eugene Lovinescu. He has a wide range of knowledge about the Romanian literary scene during the inter-war period. Politically, he says he is a liberal from a family of liberals. He asks me to send him Lord Acton's history of liberalism. I like him. He is an endearing eccentric. He comes to visit me, never wants me to go to his place. He forbids me to call him under the pretext that his phone is broken. He called me one day literally out of the blue. That's how we made contact. Someone on the literary grapevine had told him that I was in Bucharest working on Cioran, and he called to offer his help. He is a lonely man, and part of his willingness to talk comes from his need to have people to talk to. I hear he lives in very poor conditions. He arrives, in a patched sweater under a worn-out brown trench coat, unshaven. First he wants me to give him a drink of "something special." He means a foreign drink, though he does not ask for alcohol. I have a bottle of fresh juice ready now whenever he comes. He is very loquacious. He saw my little tape recorder and was entranced by it. I turned it on, and he just let himself go. The opposite of Relu in this respect. One day, when he saw I was not taping him, he pointed to it and asked me, "Why aren't you taping?" "Well, I thought we were not ready yet, we're still chatting." "No, I want you to start taping right away!" So I did, and it seemed to make him so happy.

October 24. I've fallen behind with my notes. A week of what I had forgotten was typical Bucharest weather: gray, fog, wet, cold. Coming home last night, out from the damp cold into the cold drabness of my apartment, I remembered Ken and his boots. Twenty years ago, during our courtship, when we used to walk the cold streets of Bucharest because we had nowhere else to go, he had found the cold so unbearable that, in most unromantic fashion, he put on sturdy winter boots in order to keep on walking with me. Used to cold rooms, cold bathrooms, cold streets, I found his confession of weakness so endearing and so strange! I don't find it strange now. I wish I had thicker boots and more sweaters. American comforts have spoiled me. Yesterday we had no heat in the apartment building. There was some feeble heat coming through the pipes this morning, but I am forced to use the gas stove to be able to sit at the table and write.

My next-door neighbors. I met them yesterday as I was coming out of the apartment with Alexandru George. My neighbor was on the landing with his brother. Both in suits and hats, the Securitate officers' trademark. One in black, the other in light brown. Alexandru wanted to know the way to the nearest metro station and asked one of them for directions. They ignored him completely and shamelessly stared at me. Questions came like rapid fire: Who am I? From where? They were very confused because I spoke Romanian as well as they, yet they knew the apartment was reserved for foreigners. They couldn't place me accurately, and they were annoyed. I deliberately answered in a mysterious way, and they were like two hounds on a trail of blood. Meanwhile, Alexandru kept asking his question about the metro station, but nobody paid any attention to him. He craned his long scrawny neck, fumbled with his glasses, looked bewildered. The whole thing was rapidly becoming a comedy of the absurd. I finally appeased my inquisitors by telling them I was a Fulbright scholar. They became obsequious. The dark suit introduced himself as former desk officer at the Ministry of Foreign Affairs. He did a stint in New York, he said, obviously proud of it. Not because as a spy he served his country, but because he too had been in America, where his "two beautiful daughters" were studying now. He wanted me to meet his daughters, he became quite chummy. "We have many things in common," he said. I shuddered at the thought.

Sunday. Met Dan C. Mihăilescu, his wife, their seventeen-year-old daughter, and their cat, Mowgli. We hit it off very well. All three are bright and pleasant. He knows a lot but writes in a fragmentary manner, he is spread over too many jobs: the literary supplement of *Cotidianul,* the literary reviews of *22,* translations, research at the Călinescu Institute. His wife also works two jobs, one for the Soros Foundation and the other for Radio Free Europe. Thus they make ends meet and put their daughter through the French school. He is very generous with the Cioran stuff he has.

October 27. Melancholy fall day. Today I walked to the Fulbright Commission office housed in the former Zambaccian Museum, along badly paved streets lined with beautiful mansions, many of them embassies. The "Şoşea" is still one of the most elegant neighborhoods of Bucharest.[5] The discreet charm of a Bucharest full of potholes. As I was coming around the corner of an usually quiet street, I was startled by a loud, aggressive male voice shouting: "Can't you see that they are all facing this way? Why do you put yours the other way? I could have parked that way myself. Do you think I didn't know I could? Damn it, you are a driver, can't you see there's a logic here!" I looked to see why all the shouting. One man had parked his car at the end of a line of cars all facing in the opposite direction. Or almost all, because further up the street there were some exceptions. But the guy who was shouting seemed to take it very badly, as if it was a personal insult, and kept repeating that he too knew how to park facing the other way if he wanted to, despite the "logic" of the pattern. Romanians hate to feel inferior, no matter what, and it was hard to tell which infuriated the man more, the violation of the pattern or the implied suggestion that he couldn't violate it himself if he wanted to! One of those "Kafkaesque" moments of absurdity that are simple realism in Romania.

Later on, I went to the Writers' Union on Calea Victoriei for another book launching. I recognized the faded sumptuous glory of the building. I had been there once before, a long time ago. Trying to remember. With whom? My old boyfriend, son of a writer of Romanian children's novels. And why? A dinner in the restaurant? The restaurant is still there, downstairs. As smoky as ever. How forgetful can I be? It all comes back with the vagueness of a dream that one tries to piece together in the morning.

Upstairs. Speeches from a tribune, old ladies and old gentlemen—who are they?—sitting in the front row. I stared at the brocaded walls, the faded golden-framed mirrors, the gold leaf molds on the ceiling and listened the meanwhile to Mircea Martin, my former prof at the university. Humorless and stiff as if he had swallowed a stick. I remembered him as open-minded and fun, what has happened to him? The Indiana University English department at a memorial service for a deceased colleague is a million times more entertaining than this.

Liiceanu, director of Humanitas Press, the successful publishing house that reprinted all of C.'s work, including the infamous *Transfiguration*, was among the speakers. Short, stocky, with the head of a Roman emperor like the heads one sees on old coins. A smooth, smart talker, a quick intelligence. Asked to say something on the spur of the moment, he picked out a few of Martin's better themes and delivered a pleasant little speech. He has a particularly beautiful voice, low, enveloping, caressing, and authoritative at the same time, slightly pompous too, but beautiful nevertheless. I talked to him briefly, introduced myself. He was unnecessarily and ostentatiously polite to me, so much so that he was rude to other people, and I was shocked, almost insulted. As we were talking, someone came up and introduced himself, but Liiceanu cut him off abruptly, "I'm talking to this lady now!" Very embarrassing, since I had stepped up to him in similar fashion just minutes before. One does so at cocktail parties. Why this display of deliberate rudeness?

October 29. Good working morning at the Museum of Romanian Literature. Everything upside down there since they are renovating the building, and everybody is stuck in little back rooms, cold as hell in spite of the nice autumn weather outside. C.'s letters are very entertaining. He can't even write a boring post-card: everything is exciting and intense with him, he finds striking formulations, and since he always talks about himself, he's an ideal subject for a biographer. It is obvious that his addressee is more or less a pretext, and his letters, like his books, are a mode of self-expression, only more intimate.

At the museum, they let me look at the material they have on my great-uncle, Paul Zarifopol, a comparatist like myself, literary critic, good friend of Caragiale.[6] Besides the photographs, letters, and manuscripts donated by the family, I discover a secret donation of fifty-five letters to his last lover, a young woman of Armenian extraction almost thirty years his junior. The friendly museum staff lets me borrow the letters to read at home. The donation papers stipulate that they are not to be published until fifty years from now.

Lunch with my father. He's in a good mood since he had been receiving a lot of praise for his book. Newspaper articles, radio interviews, fan letters: the works. His few weeks of fame. But he does not want me to think that all this success and publicity is going to jolt him out of his existential unhappiness.

Home by taxi loaded with shopping bags. Phoned Ken. Lonely. The melancholy end of a day that started with a dead body under a white sheet in the dusty patch of grass between our building and the one next door. A few candles flicker in the grass near the corpse, policemen and passers-by gaping curiously. Falling accident? Suicide?

October 30. Wet and cloudy, tufts of fog scattered in the darkening air. It suits Bucharest better. Yesterday's sunny warmth clashed too much with the grim surroundings. I came across large groups of deaf people both in the morning and the evening. I wonder what they were doing in my neighborhood—maybe attending a conference at the Youth Sports Palace, not far from here? Their agitated silent gesturing added to the weirdness of the street. I forced myself to take a walk around the lake in the park across the road. Muddy, unkempt paths, scattered groups of pale-faced, skinny people, looking like convalescents from tuberculosis, two boys playing tennis over a string attached to two trees, the court marked in chalk on the asphalt path; farther up the path, a few boys with an old soccer ball, and another little boy with an improvised fishing rod—or was it a whip?—his parents watching in silence as he tirelessly hit it against the ground; a man washing his hands in a sewer pipe; adolescent girls, and a young man making obscene gestures at me. I look with wonder at this devastated landscape, surrounded by decayed apartment buildings and the carcasses of yet more unfinished, and never-to-be-finished, buildings, at the rows of bushes and roses planted in a onetime attempt to make this a people's park. I feel like an inmate in an asylum. Why am I here? How can I get away? I panic every time I hear my father, imagine cataclysms (planes falling, a war, an earthquake) that will force me to stay. I escaped once; I may not be so lucky a second time. Back in the apartment, I overhear my neighbors fighting and swearing at each other. I can't help it—the walls are so thin. Father (presumably the same man I met on the landing) to the son who did not get the top grade in math: "Fuck you! Do you think that anybody bothered to send me to school when I was your age? Shall I tell you what I was doing? I was sent out to guard the sheep!"

I divide my evening between my great-uncle's love letters, Manzoni's *The Betrothed,* and Sofia Tolstoy's painful account of her marriage to Tolstoy. All of them fantastic reads. Cranky old Tolstoy hated sex, but his vitality was stronger than his will. So he would have sex with his wife and then punish himself and her for their shared weakness.

From Manzoni, chapter 10: "There are certain moments when the human heart, especially in youth, is so disposed that only the faintest pressure is needed to persuade it to undertake any action that has something to do with virtue and self-sacrifice; just as a newly open flower nods softly on its stem, ready to grant its fragrance to the first air that breathes upon it. Those moments should be treated with admiration and the tenderest respect by the rest of us; but cunning and self-interest carefully spy them out and catch them on the wing, binding in chains the will which they have taken off the guard."

Relevant in relation to Cioran and all of our youthful follies.

Paul Zarifopol's letters reveal a sensual, passionate man, haunted by premonitions of death. Unlike Tolstoy, no trace of remorse in them about sex. I think of his photographs, the beautiful, though severe profile, the closely cut balding hair that exposed the strong bones of an imposing, tall forehead, the icy cool blue eyes and the thin lips pressed together in a faint ironic smile. Nothing in them betrays the mixture of passion and despair unfolded in these letters, the sheer physical joy he finds in his young lover's body, the energy he spends in thinking about her and writing to her. And then there is a letter in which he describes to her how he looked at himself in a mirror while visiting his aunt's house (the house where I grew up, I know the mirror he is talking about!) and sees himself pale and ghost-like, life drained out of him.

Cioran allowed me to translate his books when he learned I was Paul Zarifopol's grand-niece.

November 1. I walked around my old childhood neighborhood again. This time I took pictures, though what's the use? I don't want my mother to see them, it would make her terribly sad. Shall I show them to my son? And what shall I tell him about the dilapidated buildings that would mean something to him? I try to make sense of our lives; this "here" was a reality for a long while, and now, nothing. In true romantic fashion, I look for signs, for correspondences, for a secret language that would all of a sudden be revealed to me as I wander about looking at the house, retracing my steps through familiar streets, recognizing familiar trees, backyards. This is my past, and like Ozymandias—though not so grand, of course—it lies in ruin in front of my eyes, but it refuses to speak. There is no moral awaiting me as in Shelley's poem. This silence scares me more than the sternest of warnings about the vanity of things.

Lunch with my father, who was in a storytelling mood. He tells me family stories I had never heard before. How, when my grandparents heard from a man in the village about the expropriation act of March 2, 1949, my grandmother panicked, ordered the carriage, got everybody into it, and, leaving everything behind, drove to the station and took the train to Bucharest. After their dash to the station, they never saw their old house or their things again. In April 1949, they went to another nearby provincial town where they lived under police surveillance at home, while, little by little, their other friends were getting arrested and disappearing. My grandfather died in February 1951 from a blood clot, just in time to avoid his own arrest and imprisonment.

Another story: how Alexandru Voitinovici, prosecutor of Marshall Antonescu, used to come to our family country house in the days before the war, when he was a young prosecutor in Roman, and my grandfather was president of the tribunal. He showed up uninvited in September 1946 at my aunt's wedding, where he was coolly but politely received (Antonescu's execution had taken place in June). In the morning, my uncle Paul, or Lulu, as we called him, the youngest of the three brothers, ran after Voitinovici's car shouting, "Long live the marshal!" My father attributes my uncle's later persecution at the hands of this same man to this particular incident, but I think the man didn't need any pretexts.

My father has been rereading his novel in its new (to him) and marvelous (though to me so poorly done) printed form. He reads and rereads and cannot have enough of it. He is on his fourteenth reading now. And he confides to me: "You know, I really think I am a good writer! The more I read the more I admire myself." He does not edit his text, however. Leaves everything as it is. What a pity!

November 3. At the offices of Humanitas, the most successful publishing house in Romania, to have my interview with Gabriel Liiceanu, its director, a philosopher and disciple of C. Noica, friend of Cioran. A bulky man, built like a bull, acting like a bull. Impressive head, big jowls, balding forehead, aquiline nose. An extremely cultivated voice, velvety with fleeting steely inflections, and brusque manners that betray the authoritarian, velvet glove and iron fist. Sharp, impatient and very self-preoccupied. With me, distant, polite, something undefinable but deliberately insulting in his manner. Today I arrived about ten minutes before my appointment and was waiting in the secretary's office. When he came in, he looked at his watch as if to reproach me for an early arrival, and then busied himself with things for exactly ten more minutes. He loves to play the role of the busy and efficient man, always on the run, always with something weighty on his mind, much more important than talking to you. Precisely at 10 a.m., he ushers me into his office, and without even attempting to talk to me, he just took out the manuscript of C.'s letters he had promised to let me photocopy and was about to hand it to me. But I, at the same time, was bending over, looking for my translation of Cioran's *Heights of Despair* to offer to him as a present. So I am not "at attention" for him as it were. He gets impatient and says in an annoyed voice as if I were a naughty child: "Are you going to look at this or not?" "Oh, yes, yes, of course," I reply straightening myself up, "but here's something that might interest you." He takes it, looks it over, and then with a sneer: "But how come you know English so well, because, you know, one must know it *to perfection* to translate this. It can't be anything less than perfect." I mumble something inept about my seventeen years in America, to which he counters: "Yes, but still it must be *perfect,* and how can that be?" I didn't insist; the deliberate insult was floating between us like foul breath. I took the letters and went out to copy them. When his secretary offered to help me, he yelled: "No, no, the lady will do it all herself!" Thus making sure I understood that I couldn't expect anything more from them. But he must have some interest in me, for Dan C. came later to tell me that Liiceanu had shown him my translation. Envy? Marking his territory? Power games? Next morning, in what I think may have been an attempt at friendliness, he addressed me less formally and asked twice in a chummy voice whether I was all right and if my work went well. But, beyond that, he couldn't find anything more pleasant to say. I didn't try to engage him either. Under all that intelligent polish, I sense a vulgar arrogance. To me he is just another Romanian bully.

Dinner last night with my cousin, Tess Petrescu, and her husband, Dan. Dan, a fastidious man with an impish glint in his eye, was one of the few vocal dissidents in Romania during Ceauşescu's last year. He lived several years under house arrest in Iaşi. He held for a brief period of time a ministerial position in the provisional government but has now retired from politics. He disapproves of his former friends Liiceanu and Pleşu. Liiceanu, they tell me, is very visible. He has just published an open letter to Andrei Păunescu, the detested former official "court poet" for Ceauşescu. The letter, Dan maintains, is designed to increase Liiceanu's popularity. Things are going badly for intellectuals in Romania right now; there are restrictions on the freedom of speech and the press, and the committee for historical monuments has just been disbanded. Romanians haven't yet learned how to live in freedom; intellectuals are narcissistic and obsessed with power. They become autocratic as soon as they get it. Liiceanu is a case in point.

Dan is an epicurean. He gives wonderful little dinner feasts. Very fastidious, he cares for his body like a woman: his nails and cuticles neatly cut and pared, fussy about shampoos, uses only Armani cologne for his beard. Short, with a rotund potbelly, he reminds me of a little ribald monk from Chaucer's *Canterbury Tales.*

Ilenutza, Tess's mother, is a ghost of former times. She rose from her bed to greet me in the semi-dark room where on a bedside table she keeps photos of her murdered son, Ion "Néné" Culianu.[7] She tells me family stories. Some about Paul Zarifopol, my great-uncle, and his youthful passion for Ada Culianu, his first cousin, and his mother's opposition that nipped the relationship in the bud. Also about PZ's idyll in Germany with Tania Dobrogeanu-Gherea, daughter of Romania's socialist writer Constantin Dobrogeanu-Gherea; she later became his wife. Ilenutza evokes scenes in a park at a German spa at the turn of the century, where visiting relatives from Romania felt left out because "Pavaluca," as he was called, spent all the time with his future father-in-law, who was indoctrinating him with his socialist views. The abandoned, discomfited relatives sat on a bench in the park, from where they spotted Emperor Wilhelm II, the Kaiser of World War I to come, passing through a nearby alley. They found some comfort in the sight.

Ilenutza tells her stories with great verve, chuckling to herself as she goes along. She had another good story about our Tante Sophie, the old maiden aunt who lived on the first floor in our house in Bucharest and used to give me piano lessons. She had been jilted by her French lover. He went to France and promised to come back, but he married there. Years later, when she was in her seventies, a man came to visit. As she couldn't see very well, she got up from her armchair, came closer, peered at him, and exclaimed: "Is it only now that you are coming, idiot?" They renewed their friendship, however, and he came to eat his lunch with her every day.

November 8. Nine o'clock. Lonely. Listening to Radio Free Europe, waiting for a broadcast on Ion Petre Culianu. Home earlier than usual, happy to be out of this dusty, polluted city. This morning I thought it was foggy, but later, as the fog persisted at the street level in spite of the sun, I realized it was smog. My eyes bother me a lot. Earlier today I went to Romania's Cultural Foundation, an umbrella organization that comprises a publishing house and a newspaper and basically manages government money for cultural activities and propaganda. Zigu Ornea, the historian who writes on the Romanian intellectuals in the 1930s, runs the publishing house there. I couldn't help but be struck by his quirky appearance. He looked like a character out of Dickens: very short and bald, with a prominent bump in the middle of his forehead like an ostrich egg, glasses on a floppy sort of face, all lines curving downward, and stubby fingers with open sores around their tips. A smooth talker, very knowledgeable, but slightly hypocritical. He told me he never meant to embarrass Eliade, Noica, and Cioran with the incriminating evidence of their participation in the fascist movement in their youth. How am I expected to believe that? He talked about the historical truth which must out, and they are dead anyway, he said, and moreover, they had published enough. I mentioned having read his 1980 book on the intellectual scene of the 1920s. Although I did not mention its fawning first chapter on the Romanian Communist Party, he must have a guilty conscience, since he was quick to defend himself.

On the way home, I stopped at the duty-free shop. Hard to find, windows with thick patterned glass through which you couldn't see anything, a minuscule sign above the door. Inside, two policemen reluctantly let me pass when they saw my embassy card. They wrote down my name on a list. I felt uncomfortable. I still get tense when confronted with people in uniforms. Some habits are hard to shed. I bought a few things for my father and left. Further down the street, on a dusty piece of grass in front of a gray apartment building, a big black rooster with its head cut off jerks around spraying blood. I did not go to see my father today. I must space out my visits and presents because he's too obsessed with money, what I buy, how much I spend. He says I am a big spender. As if it weren't all for him! On the bus, young teenagers on their way from school, sharing trashy magazines bought on the street, with pages full of prostitutes in various explicit positions. This is called freedom here. Coming out of the elevator, I meet a man waiting in front of its door. Suit and hat de rigueur. He shouts at me: "Why do you bang the door?" I don't reply, and he keeps shouting insulting words. There's a lot of pent-up anger in everybody around here. Or maybe he's a brute who wants to flex his muscles at someone that looks different, an easy victim.

November 18. Foggy, foggy day. Fog thick enough to cut with a knife. Stray dogs everywhere. One lucky dog on Bulevard Ana Ipătescu had a doghouse and a bowl of food. The doghouse was made of rough planks and set against a fence. A boy was playing with the dog; he must be the dog's protector!

It's been raining for about a week now. An early winter. From my apartment window on the eighth floor (Boulevard of Youth No. 21), I see the paved streets below full of dirty puddles, the melancholy park across the street with its trees not all dead yet but swathed in sheets of fog, the battered cars, so many nowadays, and the hurried passersby with their perennial plastic shopping bags. And I remember another time—I woke up this morning with this memory vivid in my mind—a late lunch on a felled tree trunk up at Vovidenie, the little hermitage not far from the monastery of Neamţ. It was simple and delightful: *brînza de burduf* and the *zacusca* given us by the good peasant of Borsa (Maramureş), and green walnuts so hard to break loose from their shell. Sounds: the *toaca,* the wood bars the monks use to drum out their call to mass, the noon bell clanging, and the rumble of a tractor bringing wood from the forest. Sights: the hill of Pocrov, the hermitage further up into the mountains, sloping downward toward the Sadoveanu house, where once I spent three days visiting with friends.[8] Here I am at the window, sick with longing like the hospital inmate in Mallarmé's poem.

Later. Yesterday, as I was walking home at loose ends, I met Horia Patapievici, who seemed very happy to see me. He took me to the offices of the journal *22* and then to a performance artist's show in a hall at the back of the National Theater building. We walked along a narrow corridor, he rushing in front, I lagging behind, vaguely aware that the corridor *was* the show, but Horia still looking for it at the end of the corridor somewhere. Some people we passed by warned us against the pipes hanging from the ceiling. Along the walls, tiny photographs were lined up, so small you had to go up very close and peer at them. They were photographs of mass scenes. "Witness" photos: bits of film with scribblings that indicate what's on the reel. The idea of half-finished, unpolished material that is not made by the artist himself but with which he worked. Same idea for the pipes on the ceiling, unfinished task or job. Title of the show: "It's your turn!" At the end of the corridor, a TV with a bit of fuzzy film on the screen showing the map of Europe. In various languages, it said "go east, go west!" General idea of the show: stop being an amorphous mass, go and see the world and make yourself known. Thank God the artists, a husband and wife team, were there to explain! The man then showed me some other work of his: a big canvas covered with tiny bits of paper drawn in ink with heads and fingers pointing mainly (the fingers looked like so many penises to me), stacked up so that they formed many tiny books. Its significance: guilt. Yet another piece, a whole wall covered with tiny drawings of heads, each with a different expression, rows and rows of them, from afar it looked like a printed page.

Finally, "Dracula Land," a bunch of wooden spears set in a square space, and on the wall around, projections of naked men's bottoms.

Afterwards, Horia and I had coffee in a little bar across from the American Embassy, next door to the former house of Soviet-Romanian friendship. He told me that he felt "light, ready to jump around like a kid," and that he was "available." I didn't ask in what way because I'm afraid I know. The last few years have been very good for him, ever since the gurus of Romanian intelligentsia, Liiceanu and Pleşu have decided to take him up as the bright new hope of Romanian letters, the bright new kid on the block. They compare him not only to Cioran but also Kierkegaard! A former physicist, a self-taught man, he's now doing a doctorate in philosophy, writes essays for *22*, and has his first book coming out soon. Everything's going his way, so he's elated. For years, he tells me, he lived like a hermit, going to work in a factory outside Bucharest, coming home and throwing himself into writing. He has a nice, simple, good-hearted wife and a five-year-old kid but seems eager for a sexual adventure, since he imagines it goes with the newly conquered territory of fame. Noica and Liiceanu have a reputation as philosophers-and-lovers around town. Maybe he thinks I fall into the pattern of good luck he's describing; maybe that's why he was so happy to meet me today. He was very insistent that I describe to him the contents of PZ's love letters. What kind of sex were they having? He wanted details.

November 20. A week, a whirlwind. I'm very tired from staying out so late every night. American Thanksgiving party at the American cultural attaché's house. Small group: the Fulbright people, the attaché and her husband, who is also employed by the embassy. Security? They are both from Chicago. Very middle-class, middle America. Reminded me of Ken's family, but blander. Dinner consisted of a previously frozen turkey and a few dishes of the customary vegetables or fruit (corn, green beans, yams, and cranberries) taken straight out of cans shipped from the States. (I did better at the little Thanksgiving party I organized for my father.) Frozen pumpkin pie. Afterward we watched last year's football games on tapes. The house, however, is beautiful: spacious, comfortable, all on one floor, with a graceful entrance way, a curved driveway that sweeps up in front of a door covered by a shell-shaped glass awning. They complain that it is too big, not practical enough; they'd rather live in an apartment like other embassy employees. They obviously don't give many parties, but the house is ideal for entertaining on a large scale. They drive around in their air conditioned Volvo and have not learned one iota of Romanian. How insulated can you be when you have to represent the most powerful country in the world?

November 25. Reading at the Archives of the Ministry of Foreign Affairs. Housed in a Soviet-style building, surrounded by policemen and soldiers. They give you the third degree before they let you in: one must first call an in-house number, then someone comes to get you, your bag is checked, and you pass through an electronic gate as if it were an airport; then you fill out some forms and are given a badge in exchange for your passport. Five or six security officers stand around joking, doing nothing much except flirt with the one woman officer who is the only one who checks your bags. When I had to go to the bathroom, a man in a dark suit came along. Seedy, dirty, gray dusty corridors, and small wooden doors with frosted glass that have no signs on them. The bathrooms have no toilet paper—there is a string dangling where the missing roll should be; the door didn't close properly, so I had to hold shut it with one leg while peeing. I was taken to a small room with two wooden tables and a few chairs, where a number of "researchers" sat me down and fired off questions, supposedly meant to be helpful, but it was clearly another sort of security check. They all wore the invariable suit, and they all disappeared after a while. The real archivist finally came and really did help me: I found some interesting stuff on Cioran's brief stint as cultural attaché in Vichy.

I also went to the Library of the Academy. The premier library of the country is housed in a utilitarian-looking building, something like a factory, all in gray cement. At the entrance, dominated by huge black heating pipes sprouting from a shack in the once beautiful park around the building, there are broken cement steps and dirty, worn, pale green linoleum rugs. As you come in, you almost stumble into the men's urinal whose door stands open right next to the entrance. The main reading hall resembles a hangar for storing airplanes rather than books. It must have been terribly cold in the years when they had no heating. There are rows of black-topped tables with steel legs and, at the far end of the room, on an elevated platform overlooking the room, an angry librarian—always angry, even when it is not the same person. Always a woman, she shouts impatient orders to the young people employed in bringing the books.

November 28. Busy finishing up research work and seeing people. My old high school friend, now a successful lawyer, Adrian Vasiliu, was a delight: bright, with a strong, sharp mind. I remembered him as a tall, thin adolescent, always with a big grin on his face. He has grown thick like a tree trunk and has huge tired bags under his eyes. He used to be a math whiz; he also wrote poetry. Still writes poetry. Thinks about going into politics, would like to see a supreme court on the American model, independent of government politics in Romania. If only more people like him got involved in politics, things would maybe change. A pleasure talking to him.

Translating for Ted Anton and Tess.[9] Tess adored her brother, Ion Culianu. In Romania, he was surrounded by adoring womenfolk: Tess; his mother, Ilenutza; his maiden aunt, Anutza. Naturally, Tess guards his memory jealously. She and Dan are editing his work; he is editor-in-chief at a new publishing house that publishes all of Néné's books. They think of him as the only genius Romanian letters produced after Eliade and Cioran's generation. I'm still undecided as to how much was genius, how much shrewd self-advertisement, how much sheer weirdness. His writings are very erudite, but there's not only a fantastic side to them, but also something *fantasmagoric*. In many ways, he simply copied Eliade. At the Academy Library, I glanced at an Eliade bibliography and was struck by how many of Néné's topics of interest repeat Eliade's. Take, for example, their common interest in magic, the manipulation of minds and space. Only for Néné it becomes translated into a modern-day conspiracy of the media, to which he adds the discoveries of cognitive science, math, and so on. The strange, apparently incoherent world that in fact coheres to the smallest and most incredible detail reminds me of Umberto Eco's novel *Foucault's Pendulum*. I hear that Eco, who knew Néné, used him as a model for one of his characters in his book.

Evening with my cousin Miron, his wife Marianne, and one of their women friends. They all reminisced about 1989–1990, trying to make me understand what happened then. The high points of the so-called revolution they called "moments of grace." Their friend described the enthusiasm that had taken hold of them all, then the unwinding and disappointment that followed; the miners' march on Bucharest and their attack on intellectuals and liberals; the conspiracy theory. Everybody I talk to seems to focus on two things: the goodness of the initial explosion and the loss of that goodness which followed soon afterward. Especially interesting is their resigned acceptance of that loss, as if it was natural to lose, as if loss is a matter of fact. Those "moments of grace" so nostalgically evoked seemed to have been the only pulsation of life for this forty-something generation, after which they fell back into old patterns. Things have loosened up a bit, but everybody is in his niche, busily surviving.

November 30. Wrapping up business at the Museum of Romanian Literary History. It's being renovated, so people crowd into a few cold back rooms. Looked at PZ pictures. Some date from around 1885. PZ as a young teenager with another boy (his brother?), my great grandfather. And many girls (his cousins) in the woods behind our old family home at Cirligi. He had a small frame and very sharp features. Another picture from the Leipzig years when he was a student: a sharp bony head, long straight nose, a mustache, crew cut hair, already balding. Several pictures from the same period, with Ştefania, his wife, who looks so much bigger, rounder, than him, near her he is almost dwarfed. Another picture shows him with his family and Caragiale's in Viareggio: wiry thin arms, a well-shaped torso in black trunks. One in particular strikes me: it dates from 1930, the time of his affair. He is in the mountains, probably Sinaia, where he used to go often, because they had a house there. He's in a golfing or hiking outfit accompanied by a lady, again too big for him. He seems to try to straighten himself to make himself bigger, and tilts to one side in a strained position. His thin lips are compressed to a line, giving him almost a mean look, his gaze is narrow and intent. His eyes are very sad—he is like the ghost of himself which he saw in his aunt's mirror and described to his lover.

### Off to Iaşi and Sibiu

December 2, 1994. Driving to Iaşi with Ted Anton and Tess on a cold clear day: a black, flat landscape dotted with frozen patches of snow. Stopped at a "non-stop," as the roadside restaurants are called, near Maraşesti, the old World War I battlefield. We briefly looked at the memorial and then had lunch in the car surrounded by hungry dogs, watched with great interest by a poor little boy who ate the sandwiches we gave him leaning against our car.

We stopped in the village of Cirligi to see my grandparents' former house. A huge manor house, stuck among fields of beets. The front porch has a row of white columns. What *folie de grandeur* prompted its original owners to build this palace in the middle of nowhere? My great-great-grandfather bought it from a boyar who wanted to become ruling prince of Moldavia. The house was meant to be his summer residence. But in the political auction games at the Ottoman Porte in Constantinople someone else must have paid a higher bribe for the throne, and the boyar never became prince. So the house was sold to my great-great-grandfather.

An old woman living in a house nearby came out and talked to us. She remembered the family well, the boyar and the "little boyars," my father, my aunt Ileana, and my uncle Paul. Paul used to take her dancing to the village balls along with children from the Anghel family, my great-grandfather's illegitimate offspring. She also remembered my grandmother, a big peasant woman, who used to wear a white scarf and Romanian peasant clothes, and who used to sing while weeding in the fields. The boyar (my grandfather) went around on horseback and was often spotted in the fields where she was working. He used to push her with the horse toward the bushes at the edge of the field where he would make love to her. He preyed on her until she gave in. She bore him three children, divorced her husband, the village policeman, and my grandfather married her against his father's will. She and the children were not allowed at the manor house while my great grandfather was alive. After he committed suicide, she moved in and ruled the whole place with an iron hand. She liked to order people around. She became godmother to many people from the village and was always singing. She was a good cook and gave big parties.

An old man minding a cow in the nearby meadow joined us. He is the caretaker. He offered to let us see inside the house. The lower floor is now used as a grade school: the long, narrow corridors with shiny wooden floor planks and high ceilings give off to little classrooms. Before, they had been the kitchens and the pantries and servants' quarters. This is the best-preserved part of the house. The rest, the front rooms and the upstairs, are falling slowly into ruin, rain is coming through the crumbling roof, and the plaster has fallen off, exposing bright red bricks like raw wounds in the walls. The old sweeping spiral staircase that goes to the second floor is wobbly. The old man opened a door off the first floor corridor and casually announced: "This is the room where *conaşu* [the old gentleman] hung himself." My great grandfather's ghost, so suddenly thrust upon us, drove me out of the house and into the pale evening light.

At sunset, back on the highway, the sky is all streaks of gray and pink. Black, naked trees are silhouetted against the flat frozen land all around us. The melancholy of this God-forsaken land goes to one's head like the fumes of a bad wine.

Tess's house in Iaşi is built on a corner, a low L-shaped structure, with rooms all in a row like the carriages of a train, and a wooden verandah all around it. In the winter garden the names of the trees—walnut, wild cherry, lilac—evoked visions of lost, lush summer vacations. An old actress, now working as a puppeteer, and her daughter, an aspiring actress but less good-looking than the mother, rent part of the house: two middle rooms, an improvised kitchen in a hallway, and a big, cold bathroom also used as storage space for wood and broken household goods.

The last time I was in Iaşi was twenty years ago, when I came to collect the prize I had won in a National Student Essay competition. The place is getting on my nerves. As a result I'm chatting a little too unguardedly with Ted, with whom I'm stuck at the hotel *Unirea.* Ted is totally out of place here, but his rambling presence is also a relief. He is living proof that a solid, well-meaning, but not very subtle world, Chicago, still exists somewhere else. The hotel is a high-rise building from the early 1960s. When I was nine, on a visit to Iaşi with my mother and sister, we had steaks in its drearily imposing restaurant. Ted and I are having dinner now in the same restaurant. A woman in a severe suit and a big fur hat placed us at a table facing the live orchestra across the dance floor. The dining room is a big square room like a waiting room in a railway station. It is furnished with drab Stalinist-style furniture, its cement walls covered in rough stone veneer. Four square, paneled wood pillars, decorated with wreaths of dry flowers, occupy the middle of the room. The heat was off, so people sit with coats and hats on. Only one woman, in a flashy red and black lace dress, once in a while got up from a nearby table where she sat with a man in a coat and a woman in a sweater, wandered around, and occasionally danced like a belly dancer with three other women. A drunkard standing in front of the orchestra, waved at them as if he were conducting, then wanted to climb up on stage and kiss the singer. Ghostly women waiters in black bring in the tasteless food. Over it, Ted and I talk about Ion Culianu and his family. It all seems so unreal.

Next Day. Crossing the Eastern Carpathians into Transylvania. I drive while Ted tapes Tess, who is telling stories about their childhood in Iaşi. She sits in the back and bends forward toward us, speaks in a low, plaintive voice. I translate. Driving on winding, narrow country roads half covered in snow through the Carpathian forests at an altitude of five thousand feet, translating this tale of woe, is too much for me. In fact, I feel I'm going slightly mad, and I'm surprised we don't end up in a ditch.

December 4. Back in Sibiu. Dinner at Cioran's brother's house with the Romanian triumvirate: Andrei Pleşu, Gabriel Liiceanu, and their painter friend, Horia Bernea, all there for Noica's memorial service. Pleşu and Liiceanu are like a pair of experienced comedians. Pleşu is obese, a bearded gourmand with a heart problem. A Byzantine Falstaff. He has a cunning look in his eyes but a pleasant, smooth and jovial appearance. Minister of culture right after the revolution, he's out now, yet keeps his irons in the political fire. He is editor of *Dilema,* a government-funded paper. He plays the buffoon to Liiceanu's voice of doom. Liiceanu always looking like an effigy, an emperor without an empire. As we were having a smoke out on the landing, he launched himself into a tragic diatribe against Romania and life in a society that denies the possibility of normality. It was a monologue: talking to him means one has to listen to a mixture of complaints spiced up with bragging. He seemed to enjoy himself in the part of the indignant, tragic victim of a corrupt regime. Striking, calculated theatricality.

Discussion of Romanian politics. To illustrate the Iliescu's government's unfair policies, Liiceanu tells the story of Radu Greceanu, the Romanian pilot who spent many years in prison, was tortured, had his legs amputated after they froze during the cold water torture, now living in utter misery on the outskirts of Bucharest, while the Securitate's former chief torturer lives undisturbed in comfortable housing for the party's *nomenklatura.* I ask them how such a thing is still possible? Pleşu's answer: "Because the people aren't with us." He also quoted Adam Michnik on the people's enthusiasm, which lasts only twenty minutes. Like everyone in Romania, they too are nostalgic about the "revolution."

December 5. Back in Răşinari with Relu for the day. Strolled around the muddy streets of the village, back to the house, the church, the cemetery from where I took a long look at Coasta Boacii, the wide slope descending from the forest of fir trees where the Cioran children used to play. One of C.'s mythic places. The slope ends at the wall of the little village cemetery. I remember C.'s anecdote about a skull they used to play soccer with. Stopped for lunch at the house of a rich hide tanner, an old friend of Relu's. Hot brandy, wine, sausage, and pork cutlets thick with fat in a small smoky kitchen. The world outside became a pleasant blur.

December 11. Back in Bucharest, I'm at Liiceanu's press for some last-moment business. His attitude toward me is still the same mixture of politeness and aggressiveness. His parting words to me: "I don't know how you will write this book of yours. This is a book that cannot be written."

# Paris, 1995

January 11. A month later. After Bloomington and California, now Paris. Listening to music on Radio Classique on a dark, rainy afternoon, cozy in this quaint but slightly ghostly apartment—Mircea Eliade's Paris apartment, lent to me by his (second) wife, Cristinel. His spirit seems to be floating around. The room is filled with pictures of him; there is a big one on the mantel from which he stares with forbidding eyes. I prefer to sit so that I don't see it. His library is so impressive I want to cry. I picked up a collection of mystical texts. Since translating *Tears and Saints,* I've become very interested in mysticism. Odd to be in this apartment as a chronicler of these people's lives. Eliade. Cioran. I feel like an intruder; I hope I shall do them and myself justice. A difficult task lies ahead of me. Simone has promised to let me read Cioran's papers before she donates them to the Doucet Foundation. But when is the appropriate moment to ask her? She's so preoccupied with Cioran in the hospital, all her energies focused on keeping him alive. Tactics, wait and see. Patience.

March 6. Back from Switzerland where a four-day snowstorm turned the sublime but civilized landscape into a muffled, white claustrophobic world. Felt the last lines of Joyce's "The Dead": "His soul swooned softly as he heard the snow falling faintly through the universe and faintly falling, like the descent of their last end, upon all the living and the dead."

Today I went to see C. at the hospital. I find him disturbingly weaker, with a pale, thin face, the cheeks sunk in, the chin protruding like a bird's beak, his green eyes like washed watercolors. He's been running a low fever for ten days now. His eyes stare intently into space without a particular object to focus on. Sometimes, a glint of recognition and a smile at a familiar face—or is it just a pleasing face? Does he recognize and identify? When Ken came to visit, he stared at his face, a strange man's face, very intently, searchingly, with a worried look as if trying to place him in time and not succeeding. The private nurse, Ana, a stocky, no-nonsense woman, tries to engage him in simple conversations. He answers docilely or politely with a "yes" or "no" or just a move of his head. He is like a little boy who wants to be good and then maybe the nightmare will go away. The impish spirit is still there, though. Ana jokes about the many women eagerly coming to visit him, he smiles and gives her a wink. I hear about one admirer I haven't seen yet, a pale, almost albino blonde Austrian who once in a while arrives from Vienna, stalks the hospital, sneaks into his room when nobody is around, sits staring at him or smothers him with kisses. She is apparently a crazed fan who for years has kept coming back, followed him around in the streets or waited at his door for a glimpse of him. Once, on a cold winter night, Simone noticed her as they went out for dinner, and she was still at the corner of the street when they returned, so she took pity on the poor woman and asked her up for a cup of tea.

March 11. Dinner out with Ken and Simone. She tells about the summer of 1947 in Dieppe. After some time together, she left to go and visit her parents, and he went to a nearby village to translate Mallarmé into Romanian. Failing to do so, he decided to give up Romanian and rode his bicycle back to Paris, where he started the *Précis de décomposition.* He has mentioned this episode of his "conversion" in many interviews. It is part of the Cioran lore, so to speak. The year is different, however: 1945 for him, 1947 for her. She also mentions something I have not heard before. That same year, they went to a lecture by an Indian mathematician at the Sorbonne. As they came out, C. reasserted his decision to give up Romanian. His mind was made up, he said. Had Romanian been universal, like a mathematical language, things would have been different for him. As it is, he no longer could afford to waste his time writing in Romanian. The confrontation with a pure, abstract language, Mallarmé's or mathematics, was the decisive factor for this ambitious aspirant of the absolute.

March 21. Spring is slowly coming to Paris. Lovely walk last evening on the right-hand side of the Butte Montmartre as one goes up from Place St. Pierre. Bright yellow daffodils and red tulips already in bloom dotting an otherwise still bare garden. Pale blue sky after rain, pink and gray clouds over the panorama of Paris. The streets behind Sacré Cœur are steep, with a provincial air about them. Ken is gone, I feel melancholy.

At the hospital, C. is growing weaker, paler, thinner by the day. He hardly eats anything and is often abstracted, with his eyes closed, or vacant, the mouth open, chin protruding. Yet even in his immense isolation, he has a thoughtful air. Sometimes his eyes are turned up toward the ceiling or the sky, reflected in the window of his room. At such moments, he looks the picture of a crucified saint. The impression is not of pain but of transcendence. Though he is gone, literally so, he does not look like a madman or an empty vessel like so many of the other patients. Even his weakness is impressive. And when he comes back to himself, he is so friendly, so courtly in his eagerness to please Ana or Simone, and the other people surrounding him. If it were not for Simone, who feeds him like a baby every day, he would not have resisted for so long. Her will to keep him alive is incredible. And she also feeds his mind: she talks constantly to him about his past, it is like a sort of mental gymnastics she does with him. But I can see that it's working less well lately. He used to listen with interest and laugh and participate as much as he could through broken phrases and facial mimicry. Now he often lies silent, out of touch.

One day I told him about our trip to the Alps. He likes to hear descriptions of mountains in the snow. He was invigorated and pleased by my descriptions of our skiing holiday, and even more pleased when I talked about Răşinari and his brother. His family used to spend their winter and summer vacations in a tiny hamlet hidden in the woods of the mountains above it, a place called Santa that barely had two or three houses. Relu had shown me pictures of C. skiing. That day, when Simone came, she found him as if revived. She was so happy she exclaimed, "I'm so glad to see you!" He opened his arms, embraced her, and answered, "moi aussi!"

Meanwhile I'm still waiting for Simone to make up her mind and let me see his papers. It's embarrassing: the man is dying, and I, like a jackal, am lying in wait to pounce on his papery remains. At moments like this, I wish I didn't have to write this biography.

March 26. Mini-dramas around the dying man's bed.

Liiceanu is in Paris with a second movie on C. and a book he seems to have put together hastily since I last saw him in Bucharest. A patchwork of his TV interview with C. and his earlier article in the *Secolul 20* [20th Century]. An enterprising man. He must have feared that I would beat him to it. Nothing to fear there, alas! I'm slow and haven't even managed to see C.'s papers yet. Liiceanu mentions, lightly of course, a difficult topic, C.'s link to the Iron Guard. To think that his last words to me were "such a book cannot be written"! He was referring to C.'s fascist past. He is the first to open the door. Fine with me. It makes my task that much easier. Now he is peddling his book to interested editors: he already has an offer from an obscure little publisher but probably hopes that Gallimard, who is bringing out C.'s *oeuvre* this spring, as well as C.'s interviews, would also want his interview, and therefore his book. He had sold the anthology of interviews to Gallimard but shrewdly kept this last one for his own book to make it saleable, especially now that things are getting hotter. A smooth player, a businessman.

Another character, Bill, a gay American journalist, now an expatriate in Paris, who's written some articles on C. and a book on musical references in C.'s work. I only saw a preface of his to an English paperback edition of one of Cioran's works, in which he talks as much about himself as much as about C., even quoting a letter of recommendation C. once wrote for him. Somehow he manages to work in even a poem he wrote. Irrelevant to the topic but good advertising of himself. He is on intimate terms with Simone. The only one of us that uses the informal "tu" in addressing her. What he is doing here now is unclear to me. Maybe he too is waiting.

March 30. Ionesco Symposium at Sorbonne IV. The community of Romanians in exile all present: mostly old ladies and old gentlemen in fur hats and galoshes. Liiceanu's long philosophical lecture on responsibility and freedom, to which he stuck on at the end a few remarks on Ionesco, was nevertheless a relief, coming as it did after an extremely boring Frenchman who had absolutely nothing to say except clichés. I don't like the man, but at least he is entertaining.

Met Liiceanu as I was walking out with Simone. Very cool toward me, hardly an inclination of the head by way of acknowledging me. His defensive/aggressive attitude hasn't changed, but now I see that it may be linked to his attitude toward Simone. Relations between them are very tense. Apparently his book has pictures of C. that overlap with those she gave Gallimard. She can't remember how he got hold of them, but I suspect Relu. He must have had duplicates of those pictures. She resents his publishing these pictures and also C.'s letters without even asking her for permission.

Simone is in a delicate position. Gallimard treats her as C.'s rightful heir, but not so the Romanians, especially Liiceanu. As publisher of C.'s works in Romania, his opinion counts. Since C. is still alive, and S. is neither married to him nor his legal guardian, the question of permission, of the right to decide what happens with the work, is left open to interpretation. Liiceanu has C.'s brother to milk for material in Romania and appeals less and less to Simone since she opposes him too much. Naturally, she feels cornered and exasperated, and doesn't trust anybody anymore, not even me.

This situation *in limbo* affects my prospects. For months now Simone has promised to let me look at C.'s papers before she gives them away to the Doucet Foundation, yet she hasn't done it yet. I'm just hanging around, getting quite fretful, for time flies, and if and when she lets me go there to read I will have a lot of work on my hands. She says there are about twenty volumes or more of a diary he kept. Not to mention the rest, manuscripts, letters, and so forth. She is not unaware of my plight. Yesterday she herself referred to Henry James's *The Aspern Papers*. Before C.'s illness, she said, she used to be on the journalist's side of the story—that is, for the man who was trying to get the papers. But now all of a sudden she finds that she has become the old lady who in the night finds him snooping around in the library. Why does she tell me this? Of course, I'm the journalist or the scholar, and often I feel like a thief, an intruder, just as the character in James's story. She is sly, playing a game of cat and mouse with me, some kind of flirtation. She likes me a lot, and I like her. But is this also a way of buying my affection? Sometimes I worry so much about this difficult human situation that I wake up and lie awake in the middle of the night, feeling time slipping through my fingers. I wish I could give the whole thing up, but I've already invested too much time into it, all those months in Romania, the translations, and so on. It's too late. The trouble is I sympathize with her plight. I see how everybody—just like myself—has an interest in getting something from her. I see that she cannot trust anyone; her vagueness and her forestalling are ways of protecting herself. But I'm afraid it only works with hesitant persons like me, not with bullies like Liiceanu.

C. looked better yesterday. Some color in his cheeks, more alert, he even kissed me good-bye. As we laughed and talked around his bed, the shadow of a smile would sometimes cross his face as if the distant echo of our laughter reached him in the transcendental regions where he floats now most of the time.

April 2. Still anxious about the C. papers. Simone continues to procrastinate; I don't dare mention it any longer. She has explicitly said that she would let me see them, but she keeps putting off the date. I feel tired. Paris is gray and wet, but unlike

New York, it's a city in which one carries the burden of one's loneliness lightly, without resentment. I see why C. loved it so much.

April 6. Dinner with Simone and Sanda Stolojan at Simone's apartment. Simone is beside herself with all the events, plots, and rumors going on. She bubbles over with new developments of various story threads. She tends to get too worked up, exaggerates, sees plots everywhere. It's understandable, though. On the one hand, she's tending to her life-long companion on his deathbed;, on the other, she is weighed down with the new responsibility of representing him and his rights.

Before C.'s sickness, they led quite separate lives, and she never took any part in his social life, nor did she influence his decisions concerning his work. But now she is left to replace him and defend him as best she can. She tries to protect him from prying journalists and photographers (especially Romanians) who try to get a glimpse of him at the hospital. She is also trying to keep some control on things in this general rush to publish everything he ever wrote. Gallimard is about to come out with C.'s *oeuvres* in the Quarto edition, a sort of Everyman's Pléiade, at 200 FF, much more affordable than the real Pléiade. Cioran would have liked the idea. He once told me his fame grew once he was published in *livre de poche*. The catalog lists *Schimbarea la fața a României (Romania's Transfiguration),* Cioran's mad dream of a Romanian fascist state, as one of the works to be published. Gallimard, however, had assured Simone that they were not going to publish it. A mistake? Whose? Why? Could a big press like Gallimard make such mistakes? Could it be intentional? It has certainly stirred up some people. Simone has never read *Romania's Transformation,* but she knows it is a dangerous, compromising text. C. told her he was afraid it might get published, but he didn't want it published abroad. She feels it is her mission to respect his will. As Iris Murdoch once said, "It is always significant to ask a philosopher: what is he afraid of?"

Another plot: a Romanian woman married to a pilot has appeared out of the woodwork. Apparently she too is writing a biography of C., by way of a dissertation. She keeps telling Simone that I bought C.'s letters from Liiceanu with dollars! The implication is that I'm dishonest, part of a Mafia-like network trying to get access to the documents in her possession. The woman is naturally jealous and complains that nobody gives her anything. Simone does not like her very much and is hard on her. I don't envy the poor woman. She comes to the hospital laden with cakes and cookies she baked at home, and tries to ingratiate herself the best way she knows. But still, she is not too shy to vilify me.

Another story: Verena von der Heyden-Rynsch no longer talks to Simone and snubs her, coming to visit only on Sundays at the hour she knows C. will be alone. She wanted to edit the *œuvres* and was offended when she didn't get to do it. I sometimes think Simone a saint to have put up with all the women admirers all her life, not to mention the Romanians and the crazies that C. seemed to attract. What a circus!

As we were leaving, Simone came with us to the elevator and recalled how C. did not like the elevator in their building, and how she would leave her shopping bags downstairs and he would run up and down "like a squirrel" to fetch them. He was very agile, she said. The image she conjured was so full of love, I could feel her pleasure in watching him go, and for a moment he seemed to be there, ready to pop around the corner.

May 8. Victory day for Lionel Jospin, the Socialist candidate for Prime Minister. Last night, post-election celebrations at the Place de la Concorde. Teddy [IZJ's son] wanted to see them, so we stopped and milled about with the crowd.

Dinner Thursday at Simone's celebrating C.'s *Œuvres,* which are finally out. Present are the PR man from Gallimard and a retired lawyer friend of his, and Bill, the American freelance journalist. The Gallimard man was very entertaining, bubbling over with stories about the Gallimard family. The American, very taken with the other two men, kept his back half turned on me most of the evening. Rude out of eagerness, I guess. Naturally I did not interest him.

Gallimard strongly advises Simone to obtain a legal guardianship over C. She's very reluctant.

At the hospital, I found C. paler, weaker and more absent than ever. The mouth open, the chin protruding, the eyes thoughtful. Only once in a while the shadow of a smile crosses his face like the faint echo of his old joviality. Simone told me how, when C. was translating *Tears and Saints* into French with Sanda Stolojan, he came out of his room early one morning very happy because he had worked hard through the night and managed to cut about thirty repetitions of the word "God."

May 11. We chat and laugh around C.'s bed or his armchair. He's partly there and partly not. Sometimes, Simone bends toward him and caresses his face and calls out to him "Cioran!" with so much tenderness in her voice. He likes us to hold his hands.

Bill the American apparently told Ana that he doesn't like me. I had sensed that, but I wonder why? The other night at dinner he snubbed me openly, while talking to the other two men. He was downright wooing them.

May 21. Saints' day for Constantine and Helen, my name day and Teddy's (Theodore Constantin). Cool Sunday in Montmartre, everybody out in the streets, children, dogs, tourists, tramps. In the evening, a call from Simone inviting me for dinner on Wednesday. She tells me she upbraided Bill on my account yesterday and that he was very upset. I think it a bit out of place for her to make such a fuss over the dinner incident. She has such a high-handed way of doing things sometimes. It didn't bother me that much, why should it bother her? Are we playing some game of affection here? Taking sides, showing our loyalty, flexing our muscles and authority? I'm sorry for the guy; I know how she can hurt when she chooses to.

Friday at the hospital, C. was dozing, pale, thin, mouth agape, sunken cheeks. It was really hard for me to look at his devastated face. Trying to engage him in conversation, I mentioned again Răşinari, Sibiu, and the Carpathian mountains. It's one strategy sure to work. The transformation was striking: his eyes all of a sudden focused and pierced me with great intensity, his head nodding approval every time I pronounced what now seemed like magic words of an incantation: Răşinari, Sibiu. All I had to do was repeat them like a mantra. He held my hand until I left an hour later; in fact, he wouldn't let go when I wanted to take my hand away. He also listened carefully and seriously when I read his "fan" mail.

Big event. Simone has finally decided to let me see C.'s papers. After four and a half months of delays and procrastination. I'm leaving in three weeks, and, in fact, I don't even have three weeks at my disposal because she has already started to give the papers away to the Doucet Foundation. I wonder if the recent slight I incurred at the hands of the American has prompted her to do something good for me, and thus let me into the inner sanctum. Making up for his so-called rudeness, showing herself protective and affectionate. Whatever. It works in my favor, just as I was starting to lose all hope.

The task is daunting. The first day, when I arrived, she led me to the study and said, "Here you are! It's all yours!" I felt like crying. There was a barely detectable note of mockery in her offer. His little attic room, painted white, sparsely furnished. There are a few shelves, a table, one chair, a sagging single bed, small and simple like a monk's, an unused fireplace, plastic tiles on the floor, a rug with brightly colored animals, a drawing on the mantelpiece, a small black filing cabinet. The tiny room crammed with papers everywhere: in old suitcases, on the bed, on the uneven wooden floor. I turned on the lamp and sat at his little table right under the window leading to the roof. I was overcome with awe at the task before me. I'm sitting in the great man's chair, imagining him there reading, scribbling, and furiously erasing his sentences, over and over again till he found the right word, the pure aphorism. I looked around wondering where to start. I went through a folder with miscellaneous papers, drafts of essays, fragments of letters, quotes from books including his own, which he had written down. Hours went by. Once in a while I would enter some of it in my computer, but I suddenly realized that would not do. I would never be able to finish and go through everything in time. I was getting sweaty and frantic. I had to make a choice: what was the most important thing to look at, the one I would not otherwise see anywhere? His journal. The letters have largely been published, so have his books. But the Paris journal, neatly stacked on a bookshelf in the corner of the room, is something unique. Here's a chance to see what he thought about events in his life both before and after his "conversion." A writer's journal is a treasure trove for a biographer, and this one would probably not see the light of print for quite a while. Simone was already talking of giving it to the Doucet Foundation. There will be two or three years before it will be available to the public there. If at all, because she was donating it with very strict conditions. So I decided that the journal should be my main priority. I asked Simone if I could take it home with me to read at leisure. She agreed.

Next day. I've been reading now, or rather leafing through his journal—some thirty school notebooks from 1956 on—at great speed. Fascinating, his hypochondria, his obsessions, this whole dramatic persona he created for himself and inside which he lived in order to write.

I don't have much time. Simone wants the notebooks back soon to give to the Doucet Foundation. I'm bleary-eyed from reading and taking notes on the computer. Working like a madwoman. I wish I could photocopy this thing but no store will do it for me—it's too long. Of course, it would also cost an awful lot.

Saved! A miracle. The parents of one of Teddy's friends drove him home today and came up to the apartment. Saw me swamped in Cioran's notebooks. We chatted for a while, then, out of the blue, she volunteered: "I can copy them for you!" "No, really, where? How? It's a huge task." "No," she insists, "I can do it very easily. I am used to photocopying a lot of material." She works for a lawyer. So we did it. I would take her a batch in a bag, she'd return them to me an hour later in two bags, the copies weighing more than the real thing. And bulky too. It will fill up a whole suitcase. But what a relief! Not to have to go through that reading marathon. The whole adventure seemed taken right out of a thriller. There I was with my bag, waiting for her to appear in the little garden in the Parisian square where we had our rendezvous. The exchange of bags, as if they were secret documents. We only lacked the trench coats, the sunglasses, the fake mustaches, and the hidden dead-letter drop-boxes! What sheer luck. I'm breathing with relief, I'm exhilarated. I haven't entirely wasted my six months of "research" in Paris after all. I was getting pretty desperate back in March. Waiting has paid off.

Teddy and I had dinner one night with Simone at the little Italian restaurant near the hospital. I asked her about the sicknesses that Cioran complains of so much in the journal. In reply, she told us a story about their trip to Corsica one summer. C. wouldn't fly, so they went by boat, then by train, crossing the entire island, burning in the sun. They trekked across the *maquis* to a little place they had heard about, a little lost village in the most remote corner of the island. On their way there, they saw not one single person, nothing except a mule attached to a tree which, as it turned out, belonged to the mailman who had stopped and was swimming in a creek down below. Since C. never made any plans about where they would sleep, that night they almost ended up in a cave full of rats with straw for a bed. His stomach aches started there; it was an ulcer he had had for a long time but hadn't known about it. He used to drink enormous quantities of coffee and was a heavy smoker. In Paris, when Simone would come home at midday from school, she couldn't see him in the room for the smoke. She remembers him staying up at night, suffering from stomach pains and chain smoking on the terrace of the hotel. Always prone to colds, too. Never took a taxi, if he could help it, for fear of drafts.

May 22. Today I walked about in the Quartier Latin, visiting C.'s old haunts. First rue Jean de Beauvais to see the Romanian church. The street connects boulevard St. Germain and rue des Écoles. In front, a sort of paved patio bordered with young acacia trees. It must have been in this patio (*parvis*) that the young C. once burned the effigy of King Carol II. C. lived until 1941 at the Hôtel Marignan, rue de Sommerard, right around the corner from the church. The hotel is still there. Crossing rue des Écoles, I walk into a little square with a bit of greenery, some benches, and a statue, like so many that dot Paris. But the statue, to my surprise, is of Mihai Eminescu, our Romanian national poet.

The church is closed at the moment. Torn by internal dissensions, its priest was suspended and his supporters banned by their Russian Orthodox superiors in New York, with whom this church-in-exile is affiliated. Reason for the fight: President Iliescu's visit to the church in November 1994, when he was received with due pomp. Many Romanian exiles were outraged. On the door, there is the printed suspension order and excerpt from the Apostolic Canon about punishment for heretics. A number of suspicious-looking men are prowling around the locked-up church in this quiet and very little square. One asked me if I spoke Romanian. He had a heavy East European accent. Securitate?

I left in a hurry. Further up, just past the Pantheon, other "Cioran streets," as I call them: rue Amyot, rue du Pot de Fer, rue Cardinal Lemoine, and rue L'homond where his childhood friend Bucur Ţincu lived. That street must have changed a lot; it has many new utilitarian-looking buildings, among them the Physics Lab of the École Normale Supérieure. The whole area is dotted with university buildings belonging to the École Normale, the Sorbonne, and the Curie Institute for cancer.[1] The main Sorbonne building is just a few blocks down toward the boulevard St. Michel. There C. used to have his meals at the student cafeteria until he was forty years old. He read at the Bibliothèque Ste. Geneviève across from the Pantheon.

May 29. Dinner at Simone's with Alain Paruit, C.'s best translator into French. Good-looking, tall, mid-fifties. Pleasant and rather quiet. We touched on C.'s fascist past, and he said that one had to consider the historical context, C.'s young age, the fact that everybody at the time was going either toward the extreme right or left in search of the "new man," and so on. A moderate, intelligent position.

June 1. Back from a long chat with Monica Lovinescu and Virgil Ierunca. A little house full of books and records. Both nice, very engaging, but too gossipy. All this gossip, so typically Romanian. Given their work at Radio Free Europe, they are the gossip-processing center of the Romanian expatriate world. They know everyone, they know everything. As I talked, I felt as if I were walking on broken glass. I had to be careful where I put my foot next, or rather what I said when I opened my mouth. With people like this you feel as if you are in an Indiana Jones movie; you have to have a special sense for divining which stone not to tread on, for a trap might open up underneath you, and you fall, impaled on their sharp tongues!

Monica and Virgil are also taking sides in the war raging around the dying Cioran. They defended Liiceanu and accused Simone of having become full of self-importance. "She used to be so self-effacing!" they said regretfully. They are against her because of her efforts to stop Liiceanu from showing his movie on French TV. She has no legal rights to do so since she is not married to Cioran, and in any case both the movie and *Romania's Transfiguration* will sooner or later appear in spite of her. I had an uneasy feeling they had invited me to sound me out since they knew I was close to her. At some point they said that although Simone was well disposed toward me now, she might change. Was that a warning? Were they testing my loyalty to her? Or trying to break it? What they say is, of course, quite possible. Simone flares up so easily and gets carried away so quickly, passionately embracing or dismissing a cause without giving it much thought. She is an impulsive woman. She is also under enormous pressure. C. should have thought better than to leave her alone to cope with all this. He should have made some more specific arrangements, given her legal rights, even married her.

The afternoon was entertaining, however. They told some anecdotes about Cioran.

One: At a Romanian funeral in Paris, while the priest is chanting, "God is with us, God is with us!" C. turns to a friend and exclaims "Ça, c'est le comble!" [That's too much! or, He must be kidding!].

Another one: At a party in Paris, Mircea Eliade was praising Nae Ionescu, their former teacher, a Mephistophelian character on the political and cultural scene of Bucharest in the 1930s. Cioran interposes: "He was paid 5 million francs by a German chemical company." Eliade: "Emil!" C.: "Well, then, maybe not quite so much, 500,000 francs, shall we say?" Eliade: "EMIL!" C.: "OK, then, 5 francs and let it go at that!"

And more: At a Romanian poetry reading, a bad poet from Bukovina exclaims when he meets him: "Oh, M. Cioran, how happy I am to meet you, because now I feel that I can touch the universe with my fingers!" C.: "Take it easy now, you're being indiscreet!"

They also mentioned C.'s sudden fits of violence, how he used to drink a lot, his chain smoking, and how, all of a sudden, he gave it all up.

June 4. Afternoon at the hospital. C. is looking much worse: he's lost a lot of weight, his face is all skin and bones, the eyes half-closed in a sort of heavy slumber. He refuses to eat, he keeps his lips shut tight, his teeth sunken into them with the effort. Simone continues to read him his fan mail, which is both touching and amusing; his work provokes such passionate "gut" reactions. For example, a woman writes to say that she identifies with what she calls a "fracture" in C.'s life—I guess she's referring to his exile in Paris—and complains about all the pictures of C. and his family that have recently been published in Liiceanu's book; she finds them indiscreet. Also, two Italian painters who live in Montparnasse say that they find his writings hilarious and would like to have a photo with him and them strangling each other! This, according to Simone, is an allusion to a photo by Richard Avedon where C. is shown grasping his neck as if to choke himself to death. But this time, the letters don't seem to impress him; he isn't listening anymore.

It's so hard to tell Simone without offending her that she must take some legal steps that will officially give her rights over C.'s work. How can one tell her, without appearing indiscreet and indelicate, that many people, especially the Romanians, do not recognize her rights to dispose of the C. legacy since she isn't married to him? The insidious comment of ML and VI about how self-effacing she used to be and how much she has changed lately sticks in my mind. In some quarters, she is thought to be a nuisance.

June 12. Soon the end. For me here; for C., in life. Yesterday I found him in bed, so white and thin, with flushed cheeks and his big eyes staring at the ceiling, looking so concentrated into the beyond. Listening to a harp concerto by Handel. How much C. liked to listen to music, especially Bach. My last days here. It's over, all over. *À la dérive.*

June 13. Haunted by the image of C. in his sick bed. His huge green eyes staring with such intensity. He who has always raved and ranted about the mystery of this moment can't tell us anything about it now. And yet he looks more of a visionary than ever. What does he know?

June 24. Cioran died Tuesday, June 20. Alone at the hospital while Simone, who had spent the night near him, had gone home to change. They called her, but when she arrived, they had even closed his eyes. A small, wasted white figure where the eyes had been like gates into the beyond. She says he'll be buried in the Romanian Orthodox rite. I'm surprised but don't dare ask what made her decide it. She says that the date is not set yet since it's not sure when the priests will be available. There's been a power struggle in the church, and the priests are busily employed at the tribunal.

Cioran was buried yesterday, June 23, at the Romanian Orthodox church in Paris. Simone said to me this morning that it was not she but Marie-France Ionesco who was burying C.! Strange that he would end this way. He must not have left any instructions about how he was going to be buried, so the Romanians reclaimed him at the end, in the form he most abhorred: the priests and patriarchs, the nasal chanting, the incense, in the midst of a crowd of Romanian gapers and dubious characters: representatives from the Romanian embassy, Dan Hăulică, Virgil Tănase, even Professor Chitoran, former dean of the Department of English and Germanic Languages in Bucharest at the time I was a student! I had not seen him since my last year at the university, 1975. I remember our last encounter. In the street in front of the English and German faculty building I waited one morning to plead with him to intervene on my behalf so I could get a visa to go to West Germany to study on a German government scholarship I had won in a competition. He said I was not to be trusted, and that he could not risk his career for me. And here he is, twenty years later, attending Cioran's funeral! I wonder in what official capacity. His career was obviously not impaired by the fall of communism; how much would it have been damaged by my fellowship?

Cameramen and photographers climbing into the pulpit to take pictures, policemen cordoned off the *parvis* in front of the church. What an irony for this modest man who always shunned publicity and who scribbled as a dedication on one of his books for me, "Je suis un ennemi de la gloire"! A mediocre sermon by one of the Romanian priests. A message from King Michael read by Marie-France Ionesco. Nothing from the French cultural authorities. Jean d'Ormesson, a few people from Gallimard (including Antoine Gallimard), and the press, were in attendance. Otherwise, it was an entirely Romanian affair. Ironical ending for a man who had stridently and vehemently broken his ties with Romania. The C. in the coffin had nothing to do with the ceremony around him. I expected him to pop out of the coffin and protest. The Romanians' reappropriation of C. had started while he was already too sick in mind to resist it, and now that he is dead, they took over completely. I am surprised at Simone's behavior. She had fought these very same Romanians to the bitter end. Why did she give in now? Her resigned voice over the phone a few days ago rings in my ear: "It is Marie-France's funeral. She is burying Cioran the way she buried her father." I heard the priests intoning over and over, "Let us pray for the one who has gone to his rest": *adormitul,* literally, the one asleep. I wondered for whom this refrain was more appropriate, Cioran or the old man next to me in the pew, who had fallen asleep and was snoring? I had to shove him back so he wouldn't land on the floor.

At the cemetery, a more sobering moment. The lowering of a coffin into an open grave is always sobering. A frail old man, Barbu Brezianu, spoke a few trembling words. I glanced into the grave as we all walked around it throwing handfuls of earth and flowers. I felt slightly sick and dizzy. It was a look into the abyss C. courted yet clamored against so often. He finally lies in it.

As we came away from Cioran's grave, meandering among neighboring tombs, I saw Marie-France distributing wine and *coliva,* the Romanian sweet funeral bread. She had run out of paper plates and plastic glasses, so the remaining stragglers had to be content with paper napkins and no wine. So much for the end.

# Romania, 1995–1997

### 1995, Bucharest

July 2. Off to Romania again. As I embark from Barcelona, in a battered old plane piloted by a Captain Turkey (!), I start to wonder if I am going to make it all the way there, and why I'm going back. What masochistic impulse drives me back to the dusty, dirty place that was my place of origin? Poverty is degrading, and Romania is a degraded and profoundly humiliated country. First impressions before landing confirm my misgivings: a wintry landscape in full summer, enveloped in mist (not autumn mists but pollution), and dust endemic everywhere. Obligatory features of all Romanian landscapes: dirt, dust, rust, black, and gray.

July 12. Back in Bucharest following my Cioran trail. I feel like a prisoner here. At least my "cell" is pleasant this time around, a roomy apartment with all the American comforts. A fortress, above the din of Bucharest traffic and all the sore sights of this city's streets. I'm wasting my time. For three days, I've been trying to get in touch with the director of the French Institute in Bucharest that awarded C. his scholarship in 1937. Impossible to get him on the phone or get an appointment. One would think he was a government minister or something, rather than a French civil servant supposed to make himself available to the public. Nasty secretary trained to keep people at bay. Very evasive, not sure that I can see him at all, I should call back the next day. So next morning I call again, but no, he is not available. I call the director of the Fulbright Commission and ask her to intervene on my behalf. She does so, and I get an appointment, but the following day it's cancelled. Message: M. Norbert Dodille is too busy to see me, and he's sure he has nothing to tell me besides. However, I may speak to the head librarian, although she probably does not know much about the history of the institute and its archives, where I could find C.'s application for a fellowship dating 1937, and so on. It sounds like they don't know anything. Or don't want to cooperate? Very discouraging. I call back to see if the secretary could find out at least whether the Institute's files are in Romania or in France. Again, they don't know. Still, I insist, there must be such a file, for I saw a quote from it in Liiceanu's book. She goes back to ask. All of a sudden, a squeaky male voice comes on the phone, speaking Romanian well and rapidly but with a faint accent. I suspect it is the mighty invisible Dodille himself: "We do not have anything on EC, we do not know anything." I: "M. Dodille, is this M. Dodille?" Voice continues to repeat with its mechanical and hysterical shriek: "We don't have anything on C. Yes, it's me." I: "I'm sorry to bother you, M. Dodille, but . . ." "Yes, you're bothering me very much!" He hangs up abruptly. Of Dodille, I only know from Simone that he wears loud neckties. Now I also know he has a high voice.

I'm shocked, offended, angry. I call the commission to complain. The person in the office who is the cause of all my trouble, since she failed to make an appointment with Dodille as I had asked her to do two months in advance, is too busy with her own travel plans for the States to care. She's also too limited to see beyond schedules and papers. I call up the director again, and she promises to speak to the new cultural attaché with whom she has an engagement to dine in the evening. She is on the *mondain* Bucharest circuit. She might well complain for me, because this indirectly affects her as well, since she had personally asked for an appointment for me, and he snubbed her as well as me. On the other hand, everyone is polite on the dinner party circuit, and they may not want to stir up things for Dodille. Two Americans who have the right reaction, Julie and Ken, are both indignant that a civil servant behaved so uncivilly. But Julie's Romanian friend is right, we are in the Balkans here, and this is a Frenchman behaving accordingly. I, naturally, think of plots: Nobert Dodille in league with Gabriel Liiceanu, who no longer wants to let me have any information on C. since he sees me as a competitor? I'm also a friend of Simone's, who is causing him trouble.

July 13. Boredom, or as Cioran defines it, "melancholic stillness." Saw Relu today. Took him out for lunch, an outrageously expensive mediocre meal in a summer garden near the Statue of the Aviators. We talked about Relu's TV appearance the previous night. I complimented him on it, but I didn't have my heart in it because the interview had been rather bad: a slow, ponderous, dull interviewer who had no interesting questions to ask, short of ideas but very long on words. The one question he did ask that he shouldn't have was apparently prompted by Relu himself, who has his own agenda: he wanted to defend the memory of Nae Ionescu, the famous philosophy professor who had been accused of plagiarism in the Romanian press. Relu, of course, didn't know much about the issue itself but was outraged by the attack and felt he had to defend Ionescu's memory. So he asked the interviewer to ask him about Ionescu, and the high point of the interview was Relu getting violent, banging on the table, and blubbering incoherent words in Nae Ionescu's defense. Violence, a family streak. In Cioran, violence mixed with a subtle mind and a good sense of humor. Not so in poor Relu.

Relu tends to get violent once in a while, and he is then intractable. He became so today at lunch when we started to talk about Liiceanu's edition of Cioran's letters and his new film on C. Relu is totally wrapped around Liiceanu's finger: Liiceanu is his best friend, a great mind, a generous heart, and an innocent victim of Gallimard's. For example, Gallimard pays Liiceanu peanuts for all the work he's done on Cioran, the anthology of articles, the letters. In Paris, I heard that Liiceanu had asked Gallimard to pay him for secretarial work. From what Relu says, Liiceanu resents Gallimard because he offered them his book on Cioran, and they gave him less money than Michalon. Liiceanu also tells Relu that he has never seen any money from Michalon whereas Simone has, so she's the one to profit, not he! Simone is the other sore spot in Liiceanu's outlook. So he denigrates her to Relu, subtly, lightly, nothing too strong to arouse his suspicion. He was hurt by her registered letter to him in which she forbids him to show the movie in France. Says he was hurt by the fact that it was sent registered! He took it as a slap! As to the movie controversy, Liiceanu maintains that C. had asked that the movie not to be shown until after his death. He's waited quite patiently; now he'd like to show it. Poured a lot of time and money into it, would like to get it back. He feels wronged by Simone's stubbornness on the matter. Relu thinks the movie is good, especially since he was told that Lucian Pintilie, the movie director, had said so, too. As we talk, he gets quite wound up and more and more strident. The wine and the heat contribute to his state of excitement. Liiceanu has all the rights to publish the letters he has gathered, and also to show the movie: "They shouldn't tell me how the law is in France. I do what I want here. I publish whatever I want; I don't need their permission. I'm tough, I am from Rășinari, you know!"

No way to make him see that he should collaborate with Simone on these matters. Since he's given Liiceanu permission to publish, that's enough. Simone, though Relu knows she is the executor, has no say in it as far as he is concerned. For him, Liiceanu is a sensitive victim, misunderstood and mistreated by Simone and Gallimard. Poor man, who does all this work and gets no reward, only slaps! Poor Relu, so naive, so blindly faithful. Liiceanu brings him to Bucharest, asks him for dinner at his house on a night off, pretends to let him into his secrets, and Relu, lonely and forlorn, eager to get away from his wife, laps it all up. Simone was concerned about the fate of the manuscripts Relu still has in his possession. She asked me to encourage him to donate them as soon as possible. He says he has willed them to the Astra Library in Sibiu where his brother used to read, but Liiceanu has now suggested that he should send them to Bucharest. Where? To whom? Will they fall into Liiceanu's hands then? Most likely.

Details of Cioran's life gleaned from Relu today: their older sister was married to a well-to-do notary public in Ineu, in Transylvania, and they had one of the best looking houses in town, which during the Communist period became the county courthouse. The sister did many years in prison later on, her son hanged himself, and two of her grandchildren, good for nothings, died from alcoholism and despair.

On their mother's side, there were six daughters and one son, a mill owner and champagne maker, who used to send them champagne by the case. A big strong man who could raise heavy flour sacks at the mill, and who was pathologically jealous of a very ugly and faithful wife.

At the high school in Brașov where C. used to teach, he would walk into a classroom, take his hat off, bang it on the table, and exclaim: "That's our history, in a nutshell!"

Cioran apparently bought the plot where he was buried in Montparnasse a few years before he died. He used to go there and stare at it long and hard.

July 14. Two hours today with Arșavir Acterian, a sprightly eighty-seven-year-old man, slightly hard of hearing but shuffling energetically on his two-hour constitutional through the Herăstrau park. He must have been a handsome man; he still has a nice white curly head of hair, long olive-colored face with a big aquiline nose and bright, black, amused eyes. He went to prison twice, once in Dobrogea for four years, then a second time, condemned with the Noica group for twelve years, out of which he did six. Freed in 1964, the year of the amnesty. Studied law, but made a living as an antiquarian. He had at one time his own store in Bucharest; later he lived on selling papers and letters to museums. Never married because of his precarious existence. He cared for his sister, Jeni, and discovered her secret diary after her death in a locked drawer that had no key. He published parts of it, but the whole manuscript is either at the Academy or at what he kept calling the museum "of old things," couldn't remember which. Very friendly and willing to talk but sometimes distracted, either by his hearing problem or for fear of getting lost in the park if he abandoned his usual path. After a while, he seemed eager to walk alone, so I left him.

He talked charmingly, urbanely, and sounded like a young man. He had an ease and grace that is rare nowadays. At some point during the walk, he told me that he had brought me one of his books. I was surprised to hear it since he wasn't carrying anything in his hands, and I didn't remember him leaving anything in the car. So I thought maybe he had meant to bring one but forgot. Then, as we were about to part, to my great surprise, he unbuttoned his shirt and from between shirt and undershirt took out a book. He must have carried it under his arm underneath the shirt. It was in an envelope, all sweaty. I took it out of the stained envelope and looked at it. But he was eager that I put it back. I wonder why? Why was he hiding it like that in the first place? Habits from old Communist Romania. I let him walk away, and from a distance he didn't even look too old!

In the afternoon, hanging around the Fulbright office waiting to get my money. Drinks with Luri Berza and others. Luri, a good-looking woman in her fifties. Tall, blond, blue-eyed, strong profile. I see her as "one of us"; that is, belonging to a class which has largely disappeared from Romania. She is one of those rare species who managed to survive by a sort of steel ambition and determination. She did not go abroad; why, I wonder? She moves in Bucharest high-society circles, a mixture of foreign diplomats, intellectuals, remnants of the old bourgeoisie, the new intelligentsia, and political figures. She's smart, polished, but as I look at her she strikes me as unhappy. I could vividly picture her despair and sensed in her a great potential for discontent.

July 16. Stores, like little holes in the wall, selling beer, cola, toilet paper. Brown, coarse toilet paper rolls arranged in towers on a table as centerpiece, surrounded by ramparts of beer bottles and coke cans. Budding commercial art in Bucharest.

From my kitchen in the "fortress" I spent a very pleasant, silent Sunday morning, watching the rooftops of Bucharest. They are picturesque, red tiles or green, rusty sheets of metal, not very high above the ground, their monotony interrupted by trees, of an unusually vivid green this wet summer. There are a lot of unusual architectural features in this neighborhood: old Romanian style houses, with arched arcades and porches, apartment buildings from the 1930s and 1940s in the Bauhaus style. I remember looking at the rooftops of Paris from the Beaubourg earlier this spring: they were more imperial, more uniform, gray, and less picturesque. Bucharest from above is almost pleasant to look at on this Sunday morning. But from below and close up: the potholes, the mounds of dirt and rot, the smells, the leprosy of the decaying walls, the old junk piled up and obstructing windows, balconies, gardens! It looks more like Bombay than Bucharest, though perhaps Bombay is better.

July 18–20. Relu tells me confidentially what he had been too shy to tell me when I was taping him. His religious crisis ended not because of his brother's vehement opposition to it, but simply because after a year and a half of abstinence he could no longer hold out; he discovered that he could not do without women. He also talked about the three prostitution houses in Sibiu where the young high school boys would often encounter their teachers. Prostitution, of which he warmly approves, was the only way to solve their sexual needs. He extolled the virtues of prostitution: experienced women, who had techniques and "were not like logs"—something that often happens with ordinary women, he said. He knows what he's talking about because he's been a womanizer all his life. And prostitution was so much more efficient: there was no need for love, commitments, no long-term involvements with a woman one does not know and could be mistaken about, as often happens in marriages. Plus, it was safe. According to Relu the prostitutes were checked by a doctor weekly and had special papers attesting to their health. Both he and his brother benefited greatly from the system. He then talked about his brother's disappointment with a high school sweetheart, Cella, which, given his intense character, may have affected him in his view of women. Cioran has talked about this early episode in his love life; in fact, it is the only one he ever mentions, besides the prostitutes. Another fragment of Cioran mythology. Relu says the event may be the cause of his brother's misogyny. The nickname of the boy the girl preferred over Cioran was "Pizdulici" [Little Cunts]. (C., in his interviews, softens the name to "Păduchi" [Louse].) Cioran, who was very proud, was offended by the girl's bad taste. Relu also mentioned that there had been a young math teacher in Sibiu whom Cioran almost married. Her first name was Minerva. She, however, left no trace in the Cioran mythology.

July 22. My revulsion toward Romania is a mixture of love and hate. I'm offended by all its sights and sounds: the dirt, the poverty, the decay, the stench of fecal matter wafting through the streets from open sewer pipes, the potholes like small volcano craters, the aggressive swagger of the people. I'm also so affected by it. It is like a wound I'm carrying within myself, whose festering infection has fatally afflicted and shaped my identity.

A country of troglodytes. I didn't belong, not even when I lived here. Leaving it was the most natural thing in the world for me. And I distinctly feel that part of my problem with Romania is a question of class: the class I belonged to has long been extinct, wiped out. Executions, prisons, exile, the years of terror worked wonders, and a new people was born. So, I don't belong and should stop agonizing over the same old question, "How can one be Romanian?"

**1997, Sibiu**

May 5. Back in Bucharest after three days in Sibiu at the Cioran Colloquium. A patriotic affair with folklore thrown in for local color. Not an academic conference, though pretending to be one. Cioran has become a national monument. In his honor, we sing hymns and give grandiose speeches. We are all oh so proud to be his compatriots. Basking in his glory which rubs off on us, all of us, little Ciorans, little budding, undiscovered geniuses. We congratulate each other for belonging to his race, his country, for being in this town, for rubbing shoulders with his brother. Etc. What a circus!

The opening of the conference was like a mock opening of Parliament. A multitude of platitudinous political speeches from the mayor of Sibiu, the parliamentary representative, the head of the Youth League, the head of the tourist office, and a number of other heads and dignitaries. It took place in the main reading room of the Astra Library, where Cioran used to read. I spent the entire time looking at the people around me and up at the ceiling. A high-ceilinged room in neo-classical style with freshly repainted gold trim on the walls and the busts of mythical-looking women supporting the ceiling vault in its four corners. The public was mixed, but in great numbers, for Cioran is the brother of us all. There were a few students, about thirty invited guests, and the rest were retired people, many probably former Iron Guardists, possible friends of Relu, but not necessarily. Cioran, I have noticed from the odd correspondence I get as his American translator, attracts a mixed bunch; he has a widespread and varied appeal.

The papers and discussions were held in the same room and proceeded in haphazard fashion. The atmosphere was that of an Oriental market, people milling about, talking loudly, shouting to each other from one far corner to another. The program was not respected, people kept dropping off and popping up on panels, papers were added, others were not given. I didn't give mine. I just ad-libbed a bit about Cioran in America. It was not an audience for an academic paper.

One speaker, a former priest apparently, a university professor and now Romania's designated ambassador at the Vatican, a pompous little man, folded his hands on his stomach, rolled his eyes toward the ceiling, and talked soaringly for what seemed like hours on end. As if God had forgotten him there, speaking in the desert. Another, a

Greek woman artist whose multi-media sculpture was unveiled afterward, launched herself into an interminable Swedenborgian kind of paper connecting Cioran with everything else in the universe, but especially with Greek myths, which she proceeded to recount in detail. Things got rather heated when the structuralists attacked just about everyone else for talking about Cioran in terms other than the purely formalistic. People were jumping up from all over, invoking names *à tort et à travers:* Heidegger, Gadamer, Barthes, Lacan, Kundera, flying right and left without making much sense.

After a long afternoon session in the presidium, I kept to the back rows of the conference room for the rest of the time. This, however, did not prevent someone for asking me to deliver the final word at the conference. Our woman in the USA. Afterward, interview with the Sibiu daily, *Tribuna.* Cioran's reception in the States, my future projects, and so forth.

I was lodged in the Hotel Boulevard, a cavernous building of vaguely Stalinist architecture, in a shabby room with a peeling shower stall, broken mirror, and a TV set which had a note asking guests to handle it carefully. However, it was not working, so it didn't require any handling at all. I called the front desk to let them know it was broken so they wouldn't blame me later. They asked if I wanted it repaired. I said no. I can't complain about the lodging. We were invited as guests, but it turns out that the organizers have run out of the few funds they had, and so Relu ended up paying the foreigners' bill, pretty hefty by Romanian standards. I felt very embarrassed and insisted on paying for myself, but Relu is an old-world gentleman. I had to find another way to make up for it.

Trying to call Ken in the States. I ring up the operator and say, "I'd like to dial . . ." She cuts me off: "You can't dial, I dial for you." "Well, OK, but I'd like to . . ." "No, you can't, I'll do it." I give up trying to talk to her, just give her the number and, miracle of miracles! I get through to Ken. I want to tell him about my horrendous drive from Bucharest to Sibiu in a little rented Citroën Visa. I consider myself lucky to be alive. After twenty-four hours of airplanes and airports, I drove for hours in the dark and rain, on an unmarked, unlit road, no trace of a median strip, and the shoulder, simply a ditch. Potholes and construction sites are not signaled. At one point, I found myself facing a truck across a huge crater in the road. I declare myself a very good driver and want Ken to know it. I'm proud to have survived. Badge of honor.

Last afternoon at the conference spent at the mountain resort of Păltiniş. Though it is May, there is still snow on the ground. Ladies in high heels and tight mini-skirts flounder through the mud and snow. A small wooden chapel with a pointed bell tower, and a lonely nun chanting in front of the altar. There are only three nuns living at the hermitage. I look at the woods, trying to imagine how they spend their winter surrounded by a wall of snow two meters high. For weeks, they are walled in their snow prison, can't even go out to buy bread.

We have supper prepared by the nuns: a welcome change from the chips and cola we pretended was dinner for the last few days. Goat cheese and roasted sausages, roasted chicken and spring salad with French fries. It all tastes delicious. There are speeches again. Tearful, sentimental, patriotic, sometimes on the aggressive, belligerent side because of the wine. The nuns come in to sing "Christ is risen," though it's not Easter, and "Happy Birthday" to no one in particular. Then they approach Relu, a familiar visitor and patron, and beg discreetly for money. One has fourteen brothers in a god-forsaken village, another has no money to buy a pair of boots. I jump at a chance to help out and pay him back for the hotel. The nuns keep on talking to him, but they also keep one hand stretched toward me, with which they quickly grab the money without even looking at it. It was like a magician's act, the money disappearing into the folds of their black robes as if it had never existed.

All in all, the dinner is a grotesque scene, a mixture of comedy and melodrama, minus the tragic-pathetic dimension of a scene from Dostoevsky (like Marmeladov's funeral in *Crime and Punishment,* for example). As a people, we Romanians tend toward the comical: we all end up kissing and loving each other. *Pupat Piața Independenței,* as Caragiale said [Kissed and made up in Independence Square]. I feel sick with pity, love, and despair.

I mention to Relu that I have a copy of Cioran's journal. He asks me to send him a page from it. Says he has been asking Simone for months but she has not responded. On the way back to Bucharest, I also tell Dan Mihailescu that I have a copy of the journal. I may have spoken too openly. Dan's ears perked up when he heard it. He spoke enviously of how much he would like to set eyes on the whole thing rather than Simone's selections. See what Cioran thought of the Paris intellectuals, his contemporaries.

## 1997, Bucharest

Dust, dogs, and potholes. A dirty Danubian city. Big heat wave. As I was looking for a parking space in my father's neighborhood, a little old man in a doorway beckons to me, calling out, "Over there, over there." There is indeed a space around the corner, in front of a big house with an iron fence. "Make sure your car alarm isn't on," he warns me, "otherwise you'll find the car without its wheels when you come back." I thank him, park, and then stop to talk. I ask him why the car would lose its wheels if I had a burglar alarm; it doesn't seem to make much sense. He explains that in the house lives a doctor who works night shifts and therefore is very keen on his sleep during the day.

He gets mad at cars parked in the street whose alarms go off at the smallest vibration. When heavy trucks pass by, often these car alarms start ringing, and he dismantles the car to avenge himself. Vagaries of Bucharest life.

I find my father in his pajamas, unshaven, in his ratty armchair. Crying, he tells me horror stories about people imprisoned in Romania in the 1950s. He's been reading these stories and lives through them vicariously. He says with awe, and he's probably right, that it was a miracle he did not go prison. His brother Paul (Lulu) did, spent six years in the lead mines, and his uncle, Paul Zarifopol's son, was in prison for sixteen years. My father feels sorry for himself as if he had actually gone to prison. He has a very lively imagination and knows he would not have made it out of there; this makes him terribly sad and frightened. The worst that ever happened to him was being fired for being the son of an aristocrat and being unemployed for three months right after my birth. My mother got him his job back from her vast networks of connections. The wife of a dentist knew someone who knew someone with influence. My father says he will always be grateful to my mother for that.

I try to cheer him up. Got him to talk about the time he was a soldier at the end of World War II, 1943–44. He is such a good storyteller. As he talks, he forgets his fright and becomes engrossed in his own tales. Stories about his time in the army are hilarious, mock-heroic. He never saw a real battle, only moved from training post to training post, lost his division in the general chaos of the end, played poker all the time and got cheated, got infested with lice. His most heroic action was walking through the mud and rain for twelve hours to go and see his newborn daughter, my sister, whom he jokingly wanted to name Stalinica (Little Girl Stalin) because she was born in September 1944, after the Russian invasion of Romania.

Bucharest. I can't get over the heaps of garbage amassed in the middle of the streets and the life-endangering potholes. Besides the stray dogs, a fixture of everyday life, there are pet dogs. Especially Great Danes. The size of Romanians' favorite dogs seems to match their megalomania. Great Danes, huge, costly animals that can barely fit into apartments where the human inhabitants were once entitled to only eight square meters, are the canine expression both of Romanians' insecurity and their inflated sense of self.

Some signs of progress: there no longer are so many vending tables in the streets. The small businesses have moved to kiosks and one-room stores that spring up in the most unexpected places. A grotesque mixture of decay and modernization; here and there, there are attempts at restoration. Even my old home has changed a bit: the downstairs is now newly repainted and has a shiny plaque on the facade that says

"Monopoly Media: Outdoor Advertising." A brand new Mercedes is parked in the courtyard. The upstairs remains ruinous.

I finally met Lizette Georgescu, Paul Zarifopol's last love. Ninety years old, dark-eyed, bright smile. Armenian, educated in Dresden: music, piano, canto. Worked as voice trainer at the Romanian State Opera during the Communist years. Paul Zarifopol died in her arms. What a shock it was. She had an understanding husband, though, who helped her get the body out of the house and onto a park bench where it was found later. Then her son was born, and life went on. Showed me pictures of herself with her son. She says Paul Zarifopol was the love of her life. Shall I believe her? Why not? She keeps copies of his letters and recites portions from them to me by heart. She met him at a friend's house. He was lying on a sofa, dressed in a Russian-style shirt, trying to look Socialist like his father-in-law, Dobrogeanu Gherea. They looked at each other, and the attraction was instantaneous. He came over and asked, "Do you like exhibitions?" "Yes," she answered, and they made an appointment for the next day to go and see a new exhibition at the Dalles Hall. Then the passion he documents in his letters bloomed.

My father is stuck in his apartment. The lift doesn't work, and he can't climb down all eight flights of stairs. He barely drags himself around. He cries and tells me that he cannot stand this waiting for death—he doesn't have the heart for it. Old age, sickness—the punishment is too hard. He's a weak but pitiable man.

Next day. The lift works, so we go to the Lakes and have lunch at an outdoor restaurant. He has his favorite meal of succulent Chateaubriand. He's happier. He says he ate "like a king." I promise to take him grocery shopping. That makes him happy, too. Tells me a story about his uncle taking him to a toy store when he was five. In the store, his uncle said, "Here you are, you can buy anything you want." It made a big impression on him; he anticipates the trip to the grocery store as if it were a repeat of that miraculous childhood trip to the toy store.

Trip to the store. Shopping bags of all sizes, on wheels and off, waiting at the door in preparation for the big expedition. I tell my father and his wife that I don't want any fuss, the trip should proceed in an organized quiet fashion. Simple rules: we buy whatever they want, and we don't comment on prices within the shopkeeper's hearing. They promise, but once in the store, it's as embarrassing as I feared. The store is one of the new, modern Western-style grocery stores that have popped up all over Bucharest. With Western prices. Wide-eyed, my father and his wife meander through the store, picking things off the shelves, turning them upside down to check the price. Then they call to each other: "Look how much it costs! At such and such a store it's half the price!" Or, "We can't buy anything here, it would be such a waste of money." Apostrophizing and accusing me at the same time: "You are such a big spender!" Or she, "I'd love this, but we can't really afford this, can we?" At the end, my father fusses over the amount of things they've bought and the mode of transportation back home. We have to make two trips. He wants to stay behind to make sure nothing disappears from the bags. He is as delighted as a child with his collection of colorful packages. The toy store experience all over again. I'm happy I could play that favorite Romanian character, the good uncle from America. At least my father lets me give him these small pleasures. With my mother, it would be unheard of. I can never make her happy, no matter how hard I try.

# Postlude

Bloomington, May 27, 1997. Relu Cioran sent me a copy of my interview in *Tribuna.* I am horrified. They adapted or rather mis-adapted my words to suit their purposes. It makes it sound as if I plan to publish the entire, uncut version of Cioran's journal in competition with the Gallimard version prepared by Simone. All I had said to the interviewer was that one of my future projects was a translation of the *Journal* (by which I meant Simone's selections), but that there was a longer version deposited at the Doucet Foundation, which interested scholars would want to consult in the future. I inadvertently let it slip (to Relu) that I had a copy of this other version. I had made clear to him that his copy was for my personal use only. They jumped on that bit of information. Did Relu tell the newspaperman something about it? He knows them all and talks freely with them about his famous brother.

This is potential trouble, if Simone gets wind of this, she'll have a fit. I must do something.

Later. I wrote a letter to the *Tribuna* editor with my corrections. Hope they'll publish it. Wrote to both Relu and Simone with copies of my letter to the editor and explanatory notes. I hope this will clear the matter up. Or will it get it more muddled? I fear distance and misunderstandings.

Spain, June 23. First, a letter from Relu, with pictures from the conference. Kind, does not appear to be concerned about the newspaper interview. Then, the bomb explodes. A letter has arrived from Simone. Christina reads it to me over the phone. Simone is upset, as far as I can tell, not so much about the interview as about the fact that I gave Relu a copy of one page from the *Journal.* Maybe she's right. I should have known better and not stepped between the two of them. All those months in Paris two years ago, all the plotting and jealousies should have taught me something. They are divided about what should be published and what not. Behind them, Liiceanu, the head of the Romanian publishing house, and Gallimard. It's not quite clear to me from what Christina reads over the phone, but I get the gist of it: Simone, frantic and stressed with all the publicity around Patrice Bollon's new biography (*Cioran l'hérétique,* Gallimard, 1997), does not want to give Relu and Liiceanu the rights to the *Journal.* Or some such thing. So she hates the idea of my having sent him one page from it.

I hurry to hang up and call Simone in Paris. I want to reassure her. It is all a misunderstanding, and I am very sorry I sent the page but can't believe they can do much with it. What I did not take into account was the fact that some weeks had passed from the time she wrote the letter to tonight. By now, things have escalated in her mind and have taken on horrific proportions. She screams at me that I am a thief, that I shouldn't have copied the *Journal,* that this is piracy. Impossible to talk and explain, she keeps repeating that I am a thief. I know where this comes from. Marie-France Ionesco, who totally dominates Simone, and who has taken it upon herself to control both her father's and Cioran's legacy. No love lost between the two of us. I felt her hostility from the beginning, and now she sees a way to undermine me in Simone's eyes. She must be pounding it into her every time they talk that I had no right to copy the manuscript.

But what was I supposed to do? Simone gave it to me to take home and read and take notes. She knew what it was for. She knew I was there collecting material for my book. She knew I had been waiting and waiting. She had been promising and promising and putting it off till almost the very end. Maybe she couldn't make up her mind. But she had a very clear grasp of the whole awkward situation. She referred to James's "The Aspern Papers," and she identified me as the young journalist and herself as the old woman who catches him in the library. When she finally gave me access to Cioran's stuff, and then let me take the notebooks home, she knew perfectly well what she was doing and what I was doing. She gave it to me. Thirty-five notebooks to cover in four days! That's all I had, four days, because she was just about to hand the whole thing to the Doucet Foundation and kept hurrying me as if regretting her own generosity. After six months of waiting and despairing that I would ever see anything at all! So I started taking notes, going almost crazy with the impossible task, and then a friend offers to help by photocopying it. And I accept the offer, not once thinking that I would do anything else with the manuscript but read it in peace and quiet when back in Bloomington. I had been collecting data for several years, copying wherever I went and whatever I could, when I had access to a photocopier. In Romania especially, in Sibiu, in Bucharest at the Museum of Literary History, at the Humanitas publishing house, at the Ministry of Foreign Affairs. I was copying letters, unpublished documents, that's why I had a research fellowship and went to all those places. I was doing my job, collecting documents for my book. What am I doing now, anyway? Justifying myself to myself, conducting imaginary dialogues with Simone, feeling guilty even though I shouldn't. Feeling sorry, too. I'm afraid I have lost Simone.

What Simone accuses me of now makes no sense except that she has changed her mind, or had it changed for her, and she regrets having allowed me to have the journal. So she blames me of abusing her trust. But I haven't done anything at all except, possibly, talked too freely. Since I cannot keep my mouth shut, and I blabber about it in Romania where such news is BIG news, and everybody expects me to publish the journal. Now I have to pay for it with her friendship.

July 15. Angry letter from Simone, who insists that I had no right to copy the journal. The letter sounds as if it were from a jilted lover; full of spite, venom, insults. I am now angry myself because I'm fed up with this emotional blackmailing and the insults. What gives her the right to treat me this way? I had written to her and tried as delicately as possible to make her see that it was all a misunderstanding, that I had no intention whatsoever to publish the journal and abuse her trust, that she could not have trusted a better person. I even offered to send it back. She says, yes, send it back since obviously you have such easy access—"trigger happy"—to copy machines. By which she probably means that even if I sent it I would probably keep another copy for myself, that my offer was therefore disingenuous. Well, then, I won't send it, and I'll keep doing my work and won't let all this bother me any more.

Now I wonder about those months I spent in Paris. I thought her procrastinating was due to the hard times she was going through. I was in good faith and sympathetic to her plight. But could she have actually deliberately delayed until the last minute, so that when she did make the final gesture of good will she knew it would be physically an almost impossible task? In other words, she gave me access to C.'s papers, but only so late that I couldn't possibly do much with them. She probably counted on my not being able to do much. Now that she sees that I actually did find a way out, she's mad and accuses me of stealing. Her words to me that first day when she let me in his study still ring in my ears. Only now they have an ironic tone I did not sense then, when I thought she was being so generous: "Make yourself at home. You're free to do whatever you can do here. Help yourself!" The little room was like a jungle of papers. She did not think I would be able to actually find my way through it and help myself to what was most important. She hoped I would get lost in it. She's mad at me because her scheme has failed.

And this is how I became a manuscript thief.

October 1997. Simone is dead. Found drowned on a beach near her house in the Vendée. She was buried in the same tomb with Cioran. There was a notice about her in *Le Figaro* a week after the funeral. Not a single one of her friends from the Cioran years attended. Forty days later, an Orthodox mass for the dead, organized by Marie-France Ionesco, took place at Montparnasse Cemetery, beside the grave where Cioran and Simone lie together.

# Appendix 1
## Another Family

Cioran was not a simple peasant born into an ordinary peasant family. But, besides the very considerable talents of his father, there was another family that all the Ciorans looked up to as their model. A sister of Emil's grandfather, Şerban Cioran, Stanca (Aunt Stanca), married into another Răşinari family that produced priests, men of letters, and politicians, the Barcianu family.[1] The Barcianu family history is recounted in richly interpretive detail by Cioran's father in his book *Seven Generations of Priests, Archpriests, Professors from the Same Family: Barcianu, 1699–1903,* written in 1955 but not published until 1991, by Cioran's brother, Aurel, in Sibiu.[2] The Ciorans closely identified with the Barcianu family: not only were they related, but they recognized in the Barcianus the pattern of their own lives, as well as a model of dedication to the cause of the nation. In his introduction to his book on the Barcianus, Cioran's father confesses his affinity for this family, speaking of his moral duty to preserve their memory for posterity:

> for a long time I've been obsessed with the necessity of gathering and processing documents left in the family, and held it as my moral and spiritual duty to draw a picture of these people's lives and activity, since they deserve posthumous recognition from posterity. But I also personally owe them recognition since I too have served at the altars of the Răşinari churches, where the Barcianu priests served, for 18 years. . . . This Barcianu dynasty remains a source of light and an example to follow.[3]

There is a feeling of urgency here, a need to set the record straight before he died, and it is natural to assume that Emilian Cioran, long before he wrote up the Barcianu family saga "for posterity," just two years before his death, had already held up this familiar lore as "a source of light and an example to follow" to his two sons, that he had tried to instill in them the spirit of the Romanian intellectual's national and cultural mission that he so admired in the Barcianu family.

Emilian Cioran's history of the Barcianu family begins in 1699, with Coman Birsan, archpriest of Răşinari, who lived 105 years, until 1804. His son, Sava Popovici the Elder, was a renowned copyist of old church manuscripts and a talented preacher.[4] The original family name of Birsan was changed to Barcianu by the sixth priest of the family, Sava Popovici Barcianu (1814–79), who in 1839 married Coman Cioran's daughter, Stanca. He was appointed professor at the Theological Seminary in Sibiu by the great bishop Andrei Saguna and in 1869 was elected corresponding member of the Romanian Academy. Sava P. Barcianu was not only a distinguished intellectual figure (author of numerous textbooks, among them a German grammar textbook and a Romanian-German dictionary) but also politically active: he was elected to the permanent committee of the Blaj Assembly of May 3–15, 1848, a member of the Romanian delegation to Vienna to present the Austrian emperor with the claims of the Romanians of Transylvania, and a member of a volunteer army group from Răşinari fighting alongside the Austrians against the Hungarian revolutionaries in that famous "year of revolutions."

Continuing the family tradition, his son, Daniel Popovici Barcianu, teacher, writer, and secretary of the Astra Association, was also politically active: together with fourteen other Romanians, he signed a charter of political rights for the Romanians of Transylvania which was sent to Vienna in 1892. Not receiving any official answer, the members of the Romanian delegation published the charter, with the result that its signers were arrested and sentenced to several years in prison soon after.

In his history of the Barcianus, Emilian Cioran quotes amply from family letters. He chose to quote precisely those passages that emphasize their dedication to the family and the national cause. The passages chosen from the Barcianu letters dealing with parental concern for the son's well-being, the son's respect for parental authority, the parents' longing to see the son return sooner, and, through it all, the urgent sense of a mission are themes that weigh heavily on the older Cioran's mind and must have reminded him of letters between him and his by-then estranged son, Emil, as he felt his life's end approaching. For Emil's education and career in many ways resembled that of many talented sons of Romanians sent to study abroad and who were, like the Barcianus, expected to return and work for the advancement of the mother country. Thus, for example, from a letter written from abroad in 1837–38, by Sava Popovici to his father, Cioran's father quotes the son as saying: "remember your son who *wants to be an arm useful to his country's body-politic. The time has come for us to step forward into culture, along with other nations.*" Here is an ideal close to Emil Cioran's later wish, in *Romania's Transfiguration* (1937), to raise Romania from small to big nation status.

Daniel Barcianu's career (1847–1903) is typical in this respect. He had fellowships to study in Vienna, Leipzig, and Bonn, where he obtained his doctorate, just as Emil would later go with a German fellowship to Berlin and then with a French government fellowship to Paris. But whereas Barcianu goes abroad to study and returns home to serve his people, the young Cioran can think only of ways to *escape* this pre-established pattern.

Barcianu was sent abroad with a mission summed up in Bishop Saguna's words: "Go first to Vienna, then Bonn and come home a great learned man!" From Vienna, he writes home giving minute details about his daily routine, well calculated to satisfy the curiosity of those at home, who follow in imagination his goings and doings abroad. Daniel's father writes thus: "your mother and I estimate that you must have left home about two hours ago to go to the university on the Ring. Might it be raining there as it is here? Did you remember to put on long underwear so that you would not catch a cold on the way back?" This dutiful and loving son wants not only his father's but also Bishop Saguna's permission to go to Leipzig to listen to Nietzsche's lectures.[5] But Saguna had died in the meantime, so he's trying to pry from his father what the old bishop's wishes would have been: "from talking with our dear departed, did you get the impression that he would have wanted me to return sooner?" asks this model of filial obedience. To which the father, while giving his permission, replies: "of course, my dear son. Our dear departed bishop was looking forward to your coming back to increase the number of cultivated men working for the good of the nation." When, on his return home in 1875, Daniel Barcianu was offered a teaching position at the University of Bucharest, he refused the offer because of his sense of mission, his feeling of moral duty toward the dead bishop, architect of the Romanians' national identity in Transylvania, whose work he feels it his obligation to continue: "there is a lot of work to do in Ardeal [Transylvania] and there are very few fighters!"[6]

This attitude of responsible patriotism was a lifelong value of Cioran's father Emilian, not merely the product of a belated appreciation of another famous local family. In 1934, Emilian wrote an appreciation of one of his own priestly predecessors, Nicolae Cristea (1834–1902), on the occasion of the one hundredth anniversary of Cristea's birth.[7] He specifically casts Cristea as "a *model*, a personality, who devoted himself to the welfare of his nation . . . a model of character, dignity, [who] inspires power by his labors, pride for the nation, and courage in the imitation and creation of other models." Cristea's work was humble but critical: he created the first "reunion," or cooperative organization, of Romanian handicraft workers, allowing them to improve their conditions and extend their skills through education, breaking the vicious cycle in which they were constantly replaced by foreign workers, reverting to a status little better than slavery. Nor does Emilian fail to point out the lesson for the future, in 1934: "There was a necessity for the Reunion, certainly. But that is not all; we have to continue going ahead. The fight for the prestige and glory of our nation makes any condition, social or political, of worker liberation a sign of continued progress."[8]

# Appendix 2
## Articles by Cioran Reflecting His Experiences in Germany

A certain amount of confusion surrounds Cioran's writings about Germany and his experiences there. This is understandable, given his controversial polemical stature. His detractors want to emphasize the worst pieces, those most uncritically enthusiastic about Hitler and the new Nazi regime. His defenders naturally seek to ignore or minimize these. *Singurătate și destin: Publicistică 1931–1944* [Solitude and Destiny] published in Bucharest by Humanitas in 1991, includes seventy-five of Cioran's periodical writings for the dates given, but omits almost all political articles, to achieve the book's predominantly literary and "philosophical"—that is, non-political—aspect.[1] Some, but by no means all, of these essays appeared in right-wing journals. Many are political, but the majority are not (for example, "The Vision of Death in Nordic Art," "Faith and Despair," "Style and Eschatology").

Aurel Cioran made a list for IZJ of forty-six "articles published in various periodicals by E. Cioran" (her note), which may or may not have purported to be complete for the 1930s. Thirty-one of the articles he listed appear in *Solitude and Destiny,* but fifteen do not, including three from Cioran's years in Germany, none of which are (from their titles) evidently about political topics. But Aurel had been a member of the Iron Guard and went to prison for it, and he had his own reasons for downplaying this aspect of his brother's *œuvre.*

IZJ made another list of eleven "articles by Cioran from Germany," only one of which appears in *Solitude and Destiny* ("The Historical Silence of Spain"), and none in Aurel Cioran's list. In 1999, Marta Petreu listed fourteen political and historical articles written by Cioran between November 1933 and July 1935, as *included* among a larger number of "German articles" he wrote, from which she distinguishes philosophical pieces later included in *Cartea amăgirilor* [The Book of Deceptions], 1936, and some (another fourteen or more) incorporated into *The Transfiguration of Romania.*[2] These include seven of the eleven listed by IZJ, which however also includes pieces written after Cioran's return to Romania.

These differences do not necessarily reflect editorial or authorial manipulation or suppression, or simple errors of attribution. Some arise from differences in the chronological period being covered; others, from varying categorical definitions of what constitutes "philosophical," "historical," or "political" writing.

Between the three of them, Aurel Cioran, Marta Petreu, and IZJ list over fifty articles as pertaining to Cioran's German experience in one way or another, of which seventeen derive from the time of his actual residence there. Eight of these seventeen specify German topics in their titles. From 1933: "The German Aspect," "From the University of Berlin," and "Germany and France or the Illusory Peace." From 1934: "Problematical Ethics in Germany," "Letters from Munich: Romania from Abroad," "Impressions from Munich: Hitler in the German Conscience," "Letters from Germany: The Revolt of the Villagers," and, probably, "Dictatorship and the Problem of the Young."

Looked at from the outside, without analyzing the contents of all these essays, one can draw two obvious conclusions. First, that Cioran was a very prolific writer, producing perhaps over a hundred periodical essays during the 1930s, at times under the most difficult personal and political circumstances (though he thrived on adversity), while also composing and publishing half a dozen books—several of which naturally incorporated material from some of these essays. Second, that his most vehemently fascistic, pro-Hitler articles constitute somewhere between ten and twenty percent of his output during this time.

To allow readers to form their own partial conclusions, one of the essays from Cioran's German period is printed below, and an excerpt from another, both translated by Ioana Patuleanu. [KRJ]

## Impressions from Munich: Hitler in the German Consciousness

### *Vremea* [The Times], 15 July 1934

*Mr. Emil Cioran, our correspondent in Germany, who happened to be in Munich when the recent events that shook the entire world took place, sends his report.*

*As one can see in the lines below, our correspondent merely sketches a portrait of Hitler, the way he thinks that the Germans see him at this moment.*

*As far as the drama itself is concerned, Mr. Cioran refrains from sending any details.*

*The events that took place in Munich at the beginning of last week remain, therefore, shrouded in the same mystery.*[3]

There is no politician today who inspires me with a greater sympathy and admiration than Hitler. There is something irresistible in the destiny of this man, for whom every act of his life gains significance only through a symbolic participation in the historical destiny of a nation. For Hitler is a man who does not have what is called a private life. Since the war, his life has been nothing but renunciation and sacrifice. A politician's lifestyle gains depth only when the desire for power and an imperialistic will to conquer are accompanied by a great capacity for self-restraint.

The Führer's mystique in Germany is totally justified. Even those who imagine themselves to be Hitler's passionate adversaries, who claim to hate him, are in reality caught in the waves of this mystique, which has turned Hitler's personality into a myth. When Roehm's conspiracy took place and nothing official was yet known, I encountered many of those who only the day before did not hesitate to deprecate Hitler, now exclaiming: "If only Hitler were unharmed!"

His discourses are fraught with a pathos and frenzy that only the visions of a prophetic spirit could possibly reach. Goebbels is a finer, subtler spirit, his irony is more discrete, his gestures are more nuanced, and he appears to be a refined and consummate intellectual, but he cannot explode in a violent and torrential way to the point of depriving you of your critical spirit. Hitler's merit consists in having stolen the critical spirit of a nation. You cannot dynamize something and create an effervescence unless you deprive people of the freedom of a distance between you and them. The fecundity of a vision is revealed only in the capacity to seduce. To be able to make others become irresponsible for the road they have taken, that is the dramatic destiny and responsibility of any visionary, dictator, and prophet.

As far as Hitler is concerned, the capacity to seduce is even more impressive, since it is not aided by an expressive physiognomy. His face expresses nothing but energy and sadness. Because it needs to be known: Hitler is a sad man. A sadness that is the result of too much seriousness. This is characteristic of the entire German people, a desperately serious people, compared to whom Latin nations are nations of clowns.

In Berlin, I once had the opportunity to witness some sort of a collective ecstasy in front of the Führer. On the occasion of a solemnity, at the moment when Hitler was passing on Unter den Linden, the people rushed and surrounded the car, but were unable to utter a word in their awe. Hitler is so rooted in the German consciousness that only a massive disappointment could possibly deviate the people from such a cult. It is extremely strange how after the party's recent crisis Hitler still won the nation's trust.

Those who have reservations about Hitler refer to his lack of culture. As if one needed to quote Goethe in each discourse in order to be able to rule a nation! What counts is an infinite vibration of the soul, a will for an absolute fulfillment in history, an intense exaltation bordering on the absurd, an irrational drive to sacrifice your life.

We must admit that this great tension is present to a certain extent in the dictatorships of Europe today. In order to become a [major] power, such a tension is necessary; one must seriously wonder whether small nations could possibly make a leap forward without a dictatorship.

It is also true that dictatorships represent crises of the spirit. Any dictatorship marks a lack in the historical progress of a culture. Many national-socialists admit that. The problem with the German culture is its lack of universality. With national-socialism, the illusion of universality disappeared. Judging from a strictly political perspective, national socialism is a tremendously wide movement, on a formidable scale. An extraordinary dynamism has taken hold of the nation and impressed upon it a rhythm of tremendous intensity. In just one year, national-socialism has created more [adherents] than fascism created in ten. Mussolini may be better equipped than Hitler; one must not forget, though, that Hitler had more to struggle with, was confronted with incomparably greater difficulties, and that the destiny of Germany is infinitely more complex and dramatic than Italy's. In Germany, a true social tragedy is taking place: under the circumstances, it is humanly impossible to defeat unemployment. The tension within the nation is so intense that, since it is impossible to find immediate and concrete solutions to so many problems that are impossible to solve at the moment, an atmosphere of "eternal dynamism" prevails, the dangers of which von Papen signaled in his Marburg discourse, which marked a violent criticism against the government, in the name of the Catholic opposition.[4]

The Catholic opposition is, indeed, strong. Since the Pope forbade young Catholics to become members of the Hitler-Jugend, the Hitlerists' reaction and pressure led to a severe conflict with the Catholics. The Bavarians, who are Catholic and extremely religious, if faced with a choice between Catholicism and national-socialism, would not hesitate one moment before they chose their religious convictions.

Hitler, nevertheless, means much more to the German people than some Pope who interferes in the internal affairs of a people, in the name of a Christianity, which, trivialized by politics, calls itself Catholicism.

Hitler has poured a fiery passion into political fights and has breathed a messianic spirit into a whole set of values which democratic nationalism had rendered dull and trivial. We all need such a mystique, as we are all sick of so many truths from which no flames ever spring forth.

## *from* Aspects of Germany

### *Vremea*, 19 November 1933[5]

In order to understand the spirit of Germany today, it is absolutely necessary to love everything that is exaggerated, everything that emerges out of an excessive and overwhelming passion, to be enraptured by everything that is [characterized by] irrational élan and disconcerting monumentality. I have always loved Germany for that character of *Formlosigkeit* [formlessness], which, even if it has occasionally degenerated into the grotesque, it is no less true that we owe to it part of the sublime values and achievements that temporarily bring us out of the vulgarity of everyday life. In this world, one should only love people who are excessive. Everybody else, whoever is not intelligent, is mediocre, calculated, their spirit is critical and ironic. But I am asking everyone this question: isn't it time we got rid of everything that is critical spirit, calculation, measure, or form? Indeed, there are quite a few things that we still need to deny in order for the negation to lead us to certainties, ecstasy, and the sublime.

If Germany today has managed to do something, if the Germans live a life of mad enthusiasm and admirable effervescence, it is because at some point they had the courage of annihilation, the passion for a fertile and creative barbarism, and especially a messianism that foreigners find difficult to understand. I don't want to address here either the attitude of small countries towards the Hitlerist phenomenon or my own personal attitude towards it; what interests me is whether or not it participates in the immanent sense of German history. Any man, no matter how limited his understanding of history might be, must admit the indisputable fact that Hitlerism was a *destiny* for Germany.

. . . Small cultures make no sense and have no value in the world of history. This is why they should be, if not destroyed, at least ignored.

. . . If Russian and Jewish messianism bear the colors of religion, German messianism is of a historical nature. While both Russian and Jewish messianism talk about a liberation and salvation through a people of a divine covenant, the fulfillment of which leads to a resolution of the historical process, the Germanic one starts with the excellence of a particular ethnic type amongst other ethnic types, and rests only upon an actual fulfillment within the immanence of history. The first two have an obvious apocalyptical character, an overt intention to transcend and defeat history. German anti-Semitism has its origins in the instinctive reaction of a Northern messianism of German essence against a Southern messianism of Jewish essence. The same applies to Russian anti-Semitism. (In the historical conditions in which the Jews live, they are too well endowed in order to be defeated, just as they are too well endowed in order to ever win).

Has not God suffered enough when he sent his son to die on the cross, did he have to crucify his chosen people several times over?

# Notes

## Introduction

1. Cioran, interview with Fritz Raddatz, *Entretiens,* 183.

2. The quotations are Cioran's own words. He described the scene at the Flore in many interviews, as well as to me personally, especially the detail about Simone de Beauvoir.

3. Maurice Nadeau, "Un penseur crépusculaire," *Combat* 29 (September 1949).

4. My personal interview with Simone Boué.

5. 20 January 1950; Liiceanu, *Itinéraires d'une vie,* 50–51 (italics added).

6. Cioran, Gabriel Liiceanu interview, in *Itinéraires . . . ,* 108–9.

7. Cioran, interview with J. Weiss, *Grand Street* (1983), 106, 138.

8. André Maurois, *Opéra,* 14 December, 1949.

9. Claude Mauriac, *Table Ronde,* January 1950.

10. Stéphane Mallarmé, "Le tombeau d'Edgar Poe," *Poems,* trans. Roger Fry (New York: New Directions, 1951), 108–9.

11. Two plays inspired by Cioran's texts, interviews, and journal were produced in Paris shortly after his death: *Conversations avec Cioran* (1996) and *Insomnies avec Cioran* (1999).

12. Cioran, interview with Hans-Jurgen Heinrichs (1983), reprinted in *Magazine Littéraire,* 373, February 1999, 102–3.

13. Liiceanu, "Les Continents de l'insomnie," in *Itinéraires,* 76.

14. Cioran himself explained the origin of his name to me. He has also observed, with pointed interest, how some people change their names after important or traumatic experiences (Cioran, interview with Weiss, 113).

15. Vladimir Tismaneanu, "Romania's Mystical Revolutionaries," *Partisan Review* 61 (1994): 601.

16. William James, *Varieties of Religious Experience,* 199; quoted in Erik Erikson, *Young Man Luther,* 41.

17. In *Young Man Luther* (1958), Erik Erikson describes his revisionary version of the classical Freudian "identity crisis" as it applies to "self-made" men, exemplifying it by the case of Luther. He elaborated this model in *Gandhi's Truth* (1969). The pattern is also useful for understanding Cioran.

18. Jerry Z. Muller, *The Other God That Failed: Hans Freyer and the Deradicalization of German Conservatism,* 4–11. As Muller notes, the phrase "the god that failed" has usually been

applied to communism; he cites a 1949 anthology of the same title (ed. Richard Crossman) which contains autobiographical accounts of disillusionment among leftist intellectuals, such as Arthur Koestler, Ignazio Silone, André Gide, Richard Wright, and Stephen Spender. He also notes that accounts of political disillusionment among right-wing intellectuals have been comparatively rarer, although he recognizes a tradition in this vein that extends back to the "Counter-Enlightenment," including such figures as Hegel and Schleiermacher in Germany, and Burke, Wordsworth, and Coleridge in England.

19. Ibid., 12.

20. Ibid., 19.

21. See Matei Calinescu's foreword, which compares IZJ's book to Bollon's and to two others, one by Marta Petreu, the other by Alexandra Laignel-Lavastine. Petreu's book contains valuable information about Cioran's writings from Germany, which I have added to Appendix 2. (KRJ)

22. Milan Kundera, *Testaments Betrayed* (New York: HarperCollins, 1995), 191.

23. Hannah Arendt, *The Origins of Totalitarianism,* xiv (italics added).

24. Kundera, *Testaments Betrayed,* 191.

25. William Wordsworth, *The Prelude* (1805), Book X, 692–93.

26. Cioran, *Ţara mea / Mon Pays* (1996); my translation. In her foreword to this booklet, Simone Boué, who discovered the manuscript in a brown envelope marked "Mon Pays," estimates that the undated text was written prior to 1960 when Cioran moved to his attic apartment in the rue de l'Odéon.

27. Cioran, "De l'inconvénient d'être né," in *Œuvres,* 1299.

28. Cioran, "Penser contre soi," *La tentation d'exister,* 18.

29. Quoted in Erikson, *Young Man Luther,* 13.

30. Cioran, *L'incovénient*, in *Œuvres,* 1332.

31. Cioran, "Valéry face à ses idoles," *Exercises d'admiration,* 75.

32. Sorin Antohi, *Civitas imaginalis: Istorie şi utopie in cultura romana* [Civitas Imaginalis: History and Utopia in Romanian Culture], 224.

33. Cioran, *Anthologie du portrait,* 17.

### 1. Răşinari, Transylvania, 1911–1921

1. Cioran, *Cahiers,* 32.

2. Cioran, letter to Bucur Ţincu (*Scrisori* [*Letters*], 319).

3. The memory dates from 1921, when Cioran was ten years old, just three years after the union of Transylvania, a former Austro-Hungarian province, with the neighboring kingdom of Romania.

4. Cioran, "De l'inconvénient d'être né," *Œuvres,* 1274.

5. Ibid., 1283.

6. Cioran, *Cahiers,* 769.

7. Cioran, interview with J. L. Almira, *Entretiens,* 122.

8. Cioran, interview with Leo Gillet, *Entretiens,* 70.

9. Cioran, letter to his brother, *Scrisori,* 56.

10. Cioran, *Cahiers,* 111–12.

11. Cioran, *Œuvres,* 1271.
12. Cioran, *Cahiers,* 102.
13. Cioran, interview with Fernando Savater, *Entretiens,* 19.
14. Cioran, interview with Luis Jorge Jalfen, *Entretiens,* 111–12.
15. Cioran, *Cahiers,* 137.
16. Ibid.
17. Cioran, "La Tentation d'exister," *Œuvres,* 851.
18. Ibid., 851.
19. Mihai Rădulescu, cited in Petreu, *Un trecut deocheat,* 267.
20. Vlad Georgescu, *Istoria Romanilor*, 52. Even before the annexation by Austria, as early as 1437, an act entitled "the brotherly union," *Unio Trium Nationum,* asserted the "political monopoly of the Hungarian nobility and the Saxon [German] and Secuis [Magyar] patriciate, and the exclusion of the Romanians from any rights as a separate nation." Subsequently, "the segregation policy which affected the majority of the Transylvanian population was further reinforced . . . first by effectively turning the peasant population into serfs and secondly, by limiting official recognition to only four religions—Catholic, Lutheran, Calvinist and Uniate [Eastern Catholic]—while the Orthodox religion was declared tolerated."
21. Ibid., 189. The struggle became particularly fierce after 1867, when the dual monarchy was instituted and Transylvania was annexed to Hungary. *Magyarization* meant first of all a policy of one official language. It went as far as the passing of a law in 1917 which restricted voting rights to speakers of Hungarian who had studied at Hungarian schools.
22. Ibid., 110–12; also 188–90. The pleas for reform started with the Uniate Bishopric of Inochentie Micu-Klein (1728–51) who during his lifetime wrote dozens of memoranda. In 1791, another long plea, the *Supplex Libellus Valachorum,* was sent to Vienna. In 1848, in Blaj, a "national petition" was adopted, sent both to the local authorities in Cluj and to Vienna. More memoranda were sent to Vienna in the 1860s and 1890s. They had little beneficial effect.
23. Ibid., 110, 142.
24. Patrice Bollon, *Cioran l'hérétique,* 38.
25. Păcală, 36 [source not found; see Bibliography].
26. Ibid., 106, 108.
27. Letter to Aurel (Relu) Cioran, *Scrisori,* 56.
28. Păcală, 1.
29. His father was incarcerated at Sopron, in western Hungary, on the border with Austria, his mother in Cluj, the capital city of Transylvania.
30. Cioran, interview with Max Jakob, *Entretiens,* 298.
31. Cioran, *Cahiers,* 369.
32. In an interview with François Bondy, Cioran speaks of priesthood not as a vocation but as the only profession open to an educated Romanian in Transylvania. He insists that his father was not fanatically religious, only a practicing Christian who mixed his religion with the pragmatism of a man of common sense (*Entretiens,* 7–17). But he said his mother was not a believer (interview with Lea Vergine, *Entretiens,* 130).
33. Mihai Sorin Rădulescu, "La Généalogie d'Émile Cioran," *Généalogie,*140 (August 1995), 34.
34. Ibid., 29.

35. The Romanian Orthodox population of Transylvania, as part of the Austro-Hungarian empire, was under the jurisdiction of the Serbian Orthodox church, not that of the Romanian Orthodox church in the nearby provinces of Moldavia and Wallachia.

36. This incident is recounted by Emilian Cioran in his 1955 book *Seven Generations of Priests, Archpriests, Professors from the Same Family: Barcianu, 1699–1903,* published posthumously by Cioran's brother, Aurel, in 1991.

37. Rădulescu, "La Généalogie d'Émile Cioran," 31.

38. A member of the Enlightenment movement known as *Şcoala Ardeleana,* "The Transylvanian School," Petru Maior is the author of the 1812 book *History of the Romanians' Beginnings in Dacia.*

39. Cioran, *Scrisori,* 146, 149.

40. I asked Relu Cioran if there was any madness in the family and whether he thought his brother's suspicions were justified. He assured me that there was no madness but spoke of his mother as a sensitive and melancholy person.

41. Cioran, letter to Aurel, written at the time of their mother's death in 1966, *Scrisori,* 50.

42. In letters to his brother, but especially in his journal, Cioran's obsession with illness and the amount of time he spends paying attention to various, but invariably small, aches and pains is remarkable.

43. Cioran, letter to his brother, *Scrisori,* 50.

44. Cioran, *Cahiers,* 957.

45. Ibid., 957.

46. Ibid.

47. Ibid., 427.

48. Ibid., 15.

49. Ibid., 232.

50. Ibid., 514.

51. Ibid., 63.

52. Cioran, *Œuvres,* 851.

53. Cioran, *Cahiers,* 687.

54. Ibid., 699.

55. Ibid., 342.

56. Ibid., 964.

57. Ibid., 83, 102 [April–July 1962]. Or again: "I am of the Slavs and the Magyars, I have nothing of the Latin [in me]." Ibid., 128 [November 1962].

58. Vlad Georgescu in his *Istoria Romanilor* (191) explains that the Romanian nationalist party in Transylvania during the war was divided in several factions: those who directly favored the union with Romania (led by the poet Octavian Goga, originally from Răşinari); those who were waiting to see the turn of events (led by Iuliu Maniu); and the federalist group favoring the solution of the Romanian question inside a federalized Austria (led by Aurel Popovici). Cioran alludes to the latter, and it is clear that it is the solution *he* would have preferred, but whether his father had belonged to Popovici's faction is less clear. Since he was one of the signers of the union and since he was from Răşinari, like Goga, with whom the Ciorans were related, it is much more likely that his father had belonged to Goga's party.

59. Cioran, interview with François Fejtö, *Entretiens,* 194.

**2. Sibiu, 1921–1928**

1. The province was conquered by Trajan during two campaigns, 101–102 BC and 105–106 BC.

2. Ovid, *Epistulae ex Ponto* ["Black Sea Letters"], trans. Peter Green (London: Penguin, 1994), I.3.49–50; II.7.63–65.

3. Cioran, *Entretiens,* 286.

4. Compare to Ulm with 17 guilds, Augsburg with 15, Cologne with 22, and Strasbourg with 25.

5. Quoted in Nicolae Nistor and Mircea Morinescu-Frotânei, *Sibiul şi ţinutul în lumina istoriei,* II.155.

6. The Romanians were allowed in the town late and in small numbers, mostly in the suburbs. Still, in 1811 they opened a theological institute; in 1861 they founded Astra: The Transylvanian Society for Literature and Culture, which opened its museum and library in 1905, and by 1906 they had also managed to erect their own church, the Orthodox Cathedral built in the style of St. Sophia in Constantinople.

7. Cioran, interview with Michael Jakob, *Entretiens,* 286. In an interview with François Fejtö, the Hungarian journalist who was also an old friend, Cioran gives a slightly rosier picture of multi-lingual Sibiu. Instead of referring to the slave status of Romanians and Hungarians in Sibiu, he said that, in spite of a German majority, "none of the three languages was especially privileged" (*Entretiens,* 190).

8. Cioran, *Cahiers,* 678.

9. The transfer of sovereignty was not officially ratified until the Treaty of Trianon, 1920 (Gabriel Liiceanu, *Itinéraires,* 4).

10. Cioran, *Entretiens,* 190, 286.

11. Cioran is not sure of the date. He indicates it may have been 1919, in which case he would have been taken there by his parents for a special outing. Most likely though, he saw the movie in 1921, after his move to Sibiu (*Cahiers,* 345).

12. Ibid.

13. Cioran, interview with F. Fejtö, *Entretiens,* 191.

14. Ibid.

15. Cioran, letter to his brother, *Scrisori* ["Letters Home"], 145. To which he added, "we wasted our youth running after delusions."

16. Cioran, interview with Fernando Savater, *Entretiens,* 18.

17. Ibid.

18. Cioran, letter to Bucur Ţincu, *Letters,* 318–19.

19. The Sunday performance at *popice* was not the only one for which Emil practiced with such doggedness. He loved music—he and his mother shared a common passion for Bach—and played the violin, practicing long hours into the night, until one day at fourteen he decided that he was not good enough and gave up playing. The violin was put away and never heard again.

20. Cioran, *Cahiers,* 571.

21. Cioran, letter to his brother, *Scrisori,* 71.

22. Cioran, letter to Bucur Ţincu, *Scrisori,* 316; cf. *Cahiers,* 753 (October 1969), for Cioran's speculation that the *raté* is a specifically Romanian type.

23. Ibid.

24. Cioran, letter to Bucur Ţincu, dated April 5, 1932, in *Cioran: Twelve Letters from the Heights of Despair,* 53.

25. The Ţincu family was so proud that their mother made it a point of honor to call after the children as they left the house: "wipe the chocolate torte crumbs off your mouth!" Thus she sent a message to any neighbors within hearing: "we're doing so well that we can afford chocolate cake every day for dinner."

26. Petru never wrote anything after his adolescent volume. The promising literary career of his brother Bucur, philosopher, journalist, and diplomat, was cut short by a triple coincidence of unfortunate circumstances: the advent of communism, which cost him his job in the Ministry of Information, a car accident, and a disastrous marriage.

27. Paul Morand, *Bucharest,* 288.

28. Ibid.

29. Cioran, *Cahiers,* 552.

30. Ibid.

31. Cioran, interview with Michael Jakob, *Entretiens,* 288.

32. Ibid.

33. Cioran, *Cahiers,* 127. Henri Frederic Amiel (1821–81), Swiss protestant writer attracted to nineteenth-century German idealist philosophy.

34. Cioran, interview with Jakob, *Entretiens,* 288.

35. Ibid., 287.

36. The exact moment when he started suffering from insomnia varies from interview to interview, but judging from the evidence in his journal, age seventeen seems the more likely candidate for the watershed year.

37. Cioran, *Cahiers,* 33.

38. Cioran, interview with Lea Vergine, *Entretiens,* 134.

39. Cioran, interview with Jakob, *Entretiens,* 287.

40. Cioran, *Cahiers,* 98–99.

41. Ibid., 776.

42. Ibid., 685.

43. Cioran, from a letter to "Mon cher Maître" [unidentified] of 29 April 1957.

44. Ibid.

45. "Astra" is short for the Transylvanian Association for Romanian Literature and Culture; its library was established in 1861. The "Metropolitan" was the library of the Romanian Orthodox Bishopric of Sibiu, founded in 1656.

46. Cioran, *Cahiers,* 334.

47. Quoted in *Cioran: Twelve Letters from the Heights of Despair,* 68.

48. Cioran, *Cahiers,* 334.

49. Ibid.

50. Cioran's version of the incident gives the boy another nickname, "The Louse." But according to Cioran's brother Aurel, who was present during the park incident, the real nickname was the more explicit one.

51. Information from Cioran's brother, himself a customer of the same houses, often in

company with his brother. According to Aurel, the houses enjoyed the reputation of being safe. The women were checked weekly by gynecologists and carried at all times papers attesting to their good health.

52. Cioran, interview with Gerd Bergfleth, *Entretiens,* 147; but the laboratory test was negative (Liiceanu, *Itinéraires,* 13).

53. Cioran, *Tears and Saints,* 29.

54. Cioran, letter to his brother, *Scrisori,* 142.

55. Cioran, *Twelve Letters,* 75.

56. Ibid., 76.

57. Ibid., 77.

### 3. Bucharest, 1928–1933

1. Paul Morand, *Bucharest,* 146. Morand was a conservative modernist writer and diplomat who later collaborated with the Vichy regime, but his views of inter-war Bucharest, though sometimes condescending, do, in the opinion of members of my father's generation, capture its atmosphere well.

2. Ibid., 140.

3. Ibid.

4. All the quotations are from ibid., 172, 284–85.

5. A still-popular Romanian expression for rampant corruption is "like thieves in a Wallachian forest."

6. Morand, *Bucharest,* 76.

7. Ibid., 128–29.

8. Ibid., 290 (my translation).

9. The other two leaders were Ion C. Brătianu, one of Romania's most liberal prime ministers (died 1927), and Vintila Brătianu (died 1930).

10. Georgescu, *Istoria Romanilor,* 235.

11. Cioran, unpublished manuscript, "Ferveur d'un barbare."

12. Cioran, *Twelve Letters,* 34.

13. V. S. Naipaul, *Reading and Writing,* 2.

14. Cioran, *Cahiers* (?). [Reference not found. *Cahiers* 334 (January 1966) has a similar formulation, but this one is more polished, suggesting that it comes from one of Cioran's published works. KRJ]

15. Ibid., 886–87.

16. The street and its buildings were torn down during the Communist period.

17. Arşavir Acterian, quoted in Zigu Ornea's "Ultimul prieten al lui Cioran şi Eugen Ionescu" [The Last Friend of Cioran and Ionescu].

18. During the Communist era the King Carol Foundation was known as the Central University Library. It burned down during the 1989 street disturbances that led to the downfall of Ceauşescu.

19. Morand, *Bucharest,* 210.

20. *Shelley's Poetry and Prose,* ed. Donald Reiman and Sharon Powers (Norton, 1977),

127–28. The "sage" in ll. 22–23 has been conjectured to be the Stoic philosopher Marcus Aurelius.

21. Cioran, *Cahiers,* 98.

22. Dan Petraşincu, "O mistică necesară" (1934), in *Pro şi Contra Emil Cioran,* 12.

23. Leon Şestov, or Chestov (1866–1938), Russian-born Jewish Romanian philosopher, author of *The Idea of Good in Tolstoy and Nietzsche* (1900) and *Dostoevsky and Nietzsche: The Philosophy of Tragedy* (1903).

24. Cioran tells the story of this revelation in various places: *Cahiers,* 114; *Entretiens,* 40–41.

25. Cioran, *Twelve Letters,* 23.

26. Georg Simmel (1858–1918), German philosopher and sociologist; author of, among other works, *On Individuality and Social Forms.*

27. Cioran, *Twelve Letters,* 21.

28. Ibid., 34.

29. Ibid., 29.

30. Ibid., 39.

31. Vladimir Tismaneanu and Dan Pavel, "Romania's Mystical Revolutionaries: The Generation of Angst and Adventure Revisited," 432.

32. My interview with Relu Cioran.

33. Arşavir Acterian, "Amintiri despre Emil Cioran [Recollections of E. C.]," *Pro şi Contra Emil Cioran,* 286.

34. *Du sang, de la volupté et de la mort.* Barrès's trilogy of novels, *Le Culte du Moi* (1888–91), would have attracted Cioran. Barrès (1862–1923) was, with his chauvinistic nationalism combined with extreme individualism, a sort of proto-Cioran, except that his patriotism was fueled by an intense hatred of Germany.

35. From Cioran's reading cards in his brother's archive.

36. Cioran, *Twelve Letters,* 49.

37. Ibid., 39 (24 January, 1931).

38. Zigu Ornea, *Anii treizeci: Extrema dreaptă românească* [The Nineteen Thirties: The Romanian Extreme Right], 146.

39. Malraux, quoted in Gaëtan Picon, *Malraux par lui-même,* 29.

40. Petru Comarnescu, *Jurnal: 1931–1937* (1994), 12.

41. Mircea Vulcănescu, "Generaţie," *Criterion* (Nov. 15–Dec. 1, 1934), 6.

42. Cioran, *Cahiers,* 98 (1962).

43. Cioran, *Tears and Saints,* 42.

44. Petreu, *Un trecut deocheat,* 270–71.

45. *Gândirea* [The Thinking], founded in 1921 in Cluj, moved to Bucharest in 1922, where it came under the influence and directorship of Nichifor Crainic (1889–1972), a neo-Orthodox theologian and nationalist who based his anti-Semitism on the Gospels rather than racial stereotypes. Originally dedicated to promoting cultural forms that could be defined as both modern and nationalistic, the journal became increasingly traditional, mystical, and Orthodox. By the 1930s it was suspected of supporting the Iron Guard, and it endorsed Romania's dictatorial regimes during World War II. Its ideological shifts parallel those of many members

of Cioran's generation. It folded in 1944, when Romania left the Axis and joined the Allies. Crainic was imprisoned for fifteen years by Romania's post-war Communist government.

46. Mihail Sebastian, *Depuis deux mille ans,* trans. Alain Paruit, 202–4 (my translation into English, IZJ).

47. Ibid., 207–9.

48. Mihail Sebastian, *Journal: 1935–1944,* 303.

49. Ibid., 311 (25 January 1941).

50. Ibid., 309. Whether Cioran was posted to Paris or, as both he and IZJ say, to Vichy, remains unclear, although Vichy, as the seat of the Pétain government, would be where any diplomat posted to Nazi-occupied France would have had to report first. (KRJ)

51. It is in this same month of 1941 that Sebastian begins recording rumors, then confirmations, of murders, executions, assassinations of, at first hundreds, then thousands, of Jews, some in Bucharest but many more in the northern parts of the country, Bukovina and Moldavia, particularly in and around the provincial capital, Iaşi.

52. Sebastian, *Journal,* 323. Horia Sima (1907–93) was briefly vice-president of the Antonescu-Legionnaire government. He had been a fellow student with Cioran in the philosophy faculty of the University of Bucharest, 1926–32.

53. Ibid., 321, 335.

54. Ibid., 304 (8 January 1941).

55. Ibid., 198 (17 January 1939).

56. Ibid., 334.

57. Dimitrie Gusti (b. 1880) was both a sociologist and an ethnographer. Founder of the Village Museum, which is still one of Bucharest's best tourist attractions, Gusti was made a member of the Romanian Academy in 1919.

58. But there is one very particular compositional note, in his parenthetical observation at the end of "The World and I": "(These lines were written today, April 8, 1933, when I turn twenty-two. It is strange to think that I am already a specialist in the question of death.)"

59. Fernando Savater, "El ultimo dandi," *El Pais,* 25 October 1990.

60. Cioran, *Syllogismes de l'amertume,* 22.

61. Cioran, *Twelve Letters,* 49.

62. Ibid., 49.

63. Ibid., 25.

64. Fernando Savater, *Ensayo sobre Cioran*, 136.

65. Cioran, *Twelve Letters,* Letter 11 (April 1933).

### 4. Berlin, 1933–1935

1. The author was working on this chapter at the time her illness prevented her from undertaking any more extended research or writing. I have composed it from her drafts, her reading notes, and her marginal comments in Cioran's published writings. (KRJ)

2. Cioran, *Twelve Letters,* 53 (5 April 1932).

3. Cioran, *Tears and Saints,* 10.

4. Lewis Coser, *Masters of Sociological Thought,* 198.

5. Cioran, *Cahiers,* 158.
6. Ibid., 127 (1962).
7. Lessing was assassinated by the Gestapo at Marienbad on 31 August 1933, an event that is said to have convinced Albert Einstein of the danger of trying to return to Germany. The murder must have been a topic somewhere in Cioran's introductory conversations with his new mentor Klages, Lessing's old friend, little more than a month later.
8. Cioran, *Cahiers,* 764 (1969).
9. Ibid.
10. Ibid., 383 (1966).
11. Ibid., 646–47 (1968).
12. Ibid., 579 (1968).
13. "À la veille de la dictature," *Vremea* [The Times], 21 February 1937; quoted in Liiceanu, *Itinéraires,* 26.
14. Ibid. In a somewhat similar way, after he published his own fascistic book upon his return home (*Romania's Transfiguration*), he records that he fell into a *religious* crisis, the result of which was *Tears and Saints* (1936), an attack on Christianity and clericalism infused with a passionate *spiritual* admiration for the "tearful" disciplines of radically individualistic saints and martyrs.
15. Cioran, *Cahiers,* 833 (September 1970). But by the time he wrote this, he was eager to distance both himself and his country from it: "Not a Romanian phenomenon. Besides, the chief of the Iron Guard was a Slav."
16. Cf., for example, the Romanian military officer in Thomas Mann's *The Magic Mountain.* The first two volumes of Olivia Manning's "Balkan Trilogy," *The Great Fortune* (1960) and *The Spoilt City* (1962), have a full cast of decadent Romanian aristocrats, though most Romanians find it overdrawn.
17. This paragraph is paraphrased from Liiceanu, *Itinéraires,* 32–33.
18. From Cioran's *Romania's Transfiguration* (1936), quoted in ibid., 113–14.
19. Cioran, *Cahiers,* 17–18 (1958).
20. Ibid., 203 (1963).
21. Ibid. (1964).

## 5. *Romania's Transfiguration,* 1935–1937

1. Mircea Eliade to Cioran, unpublished letter, archive of Aurel Cioran.
2. Cioran, *Scrisori,* 273.
3. Ornea, *Anii Treizeci,* 149.
4. Cioran, *L'incovénient,* in *Œuvres,* 1285.
5. Cioran, *Anthologie,* 26.
6. E. M. Cioran, *Schimbarea la faţă a României,* 95. This and all following translations from *Romania's Transfiguration* are my own. Page numbers included in the text are from the original Romanian edition of 1936.
7. Another, more intimate tension is between his "right" to criticize Romania versus anyone else doing so: "I detest, it is not too much to say, my country and especially my

compatriots. But if a stranger speaks badly of them (of my country especially), I feel that I have been directly attacked, provoked. This reaction is banal enough; it hinders me each time that I discover it in myself, it surprises me and makes me pause and reflect" (Cioran, *Cahiers,* 68 [1960]).

8. Erikson, *Young Man Luther,* 102.

9. The document was found in an envelope with this title by Simone Boué after Cioran's death.

10. Cioran, *Mon Pays,* 137.

11. Antohi, *Civitas imaginalis,* 221.

12. Erikson, *Young Man Luther,* 13.

13. E. M. Cioran, unpublished letter to Petre Comarnescu, courtesy of Romanian Museum of Literary History (Cioran's emphasis).

14. Cioran, *L'inconvénient,* in *Œuvres,* 1279.

15. Ibid.

16. Or downright begging for them. In a letter to Mircea Eliade of 1937, the year he left Romania, Cioran confesses his unsuitability for the Romanian nationalist movement and begs Eliade to help him win a fellowship to Italy, but fears it may be too late, for otherwise "letters of recommendation I will ask even from God himself. . . . Be so kind and send me to Italy" (*Scrisori,* 274–75). This letter, coming after the publication of *Romania's Transfiguration,* and four years after the letter to Comarnescu, contrasts sharply with the latter. His opportunism is no longer disguised and entangled with high talk about a saving mission, nor is his fascination with suffering going to keep him tied to his fatherland and turn him into a willing sacrificial victim: "nor can all of St. Teresa's ecstasies extinguish in me the maddening desire to go abroad. There's in me a longing for space which is becoming pathological." Holding fellowships as an "eternal student" becomes, in effect, Cioran's next "career," an idea which first occurred to him in Braşov, and which he realized at the end of 1937, when he went to Paris on a three-year fellowship. Much of his later life in Paris follows the same pattern: living like a perennial graduate student and, later, dining out perpetually on the basis of his literary reputation.

17. Matei Calinescu, "'How Can One Be What One Is?' Reading the Romanian and the French Cioran," 199.

18. Irina Livezeanu, *Cultural Politics in Greater Romania: Regionalism, Nation Building, and Ethnic Struggle, 1918–1930,* 19.

19. Ibid., 7.

20. Ibid., 134.

21. Ibid., 16.

22. Ibid., 14.

23. Calinescu, "'How Can One Be What One Is?'" 214.

24. Antohi, *Civitas imaginalis,* 222.

25. Cioran to Eliade, letter 549, *Scrisori,* 270–71.

26. Cioran to Eliade, letter 554, ibid., 275.

27. Livezeanu, *Cultural Politics,* 147.

28. Source not located. Neither letter appears in *Scrisori către cei de-acasă,* nor in *Scrisori*

*din tinerețe*, ed. Alexandru Condeescu (Bucharest: Muzeul Literaturii Române, 1999). There is no complete edition of Cioran's letters. IZJ made copies or transcriptions of many, in the Bucharest archives; these may be among them. (KRJ)

29. Zigu Ornea also makes note of the common-sense difficulty among these young men, for all their apocalyptic conversations and ideals, of finding work by which to maintain themselves. Although Cioran hated it, getting his teaching job was no easy matter, despite his holding a doctorate in philosophy and having nearly two years' experience in Germany. His letters repeatedly ask his parents to use their influence to get him interviews and letters of recommendation, from the right wing politician Octavian Goga among others (Ornea, *Anii Treizeci*, 187).

30. Cioran, interview with Gerd Bergfleth, *Entretiens*, 148.

31. The Barcianu family's political activism as recounted by Cioran's father is an example of such pragmatism and prudence. Young Emil must have had such stories very much in his mind at the time he was writing *Romania's Transfiguration*. Thus, his father recounts how Sava P. Barcianu urged compromise when he went in 1848 as a member of the Romanian delegation to Vienna to present a Romanian Bill of Rights at the Imperial Court. Reporting back to Răşinari, he insistently advised patience and restraint at a time of revolution and war: "We shall obtain all the rights enjoyed by the Saxons, and what else do we want? This will be determined at the Hungarian council which will be held pretty soon, namely next month in Pesta [Budapest], and where our bishops have also been invited to work out a plan and set the foundation for the political existence of our nation, of that there is no doubt. *A little patience and caution, so that we don't take a wrong step (I hope you understand me), of which we shall later repent ourselves. Thus I say again, watch that you don't fall into temptation.*"

32. Just how complicated and ambiguous Cioran's stance on nationalism was can be judged if one simply compares him to his younger and less complicated brother, Aurel, who was openly nationalistic, joined the Iron Guard, and went to prison for his convictions and Guardist sympathies.

33. Emilian Cioran, *Seven Generations*, 92.

## 6. *Romania's Transfiguration*, Continuing Controversy

1. Milan Kundera, *Testaments Betrayed*, 229. Kundera is speaking of the example of Victor Farias's biography of Heidegger, *Heidegger and Nazism*.

2. Slavoj Žižek, "The Two Totalitarianisms," *London Review of Books*, 17 March 2005.

3. Bollon, *Cioran, l'hérétique*; Laignel-Lavanstine, *Cioran, Eliade, Ionesco*.

4. Sanda Stolojan, in her book of memoirs, *Au balcon de l'exil roumain à Paris: Avec Cioran, Eugène Ionesco, Mircea Eliade, Vintila Horia . . .*, recalls the savage way in which Cioran altered the original text of *Tears and Saints* (1937) when he worked with her on her French translation of it in 1985. He was obsessed with the impression the book would make on the French public and afraid of its being too "morbid" (215). One could argue that a similar concern determined Cioran's decision not to allow the translation of *Romania's Transfiguration*. Anchored as it (apparently) is in history and politics, the book would have been perceived as too "specific," whereas the French Cioran always aspired to universality. Even worse, of course, was the book's hysterical tone of enthusiasm for political extremism.

5. Cioran, *Schimbarea la față a României.*
6. Kundera, *Testaments Betrayed,* 227, 229.
7. Cioran, *Scrisori* [Letters Home], 114.
8. Ibid., 173.
9. The page numbers do not correspond to either the 1934 or 1990 editions, so, unless Cioran got the numbers wrong, they might be from the 1941 edition, which I have not been able to locate.
10. A "general paralytic" does not mean a completely paralyzed person, but rather someone afflicted with "a disease characterized by a stage of mental excitement with exalted delusions, followed by dementia" (*The Oxford Universal Dictionary*).
11. Since the "my" is feminine (*ma*), perhaps the illegible/deleted word is *femme:* i.e., Simone Boué. Petreu quotes almost exactly the same statement, attributing it to the reaction of Cioran's mother (Petreu, *Un trecut deocheat,* 135).
12. Calinescu, "'How Can One Be What One Is?'" 206–7.
13. Viorel Cosma, *The New Grove Dictionary of Music and Musicians,* vol. 2, 2nd ed., 521–22. Bălan's books include *Arta de înțelege muzica* [The Art of Understanding Music] (1970) and *Musicosophia* (Neustadt, 1981).
14. E. M. Cioran, *George Bălan: In dialog.* (Bucharest, 1996).
15. *The New Encyclopedia Britannica,* vol. 12 (2003), 562–63.
16. Cioran, *Tears and Saints,* 37.
17. Calinescu, "'How Can One Be What One Is?'" 207.
18. Ibid., 207–8.
19. Turning the situation the other way round, he reports in a late journal entry that a Jewish friend of his ("un juif fier de l'être") called him the Wandering Goy ("le 'goy errant'") when he learned of Cioran's habit since the early 1940s of living only in hotels and student dormitories (Cioran, *Cahiers,* 60 [Spring 1960]).
20. Unpublished letter, courtesy Romanian Museum of Literary History.
21. Calinescu, "'How Can One Be What One Is?'" 200.

### 7. *Tears and Saints,* 1937

This chapter is adapted with minor adjustments from my introduction to my translation of *Tears and Saints* (University of Chicago Press, 1995). All quotations are from this text.

1. Cioran, *Cahiers,* 63.
2. The Sibiu seminary contributed substantively to the book as well, for Cioran spent hours in its library during vacations from Brașov, poring over musty old volumes of saints' lives, literally searching for his cast of characters. For it is notable that almost all of them are Catholic, not Orthodox—that is, not "native"—saints, and several are Muslim.
3. Nietzsche, *Beyond Good and Evil,* trans. Helen Zimern, 56.
4. Cioran, *Romania's Transfiguration,* 47.
5. Ibid., 49 (emphasis added).
6. Ibid., 41.
7. Leon Volovici, *Nationalist Ideology and Antisemitism: The Case of Romanian Intellectuals in the 1930s,* 62.

8. Michel de Certeau, *The Mystic Fable,* trans. Michael B. Smith (Chicago: University of Chicago Press, 1992), 153.

9. Ibid., 77–78.

10. Ibid., 14.

11. Ibid., 24.

12. Ibid., 229.

13. Ibid., 170.

14. Ibid., 235–36.

**8. Stranger in Paris**

1. This is the point at which IZJ's continuous, concentrated writing of her book stops. (KRJ)

2. The following pages have been drawn together from four sources: Gabriel Liiceanu's *Itinéraires d'une vie,* 36–38; IZJ's transcriptions from Cioran's notebooks (not yet published at the time she read them); IZJ's citations from *Cahiers, 1957–1972;* and IZJ's references to Cioran's and Simone Boué's comments about wartime Paris in her "Memoirs of a Publishing Scoundrel." (KRJ)

3. Petreu, *Un trecut deocheat,* 278–79.

4. When he moved into his first (and only) real apartment, on the rue de l'Odéon, in 1960, he said, "for ten years, I've dreamed of an apartment. My dream is realized . . . I already regret the hotel years. Possession makes me suffer more than destitution. In fact, I lived in hotels since 1937!" (*Cahiers,* 61).

5. Liiceanu, *Itinéraires d'une vie,* 36.

6. Cioran, *Cahiers,* 83. In spring of 1935 Cioran, coming from Germany, spent some time in Paris visiting his friend Bucur Ţincu, who was there on a scholarship.

7. Liiceanu, *Itinéraires d'une vie,* 36.

8. Cioran, *Cahiers,* 187 (ca. 20 October 1963). There is still a Romanian Orthodox Church in rue Jean de Beauvais.

9. Cioran, *Cahiers,* 216 (March 1964).

10. Petreu, *Un trecut deocheat,* 280. In 1948 Cioran wrote to the committee in charge of memorializing (in the Pantheon) French writers who were victims of the Nazis, urging that Fondane be included (ibid., 281).

11. Cioran, *Exercises d'admiration,* 213.

**9. Conclusion**

Since IZJ did not live to provide a proper conclusion to her book, this essay is offered in lieu of one. It is one of a number of critical essays she was working on to supplement her biography of Cioran. See also her last scholarly essay, "Found in Translation: The Two Lives of E. M. Cioran; or, How Can One Be a Comparatist?" *Comparative Literature Studies* 44 (2007): 20–37. (KRJ)

1. Cioran, *The Temptation to Exist,* trans. Richard Howard, 48–49.

2. Cioran, "Sur les deux types de société," *Histoire et Utopie* (1960), 26–27; translated as "Letter to a Faraway Friend," by Richard Howard, in *History and Utopia.*

3. Cioran, "Sur les deux types de société," 25–26; "Letter to a Faraway Friend," 14–15.

4. Cioran, "Sur les deux types de société," 27; "Letter to a Faraway Friend," 16.

5. Cioran, *Histoire et Utopie,* 52; "Learning from Tyrants," in *Temptation to Exist,* 38.

6. Ibid., 51.

7. Ibid., 52.

8. Horia Patapievici, "Despre intoleranţa: Un studiu de caz" [On Intolerance: A Case Study], 22 (September 9–15, 1997).

9. Cioran, "On Being Lyrical," in *On the Heights of Despair,* 4.

10. Milan Kundera, radio interview with Norman Biron (Radio Canada, Summer 1976), quoted in *Milan Kundera and the Art of Fiction.*

11. Patapievici, "Despre intoleranţa," 12.

12. Cioran, "On Being Lyrical," 5.

13. Cioran, "Dictatura şi problema tineretului" [Dictatorship and the Problem of Youth], *Vremea,* October 7, 1934.

14. Cioran, "Revolta sătuilor" [Revolt of the Villages], *Vremea,* 5 August 1934.

15. Cioran, "Ardealul—Prusia Romaniei" [Ardeal (Transylvania)—the Prussia of Romania], *Vremea,* 1 January 1941.

16. Cioran, "On Being Lyrical," 37–38.

17. Cioran, "Advantages of Exile," in *The Temptation to Exist,* trans. Richard Howard, 74.

**Paris, 1992–1994**

1. Norman Manea, "Felix Culpa," in *On Clowns: The Dictator and the Artist,* 91–125.

2. Pierre Beregovoy (1925–93) headed several ministries in François Mitterand's Socialist government, becoming premier in 1992. He resigned the next year amid charges of corruption and committed suicide 1 May 1993.

3. Sergiu Celibidache (1912–96) the famous Romanian conductor.

**Romania, 1994**

1. This source is not identified other than as Miller, 11. However, the quotation is identical, word for word, to a sentence in Audre Lorde's "biomythography," *Zami: A New Spelling of My Name* (Persephone Press, 1982), 199. Lorde's book concerns her search for her identities, familial, sexual, and geographical, through her Caribbean past and her New York City present—very much the kind of work that interested IZJ (cf. her use of V. S. Naipaul). "Miller" may be the name of an editor of an anthology or of a critical work on these subjects. (KRJ)

2. This is probably the book by Păcală referred to in chapter 1. (KRJ)

3. Corneliu Zelea Codreanu, the charismatic leader of the Iron Guard, murdered in prison by order of King Carol II.

4. Ion Moţa (1902–37), deputy leader of the Iron Guard, killed in battle in the Spanish Civil War, leading a Legionnaire unit. Jailed twice in the mid-1920s for assassination conspiracies against Jews and Romanian politicians.

5. Boulevard Kisseleff, near the north edge of Bucharest, known universally as "La Şosea" to residents. A *şosea* means simply a large road leading out of town, a highway.

6. Ion Luca Caragiale (1853–1912), Romanian satiric playwright and theatrical manager, called "the greatest unknown dramatist" by Eugène Ionesco.

7. Ion Culianu was professor of the history of religion at the University of Chicago. He was shot to death there in 1991, a murder never fully solved or explained, but widely believed to be connected with his public criticisms of Ceauşescu's regime. He was called "Néné" in the family. (KRJ)

8. Mihai Sadoveanu (1880–1961), Romanian writer, novelist, and theater director. In his last years he became enthusiastic for socialism and briefly joined the new Communist government. (KRJ)

9. See Ted Anton, *Eros, Magic, and the Murder of Professor Culianu.*

## Paris, 1995

1. IZJ was first diagnosed and treated for cancer at the Curie Institute, in 2000. (KRJ)

## Appendix 1

1. Rădulescu, "La Généalogie d'Émile Cioran," 30.

2. Relu Cioran gave me his father's book, which he had published at his own expense, to help me understand the atmosphere and circumstances of the larger Cioran family.

3. Emilian Cioran, *Seven Generations,* 5.

4. Some twenty of Sava's manuscripts could be found in Leipzig, St. Petersburg, and the Romanian Academy in Bucharest.

5. From 1865, Nietzsche studied in Leipzig. In 1869, he was appointed professor of classical philology at Basel, Switzerland. Emilian Cioran does not give the exact date of Barcianu's letters, but they seem to be from the early 1870s so it is questionable whether they really refer to Nietzsche. Nietzsche may have returned to Leipzig to lecture, or the letters may be from an earlier period.

6. Emilian Cioran, *Seven Generations,* 80, 82.

7. Emilian Cioran, *Comemorarea lui Nicolae Cristea.* Sibiu: Tiparul Tipografiei Arhidiecezane, 1935.

8. Ibid.

## Appendix 2

1. Edited by Marin Diaconu, with an eighty-word foreword by Cioran (dated 16 July 1990) that diverts questions of identity and intention with his by-then trademark interrogatory mode. It begins, "Am I? Am I not?"

2. Marta Petreu, *Un trecut deocheat sau "Schimbarea la față a României"* (1999); published in English as *An Infamous Past: E. M. Cioran and the Rise of Fascism in Romania* (2005). In the English edition, Petreu's lists of Cioran's German essays appear on pp. 290–92, notes 27 and 52.

3. On 29 June 1934, Hitler invited Ernst Roehm, head of the SA (storm troopers) and its leaders to a meeting at Bad Wiessee, near Munich. There, he personally arrested Roehm for conspiring against him, as well as many of Roehm's closest associates, some hundreds of whom were summarily executed. So was Roehm, though spared for a while. Hitler liked him personally, because Roehm's manipulation of army finances had helped Hitler's rise to power. This was the "Night of the Long Knives," so named from an old German folk song. The affair secured Hitler's absolute power, though historians have shown that it was engineered by Goering, Goebbels, and Himmler, rivals with Roehm for Hitler's favor. Roehm's SA—at four million strong, larger than the German army—was hereafter marginalized, and his socialistic influence diluted, to the relief of German industrialists, like Albert Krups, who were trying to learn to live with Hitler.

4. On 17 June 1934 Chancellor Franz Joseph von Papen (1879–1969) gave a speech at the University of Marburg urging the restoration of some of the civil rights suspended by the Nazis in the present time of emergency. He too opposed Roehm's SA, although from a perspective nearly diametrically opposite to Hitler's. Some of his associates were shot in the "Night of the Long Knives," but von Papen was judged useful to the new regime and lived on, in a variety of roles.

5. This is the first of Cioran's essays sent back from Germany after his arrival there. Almost all these essays are like op-ed newspaper pieces, taking up half a page or less in tabloid-size publications. This is also one of the few in which he says anything, even indirectly, about Jews.

# Bibliography

## Cioran's Writings


*Amurgul Gîndurilor* [The Twilight of Thought]. Sibiu: Dacia Traiană, 1940.

*Le crépuscule des pensées*. Trans. Mirella Patureau-Nedelco. Paris, L'Herne, 1991.

*Anthologie du portrait—De Saint-Simon à Tocqueville*. Paris: Arcades, 1996.

*Antropologia filosofică*. Ed. Constantin Barbu. Craiova: Pentagon-Dionysos, 1991.

*Aveux et anathèmes* [Praises and Anathemas]. Paris: Gallimard, 1987.

*Cahier de Talamanca. Ibiza (31 juillet–25 août, 1966)*. Preface by Verena von der Heyden-Rynsch. Paris: Mercure de France, 2000.

*Cahiers [Notebooks]: 1957–1972*. Paris: Gallimard, 1997.

*Cartea amăgirilor* [The Book of Deceptions]. Bucharest: Editura Cugetarea, 1936; Humanitas, 1991.

*Le Livre des Leurres*. Trans. Grazyna Klewek and Thomas Bazin. Paris: Gallimard, 1992.

*Cioran: 12 Scrisori de pe culmile disperării* [Twelve Letters from the Heights of Despair]. Cluj: Biblioteca Apostrof, 1995.

*Cioran și Muzica*. Ed. Aurel Cioran and Vlad Zografi. Bucharest: Humanitas, 1996.

*De l'inconvénient d'être né* [The Inconvenience of Being Born]. Paris: Gallimard, 1995.

*Écartèlement* [Dismembering]. Paris: Gallimard, 1979.

*Entretiens* [Interviews]. Paris: Arcades, Gallimard, 1995.

*Entretiens avec Sylvie Jaudeau*. 2nd ed. Paris: José Corti, 1990.

*Eseuri*. Trans. and ed. Modest Morariu. Bucharest: Cartea Românească, 1988.

*Essai sur la pensée réactionnaire: À propos de Joseph de Maistre*. Paris: Fata Morgana, 1977.

*Exercises d'admiration*. Paris: Gallimard, 1986.

*Historie et utopie: Les Essais XCVI*. Paris: Gallimard, 1960.

*History and Utopia*. Trans. Richard Howard. Chicago: University of Chicago Press, 1998.

*Îndreptar Pătimaș* [Primer of Passions]. Bucharest: Humanitas, 1991.

"Je ne suis pas un nihiliste: Le rien est encore un programme." Unedited interview with Hans-Jürgen Heinrichs. *Magazine littéraire*, 373 (Février 1999): 99–103.

*La tentation d'exister*. Paris: Gallimard, 1956.

*The Temptation to Exist*. Trans. Richard Howard. Chicago: Quadrangle Books, 1968.

*Lacrimi și Sfinți* [Tears and Saints]. Bucharest: Editura Autorului, 1937; Paris: Ioan Cusa, 1972.

*Des larmes et des saints.* Trans. Sanda Stolojan. Paris: L'Herne, 1986.
*Tears and Saints.* Trans. Ilinca Zarifopol-Johnston. Chicago: University of Chicago Press, 1995.
*(Lettre à) L'Ami Lointain. Paris-Bucarest.* With Constantin Noïca. Paris: Critérion, 1991. [Cioran's text extracted from *Histoire et Utopie,* 1960]
"The New Gods." Trans. Frederick Brown. *Hudson Review* 21 (Spring 1968): 39–52.
*Œuvres.* Paris: Gallimard, 1995.
*Pe culmile disperării* [On the Heights of Despair]. Bucharest: Fundația pentru literatură și arta "Regele Carol II," 1934; Humanitas, 1999.
*Sur les cimes du désespoir.* Trans. Sanda Stolojan. Paris: l'Herne, 1990.
*On the Heights of Despair.* Trans. Ilinca Zarifopol-Johnston. Chicago: University of Chicago Press, 1992.
*Précis de décomposition* [Treatise on Decay]. Paris: Gallimard, 1949.
*Tratat de descompunere.* Bucharest: Humanitas, 1992.
*Revelațile Durerii: Eseuri* [Revelations of Durer: Essays]. Ed. Mariana Vartic and Aurel Sasu. Cluj: Editura Echinox, 1990.
*Schimbarea la față a României* [Romania's Transfiguration]. Bucharest: Humanitas, 1990.
*Scrisori către cei de-acasa* [Letters Home]. Bucharest: Humanitas, 1995.
"Sensibilitatea mistică." *Viața Ilustrată,* 10 (1934): 6.
*Sfîrșitul care începe* [The Beginning of the End]. Ed. Constantin Barbu. Craiova: Pentagon-Dionysos, 1991.
*Singurătate și destin* [Solitude and Destiny]. *Publicistică 1931–1944.* Ed. Marin Diaconu. Bucharest: Humanitas, 1991.
*Syllogismes de l'amertume* [Syllogisms of Bitterness]. Paris: Gallimard, 1952, 1980.
*Țara mea / Mon pays.* Bucharest: Humanitas, 1996.
*Valéry face à ses idoles* [Valéry Confronts His Idols]. Paris: L'Herne, 1970.

## Archival Materials

Biblioteca Academiei, Bucharest
Archives of the Romanian Academy
Romanian Foreign Ministry
Muzeul Literaturii Române, Bucharest
Dosar 29 No. 282 (19 June 1941): 62–63 (Students exempt from military service)
Dosar 30 Students repatriated from France
Dosar 32 Report concerning the press of the Romanian legation, February–August 1941
Dosar 35 Romanian Consul at Vichy; list of Legionnaires in Paris, 1941
Dosar 356 Association of Romanian Students in France, 1911–1941
Dosar 358 Romanian Colony in France, 1909–1944
Dosar 365 The Romanian Church, 1896–1944
(Information on Individuals, 1923–1944)
(Census of students, 1882–1943)
(Special investment fund, 1882–1944)
(Romanian Legation, Fontenay-en-Roses, 1940)

Dosar 697 List of Romanians in France, 1942
Dosar 702 Correspondence on life in Romania, from Romanians and foreigners, 1940–44
Dosar 709 Reports on individual expatriates (pp. 933–44)
Astra Library (Sibiu)
Archives of the Romanian Orthodox Bishopric of Sibiu.

**Books**

Acterian, Arşavir. *Jurnal în căutarea lui Dumnezeu.* Iaşi: Institutul European, 1994.

———. *Privilegiaţi şi Năpăstuiţi.* Iaşi: Institutul European, 1992.

Antohi, Sorin. *Civitas imaginalis: Istorie şi utopie in cultura română.* Bucharest: Litera, 1994.

Anton, Ted. *Eros, Magic, and the Murder of Professor Culianu.* Evanston, Ill.: Northwestern University Press, 1996.

Arendt, Hannah. *The Origins of Totalitarianism.* New York: Harcourt Brace, 1976.

Arendt, Hannah, and Martin Heidegger. *Lettres et autres documents, 1925–1975.* Paris: Gallimard, 2000.

Bălan, George. *În dialog cu Emil Cioran.* Bucharest: Cartea Românească, 1996.

Berdiaev, Nikolai. *Împărăţia Spiritului şi Împărăţia Cezarului.* Timişoara: Editura Amarcord, 1994.

Birnbaum, Pierre. *"La France aux Français": Histoire des haines nationalistes.* Paris: Éditions de Seuil, 1993.

Bollon, Patrice. *Cioran, l'hérétique.* Paris: Gallimard, 1997.

Bondy, François (and 15 others). *Convorbiri cu Cioran.* Bucharest: Humanitas, 1993.

Bossy, Raoul. *Amintiri din viaţa diplomatică (1918–1940),* ed. Stelian Neagoe. Bucharest: Humanitas, 1993.

Calinescu, Matei. *Despre Ioan P. Culianu şi Mircea Eliade. Aminitiri, lecturi, reflecţii.* Iaşi: Polirom, 2000.

Chirila, Traian. "Reuniunea culturală naţională a meseriaşilor români din Sibiu—la optzeci de ani," cu o prefaţă de Pret. Staur. Emilian Cioran. Sibiu, 1946.

Ciachir, Dan. *Gînduri despre Nae Ionescu.* Iaşi: Institutul European, 1994.

Cioran, Emilian [Cioran's father]. *Comemorarea lui Nicolae Cristea.* Sibiu: Tiparul Tipografiei Arhidiecezane, 1935.

———. *Seven Generations of Priests, Archpriests, Professors from the Same Family: Barcianu, 1699–1903.* Ed. Aulerian Cioran. Sibiu: [n.p.], 1955 (1991).

Codreanu, Corneliu Z. *La garde de fer.* Paris: Éditions Prométhée, 1938.

Comarnescu, Petru. *Jurnal: 1931–1937.* Iasi: Institutul European, 1994.

Constantiniu, Florin. *O istorie sinceră a poporului român.* Bucureşti: Univers Enciclopedic, 1999.

Coser, Lewis. *Masters of Sociological Thought.* New York: Harcourt Brace Jovanovich, 1977.

Crainic, Nichifor. *Nostalgia Paradisului.* Iaşi: Moldova, 1994.

Eakin, Paul John. *How Our Lives Become Stories: Making Selves.* Ithaca, N.Y.: Cornell University Press, 1999.

Erikson, Erik. *Young Man Luther.* New York: W.W. Norton, 1958.

Galeriu, Părintele, Gabriel Liiceanu, Andrei Pleşu, and Sorin Dumitrescu. *Dialoguri de Seară*. Bucharest: Harisma, 1991.

Georgescu, Vlad. *Istoria Romanilor.* Oakland, Calif.: Ara, 1984.

Goma, Paul. *Jurnal de Căldură-Mare (29 iunie–11 iulie 1989)*. Bucharest: Editura Nemira, 1997.

———. *Jurnal de Noapte-Lungă. (23 septembrie–31 decembrie 1993)*. Bucharest: Editura Nemira, 1997.

———. *Jurnal pe Sărite*. Bucharest: Editura Nemira, 1997.

Hillgruber, Andreas. *Hitler, Regele Carol şi Mareşalul Antonescu. Relaţile Germano-Române, 1938–1944*. Bucharest: Humanitas, 1994.

Ionescu, Nae. *Fenomenul legionar.* Bucharest: Antet XX Press, 1993.

———. *Grafologie. Scrisul şi omul.* Ed. Marin Diaconu. Bucharest: Humanitas, 1994.

———. *Între Ziaristică şi Filosofie.* Iaşi: Timpul, 1996.

———. *Prelegeri de Filosofia Religiei*, ed. Marta Petreu. Cluj: Biblioteca Apostrof, 1994.

———. *Problema mântuirii în FAUST al lui Goethe*. Bucharest: Anastasia, 1996.

———. *Roza Vînturilor. 1926–1933*. Intro. by Dan Zamfirescu. Bucharest: Poligrafica, 1990. [First published in 1934 with an afterword by Mircea Eliade]

———. *Suferinţa Rasei Albe.* Iaşi: Editura Timpul, 1994.

James, William. *Varieties of Religious Experience.* London: Longmans, Green, 1935.

Jaudeau, Sylvie. *Cioran ou le dernier homme.* Paris: José Corti, 1990.

Kaufmann, Walter. *Existentialism from Dostoevsky to Sartre.* New York: Meridian/Penguin, 1956, 1975.

Kluback, William, and Michael Finkenthal, eds. *The Temptations of Emile* [sic] *Cioran*. New York: Peter Lang, 1997.

Kundera, Milan. *Testaments Betrayed.* New York: HarperCollins, 1995.

Laignel-Lavanstine, Alexandra. *Cioran, Eliade, Ionesco: L'oubli du Fascisme. Trois intellectuels roumains dans la tourmente du siècle.* Paris: Presses Universitaires de France, 2002.

Liiceanu, Gabriel. *Itinéraires d'une vie Cioran.* Paris: Michalon, 1995.

———. *Uşa interzisă.* Bucharest: Humanitas, 2002.

Livezeanu, Irina. *Cultural Politics in Greater Romania: Regionalism, Nation Building, and Ethnic Struggle, 1918–1930*. Ithaca, N.Y.: Cornell University Press, 1995.

De Maistre, Joseph. *Considérations sur la France*, ed. Alain Peyrefitte. Paris: Imprimerie Nationale, 1994.

———. *Écrits sur la Révolution.* Paris: Presses Universitaires de France, 1989.

Manea, Norman. *On Clowns: The Dictator and the Artist.* New York: Grove Press, 1992.

Mallarmé, Stephane. *Poésies.* Gallimard, 1992.

Morand, Paul. *Bucharest.* Pais: Plon, 1935.

Muller, Jerry. *The Other God That Failed: Hans Freyer and the Deradicalization of German Conservatism.* Princeton, N.J.: Princeton University Press, 1987.

Naipaul, V. S. *Reading and Writing: A Personal History.* New York: New York Review of Books, 2000.

Nanu, Frederic C. *Politica externă a României. 1919–1933*. Trans. Liliana Roşca and Emanuela Ungureanu. Iaşi: Institutul, 1993.

Nistor, Nicolae, and Mircea Morinescu-Frotânei. *Sibiul şi tinitul in lumina istoriei*, Vol. 2. Cluj-Napoca: "Dacia," 1990.

Ornea, Zigu. *Anii Treizeci: Extrema dreaptă românească.* Bucharest: Editura Fundației Culturale Române, 1995.

Ory, Pascal, and Sirinelli, Jean-François. *Les intellectuels en France. De l'affaire Dreyfus à nos jours.* Paris: Armand Colin, 1992.

Păcală. [Source not found. In *Cahiers* 485 (March 1967), Cioran mentions Păcală as the author of a local book on Rășinari, who was alive ca. 1910 when he took a photographer to a nearby village, the site of the incident of the villagers' attack recounted in chapter 1. Presumably IZJ came across this book during her visits to Rășinari and Sibiu; it is very likely the one she mentions photocopying in her "Memoirs" of 1994. Păcală is a fairly common Romanian surname, not to be confused with "Păcală and Tîndală," a pair of comic country bumpkins from Romanian folklore. (KRJ)]

Papini, Giovanni. *Un uomo finito.* Firenze: Vallecchi Editore, 1929.

Petreu, Marta. *Un trecut deocheat sau "Schimbarea la față a României."* [An Infamous Past or "The Transfiguration of Romania"] Cluj: Biblioteca Apostrof, 1999. Published in English as *An Infamous Past: E. M. Cioran and the Rise of Fascism in Romania,* trans. Bogdan Aldea. Chicago: Ivan R. Dee, 2005.

Picon, Gaëtan. *Malraux par lui-même.* Paris: Éditions du Seuil, 1961.

*Pro și Contra Emil Cioran.* Ed. Marin Diaconu. Bucharest: Humanitas, 1998.

Radulescu, Carmen-Ligia. *Emil Cioran: Conștiința ca Fatalitate.* Bucharest: Editura Recif, 1994.

Ricœur, Paul. *La mémoire, l'histoire, l'oubli.* Paris: Éditions du Seuil, 2000.

Savater, Fernando. *Ensayo sobre Cioran.* Madrid: Taurus, 1974.

———. *Nihilismo y accion.* Madrid: Taurus, 1970.

Sebastian, Mihail. *Depuis deux mille ans.* Trans. Alain Paruit. Paris: Stock, 1998. [First published in Bucharest in 1934 as *De două mii de ani*]

———. *Jurnal: 1935–1944.* Ed. Gabriela Omăt and Leon Volovici. Bucharest: Humanitas, 1996. [Published as *Journal: 1935–1944: The Fascist Years,* ed. Radu Ioanid, trans. Patrick Camiller. Chicago: Ivan R. Dee, 2000, in association with the United States Holocaust Memorial Museum.]

Șestov, Lev. *Începuturi și sfîrșituri.* Iași: Institutul European, 1993.

Sluga, Hans. *Heidegger's Crisis. Philosophy and Politics in Nazi Germany.* Cambridge: Harvard University Press, 1995.

Sora, Mariana. *Cioran jadis et naguère.* Paris: l'Herne, 1988. [Published together with *Cioran: Entretien à Tübingen* (Gerd Bergfleth interview with Cioran, 5 June 1984)]

Stolojan, Sanda. *Au balcon de l'exil roumain à Paris: Avec Cioran, Eugène Ionesco, Mircea Eliade, Vintila Horiă. . . .* Paris: L'Harmattan, 1999.

———. *Nori peste balcoane: Jurnal din exil parizian.* Bucharest: Humanitas, 1996.

Ungureanu, Cornel. *La vest de Eden. O introducere în literature exilului.* Timișoara: Amarcord, 1995.

Vartic, Ion. *Cioran naiv și sentimental.* Cluj: Biblioteca Apostrof, 2000.

Veiga, Francisco. *Istoria Gărzii de Fier 1919–1941. Mistica ultranationalismului.* Bucharest: Humanitas, 1993. [Trans. *La mística del ultranacionalismo.* Bellaterra: Universitat Autonoma de Barcelona, 1989.]

Volovici, Leon. *Nationalist Ideology and Antisemitism: The Case of Romanian Intellectuals in the 1930s.* Oxford: Pergamon Press, 1991.

Vulcănescu, Mircea. *Nae Ionescu. Aşa cum l-am cunoscut.* Bucharest: Humanitas, 1992.
———. *Ultimul cuvînt.* Bucharest: Humanitas, 1992.

**Articles**

Acterian, Arşavir. "Amintiri despre Emil Cioran," in *Pro şi Contra: Emil Cioran* [ca. 1987].
Bădescu, Lucian. "Mircea Vulcănescu de E. M. Cioran." *Ethos* I (Paris: 1973): 10–17.
De Benoist, Alain. "Un 'fanatique sans credo'." *Figaro Magazine,* 17 Novembre 1979.
Calinescu, Matei. "'How Can One Be What One Is?' Reading the Romanian and the French Cioran." *Salmagundi* 112 (Fall 1996): 192–215.
———. "The 1927 Generation in Romania: Friendships and Ideological Choices (Mihail Sebastian, Mircea Eliade, Nae Ionescu, Eugene Ionesco, E. M. Cioran)." *East European Politics and Societies* 15 (2002): 649–77.
"Colocviul international 'Zilele Cioran'." *Tribuna* [Sibiu], 9 Mai 1997, 3. (Nicolae Balotă, Sanda Stolojan, Ilinca Zarifopol-Johnston)
Ferrua, Pietro. "Exil et aliénation dans l'œuvre de Cioran." *Revista de Istorie şi Teorie Literara,* 41 (January–June 1993): 187–94.
———. "The Romanian Roots of Cioran." *Balkanistica* 6 (1980): 88–95.
Fotiade, Ramona. "Behind the Veil of Aristocracy: Cioran's Strategy for Dealing with the Painful Memories of His Nationalist Past." *TLS* (6 October 1995): 17–18.
Fumaroli, Marc. "La poétique des mémoires." *Le Figaro Littéraire,* 12 January 1995.
George, François. "L'Époque de Cioran." *Critique* 479 (Avril 1987): 267–82.
Gregori, Ilina. "Quelques remarques sur le 'Messianisme.' Pour une nouvelle lecture de *La Transfiguration de la Roumainie* (E. Cioran)." *Neue Romania.* Berlin: Berliner Romanistischer Studien, 1993. pp. 185–94.
Gruzinska, Aleksandra. "E. M. Cioran and the Idea of Admiration." *Journal of the American Romanian Academy of the Arts and Sciences* 13–14 (1990): 145–61.
———. "E. M. Cioran: Le temps humain et l'éternel présent." *Journal of the American Romanian Academy of Arts and Sciences,* 10 (1987): 192–201.
———. "Writing Our Humanity: E. M. Cioran on Friendship." *Journal of the American Romanian Academy of Arts and Sciences,* 21–22 (1996–1997): 60–64.
Heinrichs, Hans-Jurgen. Interview. *Magazine Littéraire* 373 (February 1999).
Henriot, Émile. "La vie littéraire: Penseurs, conseilleurs, déstructeurs." *Le Monde,* 25 juillet 1956.
Jacob, Michel. "Wakefulness and Obsession: An Interview with E. M. Cioran." *Salmagundi* 103 (Summer 1994): 122–45.
Jocks, Heinz-Norbert. "On the Death of E. M. Cioran." *BalkanMedia* 4 (April 1995): 42–43.
Kampits, Peter. "Cioran." *Literatur und Kritik* 205–6 (July–August 1986): 254–60.
Kimball, Roger. "The Anguishes of E. M. Cioran." *New Criterion* 6 (March 1988): 37–44.
Mace-Scaron, Joseph. "Les victimes du lynchage biographique." *Le Fiagro Littéraire,* 19 March 1999.
Matzneff, Gabriel. "Cioran? Un excellent remède contre le désespoir." *Figaro Magazine,* 31 Janvier 1987, 13–14, 18–20.
Mauriac, Claude. *Table Ronde,* January 1950.

Maurois, André. *Opéra,* 14 December 1949.

Mihăilescu, Dan C. "L'impardonable Cioran." *Euresis: Cahiers Roumains d'Études Littéraires* 1–2 (1994): 297–98.

———. "Omul gotic şi fără scăpare." *România Literară* 24 (11 April 1991): 4.

Moraru, Cristian. "Cioran Contra Cioran." *Contrapunct* 10 (1990): 4–9.

Nadeau, Maurice. "Un penseur crépusculaire." *Combat* 29 (September 1949).

Ornea, Zigu. "Ultimul prieten al lui Cioran şi Eugen Ionesco." *România Literară* 34 (28 August 1996) [Review of Arşavir Acterian, *Portrete şi trei amintiri de puşcăriaş.* Editura Ararat, 1996.]

Petreu, Marta. "Cioran în diplomaţie." *Apostrof* 12, no. 5 (2001): 16–17. ["Arhiva 'A'": five routine telegraphs from June 1941 between Romanian Foreign Ministry and Romanian Legation at Vichy, regarding Cioran's status]

Rădulescu, Mihai Sorin. "La Généalogie d'Émile Cioran." *Généalogie* 140 (August 1995).

Said, Edward. "Amateur of the Insoluble." *Hudson Review* 21 (1968–69): 769–73.

Savater, Fernando. "El ultimo dandi." *El País,* 25 Octubre 1990, 40–41.

*Secolul 20* [20th Century]: Revistă de Sinteză, nos. 328–330 (n.d., 1989?). Bucharest. [Triple special issue on Cioran]

Ţincu, Bucur. "Profiluri europene: E. M. Cioran." *Steaua* 35 (December 1984): 54–57.

Tismaneanu, Vladimir. "Romania's Mystical Revolutionaries." *Partisan Review* 61 (1994): 600–609.

Tismaneanu, Vladimir, and Dan Pavel. "Romania's Mystical Revolutionaries: The Generation of Angst and Adventure Revisited." *East European Politics and Societies* (Fall 1994): 402–38.

Troyat, Henri. "Ces statues qu'on déboulonne." *Le Figaro Littéraire,* 19 March 1999.

Ungureanu, Cornel. "Emil Cioran şi fidelitatea contrariilor." In *La vest de Eden* (Timişoara: Amarcord, 1995), 89–113.

Vernescu, Flavia. "Emil Cioran: Le philosophe et le styliste." *Dalhousie French Studies* 37 (Winter 1996): 73–80.

Weiss, Jason. "An Interview with Cioran." In *Grand Street* (1983), 105–40; also in *Writing at Risk: Interviews in Paris with Uncommon Writers.* Iowa City: University of Iowa Press, 1991; pp. 1–38.

# Biographical Note

Ilinca Marina Zarifopol (1952–2005) was born July 25 in Bucharest, Romania, the second child and second daughter of Constantin (Dinu) Zarifopol and Maria (Mioara) Economu. She was the grand-niece of Paul Zarifopol (1874–1930), one of Romania's leading men of letters in the early twentieth century. The Zarifopol family was originally Greek, having migrated from Greece and Turkey to Romania in the late eighteenth century, first as merchants and horse traders, and later as government managers for the Ottoman Turks and the minor Romanian nobility (boyars), to which they were themselves elevated in the latter part of the nineteenth century. Ilinca Zarifopol was educated in the public schools of Bucharest and graduated from the University of Bucharest in 1975, with concentrations in English and German language and literature. Her senior thesis, on speech-acts of permission in English, was awarded first prize in the national student colloquium for that year. Her parents had had to divorce in order that she and her older sister, Christina, could attend university, because they had a bad "social file" in Communist Romania as the daughters of a member of the former land-owning class. After graduation, she was awarded a fellowship for further study in (then) West Germany, but was denied a passport by the Romanian government for the same reason.

She began her teaching career at Electro-Technical High School No. 49 in Bucharest in 1975, but emigrated to the United States in 1977, after marrying (in late 1976) her husband, Kenneth R. Johnston, Professor of English at Indiana University, Bloomington, who had been Senior Fulbright lecturer in American literature at the University of Bucharest in 1974–75. She enrolled in graduate studies at Indiana, taking her M.A. in Linguistics in 1980 and her Ph.D. in Comparative Literature in 1990. Her dissertation was awarded the university's Esther Kingsley award for outstanding dissertation of the year. After teaching Romanian at Indiana University for ten years while working on her degrees, she was hired as Assistant Professor in Indiana University's Comparative Literature department in 1990, advancing to tenured Associate Professor in 1997.

She won the university's Outstanding Young Faculty award in 1993, along with a National Endowment for the Arts translation fellowship. In 1994 she was awarded a Fulbright fellowship for her work on the biography of E. M. Cioran, and in 1999 a National Endowment for the Humanities fellowship for the same project.

She translated two of Cioran's Romanian books into English, *On the Heights of Despair* (1992) and *Tears and Saints* (1995). In addition, she is the author of *To Kill a Text: The Dialogic*

*Fiction of Hugo, Dickens, and Zola.* She also published articles in *Nineteenth-Century French Studies; Comparative Literature Studies; The Comparatist;* and the *Yearbook of Comparative and General Literature.*

Kenneth R. Johnston is Professor of English Emeritus at Indiana University, Bloomington. He is author of *Wordsworth and "The Recluse"* (1984) and *The Hidden Wordsworth* (1998), and is co-editor of *Romantic Revolutions: Criticism and Theory* (Indiana University Press, 1990).

# Index

*Page numbers in italics indicate maps and photographs.*